Social Welfare in Western Society

Historical Periods, Social Developments, Landmark Events	Charity/Philanthropy	Public Welfare	Mutual Aid
TUDOR PERIOD IN ENGLAND 1485–1603	12th–16th centuries, Hospitals and almshouses established	1531, Begging by able-bodied prohibited 1551–1601, Development of Elizabethan Poor Law	
PROTESTANT REFORMATION 1517–1555, Lutheranism 1534, Church of England 1536–1564, Calvinism	16th century, Protestants reject idea that charity can gain donor salvation 1601, Statute of Charitable Uses passed to encourage charitable gifts and protect the funds from misuse	1572, Parish poor rate, first tax to support poor 1597, Parents and children responsible for each other's support 1601, Comprehensive rewriting of poor law, extending family responsibility to grandparents and grandchildren	
MERCANTILIST PERIOD 16th–18th centuries	17th century, Charity schools for poor children established by merchants 17th–19th centuries, Merchants develop associated philanthropy	17th century, First workhouses try to employ poor in profitable work 1662, Law of Settlement and Removal restricts movement of poor people	
AMERICAN COLONIAL PERIOD 1607–1789	1739–40, Preacher George Whitefield stimulates broad-based charity	Elizabethan Poor Law carried to American colonies	

Social Welfare
in
Western Society

Social Welfare in Western Society

Gerald Handel

The City College and the
Graduate School
City University of New York

 Random House | New York

Library of Congress Cataloging in Publication Data

Handel, Gerald.
Social welfare in western society.

Bibliography: p.
Includes index.
1.   Social service—United States—History.
2.   Social service—History.   I. Title.
HV91.H28   361'.9   81-11959
ISBN 0-394-32213-4   AACR2

Manufactured in the United States of America

Composed by Haddon Craftsmen, Inc., Scranton, Pa.
Printed and bound by R. R. Donnelley & Sons, Co., Harrisonburg, Va.
Cover design and text design: Lorraine Hohman

Permission to reprint the chart on pp. 127–29 by the Council of State Governments.

Dedicated to

my Mother
and
to the memory of
my Father

Preface

This book is an introduction to social welfare. It is intended for readers who have no previous acquaintance with the subject, as well as for readers who want a convenient one-volume overview and review. The book grows out of the author's experience in teaching a course on the Sociology of Social Welfare Institutions for the last several years at The City College of the City University of New York.

The social welfare institutions that exist in the United States today are bewildering in their variety and diversity. We have family counseling services, children's day-care centers, and neighborhood community centers that depend heavily on charitable contributions. We have programs for child welfare and programs for providing compensation to workers injured on the job that are under the control of the individual states; each of the fifty states works out its own approach to these matters. And we have a social security system organized and run by the federal government, the national state. How can we understand the coexistence of such diverse arrangements?

A short answer to this question can be given in three propositions: (1) Each type of social welfare arrangement is based on a distinctive idea or cluster of ideas. (2) Each social welfare idea arose at a particular time and was put into practice as an attempted answer to the problems of that time. (3) Certain ideas remain in practice for very long periods joined, by ideas put into practice at later times.

Thus, to mention just a few of the social welfare arrangements of the 1980s, we practice charity and philanthropy, ideas first put into practice by the ancient Israelites and ancient Greeks, over twenty-five hundred years ago. Our fifty states, their counties and other local divisions, are responsible for several categories of social welfare problems; the idea of local government responsibility is four hundred years old, dating from the Tudor period in England. Our national government operates a social security system to provide income to retired workers; this system is based on ideas first put into practice in Germany one hundred years ago and adopted in the United States about fifty years ago. And we have specialized occupations—social work and various counseling occupations—whose task is to provide scientifically based help to people who need help. The idea of a distinctive, specialized helping profession based on scientific knowledge was put into practice about ninety years ago. In short, some of the things we do today we have been doing for as long as three thousand years and some for only fifty years. *Nothing* done in the social welfare field today began today. It is disputable when the last new idea in social welfare was put into practice, but it is safe to say that it has been at least a few years. Newer ideas have been proposed, but no major new idea has found its way into practice for some time.

Of course, ideas do get modified over time. Our ways of practicing charity and philanthropy are not identical with those of the ancient Israelites and Greeks. Social work is not practiced today as it was when it first began. And the same may be said for all the major ideas that go back a long time and yet still form the basis of our social welfare practice today. As circumstances change and societies face new problems, ideas about how to handle these situations also change. Ideas are modified, developed, refined, and blended with other ideas to form new combinations. Knowledge develops, understanding grows. New ways to put ideas into practice are thought of. Sometimes people become dissatisfied because the ideas and practices in use are not solving problems as they were expected to, and they return to simpler, less elaborate—and usually harsher— ideas and practices. While some ideas outlive their usefulness, others simply disappear for a time and then pop up again in slightly different forms. Some apparent changes in ideas turn out, on close examination, to be old ideas dressed up in new words.

This book takes the view that the great variety of social welfare ideas and practices in use today are specific versions of five fundamental ideas about help, each resting upon a different conception of the relationship between helper and helped. These different conceptions of how to help people arose in diverse social circumstances in different periods in history. These conceptions are linked both to the more general ideas of the time and also to the way society was then organized and the problems it was facing. Some appreciation of these more general ideas, social organization, and social problems is required in order to understand the social welfare ideas. The book is organized to clarify these connections.

A brief Prologue following the Preface offers the reader a quick preview of the scope of modern social welfare. Then Part I prepares the way more systematically by offering, in Chapter I, a discussion of what is meant by social welfare and, in Chapter II, two conceptual frameworks for thinking about how social welfare is related to other aspects of modern society, since social welfare develops as part of society.

Each of Parts II through VI is devoted to defining, explaining, tracing the development, and illustrating one of the five fundamental helping ideas that form the foundation of modern social welfare. Every society runs on an accumulation of traditional ideas and practices combined with (some more or less adequate) inventiveness in modifying those traditions to meet new circumstances. The goal of Parts II through VI is to capture and clarify that accumulating tradition and its modifications that have resulted in today's social welfare arrangements. Part VII, the last part, is devoted to major ongoing issues in social welfare, issues that have a long history and that have not yet been settled.

Social welfare is itself a fundamental idea in modern Western society, but it is not an entirely welcome idea. Whereas for some people it connotes helpfulness, morality, justice, and social stability, for others it signifies the encouragement of dependency and interference with private life and personal property. Nevertheless, social welfare has proven to be a tenacious element in Western society. It is a major idea in modern life, and this book tries to cast some light on how and why this is so.

Acknowledgments

I want to thank first Jane Cullen, formerly of Random House, whose enthusiasm for this book from its inception was a source of continuing encouragement during the three years I spent writing it. She made many valuable suggestions. She was tactful and often tenacious in her recommendations, and the book is much better because of her efforts.

For helpful comments, I express my appreciation to Eleanor Brilliant, who read a draft of Chapter 9, and to Martin Seitz, who read a draft of Chapter 12. Various anonymous reviewers for Random House evaluated my plan for the book, one or more chapter drafts, or the entire first draft of the manuscript. I gained many useful suggestions from their comments. All the readers have tried to save me from error, and I hope some of them will feel they had some success. I am responsible for errors that remain.

As the manuscript was being readied for production, several people at Random House were helpful. My thanks to Kathleen Domenig, whose role was partially visible, and to others whose roles were behind the scenes. Particular thanks to Linda Reiman for a thorough and painstaking job of copyediting.

Contents

Prologue

Two Glimpses of Social Welfare

Social welfare is a world of many ideas and activities concerned with helping people. It is a world in which the meaning of help is continually being examined, discussed, challenged, and revised. It is a world of political struggle and struggle about ideas. Who should be helped? Who should pay for the help? What should government do? What should individuals do on their own or through voluntary associations?

Social welfare is also a world that mobilizes humanitarian impulses. It is a world entered by people who want to give help and want to acquire knowledge and skill in giving it. It is a world of social agencies, organized to give help, employing social workers and others skilled in giving help. The world of social agencies and social workers is part of the larger social world that makes political and economic decisions about social welfare. Who will pay to operate the social agencies? Who will decide whether a new social agency will be created to meet a new need? Who will decide whether a particular helping activity is actually helpful?

Questions and issues such as these are the subject of this book. As a preview, two glimpses of social welfare are offered.

One

Social welfare is about dreams of help, humanitarian impulses, action programs to solve social problems—and about the cost of paying for them.

One of the great social welfare dreams of modern times was announced by President Lyndon B. Johnson in 1964:

> We stand at the edge of the greatest era in the life of any nation. For the first time in world history, we have the abundance and the ability to free every man from hopeless want, and to free every person to find fulfillment in the works of his mind or the labor of his hands.
>
> Even the greatest of all past civilizations existed on the exploitation of the misery of the many.
>
> This nation, this people, this generation, has man's first chance to create a Great Society: a society of success without squalor, beauty without barrenness, works of genius without the wretchedness of poverty. We can open the doors of learning. We can open the doors of fruitful labor and rewarding leisure, of open opportunity and close community—not just to the privileged few, but to everyone.[1]

President Johnson's speech marked the beginning of an upturn in public spending for social welfare.

Fourteen years later, in 1978, a money-saving dream replaced Johnson's when a taxpayers' revolt was successful in the voting booths of California. The voters passed a law, known as Proposition 13, which cut California property taxes in half. Other states followed. The revolt was directed by a Los Angeles businessman named Howard Jarvis. Here are excerpts from his recent book entitled *I'm Mad as Hell:*

> For me, the words "I'm mad as Hell" are more than . . . the title of this book; they express exactly how I feel. . . . I can tell you, there have been thousands of people who've had heart attacks—some fatal—or suffered extreme emotional distress as they saw their lives drastically worsened by intolerable, unproductive, and unfair taxes. . . .
>
> . . . During the eight years before Proposition 13 passed, the cost of food stamps in California went up from $248 million to $5.5 billion, the cost of unemployment insurance increased from $2.5 billion to $14 billion, Medicare costs rose from $6.1 billion to $21 billion, and Social Security costs increased from $26.7 billion to $82.4 billion.[2]

Social welfare costs, as well as other government costs paid for out of taxes, were the target of Jarvis's successful campaign that developed into a social movement that spread to other parts of the country.

Two

Social welfare is about emotional suffering in individual lives and about the efforts of social workers to help people solve the problems that make them miserable.

Professional social work has existed for approximately eighty-five years. Research efforts have been made recently to find out how social work helps people. The following are excerpts from research interviews with a social worker and her client, each of whom evaluates the outcome of the help that was given.

CASE OF MISS BROWN

Client: I'm glad I went to the agency. The counselor did me a lot of good. Before I went there, I didn't know where I was headed, I felt like committing suicide. . . . It really helped to talk with her. . . . I realized I ain't so bad. . . . People liked me. . . . I had something to live for.

Worker: I think that Esther got what she wanted . . . some help to get over her immediate crisis. . . . But I wasn't satisfied. . . . I guess I didn't get what I wanted . . . to have her stick it out in treatment so that we could deal with the underlying issues. . . . especially why she kept running away from people as soon as she got close to them.[3]

These two glimpses suggest the wide panorama of social welfare. The first glimpse provides a view of the macrosphere, the society in which basic social welfare decisions are made, decisions about social welfare goals, values that are to be implemented through political decisions made both by political leaders and by citizens in their role as voters, decisions about how much money to spend on social welfare. The second glimpse provides a view of the microsphere, the realm of one-to-one relationships in which a client comes for help and a social worker offers it. In the microsphere, individuals deal with their basic humanity. They evaluate themselves, their situation, and each other. The client and the social worker are each trying to do something meaningful with their lives.

To the untutored eye, the microsphere and the macrosphere may seem very different and unconnected, but they are, of course, connected. The interaction of worker and client takes place in an agency office, which came into being as a result of decisions made outside that office. The kind of service workers will be able to offer clients also depends upon decisions made outside the office, as well as upon decisions workers make themselves. Social workers who want to understand their work situation need to know what kinds of social welfare decisions are made in the larger society, and why.

Certain similarities in our two glimpses ought also to be noted. First, social welfare involves ideas about what helps people. President Johnson believed that new government programs would help people. Mr. Jarvis believes that lower taxes will help people. Miss Brown believes that talking to a social worker helps people. Her social worker believes that helping people involves more than just aiding them to get over an immediate crisis.

Second, social welfare involves emotions, sometimes very strong ones. President Johnson had a genuine passion to improve society. Mr. Jarvis was mad as hell at the taxes paid to improve society. Miss Brown was suicidal. Miss Brown's social worker was disappointed that Miss Brown did not stick it out in treatment thus permitting her to use her professional skills.

Third, social welfare ideas and activities grow out of a clash of perspectives. The larger social welfare decisions grow out of the clash and competition of ideas about society. The help that is given in a social work relationship emerges from diverse expectations of worker and client.

Finally, social welfare events, whether occurring in the macrosphere or in the microsphere, need to be understood as linked to other events in a historical or developmental sequence. What comes next depends upon what is happening now and what happened before. Where we want to go, as individuals or as a society, depends upon how satisfied or dissatisfied we are with where we have been. Whether we can get where we want to go depends, among other things, upon knowing something about how we got where we are.

Notes

[1] *Public Papers of the Presidents: Lyndon B. Johnson, 1963–1964,* Book 1 (Washington, D.C.: U.S. Government Printing Office, 1965), p. 872.

[2] Howard Jarvis, with Robert Pack, *I'm Mad as Hell* (New York: Times Books, 1979), pp. 4, 111.

[3] Anthony M. Maluccio, *Learning From Clients—Interpersonal Helping as Viewed by Clients and Social Workers* (New York: Free Press, 1979), p. 108.

Social Welfare
in
Western Society

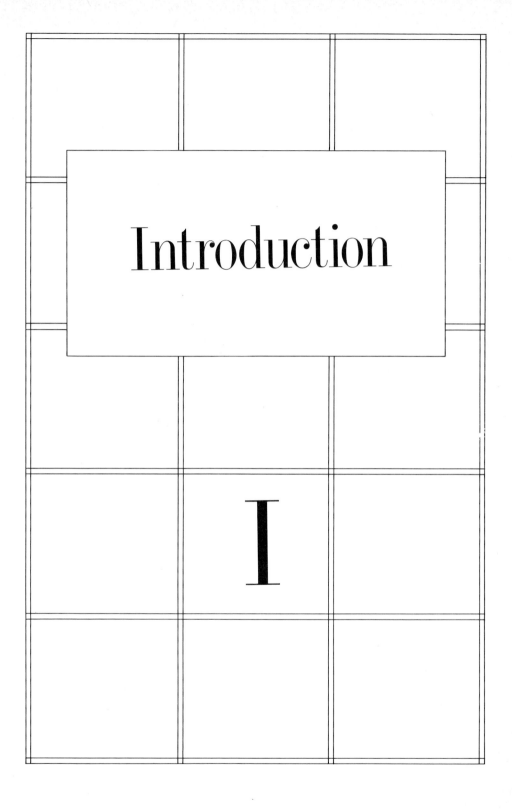

Introduction

I

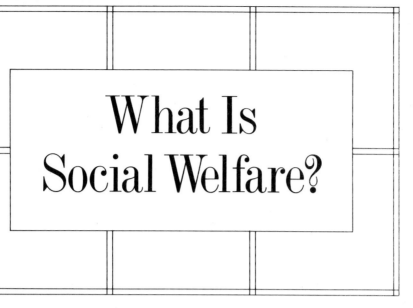

What Is Social Welfare?

1

A QUESTION OF TERMS

One of the curiosities of modern times is that in the United States the word *welfare* has come to stand for something that is widely disliked. The *Oxford English Dictionary*, which not only defines words but also provides historical information on them, gives its first citation for welfare as 1303, at which time the word meant "State or condition of doing or being well; good fortune, happiness, or well-being (of person, community, or thing); thriving or successful progress in life."[1] In 1787, the authors of the U.S. Constitution said in the Preamble that one of the goals of government was to provide for the general welfare.

Today when we hear about government providing welfare, not many people equate this with providing for the general welfare. In fact, many believe that providing welfare actually detracts from the general welfare. This is certainly an odd situation. There is a story here, but what is it?

Welfare has come to be understood in everyday speech as money given by the government to people who are poor. These people are often regarded by others not merely as poor but as different in other ways as well from "regular people." They are thought to be lazy, unwilling to work, and lacking in self-discipline. They are believed to ride around aimlessly in automobiles that they cannot afford and should not have, to drink too much and have too many babies, and to engage in other vices that outrage the sensibilities of people who see themselves as earning a living, abiding by society's rules, and otherwise doing what is "right." Thus welfare recipients are considered to be a particular subcategory of the poor; they are the people whom sociologist David Matza has described as "the disreputable poor." As Matza notes, poverty itself is considered a bit disreputable, but to be on welfare is to be in an even more disreputable category.[2]

The public dislike and distrust of the people on welfare was indicated in 1977 in a nationwide public opinion poll. A representative sample of the American adult population was asked, "Do you think that most people who receive money from welfare could get along without it if they tried or do you think they really need this help?" Only 31 percent thought the people really needed the help, compared to 54 percent who said they could get along without it. In response to another question, 58 percent said that they did not approve of most government-sponsored welfare programs.[3]

Welfare is a term in common use today. In contrast, *social welfare* is a somewhat technical term employed by a relatively small number of people: government officials, social planners, social workers, social scientists, and others who work to understand and solve problems of poverty and other social problems that will be discussed in this book. Social welfare, as the term is used by these groups, includes certain payments that most people refuse to think of as welfare. Unemployment benefits and retirement pensions, for example, are components of social welfare, but people who receive these payments do not feel they are receiving welfare. Most others in our society would share this view.

INCOME AND HONOR

Why do people receiving unemployment benefits not want to think of themselves as receiving welfare payments? The answer is fairly obvious from what has been said so far: People on welfare are widely considered to be undeserving of the help they receive, while recipients of unemployment payments are more likely to be thought to have earned the right to such payments when they were working. Furthermore, such individuals would prefer to be working now, and only as a result of circumstances beyond their control are they not. In short, having worked is moral and is even taken as proof of preferring to work; not having worked is considered immoral and is proof of preferring not to work. And moral people do not wish to apply to themselves a term ("welfare recipient") that they believe should be applied only to the immoral.

Why do social scientists, social workers, political leaders, planners, and theorists think of unemployment payments or retirement benefits as part of social welfare? The reason is that they conceive of *welfare* as the term was used in its original meaning—providing for the well-being of members of society. *Social welfare* thus is the general technical term that covers providing for the well-being of more and more groups in society. Around 1900, the term *welfare* began to be employed in the technical sense that social welfare is used today.[4] But as *welfare* took on its newer meaning of income provided to the disreputable and undeserving, a term that kept the original meaning of welfare was needed, and *social welfare* has gradually come to be the replacement.

The question of deservingness goes back a long time. It refers to more than simply who deserves welfare benefits. Under what circumstances does anybody deserve anything from society? Consider for a moment the matter of who deserves to own a piece of land. At one time in American history, a piece of land belonged to whoever could claim it and defend that claim against others who might try to take it away by force. *The People, Yes* by Carl Sandburg contains a stanza in the form of a dialogue on just this matter:

> "Get off this estate."
> "What for?"
> "Because it's mine."
> "Where did you get it?"
> "From my father."
> "Where did he get it?"
> "From his father."
> "And where did he get it?"
> "He fought for it."
> "Well, I'll fight you for it."[5]

With a touch of humor, the stanza builds to a surprise ending that suggests that personal combat is no longer an appropriate way to acquire property. The right to ownership by inheritance, established through three generations, supersedes the right to fight for property. Social conditions change, and the rules for gaining ownership of property change. Sandburg's would-be fighter seems to be trying to live according to the rules of an earlier era.

People make judgments concerning who deserves what benefits and under what circumstances. Robbing a bank, working at a job for a paycheck, betting on horse races, lending money and charging interest for its use, receiving welfare payments, investing money in a business and making a profit, accepting bribes —each of these are ways to obtain income. But each has a somewhat different official (i.e., prevailing) moral evaluation. Society considers some means better, more moral, than other means.

Sociologist Bernard Beck has argued that the only way to distinguish a special field of activity that could be called welfare is on the basis that recipients of welfare benefits are believed to lead lives that are "morally suspect and reputationally degraded." Beck seems to imply that the original meaning of the term *welfare* has been completely replaced by the newer meaning. To support his argument, he compares job training programs organized by welfare agencies and job training programs that are carried out by the military services. Both organizations, he believes, seek to impart job skills to untrained people and both attract people who enter careers that differ from the ordinary. Yet military recruits do not suffer from the same bad reputation as those who receive job training from the welfare system. Why is this so?

Beck's answer is that a certain amount of social honor is attached to the military that protects soldiers from being looked down upon in the way that welfare recipients tend to be. (He also notes that the amount of honor the military receives is related to the external danger considered to be threatening the country. Between World War I and World War II, when people wanted to believe President Woodrow Wilson's claim that World War I was the war to end all wars, a peacetime military career did not bring much honor. By contrast, after World War II, with the advent of the Cold War a military career or even a period of military service was considered more honorable.) In brief, Beck believes that the popular idea of welfare, based on the wish to maintain a clear distinction between honorable and not so honorable people, is the only sensible way to think of welfare.[6] He seems to argue that the original concept of welfare has lost out to its more restricted meaning.

It must be emphasized, however, that welfare in the narrow sense used today is part of a larger field known as social welfare. What most people understand by welfare is only one aspect of a larger social movement that has been developing over centuries, a movement to provide income to people who need it. That movement has expanded from providing income solely to the poor to providing it to virtually anyone whose earned income is interrupted—by unemployment, illness, or retirement. The movement includes efforts to train unskilled people to earn income; thus the job training programs in the military services can be understood as part of social welfare activities, even though they are not part of welfare. In recent years, efforts have been made (by Presidents Nixon and Carter) to design social welfare programs that would eliminate the narrow concept of welfare. So far they have not succeeded.

As we have seen, welfare is a method of receiving income that brings with it judgments of lesser worthiness from other members of society who receive their incomes in other ways. Similarly, individuals who receive welfare often themselves feel that, because of it, they suffer a loss of dignity. They are the modern-day counterparts of people of earlier times who felt the loss of dignity when they became dependent upon charity or upon relief. Charity, relief, welfare—these three terms, in succeeding historical periods, have represented methods of receiving income that were regarded as imposing dishonor upon the recipients. These methods of distribution of income—which will be described more fully in later chapters—did in fact set the recipients apart from other members of society; by common agreement, receiving income through these channels was considered demeaning. The recipients were marked as inferior members of society, and many came to regard themselves as such.

DIGNITY AND SOCIAL WELFARE

Social welfare can usefully be thought of as an effort that has taken shape over many centuries to provide people with income or other social benefits in ways that safeguard their dignity. This statement will require much qualification and elaboration—and that is the task of this book. For the moment, the statement will serve as a preliminary identification of the field. In addition, three of the themes to be elaborated on in the course of the book can be noted here:

(1) The concept of social welfare, as it developed over time, expanded to include a variety of activities that focused on the issue of dignity, sometimes independently of questions of income. Social welfare has come to include a variety of services to people—counseling on personal and family problems, facilitating group activities that are intended to help people lead more satisfying lives, providing community centers that, in addition to offering physical space, bring together many services in a single location and thus strengthen people's attachment to their community or neighborhood. Social welfare is, then, a sprawling combination of activities that may be roughly divided into two broad categories—*income maintenance* and *services*.

(2) While it is useful to think of social welfare as a category of human activity that has "developed" over time, it would be misleading to think of this development as always being "progress." Development is not a straight-line ascent to ever better ways of doing things. What have come to be regarded as the indignities of charity, relief, and welfare did not start out that way. These ideas were considered good—or at least not too bad—at first, and only later were they regarded as poor ideas. Poor ideas are not always replaced by better ones;

sometimes they are replaced by worse ones. The development of social welfare is a complex tangle of events, involving many indignities imposed on people in the name of "improvement" and "reform," as well as also involving new concepts and ideas that were more certainly improvements.

(3) The history of social welfare is interwoven with the changing distribution of another value, or benefit, conferred by society—the benefit of freedom. The history of Western society has involved efforts of diverse groups of people to gain more freedom for themselves. In obtaining it, some have also gained income, honor, and power. The benefits of freedom, income, honor, and power have always been distributed unequally among the members of society.

Social welfare is a set of activities that has, in part, been directed to offsetting these unequal distributions. Social welfare workers—the people who develop social welfare ideas and carry out social welfare activities—have looked for ways to increase the income, honor, power, and freedom of members of society who receive lesser amounts of these social benefits. Most of these attempts involve some *redistribution* of benefits, that is, taking some of the freedom, power, honor, and income from those who have more and finding acceptable ways of giving it to those who have less. Social welfare activities in Western society thus create conflicts among various groups in society. These for the most part fall under the major heading of the *conflict between freedom and equality*. Individuals who want to more nearly equalize the distribution of social benefits come into conflict with those who want the freedom to keep the amounts of social benefits they already have gained.

There are three main methods of dealing with such conflict: (1) continuing suppression of the less advantaged by the more advantaged; (2) compromise among competing groups; and (3) rebellion by those who have fewer benefits against those who have more, in order to change the rules for distributing benefits. Social welfare in Western societies has mostly been a set of activities devoted to compromise. Sometimes, though, the resulting compromises have been stimulated by angry protests against the established pattern of benefit distribution. In fact, some thoughtful people perceive social welfare to be a means of dealing with discontent, a strategy for preventing rebellion.

It is evident that our discussion has returned to the question: On what basis does anybody deserve anything from society? One purpose of this book is to present the activities of social welfare as a series of changing answers to this question.

Thus far, the following points have been made:

(1) Social welfare is a term designating the ideas and activities that have developed over many centuries for providing income and services to people.

(2) Social welfare includes welfare, which commonly refers to the government's provision of income to people in need. These people are widely believed

to be lazy and immoral, and therefore undeserving of welfare benefits. Although recipients must prove their need, their claims are often thought to be fraudulent.

(3) Charity, relief, and welfare are three methods that have been used to provide income to people who have proven their need for it. These people receive less social honor than other members of society. Such methods of providing income are therefore regarded as demeaning, as impairing the dignity of the people who depend upon them.

(4) The ideas and activities of social welfare cannot be understood apart from the judgments that people make about how income should be distributed. New social welfare ideas are often associated with changes in ideas about the just bases for distributing income. Others are associated with changes in ideas about how to maintain the dignity of people in need.

NEED

Need is implied in any conception of social welfare. Individuals without food and drink can be said to be in need. People must have nourishment in order to survive. But while bread and water will enable a person to survive, at least for a time, giving someone a steady diet of bread and water is likely (in contemporary Western societies) to be regarded not as meeting that person's needs but as punishing him or her. Western societies do not consider a diet of bread and water to be nutritionally adequate. Providing scraps of food to starving people, however, was once considered an adequate contribution to their well-being, and in parts of the world where starvation remains a threat, this may still be true.

A need, then, can be defined in relation to a social standard. Since all people have a biological need for food in order to survive, this need may be seen as being independent of any social standards—but only if a person is considered simply to be a biological organism. But biological existence is not equivalent to human life. When socially organized efforts are undertaken to feed starving people, the efforts are not made merely to maintain the number of live human organisms on earth. Rather, they are undertaken because of the perception that it is worth helping people to stay alive; human life has a moral value that justifies the effort. To be human is to participate, in one way or another, in society, and to feed starving people is to acknowledge that their need for food is not merely a need to remain alive but a need to continue their participation in human society. Human beings seek to survive not merely as biological organisms but as individuals who can function in the society in which they live.

Thus *a human need is a claim to participate in society in accordance with that society's standards.* According to this definition, a steady diet of bread and water would not be regarded as meeting a person's needs. People want to eat in accordance with the prevailing diet in their society. The need for food is definable in relation to a specific social standard. That standard is not met simply by the provision of something edible.

Of course, standards change, and needs change along with them. Some foods once considered acceptable may no longer be, whereas others once rejected may become acceptable. Human invention creates new needs by helping to set new standards. A telephone, or the means of communication it provides, was desired before it was invented. Once invented, it was first a luxury (as it still is in many parts of the world), but its use became so common that it began to be regarded as a need. In fact, it is a need that has been incorporated into the American social welfare system—for example, as a means of maintaining contact with elderly individuals who live alone. In the United States, at least, it would be widely acknowledged that elderly men or women living alone need a telephone. That need is, in effect, their claim to participate in American society according to prevailing standards of communication access to others.

Standard of Living

A standard of living is one way of measuring needs—needs that can be satisfied through economic means. Other types of needs will be discussed elsewhere in this book. Economic needs are focused on here because the need for an adequate income is a theme that has run through the entire history of social welfare efforts.

Societies differ in the level of comfort they are able to offer their members. Western societies have developed the ability to produce a wide variety of objects that have lifted most people far above the level of subsistence. A society exists at a subsistence level if most of its people must be occupied with producing their own food, clothing, and shelter. A society begins to rise above a subsistence level when some of its members are able to produce more food than they require for their own consumption. The extra food can then be exchanged for other goods, obtained from people who have been freed from growing their own food and therefore can devote their time to other work. In this manner, a society develops a division of labor. Increased production of a variety of goods usually follows from the differentiation of work into specialized occupations. Many factors facilitate the productivity of a society—for example, invention of labor-saving machinery, discovery of new resources, and increased ability to carry on trade with other societies. One may speak of the standard of living of a society as the expected level of comfort that it is able to provide its members.

In a society of any size and complexity, there will usually be a range of standards of living, rather than just a single standard. The level of comfort is greater for some people in the society than for others.

Over the past two hundred years, and particularly since 1860, standards of living have been measured in order to evaluate a nation's general economic situation and to compare levels of prosperity within a nation. These efforts at measurement were stimulated in part by social welfare's efforts to arrive at an adequate understanding of the needs of the poor. Sociologist Lee Rainwater has summarized a century and a half of work by various economists and social welfare specialists who attempted to achieve more accurate measurements. Rainwater has noted an interesting trend: Over this period, the very standards for evaluating standards of living were rising.

To make clear what this means: Between about 1860 and 1900, welfare specialists were interested in discovering how much money it took for a workingman and his family to subsist, that is, how much income enabled the family to meet its "physical needs" without its having to receive charity. (Income to meet "physical needs" constituted an adequate budget.) As social attention began to be directed to factory conditions and the fairness of the wages that factory workers received, the concept of an adequate household budget broadened. After 1900, expressions such as "simple decency and efficiency" were used in deciding what was an adequate budget. In 1909, the U.S. Bureau of Labor prepared a report that included two types of budgets, one referred to as "a minimum standard which met minimum physical needs" and another that presented a fair standard for "the development and satisfaction of human attributes." Rainwater has commented:

> The budget makers had a nice sense of the relation of their dry household account-ing to the styles of life it sought to capture—nothing was included in the fair standard budget "other than what some families have already attained and all families are striving to attain." The budget makers during this period were seeking to fix with various kinds of absolute standards a very rapidly changing level of consumer affluence.[7]

The difference between a minimum standard and a fair standard is a difference between two ideas of what a person or family "needs." The step from a minimum to a fair standard was taken in recognition that "all families" were making claims to participate in society at a level that provided for "the development and satisfaction of human attributes."

The U.S. government continued its efforts to clarify standards of living, and by 1967, the Bureau of Labor Statistics had drawn up three budgets. In his analysis of the bureau's recent work, Rainwater concluded that its lower living-standard budget can be regarded as a charity-class budget. This budget states how much money is necessary for the minimum food, clothing, and other physical necessities to keep someone alive and functioning on a temporary emergency basis. The moderate budget can be described as a "poor-but-honest-worker" budget:

If a person is living at the level of this budget, he can regard himself as in the mainstream of the society, although only very modestly so. If he is below it, he is out, clearly disadvantaged in terms of participation in the ongoing socioeconomic life of the community.[8]

The highest of the three budgets, which includes calculations for such things as a fuller array of household appliances and more extensive use of services for a fee (e.g., money for movies, babysitters, dry cleaning services) than do the moderate and lower budgets, Rainwater characterized as "the average American worker's budget."[9] The budget at this level enables workers to know whether they are falling behind as the society's level of affluence has increased.

The efforts of government statisticians, social welfare planners, and social scientists to formulate budgets for different standards of living within the same society illustrate the basic point made earlier about the concept of need. A budget for a standard of living is a way of summarizing "a package of needs." These standard-of-living budgets might be called "standards of needs," for, in effect, they specify what an individual is allowed to need at various income levels. For example, the lowest of the three 1967 budgets assumed that the family lived in rental housing without air conditioning. One may ask, Doesn't a low-income family in a hot climate "need" air conditioning as much as a higher-income family in the same climate? Relief from the discomfort of great heat may be assumed to be equally desired by all who suffer it. The invention of air conditioning makes possible a need for air conditioning to satisfy the desire for relief from the heat. The lack of air conditioning in the low-income family may be characterized as an unmet need, just as decades earlier the family without running water had an unmet need for it, once the society had provided this convenience to many.

Social welfare systems do not assure air conditioning to those who need it but cannot find the means to pay for it from private sources of income. The time may come when air conditioning becomes one of the needs that social welfare systems will meet. That is, they may recognize as legitimate the claim to participate in society with the degree of comfort that air conditioning allows. If this seems far-fetched, consider that some European social welfare systems now provide assured vacations to all.[10] Clearly, the concept of need has developed over time to include social benefits that were scarcely contemplated only a few decades earlier.

In discussing providing air conditioning and vacations through a system of social welfare, we have returned to our earlier question: On what basis does anyone deserve anything from society? Who should have air conditioning? The answer up to now has been that the people who should have air conditioning are those who want it and who can afford to pay for it. Air conditioning is defined as an item rightfully obtained by purchase in the market. It may also be obtained as a gift from a relative or a friend. Although such gifts are a form of help, they are not generally considered a part of social welfare. While the scope of social welfare is broad, it refers to activities for providing help through institutions other than the market or friends and relatives. What then are the kinds of help that constitute the field of social welfare?

HELP

Should the poor be helped in any way? Why? Why not? If they should be helped, who should help them? What kind of help should they be given? Which actions are truly helpful and which only seem to be helpful? If the poor are helped, should other people be helped as well? Why? Why not? Which other people? How should they be helped?

None of these questions has only one answer that is true for all times and all places. The question of helping the poor has been debated over the centuries. And the reasons advanced for helping the poor have varied at different times. As for the ways in which they should be helped—dozens have been proposed and tried.

An attempt to list all of these will not be undertaken here. But an examination of them, and of the ways in which social welfare has been expanded beyond a concern with the poor, suggests that most can be regarded as variations of five fundamental ideas. Parts II through VI of this book are devoted to presenting these five fundamental ideas, showing their development in Western society from their first significant appearance to their contemporary manifestations, including the various ways they have been implemented, that is, the kinds of organizations that came into being for carrying out the ideas. At this point, an expanded definition of social welfare can be given: *Social welfare is a set of ideas and a set of activities and organizations for carrying out those ideas, all of which have taken shape over many centuries to provide people with income and other social benefits in ways that safeguard their dignity.* It must also be noted here, and will be noted where appropriate throughout this book, that some of the ideas that were tried did not safeguard dignity and some provided little or no income.

As has been implied by the discussions of standard of living and the references to assured vacations and air conditioning, the scope of social welfare is not fixed. It is elastic, expandable. In the late nineteenth and early twentieth centuries, particularly, the concept of social welfare was enormously expanded from exclusive concentration on the poor and the disabled to a conception that includes all members of society. However, as often happens in social welfare, the expanded conception did not receive complete acceptance, nor did it totally replace the old one. In fact some influential people believe the older idea to be better than the newer one.

With regard to this incomplete change, Wilensky and Lebeaux have observed that there appear to be two competing concepts of social welfare in the United States—the *residual* and the *institutional*. According to the residual concept, social welfare help should be a last resort, called upon only when the "normal" institutions for meeting needs, the family and the market, are not functioning for a person, who then, and only then, becomes a person "in need." According to the institutional concept, social welfare institutions are part of the everyday, "normal" institutions of society, as are the family, the market, and religious institutions.[11] To illustrate this distinction, consider the contemporary issue of day care. Government-financed day-care facilities only for preschool children whose mothers must work outside the home in order to ensure an adequate livelihood for their families would be an example of the residual concept of social welfare. On the other hand, government-financed day-care facilities for young children of any families, regardless of income and of the work status of the mother, would be an example of the institutional concept of social welfare. Day care would be one of the ordinary services the society makes available to everybody, as it now makes available education at public expense. It is clear that the woman who chooses to pursue a career has a need for day-care facilities for her preschool children, but it is equally clear that this is a different concept of need from the one that applies to the woman who must work to support her family. As mentioned above, social welfare has been moving from a residual concept to an institutional one. To understand this development more precisely, five major ideas of social welfare must be distinguished.

The five fundamental ideas that have emerged in the course of social welfare history can be differentiated from one another on the basis of the type of social relationship that is built into each idea, the type of social relationship between the helper and the helped. The five main ideas are briefly identified here:

(1) *Charity and philanthropy* are forms of social welfare based upon a relationship between a donor and a recipient, a giver and a receiver, with a clear status difference between the two. The social welfare act is an act of donation, often from someone wealthy to someone poor or to an organization that acts as an intermediary between the wealthy and the poor. Historically, the donation made voluntarily has been considered the ideal, but social pressures have usually been applied to stimulate donations.

Philanthropic donations may be made for purposes other than social welfare; for example, they are given to support art museums, orchestras, theaters, universities. Philanthropic donations for purposes other than social welfare are not a prime concern in this book.

(2) *Public welfare* is, to a substantial degree, the successor to charity as the major idea for dealing with the poor, but it is also something more. Public

welfare can be described as a form of social welfare in which the public, acting through the state, provides care for the dependent members of society—not only poor people but also children, the aged, and the physically disabled. Care takes a variety of forms. Historically, provision of income has been the major form of care; today this type of provision is known as public assistance. But over the years, other types of care have been added in the form of specialized services: for example, finding foster homes for children who are homeless or whose homes have been judged unfit for the raising of children.

Public welfare, then, encompasses provision of both income and services to dependent persons by the state, financed by taxation of citizens rather than by voluntary contributions. The term *state* is used in the sense of the organized public authority that can enforce its legitimate decisions on the members of a society. The state encompasses the various levels of government; in the United States, the distinctions among federal, state, and local governments are particularly significant. The distinction between national and local levels of authority has some importance in other societies as well.

Like charity, public welfare is a modality of social welfare that is directed to significantly disabled or otherwise disadvantaged members of society. Public welfare includes public assistance, and also various services to certain categories of disabled and disadvantaged people. What is technically known as public assistance is what is popularly thought of as "welfare." Journalistic and popular discussions of "the welfare system" most often are discussions of various aspects of public assistance programs; such discussions seldom cover the full spectrum of public welfare, much less the full scope of social welfare.

(3) *Social insurance* is a relatively modern idea, arising in clear form in the nineteenth century. The idea of social insurance is similar to that of public assistance in that both involve a relationship between a government and its citizens. The funds for public assistance and for social insurance come from taxes paid by the citizens to the government, and the funds are paid out by the government to recipients. A very fundamental difference, however, is that the recipients of social insurance are receiving benefits that have been earned by work, either their own work, or work by someone else on their behalf. The amounts of the benefits to be paid under various social insurance programs are, in theory, predictable obligations of the government. Thus a person who is, say, age thirty-five, can write to the Social Security Administration and find out the amount of monthly retirement income he or she can already count on upon retirement at age sixty-two or sixty-five or seventy.

The concept is seldom realized in pure form. In other words, the benefits of social insurance to which a person is entitled are often subject to certain qualifications that are not found in private insurance arrangements. Nevertheless, predictable entitlement to government-paid benefits under specified circumstances such as unemployment, disability, and retirement is a distinctive social welfare idea. The range of circumstances under which such predictable benefits are paid has steadily broadened since the nineteenth century, and this has resulted in a new ideal in Western societies that has been called "the welfare state." The welfare state is one that provides benefits for virtually all types of hazards that any person might encounter. The welfare state does not exist in pure form, but the concept has been used by many in the social welfare field as a standard for judging progress in social welfare. The welfare state came under increasing political attack in the late 1970s and early 1980s.

(4) *Social service* differs from the other main social welfare ideas in that the benefits provided are, unlike income or material benefits, predominantly intangible services. Social service, like social insurance, is an idea that first emerged clearly in the nineteenth century. It began as a kind of offshoot of charity. Well-to-do people voluntarily donated their time, rather than their money, to helping the poor. At the turn of the century, the well-to-do volunteer was replaced by the middle-class, trained professional. In both cases, the social welfare benefits are considered to lie in the *interaction* between the helping person and the person being helped, the social service worker (volunteer or professional) and the client.

The social service idea gave rise to a number of new occupations whose practitioners provide services. The first of these new occupations was social work. *Social work may be defined as an occupation devoted to providing social services through a set of specialized techniques and procedures that are based on concepts drawn from the social sciences and from social work's own concepts and backlog of experience.* Social work is the longest-established and probably most fully developed of the social service occupations. It is also the most wide-ranging, dealing with a wider scope of problems than do more recent social service occupations such as rehabilitation counseling, marriage and family counseling, day-care work, and recreation work, which focus on more narrowly specified problems.

The first social workers dealt with poverty; others soon worked in other problem areas, and the field since has developed in a way that has carried it into new settings in keeping with an expanding concept of its usefulness. The social worker is expected to be knowledgeable about personality problems of childhood, adolescence, adulthood, and old age; about adoption procedures; about family conflicts of all kinds; about group activities as productive developmental experiences; about how to help communities organize to solve neighborhood problems; about how to help people get to specialized agencies that deal with their problems; and about how to help people deal with problems of inadequate income.

(5) *Mutual aid* is distinguished from the other social welfare ideas in that the control over the way in which help is provided rests with the people who will be helped, because helpers and helped are, in effect, interchangeable. The charity, public welfare, and social service ideas of social welfare make clear distinctions between helpers and helped. (The concept of social insurance does not fit easily into the point now being developed.) The idea of mutual aid involves

people banding together as equals to help one another. In some types of mutual aid, the people involved contribute to a common fund. Each member of the group can draw upon the fund when the need arises, but it is not known in advance who will need aid or when. Mutual aid in this form can be traced back at least as far as the Roman Empire, and it was also a prominent form of social welfare among immigrants to the United States.

A somewhat different type of mutual aid arose in the 1960s in the United States. Known as "community action," it represented an effort to develop a system of social welfare based more in and on the local community than on the national government or on professional social service. In practice, community action was not very successful, and the concept has gone into decline. Nevertheless, it retains importance because it envisions a type of social welfare based on a relationship among equals in a geographically identified community.

These, then, are the five fundamental ideas of social welfare that have emerged over the centuries. Each has undergone many transformations. Each has been put into practice in many ways, and today there are many competing versions of each idea. There are, for example, numerous proposals for expanding social insurance. The social services have changed as new needs have been identified and as the standards of the times have changed. Thus, where once the major advice given to unmarried people was that they should remain chaste, now there is a widely perceived need for counseling on the use of contraceptives. Further, any particular social welfare program may blend two or more of the five basic ideas; the combinations are numerous. For example, at times, public assistance and social service counseling have been handled by the same agency. At other times, social service counseling has been kept separate from public assistance.

It is difficult to confine the words "social welfare" to a precise set of human activities. Nevertheless, the term points to activities that have arisen as responses to certain tendencies that recur in human history. These tendencies can be stated as follows:

(1) A tendency to be concerned about what happens to other people.
(2) A tendency to be alarmed by people whose situation or whose conduct deviates too widely from what is considered "normal."
(3) A tendency to want to keep social arrangements continuing as they have been with the least disruption possible.

Throughout Western history, poor people have aroused the concern of others, alarmed them by their conduct, and have often seemed to pose a disruptive threat. The humanitarian concern for others, the fear of deviant behavior, and the fear that deprived people would take power and change things to suit themselves have blended and led to an incredibly diverse array of ideas and plans as to what to do for and about poor people.

From a central focus upon the poor, social welfare activities have expanded to take in more and more categories of people. There is no doubt that this mode of thinking about social welfare in itself causes problems: The reason is that *welfare* is a term that is applied to those deviant, disreputable, alarming segments of society. Other members of society do not like to think they are involved in "social welfare"; it brings them too close for comfort to people they do not care for. Reflecting this general fear, an electric utility provided social welfare information in the regular newsletter it sends with its electric bills. It stated:

> Many people who are eligible for Food Stamps are not getting them because they are unaware that they qualify. Food Stamps—which can boost your food purchasing power considerably—are a federal subsidy, not a welfare program. You do not have to be on welfare to get them, and ownership of an auto or a house does not bar food stamp eligibility. Deductions for rent, health, education and other costs are allowed in figuring income levels to determine eligibility.[12]

Here, then, is a message that makes fine distinctions. If you are really needy, you are entitled to food stamps, but only if you are really, really, really needy do you have to think of yourself as being "on welfare." If you are a bit better off, you do not have to think of yourself as having anything to do with anything called welfare. Food stamps can be called a subsidy; that removes the dishonor from the benefit. Businesses receive subsidies, and only a few people are willing to call business subsidies "welfare." If you can think of benefits you receive as being a subsidy, or as unemployment insurance, or as a family allowance, or as a social service, or as anything other than "welfare," you can be part of the world that does not suffer from loss of dignity for the benefits they receive.

But the student of social welfare cannot pretend that these programs and terms have nothing to do with "welfare" in its popular meaning. Food stamps, social security, and all the other terms arose, like welfare in its modern, disreputable meaning, as part of the same general concerns identified earlier as three recurrent tendencies in history. Fear and compassion are blended into these terms and into the activities they stand for. The desire to help others and the desire to control them are mixed, in varying proportions, into the whole field of social welfare and into all the versions of it that the world has seen thus far. For all the diversity of terms, for all the ambiguity that any particular term has, and for the unboundedness that the field itself has, there is nonetheless a certain overall coherence to this large area of activity that is called social welfare. Taking account of the preceding discussion and, further, taking account of the fact that the word *concern* implies both responsible care and anxious worry, the overall coherence of the field can be indicated in the presentation of a more abstract, but more inclusive, definition of social welfare than the one presented earlier: *Social welfare may be defined as the social organization of concern for persons and groups who are vulnerable to social disability.*[13]

SUMMARY

Social welfare may be defined as the social organization of concern for persons and groups who are vulnerable to social disability. Concern is expressed in ideas of what people need, ideas about how to help them meet their needs, and organizations for putting the ideas into practice. Social welfare today can be understood as being based on five major concepts of help: (1) charity and philanthropy, (2) public welfare, (3) social insurance, (4) social service, and (5) mutual aid. Each of these concepts has been modified over time and has been implemented through various kinds of organizations. The concepts are developed and combined in diverse ways in actual practice, but these five are the major ideas of help that modern social welfare is based on.

Originally social welfare was concerned with a small range of social disabilities—poverty, illness and physical disablement, widowhood and orphanhood. The scope has since widened to include other kinds of disability. Loss of income because of unemployment and retirement are modern examples. Changes in society result in new concepts of what people need and consequently in new ideas about how to give help.

A central issue in social welfare is how concerned society should be about safeguarding the honor of people who need help. People who receive government payments technically known as public assistance (and popularly known as welfare) tend to be considered disreputable, just as fifty or a hundred years ago people who subsisted on charity were considered disreputable. Other forms of social welfare do not bring a penalty of reduced honor and reputation (and charity did not originally).

Notes

[1] *Oxford English Dictionary*, Vol. 12. (Oxford: Oxford University Press, 1933).

[2] David Matza, "Poverty and Disrepute," in Robert K. Merton and Robert Nisbet, eds., *Contemporary Social Problems*, 3rd ed. (New York: Harcourt Brace Jovanovich, 1971). See also Richard P. Coleman and Lee Rainwater, with Kent A. McClelland, *Social Standing in America* (New York: Basic Books, 1978), Chapter 10.

[3] Robert Reinhold, "Public Found Against Welfare Idea But in Favor of What Programs Do," *New York Times*, August 3, 1977, p. 1.

[4] *Oxford English Dictionary*.

[5] Carl Sandburg, *The People, Yes* (New York: Harcourt, Brace, 1936), p. 75.

[6]Bernard Beck, "The Military as a Welfare Institution," in Charles C. Moskos, Jr., ed., *Public Opinion and the Military Establishment* (Beverly Hills, Calif.: Sage Publications, 1971). See also Bernard Beck, "Welfare as a Moral Category," *Social Problems,* Vol. 14 (Winter 1967), pp. 258–277.

[7]This discussion of standards of living is drawn from Lee Rainwater, *What Money Buys— Inequality and the Social Meanings of Income* (New York: Basic Books, 1974), especially Chapter 3.

[8]*Ibid.*

[9]*Ibid.*

[10]Alfred J. Kahn and Sheila B. Kammerman, *Not for the Poor Alone—European Social Services* (Philadelphia: Temple University Press, 1975), *Chapter 6.*

[11]Harold L. Wilensky and Charles N. Lebeaux, *Industrial Society and Social Welfare* (New York: Free Press, 1965), Chapter 6.

[12]Con Edison, *Customer News,* January 1975.

[13]This definition, though independently formulated, has some similarity to that offered in Mayer N. Zald, ed., *Social Welfare Institutions—A Sociological Reader* (New York: Wiley, 1965), p. 3.

Society and Social Welfare

2

During the American presidential election campaign of 1972, Senator George McGovern, the Democratic candidate, proposed a program that would guarantee a minimum annual income of $1,000 for every person in the country. While this proposal by itself did not account for his defeat in the election, it appears to have been one of the contributing factors. His idea was widely considered too radical, not in keeping with the country's fundamental political and social ideas. Of course, once unacceptable ideas sometimes later gain acceptance, and this idea may be among them. For now, this episode in American history illustrates a theme of major concern in this chapter and throughout the book. Ideas about social welfare tend to gain acceptance slowly, especially ideas that represent significant departures from what has been customary.

Ideas about how to achieve the goals of social welfare, and organizations devoted to achieving them, do not materialize out of thin air. They arise in a context of traditional ongoing relationships among people, or in recognition of the fact that traditional relationships are changing and thereby imposing new strains and new demands on people. Social welfare is best understood, then, in the context of the prevailing organization of society and in the associated context of social change.

This chapter will present two complementary frameworks for thinking about society; together they provide a context for appreciating and understanding the diverse social welfare institutions that have appeared in the course of Western history. The first framework is analytical. It identifies the principal elements of any society. The second framework is historical. It provides a brief, schematic overview of the development of Western society.

A FRAMEWORK FOR ANALYZING SOCIETY

The McGovern proposal illustrates several of the components of the framework to be introduced here.

Resources

McGovern's proposal that every person in the United States be guaranteed a minimum income of $1,000 per year implies that the country has enough resources to carry out such a program. We are not concerned at the moment with whether McGovern's proposal was a good one or not but rather with the elements that enter into the establishment of social welfare programs of any kind. A society's resources are one component of a framework for analyzing the society. What resources are implied by McGovern's proposal?

Wealth

McGovern's proposal, like any proposal for transferring income to people who do not have enough according to the standards of their society, implies that the society has reserves of wealth. It is based on the assumption that the society produces a surplus of wealth beyond what most of its people require to subsist. Proposals such as McGovern's did not arise on the American frontier, when the standard of living was defined by the amount of land that a family could clear of trees and brush and could farm by themselves. Whatever the needs of that time might have been and however they might have been defined, there was no surplus of wealth of the magnitude implied by McGovern's proposal. Many people believed that there was not sufficient surplus in 1972 either. Regardless of which view was correct, the important points here are that (1) social welfare is based on surplus, and (2) the determination of surplus is itself a complex social process.

Organization

To assure that every person in a society of more than 200 million people has a certain minimum income requires an organization that both identifies people below this level and collects and distributes the income. An effective organization for carrying out such a large-scale task is not found in every society. It may, of course, be developed in a society that does not have it. When such an organization exists, it is a resource. A society that lacks it cannot carry out such tasks.

Ideas

There are societies in which there is surplus wealth but in which no candidate for major office proposes assuring every member of the society a guaranteed minimum income. A society's resources include not only its wealth and its organization but its ideas. As we know from the fate of McGovern's proposal and, in fact, from other proposals for a guaranteed minimum income, not every idea is considered a good one. But it cannot be considered at all unless someone comes up with it. Once proposed, it may be discussed, debated, and discarded or modified and refined until eventually it gains wider acceptance, or is rejected.

Social welfare ideas have been proposed by many different categories of people. The dominant categories have differed at different times in history. For much of Western history, the major social welfare ideas were produced by theologians. From the fifteenth century through the nineteenth century, business and political leaders produced most of the social welfare ideas, although ministers continued to make important contributions. In the twentieth century, specific categories of social welfare professionals have developed—social workers, social policy analysts, welfare administrators—and they have largely replaced theologians, ministers, and business leaders as influential producers of social welfare ideas. Political leaders continue to be important, sometimes producing the basic proposals, sometimes deciding which ideas will be pursued.

Values and Beliefs

Both the McGovern proposal and the rejection of it reflect general values and beliefs. Values may be defined, following anthropologist Clyde Kluckhohn, as basic criteria for deciding what is desirable, or what is good and what is bad, what is right and what is wrong. Proposals to guarantee every member of a society an assured income depend upon some kind of idea that this is "a good thing to do." For example, they may derive from religious values: All people are children of God the Creator and therefore should be assured at least a minimum appropriate share of Creation. Or the values may be political: Justice requires that all members of a society have a portion of that society's benefits, at least a portion sufficient to sustain life. The values may be of self-interest: Assuring everyone at least a minimally adequate income reduces the likelihood that large numbers of deprived people will rebel and take away the wealth of those who have an ample supply. Thus the same social welfare proposal can be derived from different values and may be supported by people who subscribe to the different values.

Clearly, values may conflict. The opposition to guaranteed income proposals can be based on self-interest values: People should be allowed to keep the wealth they have and not be required to share it with others. The opposition can be based on political values: Income should be earned, and those who, for whatever reason, are unable to earn it should turn to their family, their friends, or to any agency that volunteers to give assistance in such circumstances. But they should not expect it to come from government.

Although a society may have prevailing values, at the same time it may have values that are different from these. Guaranteed income proposals have been incongruent with prevailing American values, but obviously congruent with the values of at least a minority of Americans. The minority can become a majority; it has happened before.

Beliefs are closely related to values. Beliefs are interpretations of how things work, how they happen. A long-prevailing American belief, for example, has been that the United States is a land of unlimited opportunity. The country permits all who work hard and have talent to realize their goals; anyone who tries can be successful. This belief provides most members of American society with an explanation of how the benefits of the society are apportioned. Again, as in the case of values, beliefs are not universally shared. Some believe that success is more a matter of whether or not a person has had good luck. According to this belief, chance, not effort, explains a person's situation in life. Still others believe that success depends on "who you know."

Power

Senator McGovern may have made a good proposal or it may have been a bad one. Whichever, for some purposes it does not matter. What matters is that he did not have the power to get this idea accepted and turned into a government program. Power is the ability of a person or group to influence the actions of others, through persuasion or compulsion. The people who did not like McGovern's idea had more power than McGovern and his supporters had. Changes in the way social welfare is carried out can be traced to changes in the distribution of power, as well as to changes in values and beliefs and resources.

Power is quantifiable in a rough way. A person or a group may have enough power to accomplish certain goals but not enough to accomplish others. Social welfare activities and programs often result when opposing groups engage in a contest of power and then reach a compromise because no side has enough power to have its ideas alone prevail. Political life is made up of such contests among different groups, each of which may have representatives of its interests in the government. The different interests may also organize as social movements, competing with each other by publicizing their views through protest marches or through other means of communication—pamphlets, advertisements, and discussions in printed and on broadcast media. A power struggle of this kind began to take place in the late 1970s between supporters and opponents of abortion as a medical service and abortion counseling as a social service.

Population

A society is made up of members, and collectively the members make up that society's population. The composition of a population is not static. Depending upon such factors as birth rate, migration, and health, a population may be younger or older, and this is a dimension that is particularly significant for social welfare purposes. One recent trend is that people are living longer. Some of the ways in which a society carries out its activities are affected by changes in the age distribution of its population. The presence of a greater number of older people may bring increased attention to their need for special facilities and services—attention that they could not command when their numbers were fewer.

The spatial location of a population is another important aspect of the way the population functions. In the course of Western history, three general types of location have been particularly significant: rural, urban, and suburban. Historically the movement has been from rural to urban to suburban living. This movement has affected social welfare, as well as other aspects of Western societies.

Migration

One of the significant characteristics of human beings is that they move from one place to another. Some of the movements they undertake are temporary, such as when visiting friends and relatives and in times of war. When a visit is over or a war concluded, most of the people who have participated return to their homes. Certain movement patterns are repetitive, as in the example of migrant farm workers who travel from one agricultural region to another, following the harvesting seasons. In the nineteenth and twentieth centuries, temporary traveling—whether associated with visiting, warfare, or work—prompted the development of social agencies to provide various services to individuals and families whose lives had been altered or disrupted by travel. The Young Men's Christian Association (YMCA) constructed housing for the men who were laying railroad track during the building of the transcontinental railroads. The American Red Cross developed significantly in wartime to help both soldiers and the families they had left behind.

Other migrations involve more or less permanent resettlement of people in locations at some distance from their place of origin. Three migration patterns have particular importance in the development of Western society generally and social welfare specifically. First was the migration that accompanied the revival of trade in western Europe between the tenth and fourteenth centuries. Second were the voyages of discovery in the fifteenth and sixteenth centuries that led to the establishment of overseas empires by western European countries and to the establishment of slavery in parts of those empires. Third was the migration of people from agricultural to urban locations, brought on by the Industrial Revolution, beginning in the middle of the eighteenth century and continuing into our own time. The voyages of discovery, for example, led to the settlement of North and South America. They also led to the European discovery of Africa, the capture of Africans by Europeans, and the shipping of the captured Africans to the Western hemisphere as slaves. The subsequent freeing of the slaves, and the freeing of colonies by Great Britain and other European countries, have led to multiple consequences that have prompted social welfare measures of many different kinds. These measures continue in the U.S. today, stimulated by migrations in the late 1970s and early '80s of Cubans, Haitians, Mexicans, Vietnamese, and others—twentieth-century consequences of sixteenth-century voyages of discovery.

Social Organization

A society consists of a population carrying on activities. The activities are not completely haphazard; they are organized. Store managers do not lead their employees in prayers; parents do not sell dinner to their children; bankers do not stand in the street directing traffic. The purpose of these slightly frivolous examples is to underline the familiar fact that human activities are organized in institutions; an institution is a pattern of activities, governed by values and norms, carried out by persons in specified statuses that entail the fulfillment of expectations, or roles. A store is an example of an economic institution, a market; the person in the status of store manager is not expected to lead prayers, nor are those in the status of store employee expected to pray as part of their role. If any of them wishes to pray, they are expected to do so in a religious institution, a house of worship. And so a society's activities are organized into various kinds of institutions—economic, political, religious, kinship—of which a market, a pattern of traffic control, a house of worship, and a family are examples. Each institution is governed by general values and by values specific to the particular institution.

The appearance (and disappearance) of various kinds of social welfare institutions will be a central focus of this book. As the discussion proceeds, it will at times be necessary to call attention to the way in which other kinds of institutions influence social welfare institutions.

Social Inequality

One of the persistent facts about societies is that their members receive unequal amounts of benefits from them. Why such inequality exists and whether it is an inevitable and ineradicable characteristic of society have been long-debated questions. Although the answers remain a matter of continuing dispute, two main explanations have emerged for the inequality that is found in all societies: (1) Differences in power enable some people to gain domination over others. Once in power, they, their allies, and their heirs tend to remain dominant and wealthy unless or until they are displaced by people who have new means of gaining power. (2) Differences in ability result in performances that are differentially evaluated by members of society and therefore differentially rewarded. Each of these two explanations has many variations; each is capable of being elaborated into complex theories of social inequality (or social stratification) and social organization.

Whatever the explanation of inequality, a basic question facing a society is that of how its benefits are to be distributed among its members. What are these benefits?

A livelihood

All people find a means of maintaining life—a livelihood—within the framework of a particular society. Whether loosely or strictly, a society exercises some control over the livelihoods of its members, with various kinds of rules governing entitlement to the assets that can be used for gaining a livelihood. Land, animals, buildings, materials in the ground and in the waters, opportunities to acquire

skills and knowledge, opportunities to gain suitable credentials for working—
licenses, work permits, certificates, diplomas—are examples of such assets. The
rights to these assets are fundamental benefits. Not every member of a society
has the same opportunity to acquire any of the assets that are usable for a
livelihood.

A share of control over one's life circumstances

Societies differ in the extent to which they intervene in the lives of their members. They differ also in the extent to which they permit their members to have
a say in how the society is run. Finally, they differ in the amounts of autonomy
and power they extend to their members. Autonomy and power can be thought
of as two distinct benefits, but here we may consider them as two aspects of
control. The idea that the ordinary members of society should have a high degree
of autonomy and a definite share in controlling their society by participating in
at least some major decisions originated in Athens 2,500 years ago, declined for
centuries, and began to be influential less than 400 years ago.

Honor

A society distributes honor to its members as a benefit. People want not only to
have a living and a measure of control over their own circumstances; they also
want "to be treated as human beings," which means to be accorded some honor.
To be "treated like a dog" is to be denied the minimum honor that is felt to be
due a human being.

Wealth and honor are frequently associated. That is, people with more
wealth generally receive more honor than people with less wealth. As noted in
Chapter 1, poverty in modern societies is considered somewhat disreputable. In
the early days of Christianity, poverty was seen by some Christians as a particularly honorable condition. And in the thirteenth century, two religious orders,
the Dominicans and the Franciscans, were established, whose members agreed
to live in poverty, gaining thier livelihood by begging, and devoting themselves
to comforting the poor and sick.

> All the miseries, all the hideous blemishes of humanity, every kind of outcast, the
> physical or moral lepers, were to have their sympathy; and the lower classes in
> return would love and venerate them, and grow morally better, owing to their
> word and example.[1]

The friars became so popular because of their poverty that they were given gifts
by pious wealthy benefactors, and the orders in time became wealthy organizations, with the result that "the respect of the multitude lessen[ed], their renown

for holiness lessen[ed]."[2] Here, then, is a situation in which increasing wealth led to decreasing honor. There are other situations in which this would also be true. But usually it has been poverty that has brought disrepute, a decrease of honor, and wealth that has brought increased honor.

A livelihood, a share of control over the circumstances affecting oneself and others, and honor—these are the main benefits that societies distribute or, at least, they are the benefits that have been most thought about and studied. Physical safety is also a benefit, and some people live closer to disaster than do others, by reason of geography, occupation, or the negligence of others.[3] The opportunity to experience beauty is another benefit that societies may be said to distribute. A full exploration of these benefits is beyond the scope of the subject of social welfare; the primary concern in this book will be with the benefits of livelihood, control, and honor, and the various forms that these benefits have taken at different times in the Western world.

THE DEVELOPMENT OF WESTERN SOCIETY

The world we live in did not begin this morning. Contemporary social welfare activities cannot be understood simply by describing them as they are. The experiences of people of the past are worked into the fabric of our own lives and institutions. American society functions under a Constitution that was written two hundred years ago; the English are ruled by a monarchy that is even older. Millions of people in many countries worship as believers in Christianity, a religion that is more than nineteen hundred years old and that derives from Judaism, which is even older. The Roman Catholic Church, with millions of contemporary adherents, is the oldest continuously existing single organization in the world. The lives of all of us are shaped by institutions that have developed over long periods of time, and it is necessary to have an overview of some of the major historical periods and their distinctive characteristics in order to appreciate the ways in which social welfare institutions have taken shape.

Every country has a unique history. Despite this uniqueness, many countries are linked together on the basis of certain similarities of tradition and identity. One such grouping is known as Western society, which is commonly thought of as including the countries of western Europe and the other countries of the world that were either settled by Europeans or have evolved values and ways of life that are predominantly European. Australia, Canada, New Zealand, and the United States are thus commonly thought of as part of Western society. These countries, despite their differences, share certain cultural features: their languages are part of the same general family of languages; they have a common tradition of religious belief and worship that differentiates Western Christianity from Eastern Christianity, as well as from other religions; they have in common a tradition of moral, political, and social thought that is most directly traceable to ideas that first emerged in certain pre-Christian Mediterranean societies, particularly those of Israel, Greece, and Rome. The societies of western Europe traded with each other more actively and fought with each other more often than they did with societies elsewhere in the world. The institutions of each Western society have influenced those of the other Western societies, as their members became familiar with each other's ideas and practices. The intellectual interaction among various Western countries is perhaps most concisely illustrated by this account of the career of Juan Luis Vives, a sixteenth-century social welfare thinker, presented by social welfare historian Karl de Schweinitz:

> During the years that England was moving toward the organization of a system of governmental relief, Europe was passing through a similar experience; and between the Continent and the island there was a considerable exchange of ideas about the problem of poverty.
> One of the men who participated in this exchange was Juan Luis Vives, a native of Spain who was educated in Paris and who made Flanders his adopted country. He developed a plan of organized relief which he addressed to the Consuls and Senate of Bruges, his adopted city. . . .
> Vives was one of the great thinkers of his day. . . . Vives went to England. Here he held a lectureship in rhetoric at Oxford. . . .
> It is interesting to oberve how many of Vives' ideas appeared in current or subsequent relief administration in England. He advocated registering the poor. This was provided for by Henry VIII in the Act of 1531. . . . He relied upon private contributions to finance his program, as did the English law of 1536. . . . His theory that relief and work should be administered in such a way as to punish the individual deemed to be in need of reform was not unlike the program of deterrence which later was applied disastrously in England. His concept of censorship over the morals and behavior of the poor was appropriate to an age which accepted sumptuary legislation and in which the poor were just beginning to emerge from a status only slightly superior to slavery.[4]

The interchange of social welfare ideas, exemplified by Vives's activities more than four hundred years ago, has continued. It is, then, justifiable to conceive of our topic as a Western tradition in social welfare. At the same time, of course, each Western society continues to be unique. No attempt will be made in this book to provide detailed accounts of the social welfare programs of the individual Western countries. Rather, the focus will be on the development of the main currents of social welfare primarily in Western society, and especially in England and the United States, as it developed from its two ancient sources, the Judeo-Christian tradition and the Greco-Roman tradition, and as influenced by various Western thinkers, such as Vives.

A brief account of the ancient Greek and Roman societies, and of ancient Jewish society, both when Jewish social welfare ideas first developed and when Christianity began to develop, will be outlined in the next chapter. Here a schematic overview of Western history beginning with the Middle Ages is presented. The social organization of three main periods, the Middle Ages (particularly the later Middle Ages, from about 1000 to 1500), the period of preindustrial capitalism (1400 to 1750), and the industrial period (1750 to the present) will be sketched out. Since the kinds of social welfare ideas and institutions that developed were influenced by the general social and economic ideas of the time, a brief overview of some of the significant ideas of the period will also be presented.

The Later Middle Ages

Medieval society in western Europe developed out of the ruins of the Roman Empire. The Middle Ages refer roughly to the period between the breakup of the Empire and the onset of the Protestant Reformation; the earlier half, from about 400 to about 1000 is referred to as the Dark Ages, and the following five centuries as the High Middle Ages.[5]

The basic settlement pattern and at the same time the basic economic institution of the medieval world was the manor. "A manor is a village community where unfree peasants cultivate a lord's *demesne* or domain (land directly managed by him) in return for the use of another portion of his estate, while a substantial part of the land remains more or less open to all parties for grazing, gathering wood, and possibly trapping and hunting."[6] The manorial system developed out of the violence and anarchy that attended the collapse of the Roman Empire. Small landowners, feeling the need for protection, gave up their land to more powerful landowners, in exchange for this protection and the right to gain a livelihood from a portion of the land.[7]

The great insecurity of medieval times that led to the manor as the basic unit of economic organization led also to a form of political and social organization that came to be known as feudalism. The lord of a manor might need warriors to help him protect his holdings from those who would fight to take it from him. To obtain a warrior, he would grant a man some land, a fief, in exchange for military service under specified conditions. A fief might be a single manor or several scattered manors. The fief holder, known as the vassal of the lord from whom he held the fief, might himself enter into similar relations of vassalage with people who held fiefs from him. Thus a man could be both a vassal of a greater lord than himself and at the same time a lord of vassals who were subordinate to him and considered economically and socially inferior. By the twelfth century, much of medieval Europe was organized in feudal relationships. The king of each country was considered the great lord and the landholders under him did not really own their land but held it as a vassal of the king or a vassal of the vassal, and so on down the innumerable layers of hierarchy. In theory, the king too did not own the land but was the vassal of God, the Lord of all Creation. In practice, effective power in feudal times lay mostly with the lords, dukes, counts, earls, and barons, who acquired the powers of justice and taxation in their fiefdoms.

The feudal world was turbulent, but in theory it offered to all a livelihood and physical protection, based on personal pledges of service in exchange for these basic benefits. In time, feudal arrangements, which had each begun as a kind of individual personal transaction, became hereditary. A father's fief could be inherited by his son, provided the son also swore allegiance to the lord and paid a kind of inheritance fee to him. Though there was strife, leading to conquest and defeat, with families rising and falling in fortune, the medieval world became relatively settled in the sense that everyone was born into a certain status, which carried with it a more or less specified amount of honor and a more or less specified standard of living. Feudal society was

> the quintessence of hereditary aristocracy, privilege by birth instead of proved merit. A virtually impassable gulf separated the ruling class of lords and their fief-holders from the masses of peasants. Whatever their virtues or their vices, the rulers monopolized wealth, power and prestige. However loyal, content or secure at best, the peasants were mostly serfs, bound to the soil, forced to work for the lord.[8]

The feudal world was thus one in which there was an emphasis on hierarchical relationships. At the same time, the major ties among people were local; ties to village and manor were more important than those to larger geographic and political units. Nations were weak. But one larger bond did have significance, the bond to the Christian religion. In the Middle Ages virtually everybody thought of themselves as belonging to one universal church, a supranational unit known as Christendom, distinguished from the world of the infidel, the non-believer. The beliefs that united them have been summarized by historian G. G. Coulton:

> All medieval thought is characterized, nominally at least, by the convictions that each man has a soul to save, and that, therefore, salvation is the main end of every human being, not a distant ideal, but the most practical duty that is set before all. . . .
>
> All orthodox medieval thought rested upon the assumption that the last moment of life marked the man for an eternity of unspeakable bliss or of torment beyond all conception. And, as this was decided by the dying man's state at the last moment, so the decisive factor in this state was his theological belief.[9]

Undoubtedly, there were individuals who did not take their religion seriously. But in his analysis of feudal society, French historian Marc Bloch has asked: ". . . who can fail to recognize in the fear of hell one of the great social forces of the age?"[10] The Christian concern for the saving of souls was to have a profound impact on social welfare throughout the centuries.

The Rise of Commercial Society

The decline of the Roman Empire had left western Europe transformed into an almost totally agricultural society. The towns were decayed, there was little commerce. From about the tenth century A.D., business gradually began to revive, and towns slowly began to take shape. Between the tenth and fourteenth centuries, a Commercial Revolution began, which ultimately transferred economic leadership from the landowner to the merchant. This shift in power and wealth was many centuries in the making, but "commerce between the tenth century and the fourteenth century became the most dynamic sector of the economy in one country after another, and merchants were the main promoters of change."[11] The merchants became town dwellers or bourgeoisie (from an old Germanic word, *Burg,* meaning settlement).[12] They also became a great middle class with a developing ideology of their own that was to set them in opposition to the landed hereditary aristocracy.

In France, the landed aristocracy was overturned by the French Revolution that began in 1789. In England, the middle class finally gained ascendance over the aristocracy in the nineteenth century, when the merchants were already joined by manufacturing industrialists. In the United States, inherited honor in the form of titles of nobility had been prohibited by the Constitution, but a kind of nontitled landed aristocracy developed through the plantation system of the old South, and lost power as a result of the American Civil War (1861–1865).

The development of commerce was the beginning of a major transformation of Western society. Although the Church resisted the change in some ways, in others it contributed to it. Herbert J. Muller referred to this influence when he noted:

> In general, the rise of a bourgeois, urban civilization—at first commercial, then industrial, and then increasingly nationalistic and imperialistic—is doubtless the major theme of Western history, and the locus of our major problems. We may accordingly note that medieval Catholicism contributed to the continuity of this story. Sombart thought that the great working order of the Benedictines laid the foundations of capitalistic enterprise by dignifying work and instituting the fixed, orderly, punctual life, which now seems very natural even though men naturally rebel against it. Their rule—practiced in forty thousand monasteries—exemplified the bourgeois ideal of being "regular as clock-work." (The mechanical clock itself

was a medieval invention.) Later churchmen contributed more directly to the development of finance, since the Church was by far the greatest financial enterprise of the age. Few have heard of Fra Luca Pacioli, the inventor of double-entry bookkeeping; but he has probably had much more influence on human life than has Dante or Michelangelo.[13]

Like any complex phenomenon, the rise of commerce to a position of great influence cannot be adequately treated in the space allotted. However, the highlights, particularly those associated with the mercantilist period, which runs roughly from the sixteenth century to the middle of the eighteenth century, will be presented.

The economic revolution began in feudal times, but it was during the mercantilist period that the expansion of trade in order to increase wealth became intense and feverish. Buying and selling flourish when restraints such as import and export taxes are few. The extreme localism of the feudal period was an obstacle to trade, and one of the significant consequences of the mercantilist period was a gradual strengthening of the nation-state and the gradual building of loyalty to it. The people of mercantilist times believed that one nation's gain had to come at another's expense. The rivalries and wars among the English, Spanish, French, Dutch, and others over control of the newly discovered territories of the Western hemisphere are part of the history of this period. National strength, based upon continually increasing the national wealth, was a concept that took form during this time.

One notion was that a country became wealthy if it exported more than it imported. In order to accomplish this, it was believed that workers had to be kept poor. The reasoning was that (1) they would only work hard if they had to in order to gain a livelihood, and that (2) they should be paid as little as possible to keep down their consumption because "when workers consumed home-grown or home-processed goods, they diminished the supply available for export and affected the balance of trade unfavorably."[14] Merchants wrote pamphlets in which they condemned workers as lazy, irresponsible creatures, indulging themselves in luxury and dissipation. Tea and sugar were both considered luxuries, and Arthur Young, a prominent commentator of the eighteenth century, condemned women and children for presuming to drink tea, with white bread and butter, twice a day; that practice he called "an extremity that may surely be called luxury in excess."[15] Young's statement (in 1771) that "everyone but an idiot knows that the lower classes must be kept poor or they will never be industrious" was taken as a self-evident truth.[16]

Mercantilists generally believed in strong government management of the economy; they considered this necessary in order to achieve their goal of increasing the national wealth. And although they were not the first to recommend work programs as a method for dealing with poverty, they were their enthusiastic promoters, at least for a time. Under the prodding and direction of the mercantilists from the sixteenth to eighteenth centuries, the nation-states tried to gain control over their societies, much as the Church had tried to control the society of Western Christendom in the Middle Ages.

The Industrial Revolution

If any social process could be said to have stimulated the development of modern social welfare in all its forms, the Industrial Revolution would have to be it. A significant increase in the number of inventions of machinery in the latter half of the eighteenth century (mostly in England) led to a drastic transformation of Western society. It changed the activity of making things from something done in homes and small workshops by families or by a craftsman and a few employees and apprentices into something done in factories—increasingly huge and impersonal places, and noisy and dirty from the beginning.

The feudal society of the Middle Ages was (in theory, though often not in practice) a world based on relationships that were mutual in obligation, even while the participants were unequal in power and in honor. The lord of the manor was responsible for the well-being of the serfs who worked his lands, even as they owed him work in exchange for protection and a livelihood. Further, serfs were tied to the land; they could not leave it (though some escaped). The Commercial Revolution brought changes in this way of life, but these came about slowly. In 1776, the same year that Scotsman Adam Smith published *The Wealth of Nations*—an exposition of the benefits of free trade and therefore a rationale for the unrestricted development of business and industry—the only manufacturing industry of any consequence in Great Britain was textiles, and that was still carried on mostly in workers' homes and in small workshops by entrepreneurs of modest scope.[17] Industrialization accelerated the process of change, uprooting people from their agricultural and village environments, pulling them into growing towns and cities, resulting in settlements of unprecedented population density.

The birth of industrial society caused extensive pain. A society based on hierarchical relationships in which each person had a place and a part to play was replaced by one in which the economic institutions of the market and factory dominated almost all other institutions. The farm laborers who were assured a livelihood in exchange for services became the industrial workers gaining a livelihood only by the type of bargain they could work out with their employers, who, unlike the medieval lord, had no obligations to the workers. The livelihoods of great masses of people became precarious because they were dependent upon the arbitrary control of employers and on the changing patterns of industry. Over and over again, once successful products—and the jobs that produced them —were superseded by newer products and newer techniques that made the old ones obsolete.[18]

This new type of society was supported by various beliefs that explained why it was the best kind of society. The dominant theme in these beliefs was that of *individualism,* the notion that the individual is the purpose for which society exists (rather than the notion that the individual exists for society). There were many varieties of individualism, some traceable to the beginnings of Christian doctrine, others to the Protestant Reformation. These varieties came together in the idea that allowing people to pursue their own self-interest with as little interference from the state as possible would lead to the maximum satisfaction of individuals and to progress for the community as a whole. Progress for the community would be a side effect of the activities of individuals, all pursuing their own interests, and being free to enter into contracts and to acquire private property.[19]

Individualism was to become a powerful idea in social welfare, underlying certain types of charity and philanthropy that were significant in the nineteenth century, and becoming woven into the basic concepts of social work. Individualism was influential in the United States in yet a third way because it retarded the acceptance of the social insurance concept.[20]

Individualism was bolstered in the nineteenth century by another strain of thought that had been developing over the previous three centuries. Known as *rationalism,* this cluster of ideas added up "to the belief that the universe works the way a man's mind works when he thinks logically and objectively, that therefore man can ultimately understand everything in his experience."[21] Thinking rationally about economic activities came to be the dominant form of "rationality" in industrial society, overshadowing rational thought about noneconomic matters.[22]

Eventually rationalism had consequences other than simply a more efficient and (when combined with the notion of self-interest) more ruthless pursuit of material gain. The developments of science, which had been a product of the rationalist outlook, came to be regarded as applicable to human affairs generally, not just to economic matters. Thus the nineteenth century saw an effort at "scientific charity," as well as a significant development of the social sciences, in an effort to understand the social problems that were being generated by the new industrial society.

SUMMARY

All forms of social welfare develop as part of the larger organization of society, and are understandable only in relation to the society in which they develop. Two overlapping frameworks for thinking about society are helpful in understanding social welfare in Western society. One is an analytical framework. In thinking about any society, it is necessary to have some idea of its resources, its values and beliefs, its distribution of power, its population, its social organization, and the nature of the social inequality that characterizes it. The second framework is a historical one, which presents the development of Western society in a series of broad historical stages. The historical framework offered in this chapter is sufficient to provide an orientation to the development of social welfare, which is the principal concern of the chapters to follow. Additional historical details will be added as needed. Inevitably, a more thorough and precise examination of all the historical developments touched on in this book requires consulting the specialized works devoted to them.

Notes

[1] J. J. Jusserand, *English Wayfaring Life in the Middle Ages—XIVth Century*, 3rd ed., trans. Lucy Toulmin Smith (London: Fisher Unwin, 1925), p. 294.

[2] *Ibid.*, p. 302.

[3] For two contemporary examples, see Harry M. Caudill, *Night Comes to the Cumberlands—A Biography of a Depressed Area* (Boston: Little, Brown, 1963); and Kai T. Erikson, *Everything in Its Path—Destruction of Community in the Buffalo Creek Flood* (New York: Simon and Schuster, 1976).

[4] Karl de Schweinitz, *England's Road to Social Security* (New York: A. S. Barnes, 1961), pp. 30–32. First published in 1943.

[5] G. G. Coulton, *The Medieval Scene* (Cambridge: Cambridge University Press, 1930), p. 1.

[6] Robert S. Lopez, *The Commercial Revolution of the Middle Ages, 950–1350* (Englewood Cliffs, N.J.: Prentice-Hall, 1971), p. 51.

[7] Marc Bloch, *Feudal Society*, Vol. I: *The Growth of Ties of Dependence*, trans. L. A. Manyon (Chicago: University of Chicago Press, Phoenix Edition, 1964), p. 61.

[8] Herbert J. Muller, *Freedom in the Western World—From the Dark Ages to the Rise of Democracy* (New York: Harper & Row, 1963), p. 67.

[9] Coulton, *Medieval Scene*, pp. 10, 20.

[10] Bloch, *Feudal Society*, p. 87.

[11] Lopez, *Commercial Revolution*, p. 86.

[12] H. van Werveke, "The Rise of the Towns," in M. M. Postan, E. E. Rich, and Edward Miller, eds., *The Cambridge Economic History of Europe*, Vol. III: *Economic Organization and Policies in the Middle Ages* (Cambridge: Cambridge University Press, 1963), p. 15.

[13] Herbert J. Muller, *The Uses of the Past* (New York: Oxford University Press, 1952), pp. 256–257.

[14] Robert Lekachman, *A History of Economic Ideas* (New York: Harper & Row, 1959), p. 41.

[15] *Ibid.*, p. 40.

[16] Arthur Young, in R. H. Tawney, *Religion and the Rise of Capitalism* (London: John Murray, 1936), p. 270.

[17] Lekachman, *History of Economic Ideas*, p. 72.

[18]Harold L. Wilensky and Charles N. Lebeaux, *Industrial Society and Social Welfare* (New York: Free Press, 1965).

[19]Steven Lukes, "Types of Individualism," in Philip P. Wiener, ed., *Dictionary of the History of Ideas*, Vol. II (New York: Scribner's, 1973), pp. 597ff.

[20]Wilensky and Lebeaux, *Industrial Society*, pp. 41–42.

[21]Crane Brinton, *Ideas and Men—The Story of Western Thought* (New York: Prentice-Hall, 1950), p. 334.

[22]Karl Mannheim, *Man and Society in an Age of Reconstruction*, trans. Edward Shils (London: Kegan Paul, Trench, Trubner, 1940), pp. 51–58.

Charity
and
Philanthropy

II

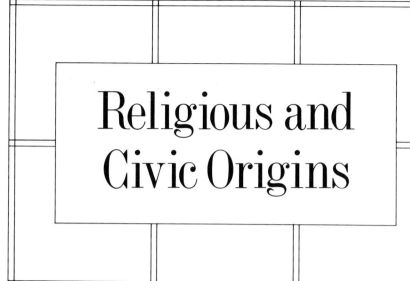

Religious and Civic Origins

3

The concepts of charity and philanthropy have had a checkered history. Today the idea of philanthropy is fairly respectable; the idea of charity, not quite so respectable. The two concepts have a common base: both involve the idea of *giving* or *contributing* something, and in both the fundamental social relationship implied is that between a *giver* and a *receiver.* Yet the two terms have different scopes and emphases. Philanthropy commonly refers to giving on a larger, grander scale than does charity. People who drop fifty cents into the container of Salvation Army Christmas carolers are not likely to think of themselves as a philanthropists but rather as someone who has made a contribution to charity. The term *philanthropist* is likely to be reserved for someone who gives thousands or millions of dollars to a cause.

In addition, the idea of charity seems to call attention to the receiver of the contribution in a way that philanthropy does not, and perhaps precisely because of the implied difference in scale of the gift. Philanthropy is a large gift to an institution. While the gift may be for a specific purpose, philanthropy in the modern sense does not seem to carry with it the idea that the money will go to people in desperate, and individually specified need. In contrast, the idea of charity carries with it a clearer implication that the money will end up, not in the general budget of some large institution, but in some more personalized benefit to people regarded as unfortunate. Charity today implies unfortunateness more definitely than philanthropy does.

Partly for this reason, there has been some turning against the idea of charity in modern times. For many, charity emphasizes the inequality of the giver and the receiver. Thus many potential receivers are likely to feel that they are "too proud to take charity." Charity has come to mean for many that the person who takes it is somehow a less worthy member of society than someone who does not accept it. As a result, the term *philanthropy* is increasingly coming to be used for all kinds of giving, large and small, when these are considered in the aggregate. The shift in terminology reflects a shift in social values.[1]

Even though charity has given way to more modern concepts of social welfare, it survives in the contemporary world. Despite its connotation (in relation to its recipients) of destitution and unworthiness, it remains a component of the social welfare spectrum. Giving on a small scale remains a part of community and church life, and the concept of giving charity retains some of its more ancient associations of nobility, generosity, and fulfillment of religious duty, particularly among Catholics.

The Western world's ideas of charity and philanthropy (insofar as they can be considered synonymous) seem to stem from two different traditions: the Judeo-Christian and the Greco-Roman. These two versions gradually became fused, and the idea underwent several transformations as society changed and new conditions called forth new interpretations and actions.

The Greco-Roman idea of philanthropy preceded the Christian idea of charity but the Christian idea derives from the Judaic, which developed before the Greco-Roman. Inasmuch as Christianity began in the Roman Empire, it will be useful for us first to discuss philanthropy in the Roman Empire and in the Greek city-states, which preceded it.

PHILANTHROPY IN THE GREEK CITY-STATES AND THE ROMAN EMPIRE

The Greek city-states, which flourished about five centuries before Christ, are important to the Western world for many reasons, not least because it was in these city-states that the idea of the free citizen first developed in a form that was to influence Western thinking. It was during this time that the concept of democracy developed. Prior to then, there was not a well-conceived, meaningful concept of the member of society as being not only free from arbitrary authority but as also having a duty to the state. Even though this concept of the free citizen later went into eclipse for several hundred years, it succeeded in entering into the Western framework of political thought and influences our ideas about human rights in the modern world.[2]

The original meaning of the Greek word from which the English word *philanthropy* derived was the love of mankind by the gods who showed beneficence to humanity.[3] By the fourth century B.C., the meaning had been extended to include rulers or other powerful men who showed kindness to their subjects or dependents, frequently by donating funds to the city treasury. In addition, the concept of citizenship influenced the concept of philanthropy. All citizens were expected to participate in the political and social life of the Greek city-state, even though there was a range of wealth among citizens. There was also a longstanding tradition that gifts should elicit return gifts as expressions of gratitude. But those who were poor could not give material gifts of gratitude to the wealthy donors. They could, however, show appreciation to such a benefactor. Since most material gifts were made either to the city-state as a whole or to clubs and associations (rather than to individuals), these groups would express their gratitude by passing a resolution honoring the benefactor. This resolution was considered a philanthropic gift, just as was the benefactor's donation of money.

Such an exchange of honor for monetary contribution was important to the social life of the Greek city-states. It was, in fact, considered essential for maintaining in the people a sense of common interest, which helped to hold the city-state together as a functioning community. The wealthy were expected to take on public offices, which were largely unpaid, and to contribute their own funds to run the government. They were willing to do this for quite a long time because of the honor they received from the populace for doing so.

In addition to their contributions to the ordinary expenses of government, the rich often received appeals to contribute "subscriptions" (solicited contributions to an emergency fund) to meet the many financial crises and food shortages that occurred. Resolutions honoring the contributors—and sometimes giving them economic benefits as well—were passed by the citizens in their political assemblies. For example, one Athenian document surviving from the fourth century B.C. read:

> Demosthenes, son of Demosthenes of the deme Lamptrai, made the following proposal: since Herakledes of . . . Salamis continues in his service of the Athenian people with his heart set upon honour . . . and in doing all that he can that is good, and since previously he contributed at a time of corn shortage 3,000 *medimnoi* of corn at five *drachmae* a *medimnos,* being the first of the merchants who entered port, and again when a subscription-fund . . . was established he contributed 3,000 *drachmae* to the corn purchase fund, and for the rest, continues in his good will and energetic service towards the people: therefore let it be resolved by the people

. . . that he be made . . . benefactor . . . of Athens, himself and his descendants, and that he have the right to own land and property according to the law, and that they serve militarily and pay property-tax along with the Athenians.[4]

The Greeks believed that good men would pursue honor. They recognized that acts of benevolence involved a combination of motives and that some donors might be more interested in their own honor while others might be more concerned with enhancing the public good. Contributors of subscriptions were listed publicly, one of the purposes being to stimulate giving from the wealthy who had not yet contributed.[5] There was great pressure on them to contribute, and those who were not as generous to the city-state as expected might be deprived of honors they desired and be assigned burdensome offices they did not want. Under some circumstances, they might even be prosecuted in the law courts and their property might be confiscated.

The Greek political assemblies, which passed the resolutions honoring philanthropic donors, used a sliding scale of honors. The amount of honor bestowed on the donor was in proportion to the size of the donation. Thus one donor might be awarded the title "Benefactor"; another, making a more magnificent contribution, would receive the title "Savior." Some donations merited honor for the donor alone, whereas others merited honor for the donor and all his descendants, as in the example in the document cited above.[6] Donors sometimes specified that they expected statues of themselves to be erected, with engraved inscriptions specifying the nature and extent of their contributions.

Philanthropy in the Greek city-states was not directed specifically to the most impoverished portions of the population. The wealthy directed their philanthropy toward the community as a whole or toward a particular club or association to which they belonged. Whether the contribution was food, money, or oil—the three most customary philanthropic offerings—it was distributed indiscriminately to the members of the association or to the citizens of the city-state. Thus membership or citizenship—not need—was the criterion for determining who received a share of the contribution.

Persons at the bottom of society—or on the edge—were expected to make their own way as best they could. Beggars—those who did not work for a living —received little sympathy. The Greeks believed that there was ample opportunity for employment and that beggars were people who were lazy and unwilling to work. Slaves, often individuals captured from other tribes during warfare, did a great deal of the heavy work of the Greek city-states; yet they were not eligible for citizenship. It was assumed that foreign merchants and artisans, who also made up a significant percentage of the population, could go elsewhere if they could not earn a living in the Greek city-state in which they had settled.

The establishment of colonies and migration to them were a frequent solution to the problem of unemployment in the Greek city-states. Expeditions to establish colonies were numerous, and the poor and landless were recruited to participate. Participants were each assigned an equal amount of land in the colony. Efforts to redistribute land at home in the mother-state to achieve the same equality were seldom attempted.[7] Another employment option open to men who had lapsed temporarily into extreme poverty was to enlist in a foreign army as a mercenary.

There is evidence that the ancient Greeks distinguished between the "worthy" and the "unworthy" poor. For the unworthy poor—those who were uneducated and whose poverty was constant—they felt little pity. There is some evidence, however, that the idea of giving to those who are worthy, of being given to, developed at this time. (The emphasis on worthiness, as we shall note later, became a recurrent theme in discussions of charity during the industrial revolution, a theme that continues into the 1980s.) The worthy Greeks were the well-reared, well-educated, formerly well-off who had fallen upon hard times. And worthiness as such might arouse the wealthy to pity and acts of aid.

Such pity was inspired by fears in the wealthy of one day experiencing a reversal of their own fortunes and of finding themselves in the same state of need. These fears stimulated the wealthy to donate subscriptions to mutual aid funds organized by clubs and associations. The donor might someday find himself a recipient. The ability of the gods to bring about changes in fate merited the attention of everyone. Pity was a sentiment offered to others on an exchange basis and was inspired by personal fear more than by genuine concern for their state of bad fortune.

Thus it may be seen that Greek philanthropy was prompted by love of honor and by fear and not by concern for the weak and helpless.

The practice of philanthropy in Rome seems to have been substantially similar to that in Greece. The Greeks had established colonial cities in Italy. Eventually the Greeks lost their political dominance in the ancient world and were succeeded by Rome, which became a strong republic and later a powerful empire that governed the lands from Britain in the West to Armenia in the East. Greek ideas continued to be influential in the Roman-dominated world, and philanthropic activity continued to be shaped by the conceptions of citizenship and of honor that had developed centuries earlier in the Greek city-states. Classical scholar A. R. Hands, in fact, discusses Greece and Rome together, without making a major distinction, since for a substantial period their practices were so similar.

There is some evidence, however, that particular concern for the poor did begin to develop in the Roman Empire. One example is Pliny the Younger, an administrator in the Empire and a writer,

who [although he] complained one time of not being a rich man, during his life gave his native town of Como six hundred thousand *sestertii*, over $75,000. Five-sixths of this was devoted to a foundation for supplying food free to the poor, the rest for the establishment of a public library. When he died he left by will half a million more for the construction of baths and the relief of the poor, besides a life pension to a hundred freedmen.[8]

CHARITY IN JUDAISM AND
EARLY CHRISTIANITY

Christianity began as a small Judaic sect in Palestine when that territory was a province of the Roman Empire. It evolved into a worldwide religion with an array of theological doctrines and social organizations that became significantly different from those of Judaism. This process of differentiation was gradual, and the early Christian teachings about charity were similar to the Judaic teachings. "In most early Christian writings there is an emphasis on almsgiving exactly as in the Judaism of the time."[9] There is, then, a Judeo-Christian stream of thought about charity that has influenced Western society. The Western world became largely a Christian world, and we shall follow further in this chapter some of the diverse forms that charity took under the influence of Christian ideas. First, however, we turn to the Judaic ideas that preceded them.

The Judaic Conception of Charity

Beginning in approximately the fourteenth century B.C., when they settled in the territory at the eastern end of the Mediterranean that became their homeland, and continuing over several hundred years, the ancient Israelites developed a religion that became known as Judaism and that affected the later development of Western society through its influence on Christianity. The doctrines of the religion were recorded in the book known to Jews as the Bible and to Christians as the Old Testament.

The central idea of the Israelite religion is that

> God is supreme above all. There is no realm above or beside him to limit his absolute sovereignty. He is utterly distinct from, and other than, the world; he is subject to no laws, no compulsions, or powers that transcend him."[10]

The will of God is the supreme law governing all of creation, and his will and command are absolutely good.[11] God gave moral laws and obligations to humanity. Among these obligations, the duty of dealing rightly with the poor and helpless was particularly emphasized.[12] These duties derive from the concept of God as merciful and compassionate, commanding the Israelites to "love your neighbor as yourself." God said to love the "alien" and to give him bread and clothes.

> All the laws that obligate men to stand by each other in the time of need, or which forbid exploiting poverty and distress, are based on this law of love. The Israelite

is required to go out of his way, if necessary, to restore lost property. . . . He is repeatedly bidden to aid the poor, the alien, the orphan, and the widow.[13]

According to the Israelites' religious laws, at harvest time they were not to collect the produce from the corners of their fields and vineyards, but were to leave it for the poor and for strangers to come and glean. The righteous person gives freely, and does not oppress the poor. Thus the Book of Proverbs states: "He that oppresseth the poor blasphemeth his Maker; But he that is gracious unto the needy honoureth Him."[14]

The practice of charity was not without variations. There is evidence from the writings of some of the prophets of social justice that the rich sometimes exploited the poor. In the eighth century B.C., the prophet Amos denounced the ruling classes in the kingdom of Israel under the reign of Jereboam II. He castigated them for defrauding and impoverishing the people, withholding their grain and thereby forcing up the price of bread.[15]

Amos and other prophets are credited with introducing a new emphasis into Israelite religion and thereby into the Western world. They are the first known speakers and writers to emphasize that morality would determine the future destiny of the Israelite nation. In ancient societies before their time, religious practice in a narrower sense—ritual—had been considered more important. It is noteworthy that the protests of the prophets Amos, Isaiah, Hosea, and Micah against oppression of the poor occurred during periods of prosperity, when the Israelite kingdom's trade with Egypt, Phoenicia, and Syria had increased significantly, and thus social and economic distinctions were accentuated.[16]

In summary, Judaism, the religion developed by the people who inhabited the ancient kingdoms of Israel and Judah, was based on the concept of a God who was the creator of the universe, whose will was the supreme law for human action, and who commanded that people be kind, merciful, and just in their dealings with one another. The poor, widows, orphans, and strangers were to be given food and clothing. Portions of each harvest were to be set aside specifically for those in need. A number of prophets arose who castigated the rich when they violated these basic religious principles by oppressing the poor. The teachings of these prophets came to be incorporated into the Bible, the basic text of the religion, thus strengthening Judaism's emphasis on social justice.[17] These teachings became part of the Christian tradition as well.

Early Christian Charity

In the earliest days of Christianity, its adherents comprised a relatively small proportion of the population of Palestine—then called the Province of Judea by the Romans—and of the neighboring provinces of the Roman Empire to which it had spread, carried by Paul and other apostles. Christians began to differentiate themselves not only from Jews but also from other non-Christian citizens and subjects of the Roman Empire. They began to establish churches, and these became the centers of their religious and community life.

During the first three hundred years of the Christian movement, the Roman Empire was becoming increasingly corrupt, ridden by class distinctions, and demanding of tax revenues from its peoples.[18] One result of this was a significant increase in poverty. Christian churches set about taking care of Christian poor, widows, orphans, aged household slaves, shipwrecked persons, and persons imprisoned, exiled, or working in mines as punishment for their Christian beliefs. Each church member was expected to place a donation, at least monthly, in a chest kept for that purpose. This monthly collection was similar to a Roman system in which the workers in particular trades and occupations were organized into associations known as *collegia* and made monthly contributions to a common fund. In addition, contributions of bread and wine were collected at the Eucharist; what was not needed for the celebration was distributed among the poor.[19]

Charity was a prominent activity in the life of the early Christian communities. One early Christian writer said: " 'We who formerly loved money and property more than anything else now place what we have in a common fund and share with everyone in need.' "[20] The sharing of funds was voluntary and was intended for distribution only among Christian believers. Each church congregation had a presiding officer who was in charge of giving out funds to needy Christian believers. As we have seen, early Christianity's ideas about charity derive from the Judaic concepts, while the organizational arrangements for implementing the ideas resemble the practices common to occupational associations in the Roman Empire.

In the early fourth century, Christianity reached an important turning point. Having been considered illegal by Roman authorities, and having suffered numerous attempts by Roman emperors to stamp it out through persecution of its practitioners, Christianity gained new status and power under the emperor Constantine who, in A.D. 313, declared the religion legal. With this official approval, many new converts came to the movement, and the volume of donations to the churches increased. In order to cope with the growth in numbers and in wealth, a new level of organization was required. Accordingly the system of distribution of charity by individual churches acting through their deacons was replaced by one in which the bishop of a diocese had supervisory control over all the churches in his district and control over the revenues, which came to the churches in greater and greater volume.[21]

It was also during the fourth century that a different theory of almsgiving became prominent—one that held increasing importance in Christianity and that was to influence not only postmedieval Europe but the nineteenth- and early twentieth-century United States as well. Early Christian almsgiving, like the Judaic, had been based largely on the conception of charity as an expression of lovingkindness, an activity necessary to the carrying out of God's will. But this concept did not offer much help with another problem that the early church fathers struggled with as they tried to work out the doctrines of their faith. This was the problem of private property and its consequences, particularly the great disparity in wealth between the rich and the poor.

Some of the early Christian writers considered the private ownership of property to be against God's will and law, but this view did not prevail. The main body of church thought considered the ownership of private property unavoidable, even if not ideal. As Christianity came to accept private property and the disparity of wealth as aspects of the real world, it also worked out a doctrine that wealth could be ennobling because it allowed the wealthy to do good works, good works that would earn them eternal salvation in the Kingdom of God. "The idea that wealth may contribute to salvation because it allows good works to be done can be found in Luke's Gospel."[22] Somewhat later, one theologian taught that almsgiving procured for the givers rewards from God through the prayers of grateful recipients. While this point of view can be found in the earliest church writings, it did not gain prominence until the fourth century, when leading Christian thinkers began to support it and to elaborate upon it. One scholar offers a brief summary of the views on this subject of two of the most important fourth-century Christian writers:

> Chrysostom praises the presence of beggars at the church door as giving an opportunity to those entering to cleanse their consciences from minor faults by almsgiving. . . . Augustine also teaches . . . the belief that almsgiving could atone for the sins of the departed as well as for those of the living. . . . He is careful to limit the efficacy of charity to those whose lives were acceptable to God. It availed nothing for living or dead who were of evil reputation.[23]

The change in the theological justification of charity and its meritoriousness was related to the social changes that were taking place at the time both within Christianity and in the Roman Empire. Although at first a religious movement especially attractive to the lower and middle strata of society, Christianity held increasing appeal for the wealthy as well.[24] Both wealthy and poor found the new religious explanations of almsgiving helpful to their own situations. Further, the church itself was becoming wealthy and propertied, particularly after it gained the right from Constantine to receive donations and bequests. At the same time, the Empire also was moving in the direction of greater concentration of wealth and property, resulting partly from the dispossession of small farmers who were pushed into choosing between working as slaves or serfs on land they had once owned or going into the cities to work, to beg, or to rob. As one historian put it:

> While this light and frivolous class of the idle rich invaded the church from above, at the same time a horde of beggars and impostors poured into the church from below, feigning poverty and faith, attracted by the new wealth and charitable practices of Christianity. The proletariat of the great cities, accustomed to public doles, scented a new quarter of supply. In a sense the Church was victimized by

this corrupt class which Rome's vicious social and economic policy over centuries had fostered; but it is a question whether the Church did not aggravate the evil which it professed to relieve by promoting a vast system of organized mendicity through a deceived philanthropy. "Never was the greed of beggars greater than it is now," complained St. Ambrose. . . . St. Basil complained of the difficulty of distinguishing between the needy poor and these imposters. Mendicancy became a profession within the circle of the Church as it long had been practised by thousands outside in the pagan world. By the end of the fourth century the Christian beggars in Rome almost formed a caste apart.[25]

During the first three hundred years of Christianity, each church congregation took care of its own poor from its own rather meager funds. With the increase in church wealth from the fourth century on, there came a change in church organization—the development of a church hierarchy. The administration of relief to the poor was taken over by the bishop of each diocese; all the churches of a city and its surroundings were under the bishop's direction. As the Roman empire and its governmental effectiveness declined, the bishops became, in effect, the governors of their territories.[26] Power and wealth gravitated to the church and its bishops, who not only accepted gifts and donations—from which they were expected to give freely to the poor—but also solicited them. Even the most sympathetic writers about the early and medieval church acknowledge that not all bishops lived up to their charitable obligations.[27] Less sympathetic historians note that some bishops exploited the doctrine of redemption from sin to increase the wealth of the church:

> . . . avarice for centuries was to be the besetting sin of the church. The famous verse "As water extinguisheth fire, so charity extinguisheth sin" was flagrantly abused to solicit gifts from the faithful. This sentiment is to be found time and again in medieval donations of land or goods. The Christians of the patristic age gave out of their poverty—for they had little wealth—to expand the gospel, to relieve the sick, to help the poor. But from the fourth century onward too many of the donations made to the Church were not primarily for the benefit of others, but to save the souls of the givers. It was a selfish unselfishness. The day was to come when a man was required in his will to leave a portion of his property to the Church, and if he had no heirs to leave it all to the Church.[28]

MEDIEVAL SOCIETY AND CHRISTIAN CHARITY

The decline and fall of the Roman Empire constitutes one of the great turning points in the history of Western society. The date of the collapse of the Empire is usually given as A.D. 476, but this was obviously not a sudden or isolated event.

Rather, it followed a series of invasions by Germanic barbarian tribes that had begun considerably earlier. The years between A.D. 400 and A.D. 1500 have come to be known as the Middle Ages. The study of the Middle Ages is a specialty in its own right. In terms of this book, the period is perhaps most significant because of the sharp contrasts between it and the period that succeeded it. Many of the changes that took place in the postmedieval period will be relevant to our discussions but for our current purposes we need only make a rough distinction between antiquity, the Middle Ages, and the modern period.

Following the collapse of the Roman Empire, western Europe was a vast territory with no strong central government. As the central government deteriorated, trade diminished and the cities shrank, until the eleventh century, when both trade and the cities began to revive. Although various kingdoms succeeded the Empire, none were effective in maintaining control over their territory.

During the Middle Ages, most people lived a rural life, with farming the dominant occupation. Because of the lack of a strong central government, people were vulnerable to economic insecurity and to attack. To protect themselves, men who felt particularly vulnerable sought out stronger men to whom they "commended" themselves. They surrendered their land to the stronger men, who became known as lords, and they surrendered their status as free people and agreed to remain attached to the land, providing to their particular lord a portion of the produce of the land. In exchange, these serfs, as they were called, received the protection of the lord and the right to stay on the land. The lord thus increased his land holdings, and acquired dependents who owed him a certain number of days of work per year and a portion of the harvest of that work, while in return he became their protector. The landed estate held by the lord came to be known as a manor. The serfs lived in houses grouped together in a village on the manor. The village included a church. The lord of the manor often had the power to appoint the priest for the village church.[29] In time, the village became a parish, one unit in the diocese of a bishop. Bishops and priests were seen as having authority over the human soul, both in its life on earth and in the hereafter. Bishops came to be "lords spiritual," in contrast with the lords of the manors, who were "lords temporal," that is, lords who governed human lives during their earthly existence.

Medieval society is, however, complicated by the fact that the churches acquired manors, so that bishops often assumed temporal power in addition to their spiritual power. One result of this was that many of the clergy developed worldly concerns, enjoying the life of well-to-do country gentlemen and neglecting their duties, including their obligations to care for the poor.

Monasticism

The increasing worldliness and materialism of the church repelled some parishioners and clergy and gave rise to efforts to rediscover religious concentration through withdrawal into secluded communities known as monasteries. Those who withdrew to the monastery and became monks sought a life of prayer and study and a revival of the early Christian concern for the poor. Monasteries were places where anyone, rich or poor, who came to the gate would be given a ration or dole of food and drink, and shelter if necessary.

Monasteries developed in somewhat parallel fashion to the church organization they were trying to escape. They evolved from single settlements into organizations of monasteries run by a particular religious order. The heads of monasteries—abbots and priors—struggled with parish priests to gain control over churches in order to enjoy the wealth accumulating from church revenues. The money left in the wills of men to be distributed to the poor or to support permanently a certain number of poor went to the churches and the monasteries. In the eighth century, churches also instituted the practice of *tithing*, that is, requiring members of the church to contribute annually a tenth of their income to the church. The church revenues were supposed to be divided into four equal parts—for the support of the bishop of the diocese, the parish clergy, the upkeep of the church, and the poor, widowed, disabled, orphaned, and aged.

Medieval Canon Law

The Roman Catholic Church was the major recognized and established religion in western Europe once the conversion of the barbarian peoples was completed around A.D. 1000. Between the fall of the Roman Empire and the rise of the colonial empires, which began around A.D. 1500, the Church also came to be the major international state in the Western world.[30] People felt they belonged to Christendom and thus to a larger, more encompassing unit beyond the local community. Except for a relatively small number of Jews and heretics, everyone belonged to the Church. The Church had its own government, courts, and taxes. The religious teachings of the Church were a major influence on what people believed. And beliefs concerning salvation were, as we have noted, a powerful inducement for the donation of charitable gifts and bequests to the Church to be used for the support of the poor.

The Church had grown into an organization whose recognized leader, the bishop of Rome, had acquired the title of pope. Yet centralized authority had not resulted in a consistent set of teachings and a consistent set of laws and regulations with respect to poverty and charity as well as other matters. The teachings of the Apostles and of the early church fathers in the first few centuries after the Apostles were not entirely consistent. Local church councils had, over the centuries, developed their own regulations. The work of eliminating the inconsistencies in canon law—the technical term for the laws of the Roman Catholic Church —was undertaken by the Italian monk Gratian, who produced his treatise known as the *Decretum* about A.D. 1140[31] Later canonists—experts in Church law —added to this basic work.

The canonists tried to resolve the issue of the cause of poverty. They made a distinction between voluntary poverty, a form of asceticism pleasing to God, and involuntary poverty. They agreed that the Church had a special duty to protect "wretched persons"—the poor and oppressed, the widowed and orphaned.[32]

A second issue addressed by the canonists was that of private property. Some of the early church fathers' statements cited by Gratian were so critical of the abuses of wealth that they could be interpreted as condemning all private property. The canonists were concerned that private property might be contrary to God's will, and felt that this possibility had to be reconciled with the existing social order, in which private property rights were valid. Their solution involved drawing a distinction between ownership of property and use of property. After a man had taken care of his own necessities out of what he owned, he was obliged to share his "superfluous wealth." A man who "accumulated superfluous wealth beyond what he needed to live in a decent and fitting fashion had no right to keep that wealth. He *owed* it to the poor."[33]

Thus, by the beginning of the thirteenth century, the Church lawyers seemed to be proclaiming a doctrine that the rich had a legal obligation to support the poor and the poor had a right to such support. In actuality, this doctrine was not legally enforceable, but it did influence attitudes toward private charity during the Middle Ages:

> The doctrine that the poor man had a right to the help he received . . . colored the whole relationship between benefactor and beneficiary in the Middle Ages, tending to discourage both sentimental self-esteem on the part of the donor and excessive humiliation in the recipient.[34]

This is a very different conception from Greek and Roman philanthropy. It also bears little resemblance to the views that developed in the eighteenth century and after, when the obligation of the rich to share their wealth with the poor disappeared in the economic doctrines that accompanied the rise of industrial capitalism. And it contrasts as well with the twentieth-century attitude that dependence upon charity is shameful and humiliating. It should be noted, however, that the medieval canonists' resolution of the problem of charity was in keeping with the property system of the time, because the right to own property was commonly accompanied by certain social obligations.[35]

The medieval canonists distinguished worthy charitable actions from unworthy ones. For example, a charitable gift made from stolen property was not worthy. Contributions that were worthy had to come from justly acquired property, and the donors had to be righteous individuals motivated by a spirit of true charity, not by a desire to gain praise or to avoid embarrassment. When these conditions were met, the almsgivers were assuring their own salvation.

The Church was concerned with the effect of charity on the soul of the donor, a concern that is much less prominent in contemporary society than it was in medieval times. But the Church was also concerned with an issue whose importance became even greater to the people of later centuries: the effect of charity on the receiver. According to some of the early church fathers, there were circumstances in which being charitable would be harmful to the recipient, and donors were urged to discriminate between situations in which charity was justified and those in which it was not. Others wrote that alms should be given to all, without investigation into circumstances or attempts at distinguishing true need from claimed need.

The thirteenth-century canonists tended to favor openhandedness in day-to-day almsgiving. They probably knew that some people would take advantage of such a practice, but they did not believe that this basic attitude would corrupt society as a whole. In understanding the sharp difference between the medieval attitude toward charity and the attitude that developed in the nineteenth century along with industrialization, it is useful to note that unemployment was rare in the thirteenth century. The majority of poorer people lived in small villages and worked their own land. Those who might become unwilling to work were subject to social pressure from priest, neighbors, and family. Thus there was little basis for concern that some people would prefer an idle life in which they subsisted on charity to a life in which they earned their own living.[36]

SUMMARY

Charity and philanthropy originated as two similar concepts that later fused into a single concept. Charity and philanthropy both refer to donations of money or property to a person or group in need. Charity originated in ancient Judaism and was incorporated into Christianity. In both religions, charity was considered a religious obligation, based on the will of God, to show lovingkindness by helping the poor and other needy individuals. Philanthropy originated in the ancient Greek city-states, particularly Athens, and was part of the concept of citizenship and civic duty. Wealthy persons contributed money to the community; in return, the community passed resolutions giving official recognition to the philanthropists, who welcomed the honor. In theory, both charity and philanthropy were voluntary, but social pressures were applied to stimulate reluctant donors.

During the fourth century A.D., the church developed the doctrine that charity could earn the donors eternal salvation of their souls. This teaching remains part of Catholic theology today. Overall, however, the concept of charity has lost favor because it calls attention to the dependent status of the receiver.

Philanthropy, a more impersonal form of giving, remains widely appreciated. Individuals often feel too proud to take charity; no one feels too proud to take philanthropy. Therefore, charitable contributions today are often called philanthropic contributions.

The early Christian churches each organized their own charitable funds. After Christianity became a legal religion in the Roman Empire, contributions greatly increased and a more complex church organization developed. Churches were grouped into districts called dioceses, each headed by a bishop, who was in charge of all contributions in his diocese. In the eighth century, churches began the practice of tithing—the requirement that members contribute one tenth of their annual income to the Church. Church revenues were to be divided into four equal parts—for the support of the bishop, the parish clergy, the upkeep of the Church, and the Church charity fund.

Church lawyers of the twelfth and thirteenth centuries concluded that the rich had an obligation to support the poor and the poor had as right to such support. This doctrine virtually disappeared after the eighteenth century, when the economic ideas of capitalism became more influential than church teachings.

Notes

[1] The shift in terminology is neatly documented by a comparison of two similar publications. The *Encyclopedia of the Social Sciences,* published in 1931, includes an article on charity; the reader who seeks an article on philanthropy finds only the cross-reference: "See Charity." The successor publication, *The International Encyclopedia of the Social Sciences,* Vol. 12, published in 1968, includes an article on philanthropy (pp. 71–76) but no entry at all for "Charity."

[2] For a brief discussion of the Greek city-states, see William H. McNeill, *The Rise of the West* (New York: Mentor Books, 1963), pp. 219–226 and 281–285.

[3] A. R. Hands, *Charities and Social Aid in Greece and Rome* (Ithaca, N.Y.: Cornell University Press, 1968), pp. 34ff. Our discussion of philanthropy in ancient Greece and Rome is drawn mainly from Hands's study.

[4] W. Dittenberger, *Sylloge Inscriptionum Graecarum,* in Hands, *Charities and Social Aid,* pp. 175–176. A *deme* is a district. A *drachma* is the Greek unit of currency.

[5] Hands, *Charities and Social Aid,* pp. 41–46.

[6] *Ibid.,* pp. 51–56.

[7] The English word *metropolis* is taken directly from the Greek, where its meaning is mother-state or mother-city.

[8] James Westfall Thompson, *Economic and Social History of the Middle Ages (300–1300),* Vol. I (New York: Frederick Ungar, 1959), p. 44. First published in 1928.

[9] Robert M. Grant, *Augustus to Constantine—The Thrust of the Christian Movement into the Roman World* (New York: Harper & Row, 1970), p. 258. See also Thompson, *Economic*

and Social History, p. 60, and R. M. Grant, *Early Christianity and Society* (New York: Harper & Row, 1977), Chap. 6.

[10]Yehezkel Kaufmann, *The Religion of Israel—From Its Beginnings to the Babylonian Exile*, trans. and abr. Moshe Greenberg (Chicago: University of Chicago Press, 1960), p. 60.

[11]*Ibid.*, pp. 73–75. The notion of the absolute power and goodness of God has led to many problems of theological interpretation in Judaism and in Christianity. For example, if God is all-powerful and also good, why are there people who suffer poverty, illness, and other misfortunes? A discussion of the theological explanations of misfortune would take us far afield. Our present concern is to describe the basic ideas from which the Judeo-Christian concepts of charity derive.

[12]*Ibid.*, p. 319.

[13]*Ibid.*, p. 320.

[14]Prov. 14:31.

[15]H. Tadmor, "The Period of the First Temple, the Babylonian Exile, and the Restoration," Part II, in H. H. Ben-Sasson, ed., *A History of the Jewish People* (Cambridge: Harvard University Press, 1976), pp. 128–130; and Kaufmann, *Religion of Israel*, pp. 347 and 366.

[16]Chester C. McCown, *Man, Morals and History—Today's Legacy from Ancient Times and Biblical Peoples* (New York: Harper & Brothers, 1958), pp. 164–168.

[17]The Judaic religious ideas received further development and elaboration in a book of commentaries on the Bible known as the Talmud. See Isidore Epstein, *Judaism—A Historical Presentation* (Baltimore: Penguin Books, 1959), pp. 150–152 and 169–170 for a discussion of charity.

[18]See Grant, *Augustus to Constantine*, p. 9, on rising taxes.

[19]C. T. Dimont, "Charity, Almsgiving (Christian)," in *Encyclopedia of Religion and Ethics*, Vol. 3 (New York: Charles Scribner, 1922), p. 362; and Grant, *Augustus to Constantine*, p. 259.

[20]Grant, *Ibid.*, p. 258.

[21]Dimont, "Charity," p. 383; and Grant, *Augustus to Constantine*, pp. 173–174.

[22]Maurice Goguel, *The Primitive Church*, trans. H. C. Snape (New York: Macmillan, 1964), p. 542.

[23]Dimont, "Charity," pp. 383–384. See Grant, *Augustus to Constantine*, p. 268, for a summary of early Christian attitudes toward property.

[24]Thompson, *Economic and Social History*, p. 64.

[25]*Ibid.*, p. 70.

[26]*Ibid.*, p. 77.

[27]See, e.g., Dimont, "Charity," p. 383.

[28]Thompson, *Economic and Social History*, pp. 76–77.

[29]Denys Hay, *The Medieval Centuries* (London: Methuen, 1964), p. 49.

[30]Harry Elmer Barnes, *An Economic Hsitory of the Western World* (New York: Harcourt, Brace, 1937), p. 120.

[31]Brian Tierney, *Medieval Poor Law—A Sketch of Canonical Theory and Its Application in England* (Berkeley and Los Angeles: University of California Press, 1959), p. 7. Our discussion of medieval canon law is drawn mainly from Tierney.

[32]*Ibid.*, p. 15.

[33]*Ibid.*, p. 37, italics in original.

[34]*Ibid.*, p. 39.

[35]A detailed account of the complexities of the obligations attached to landholding in England is given in Austin Lane Poole, *Obligations of Society in the XII and XIII Centuries* (Oxford: Oxford University Press, 1946).

[36]Tierney, *Medieval Poor Law*, pp. 62–66.

Philanthrophy
in a Business
Civilization

4

THE RISING MERCHANT CLASS
AND CHARITY

The revival of trade and town life that began in the tenth century led, over the next few hundred years, to a fundamental transformation of Western society. What had been an agricultural society, in which land was the primary form of wealth and in which most social relationships were shaped by people's connections with the land, evolved into an urban society dominated by business. The transformation to an urban society can be divided roughly into two major phases. The first phase, the Commercial Revolution, was a period in which merchants—individuals engaged in large-scale buying and selling activities—gained positions of prominence and power. The second, better-known phase, the Industrial Revolution, began around the middle of the eighteenth century. During this phase, manufacturing activities gained central importance. The rise of business and businessmen to central importance in Western society had significant consequences for social welfare.

By the fourteenth and fifteenth centuries, a well-to-do, even wealthy, merchant class had developed in the cities of Europe. In London, for example, there were craftsmen who had acquired a substantial clientele whose demand for their wares they could meet only by "putting out" some of the work to other craftsmen with fewer customers. Eventually these craftsmen devoted all their time to the managing of a business rather than to making articles for sale with their own hands. Once so launched, they often branched out into other lines of business as well.[1] In time, they became wealthy and sought ways in which to enjoy their wealth and to demonstrate their success. They ate well, they dressed expensively and colorfully, and they lived in expensive town houses. They also had lavish funerals, and these became occasions for the distribution of alms to the poor.

The merchant class developed in a society in which Christianity continued to influence the beliefs of the people. The pursuit of wealth was not taken for granted as a worthwhile activity in itself. The merchants felt the need to justify their efforts and success, and so they "were fond of texts and mottoes that expressed confidence of divine approval."[2] On the other hand:

> God approved of newly accumulated wealth, it was understood, only on condition that it was honestly won. Preachers would warn merchants against too much love of wealth.[3]

Charity became a means by which merchants could assure themselves and others that their pursuit of wealth was justified and that their business activities were pleasing to God. Opinions differed as to whether, in order to gain entrance to heaven, it was necessary for a man to distribute alms throughout his lifetime or he could wait until his estate was divided after his death.

As is apparent, the rise of a wealthy merchant class was accompanied by certain strains in society. Although the early Christian debate about private property had been decided in favor of private property, an obligation to the poor nonetheless continued to be built into the system of property holding. Further, as the discussion of feudalism indicated, since society had been primarily agricultural, even those at the bottom of the social ladder had certain well-defined rights in the use of their land. The shift to a way of life based on commerce and towns brought new possibilities of social and economic injury. Merchants might seek to increase their profits through misrepresentation of their wares or through giving short measure. They might violate other norms by doing business on holidays or by charging usurious rates of interest for loans. The clergy preached against all these practices, which were judged to violate the principles of a Christian society. Since religious norms had some force in regulating behavior, merchants strove to achieve a combination of the best of both worlds: maximum financial gain on earth and salvation in the afterlife. Through giving charity, they reduced their uneasiness about the harshness and injustice that crept into their business dealings. Whatever they did during their life on earth, they sought to make things right after death through the instructions and bequests they made in their wills. Executors of wills were often left instructions not to collect debts owed by old or very poor people.[4]

Funeral Doles

The distribution of a dole of money or food at a merchant's funeral became one of the widely accepted and expected means of providing charity to the poor. The funeral, and two associated ceremonial occasions—a feast following a memorial service one month after his death and another one a year after, following the anniversary service or "obit"—reflected on the merchant's social status. The merchant, or whoever made the funeral preparations, was often torn between the wish for a grand funeral and the pressure applied by the priest that the money be spent on alms. The merchant was concerned not only with his earthly social status but also with rectifying past misdeeds by being charitable to as many poor people as possible.

> Maximum safety would lie in the distribution of a maximum number of gifts, no matter how small they might be. The man who tried to reach more people with his charity than anyone else in London was Philip Malpas, who was one of the most popularly hated of the city magnates of his time. He left close to £1,800 to charity, most of it to be scattered in gifts of half a mark each to five thousand poor city householders.[5]

Diverse arrangements were tried in order to maximize the benefit to the soul of the merchant. One merchant left a bequest of a penny a week for ninety years to each of the poor tenants of a particular building. Another provided for the distribution of three pennies' worth of bread every Friday for a year. Still another left a shilling's worth of fruit to be given for forty years as an annual treat to young children who were able to speak well enough to ask God to have mercy on their godfather's soul.

In England, the doling out of food and money at funerals contributed to the problem of vagrancy that had been developing since the thirteenth century and that continued into the sixteenth century. In order to combat this situation, some merchants tried to have their money distributed only to the industrious poor, and "not [to] those who were astute enough to stop working in order to live by the indiscriminate almsgiving that went on at funerals."[6]

The Almshouses and Hospitals

The Middle Ages saw the emergence of an all-purpose institution that was later to become differentiated into several more specialized ones. This was the hospital, a kind of all-purpose reception center for people with various needs. In its early form, it was a guest house, free to all comers, where poor travelers, as well as the sick, infirm, or aged, could have their needs cared for. All the major cities of Europe and many of the smaller towns had them; often they were located at each gate of a town or city. Between the twelfth and the sixteenth centuries, more than eight hundred hospitals were built in England. These institutions were endowed by prominent church members, private benefactors, monarchs, towns (with all the citizens contributing), and craft and religious guilds.[7]

By the fifteenth century, all-purpose hospitals began to give way to almshouses, each of which cared for a particular group of people, as specified by the merchant donor funding the institution. Thus one man endowed an almshouse for retired and disabled soldiers and sailors, another for "decayed merchants," a third for forty poor men and women "of whom six were to be chosen from the most aged of the Fishmongers Company which administers the charity."[8]

It is interesting to note that many medieval hospitals and almshouses were designed by leading architects. They were built with considerable attention to detail and beauty, and some were "magnificent monuments of design and craftsmanship."[9] Often a statue of the founder was placed in a niche above the doorway. Thus the endowment of almshouses permitted the needs of both rich merchant and poor and aged people to be met simultaneously. The merchant's need to be considered a worthy Christian—perhaps in spite of his devoting his life successfully to the pursuit of wealth—was realized by his providing a home and an income to a group of people who needed both.

CHARITY AND PHILANTHROPY IN THE TUDOR PERIOD

The development of social welfare is marked by certain periods of change that are particularly significant for they have led to new forms of social welfare. New ideas about what to do and new types of organization for carrying out the ideas arise during such moments, and they remain influential for a long time. One era of change is the period from 1485 to 1603 in England, when the country's ruling family was the House of Tudor. The first Tudor king was Henry VII. He was succeeded, in turn, by Henry VIII, Edward VI, Mary I, and Elizabeth I. Of these, Henry VIII, who reigned from 1509 to 1547, and Elizabeth I, who reigned from 1558 to 1603, are the most significant. While Henry VIII is today best remembered for his six wives, and Elizabeth put her stamp on the United States by having the state of Virginia named in her honor (since she never married and was not known to have taken a lover, she was known as the Virgin Queen), their respective reigns require particular attention in tracing the development of social welfare. Most generally, the Tudor period is significant as the time when programs of public assistance—aid to the poor prescribed by the national government but administered by local governments—began to take shape; this form of social welfare eventually displaced charity and philanthropy in importance. The development of public assistance is treated in Chapter 5. The focus here is the changing attitudes toward charity during this period.

Vagrancy and Almsgiving

From at least the fourteenth century, and perhaps earlier, England was characterized by increasing numbers of people wandering about the countryside and into and out of the towns. While some of these people were on religious pilgrimages, and others were itinerant peddlers and tradesmen, many were unemployed, some by choice and some by force of circumstance. Some of these wanderers, or vagrants, survived by traveling from one monastery to another to obtain food at the monastery gates, as well as from other almsgivers. Others—known as rogues—were highway robbers who attacked merchants, peddlers, and religious travelers.

For a time, neither the population nor the government seemed particularly concerned about the problem of vagrancy. A law passed in 1495, during the reign of Henry VII, stipulating that beggars and idlers be punished by being (1) placed in the stocks for three days, (2) fed bread and water, (3) whipped, and (4) returned to their place of origin, seems not to have been enforced very strenuously.[10] By the time of Henry VIII, concern about the problem had mounted, and new efforts were made to deal with it. But even this loosely enforced law near the end of the fifteenth century reveals the beginnings of a change in attitude toward charity. Indiscriminate almsgiving was beginning to be regarded not as an act of Christian love but as an act that encouraged idleness. This new attitude took hold by degrees, and did not become the firm basis of government policy until the so-called Poor Law Reform of 1834 (discussed in Chapter 6). Nonetheless, the new attitude did gain ground, and one reason was that vagabonds were increasingly seen as a menace. As we would say today, they gave charity a bad name.[11]

Dissolution of the Monasteries

The rogues and vagabonds came to be feared, but it was not they alone who turned people against almsgiving. Monasteries—one of the main sources of aid to the poor—themselves came into disfavor. As a result of their practice of giving food to anyone who came to their gates, they were seen as contributing to the very problem of poverty that they were supposed to help solve by encouraging idleness and with it the menace posed by bands of wandering idle men and women.

The monasteries came into disfavor for another reason—one that seemed to contradict the first reason. Wealthy merchants—and also people of lesser means —often left money for the poor in the care of monasteries, which were supposed to carry out the philanthropic wishes of the deceased donors. All too frequently, however, instead of adhering to the instructions, the monastic clergy misappropriated the funds for their own use.[12] Legal machinery for dealing with these offenses was ineffective.

Henry VIII's marital problems had some impact on the course of social welfare. Because the Pope would not allow him to divorce his first wife, he broke with the Pope and no longer accepted his authority. Henry declared the official church to be the Church of England, or Anglican Church, with himself (and future monarchs) as its head. Henry took over all the property that had belonged to the Church (known thereafter by the more restricted name of Roman Church or Roman Catholic Church) and dissolved the monasteries, many of whose buildings were torn down and burned and the lands distributed to others.

There has been much scholarly controversy concerning the impact on the poor of the dissolution of the monasteries. The evidence suggests that, although there was considerable variation from one monastery to another, on the average they devoted not more than 2.5 to 3 percent of their income to charity[13]—a very small proportion, indeed. For this reason and also because monastic charities were uncoordinated, enabling people to receive benefits from several monasteries, monastic almsgiving was poorly regarded by the time of Henry VIII—and has been judged ineffective and inefficient by twentieth-century students of social welfare.[14]

NEW DIRECTIONS IN PHILANTHROPY

Although, historically, the Tudor period is seen as the time when poverty, unemployment, and care of the aged and infirm came to be viewed as matters of systematic governmental concern, to be financed by taxation rather than by voluntary, private donations, philanthropy particularly by merchants, but also by the rural gentry, artisans, and owners of small farms, was substantial and, in fact, remained the principal form of poor relief until the nineteenth century. According to historian Wilbur K. Jordan, who has closely studied English philanthropy for the years 1480–1660 (primarily the Tudor period, but also the reigns of the first two Stuart kings—1603–1649—and the interregnum of Oliver Cromwell—1649–1660):

> The care of the poor, not to mention other equally important charitable outlays, throughout our period remained principally in the hands of private donors, who were creating with their wealth the great social institutions which may be said to frame and undergird the liberal society. The law, the use of the taxing power, was regarded, so to speak, as a kind of co-insurance against social disaster in the event the economy was overwhelmed by forces too powerful and too abrupt for charity to master. It was the lively fear that such a period might be at hand which evoked the legislation of 1597 [Elizabethan Poor Law] and which was to result in its first considerable enforcement about a generation later. But there remained the confidence that private charity, with its rapidly mounting resources, could not only bear the burdens of the society in normal times but could raise the level of opportunity throughout the realm so that poverty might be prevented.[15]

Jordan estimates that in 1650 no more than 7 percent of the money spent on the poor came from taxation, despite the fact that this was seen as a year of large expenditure on the poor from tax monies.[16] Thus the practice of using tax monies for poor relief and prevention of poverty, first begun in 1572, developed gradually.[17]

New Motives and Ideas

The beginning of the Protestant Reformation in England, set in motion by Henry VIII's break with the Pope, affected ideas about charity. As Protestant ideas took hold more widely, people turned against many practices and attitudes of the Roman Catholic Church. One of the beliefs rejected by Protestants was that charitable contributions could gain the donor salvation in the hereafter. This was seen as a materialistic superstition not in keeping with the Protestant emphasis on faith as the basis of salvation. Catholic institutions and beliefs were repudiated, and the Catholic beliefs and practices concerning charity were regarded by the first generations of Protestants as having never been effective.[18]

The stewardship of wealth

Poverty was widespread in England throughout the sixteenth century, with particular concentrations in urban areas. Between one fourth and one third of the population of most English towns was "below the status of wage-earner, and at any moment their numbers were liable to be swelled by a slump in one of the major industries."[19] Those who were well off were sensitive to this poverty, partly because they feared a rebellion by the discontented poor, and partly because of a renewed emphasis, from Protestantism, on the obligations of the rich toward the poor.

The Puritans, who advocated an even more far-reaching Protestantism than that carried out by the Church of England, put forth a doctrine known as the stewardship of wealth. This is the idea that the rich do not really own their wealth. God owns the wealth, and the rich are no more than caretakers or stewards of it. They have been selected by God for this task, and it is their obligation to use the wealth they hold in socially constructive ways, such as for the relief and rehabilitation of the poor. Social responsibility in the use of wealth, rather than assuring one's own salvation, thus became a preoccupation of the people in the late Tudor and early Stuart periods.

This is not to say that all persons of wealth were inevitably generous. On the contrary, many were not, but the country was filled with preachers and pamphleteers exhorting the tightfisted to live up to their Christian responsibilities. Philanthropic generosity was a live and active issue, and the stewardship of wealth was the principal argument used to stimulate the sense of responsibility that would result in philanthropic activity.

The turn to secular interests

In pre-Reformation times, philanthropy and charity focused not only on almshouses, hospitals, doles, and other types of donations to the poor, but also on the construction and repair of church buildings and chantries (chapels for singing or saying Mass for the souls of the donors).[20] In the late Tudor period, there was a marked decline in these donations, and poverty became the dominant focus of philanthropy. The emphasis was on the secular, the problems of this world, rather than on the religious or spiritual, even though much of the rationale for philanthropy was inspired by religion.

Innovations in Organization

Social welfare, as noted in Chapter 1, involves ideas and beliefs about what should be done to provide for people's well-being as well as organizations for carrying out the ideas. Several innovations in organization appeared during the Tudor and Stuart periods.

The charitable trust

A persistent problem in all organized human activity is that of assuring that goals and purposes are actually carried out. It has already been noted that monasteries did not always carry out the instructions of the donors who left charitable funds in their care.

The year 1601, during the reign of Queen Elizabeth, was notable for two important pieces of social welfare legislation. One was the Poor Law, which will be discussed in Chapter V. The other, less well known law was the Statute of Charitable Uses. The goal of this statute was to correct abuses in the administration of charitable trust funds. It provided a procedure for appointing commissions of inquiry when abuses were charged in order to assure that charitable bequests were not diverted for personal profit. Trustees of charitable bequests sometimes made off with the funds, rather than carrying out the donor's wishes. Forty-five commissions of inquiry were appointed during the first year the law was in effect.[21]

The Statute of Charitable Uses "had been inspired by a national concern to encourage charitable giving," and its preamble set forth a great variety of categories of bequest that were considered legitimate and deserving of protection. Bequests of money, land, and annuities were appropriate for the aged, infirm, or poor; sick or injured soldiers and sailors; schools; young tradesmen, craftsmen, and disabled persons; orphans; the relief or redemption of prisoners and captives; and bridge, port, road, and dike repair. The law even protected bequests for bows and arrows for children between the ages of seven and seventeen. Henry VIII had imposed the duty of making this provision on parents in 1542, but "many of the parents and masters who are statutorily bound to supply these weapons are poor and not able to meet that charge."[22]

Associated philanthropy

Business activity increased considerably in England during the seventeenth and eighteenth centuries. A new form of business organization that became common during this time was the joint-stock company, an organization in which individuals pooled their funds to carry on the business. This type of organization seems to have been at least one of the influences in the creation of a new type of philanthropic organization, the charitable society—devoted to a specific worthy purpose and funded by a number of individuals joining together in what was known as associated philanthropy. "In the future, the hallmark of the philanthropist was to be not merely generous giving but also his support of worthy organizations."[23]

From the late seventeenth century until well into the nineteenth century, all manner of charitable societies proliferated, blending charitable concerns with the concerns of the mercantilists, who were interested in maximizing the nation's wealth. Thus the eighteenth century was a time when a great many hospitals (in the modern sense) were founded by charitable associations. "The mercantilist was alarmed at the effect of a high death rate on the labor force of the nation and, when he considered it, uneasy over the loss of working time through illness."[24] A retired sea captain, shocked by the sight of babies, dead or alive, left by the roadside "was able to rally notable support in the world of 'Quality and Distinction' for his project of an institution for foundlings."[25] Another philanthropist, concerned about the women who gave birth to and abandoned illegitimate children, wrote a pamphlet entitled *Proposals for Establishing a Public Place of Reception for Penitent Prostitutes,* which launched the movement to establish the Magdalen Hospital, where during the last half of the eighteenth century almost thirty-nine hundred women received religious and moral instruction, as well as training in a useful trade or craft. The Marine Society was established by shipowners and merchants to cope with both the problem of destitute boys and the problem of recruitment for the navy. Between 1756 and 1763, more than ten thousand men and boys had been prepared and equipped for sea duty by this society. The Society for the Discharge and Relief of Persons Imprisoned for Small Debts was formed by a group concerned about men who had been imprisoned for not being able to pay their debts.

The charity school movement

One of the new directions taken by philanthropy at the end of the seventeenth century was toward the prevention of poverty. As noted earlier, this concern arose as much from an interest in maintaining social stability as from humanitarian feelings. One way of preventing poverty was to send poor children to schools set up by the middle class and the wealthy. But this was not the only motive for setting up these schools:

> Among the charitable middle classes the extraordinary popularity of such schools owed a good deal to their assumed effectiveness in protecting the poor (and hence their betters) against the dangers that threatened. If the children of the poor could be at once immunized against the contagion of Popery, which was insidiously working to corrupt the faith of individuals and destroy the Protestant Succession, and drilled in habits of industry and sobriety, the gain in social stability would more than justify the comparatively modest financial outlay. Religious training was the prescription and the charity school the instrument. The easy and certain way, the Bishop of Chester could proclaim in a charity sermon, "to Reform the Lives of a Class of Mankind, which, to the utmost Degree, needed Reformation . . . is, by beginning early with Children, before any evil Habit has taken Possession of them."[26]

These schools began in England as individual local philanthropies, modeled on a school that had been established by Hermann Francke in Germany. Early in the eighteenth century, the Society for the Promotion of Christian Knowledge became coordinating agency for the schools, which by 1729 numbered more than fourteen hundred. The SPCK helped local school leaders with advice on curriculum and finances and supplied the names of prospective teachers.

The SPCK brought three significant innovations to the practice of philanthropy. First, it presented a new pattern of organization—a national committee that coordinated and guided the work of a large number of local committees. The charity school movement thus furnished a model that became the pattern of many later national-scale philanthropic and reform activities. Second, the schools developed a new fund-raising technique, the charity sermon, which also became a model for raising money for other causes. A school would get a clergyman to conduct an annual, semiannual, or quarterly charity service, at which the schoolchildren would march in in an orderly way. The special charity sermon stimulated contributions for the school. Third, the movement developed "an inspired strategem for drawing public attention." Every year from 1704 until 1877, the charity schools in London held an annual assembly, with crowds averaging forty-five hundred children and seventy-five hundred viewers.

> Like a local charity service multiplied many times over, the army of well-scrubbed children marching by parishes, each school in its distinctive garb, seemed a dramatic proof of the reality of British charity and an irrefutable argument for associated benevolence.[27]

These three innovative elements—the national coordinating committee, the fund-raising special event, and the building of public support through publicity—survive to our own time as components of philanthropic activity.

EARLY AMERICAN PHILANTHROPY

The first permanent settlement in North America was Jamestown, Virginia, settled by the English in 1607, four years after the death of Queen Elizabeth. The colonists brought to the American colonies the philanthropic ideas they had known at home. The colonizing efforts in themselves combined philanthropic motives with political motives. Georgia, the last of the thirteen original colonies, settled in 1733, was the most conspicuous instance of this. James Oglethorpe, an activist in the English movement to free debtors from prison, had the idea of helping such men to get a fresh start in the New World. The project was financed with money raised by Oglethorpe and a large contribution from the English government, which hoped that Oglethorpe's project would help solve the problem of vagrancy in England.[28]

Philanthropy was less relevant to the early colonial situation than were the English poor laws, which required local governments to collect taxes to support the poor, and they were the more direct model for colonial handling of the poor. Nevertheless, it is worth noting that some of the seventeenth-century colonial leaders expressed ideas that were similar to the ideas of their contemporaries in England and that provided a foundation for later American philanthropy. John Winthrop, an early governor of Massachusetts, and William Penn, founder of Pennsylvania, both adhered to the doctrine of the stewardship of wealth. They believed in class distinctions, regarding these as established by God. Like their contemporaries in England, they believed that rich and poor needed each other and that the rich were accountable to God for the way they used their wealth, although neither seems to have stimulated philanthropic giving.[29]

Two religious leaders loom large as active advocates of philanthropy in colonial times. In *Essays To Do Good*, written in 1710, an influential Puritan minister named Cotton Mather offered the following principal arguments for why people should engage in "a perpetual endeavor to do good in the world": (1) Performance of good works is an obligation owed to God; (2) to help the unfortunate is a reward in itself; (3) benevolent people will gain long life and business success; (4) doing good is an acceptable and effective way of reducing social tensions. "Pious example, moral leadership, voluntary effort, and private charity were the means by which competing and conflicting interests in society might be brought into harmony."[30] While Mather identified various categories of people to whom good should be done, he wrote that the most "Ravishing Satisfaction" would be obtained "'in relieving the Distresses of a Poor, Mean, Miserable Neighbour.'"[31] But in keeping with the belief in a divinely organized set of social classes, he also wrote: "To Receive Alms, with such a lowly Mind, as becomes them who need them is as great a Grace, as to Bestow them. They should thank God that He has commanded 'us' to help."[32] The theme that the poor should be grateful for what they receive from their betters was thus clearly articulated in the American colonies. Mather also recommended that reform societies, such as those in England, be established as a force for good in the community.[33]

The second influential religious leader who advocated philanthropy and charity was George Whitefield, an English preacher who made several long visits to the American colonies. The most significant, for this study, was a fourteen-month visit begun in 1739 during a religious revival, conducted by several ministers and known as the Great Awakening. Whitefield drew enormous crowds, and he was outstanding among the preachers of the Great Awakening in the emphasis he gave to charity. Whitefield had established an orphanage in Georgia, modeled on Francke's institution in Germany, and had raised great sums of money for it. Perhaps most innovative in Whitefield's approach were his appeals to conscience and altruism on the part of the people of modest means who flocked to his preachings. This resulted in "the transformation of do-goodism from a predominantly upper- and middle-class activity—half responsibility, half recreation—into a broadly shared, genuinely popular avocation."[34]

Private Charity and Public Funding

As mentioned in Chapter 1, there are five major and distinct ideas about social welfare, which have to some extent been competitive with each other at various times. Yet many actual social welfare organizations and activities have involved blendings of two or more of the five basic ideas. Some of the early blendings in American social welfare will be discussed here.

During the thirty-five-year period between the Great Awakening and the American Revolution, various social welfare organizations were financed jointly by private charity and philanthropy and by public tax funds. The main reason for this development was the occurrence of emergency situations that caused an increase in the number of people requiring assistance, so that neither voluntary charity nor tax-based funding was sufficient. Intermittent warfare between the colonies and the French and Indians resulted in a great increase in wounded soldiers and orphaned, widowed, aged, and ill refugees from frontier settlements. There were destructive fires in Boston and in Charleston, South Carolina, and two economic depressions and several epidemics.

In order to meet the needs created by these catastrophes, various patterns of public and private cooperation emerged. Private donors gave or bequeathed property to the government for charitable purposes. Public officials known as overseers of the poor asked the churches to take up special collections of alms. New institutions financed jointly by taxation and private contributions were developed, such as the *house of industry*. One of these, the Philadelphia Bettering House, established in 1766, claimed to reduce the number of beggars and paupers by employing the destitute and developing in them the virtues of industry and frugality.[35]

The joining of private, voluntary contributions with tax supported funds in the support of particular social welfare organizations or agencies is a pattern that has continued down to our own time, not only in the United States but in England and elsewhere. This pattern of joint financing should be understood as drawing upon two distinct traditions in Western history—one holding that helping people in need should be voluntary, motivated by concern for one's neighbors and a wish to carry out one's civic duty, and the other, newer one holding that the state has an obligation to care for its citizens. Throughout the nineteenth and twentieth centuries, these two traditions have been antagonistic to each other. Many battles have been fought over which aspects of social welfare are the proper responsibility of the state, using the money of taxpayers, and which are the proper responsibility of private, voluntary social welfare agencies, supported by philanthropic and charitable donations.

But, as we have seen above, while voluntarism and state obligation have remained two antagonistic principles, they have in fact been combined in numerous actual situations in support of particular social welfare programs. These compromises occur because decision makers are unwilling to make a clear-cut choice between the two practices, and they are unwilling to make such choices because each practice offers certain advantages that would be lost if social welfare were based purely on one or the other. In eighteenth-century America, there was insufficient accumulated wealth for charity and philanthropy to meet all the demands for social welfare, but social thinking of the time did not hold that the state should handle the entire job of social welfare without any input from voluntary endeavors. Throughout the nineteenth century and continuing into the twentieth, social thinkers have tried to develop clear and acceptable ideas concerning state responsibility for social welfare and the social responsibility of citizens acting in a voluntary capacity as individual donors or in association with charitable societies. And these efforts to distinguish the two will no doubt continue, just as the state as dispenser of tax-collected funds will continue to join forces with citizens contributing voluntarily from their incomes to establish and maintain certain social welfare institutions, such as the Philadelphia Bettering House.

INDUSTRIALIZATION AND CHARITY

Just as the sixteenth century was a landmark period in the development of social welfare in Tudor England, so also was the nineteenth century in England, the United States, and elsewhere. The nineteenth century is the century of accelerating industrialization in the Western world—first in England (where industrialization had actually gotten under way in the late eighteenth century) and later in the United States and other countries. Developments in social welfare were responses to the broader social changes induced by industrialization. Although there were important developments across the whole spectrum of social welfare activities (many of which will be discussed in succeeding chapters), our focus here remains on charity. In order to put the changes in attitudes toward charity in perspective, we will begin with a brief review of the impact of industrialization and some of the major beliefs that accompanied the process.

The growth of industry pulled people out of rural villages into manufacturing towns. At the same time, skilled craftspeople were finding their skills increasingly obsolete, as more and more human skills were replaced by machinery that made possible greater productivity at lower cost. The cities became ever larger concentrations of people, most depending for their livelihood on a small weekly wage, but many also unable to find employment.

Expanding industry was stimulated and supported by the general belief that opportunity for economic advancement was readily available to all. All that was required were self-discipline and hard work, plus talent. Those who prospered were considered to have combined these virtues in the right proportions. Those who did not were considered to be lacking in self-discipline, or talent.

The concentration of population, indeed the congestion, in English industrial cities was due not only to migration from rural areas but also to an overall natural increase in population. In the early nineteenth century, populations in many of these cities grew about 40 to 50 percent per decade.[36] American cities on the eastern seaboard were experiencing similar increases in population due to European immigration. Some Americans thought the immigration was part of a sinister plan by European countries to ship their paupers and criminals to the United States. Apparently there were a few instances in which European cities paid for the passage of paupers: "Thus, in 1839, in the midst of the depression, a miserable company of immigrants, many still wearing the uniform of the Edinburgh almshouse, arrived in New York; their transportation had been paid by the overseers of the poor of Edinburgh."[37] Episodes of this kind were not, however, the primary cause of immigration to the United States; the wish to flee unfavorable economic, political, religious, and social conditions was the major impetus.

Nineteenth-century cities in England and the United States became centers of concentrated distress. A large, impoverished working class lived on precarious week-to-week incomes. When economic recessions and depressions occurred, thousands were quickly deprived of income and obliged to look elsewhere than to employment for means of subsistence. Begging was widespread. Large numbers of neglected children roamed the streets.

In these circumstances, charitable societies continued to be formed. But an important new attitude showed itself. Providing relief in the form of alms to any and all who claimed to need it was regarded as destructive because of the hazard of inducing *pauperization*, that is, destroying the will to be independent and fostering unending dependence upon others. As the nineteenth century wore on, pauperization came to be perceived by the middle class and the well-to-do as a terrible threat to society. Throughout the century there was a constant confusion of poverty and pauperization. That is, there was no clear conception that people might be poor not because they were receiving charity and not through personal failing—but through being thrown out of work, being too ill or too old to work, or being paid too little to be able to set aside savings for times of illness or for old age. Charity was not to be a permanent source of subsistence. Rather, it was meant to enable people to become self-supporting as quickly as possible. Providing charitable alms for an extended amount of time was considered as adding to people's problems, not solving them, since it was believed to discourage them from looking for work. This new attitude led to what is perhaps the most significant development in nineteenth-century charity: *case-by-case investigation of need*. This technique was tried on a small and local scale early in the nineteenth century, and then in the last third of the century, it was practiced on an international scale in what became known as the Charity Organization movement, a movement that prided itself on having established the practice of "scientific charity."

The Charity Organization Movement

The Charity Organization movement began with the founding of a Charity Organization Society (COS) in London in 1869 and led, in the next few years, to the founding of such societies in many other cities. By 1891, there were seventy-five such societies in England, nine in Scotland, and two in Ireland.[38] The movement was carried to the United States by a London minister, Reverend S. Humphreys Gurteen, who organized the first American COS in Buffalo, New York, in 1877. Within ten years, twenty-five societies had been established in various cities, among them New York, Boston, Baltimore, and Indianapolis.[39] The Charity Organization movement is of considerable significance because certain of its aspects became a model for later developments in social welfare and other aspects became a kind of "anti-model," that is, an example of what social welfare should *not* be.

"Scientific Charity"

The guiding idea of the COS (the full name was Society for Organising Charitable Relief and Repressing Mendicity) was that thoughtless and unsystematic charity was the chief cause of pauperism. This idea is revealed in an essay by Octavia Hill, a leading figure in the London COS:

> I believe our irregular alms to the occupant of the miserable room, to the shoeless flower-seller, are tending to keep a whole class on the very brink of pauperism who might be taught self-control and foresight if we would let them learn it. . . .
>
> The street-sellers and low class desultory workers usually remain what they are by choice; a little self-control would raise them into the ranks of those who are really wanted, and who have made their way from the brink of pauperism to a securer place, and one where they are under better influences. Above all is this true of the children.
>
> A little self-control would enable the daughters of most of these people to rise into the class of domestic servants; and their sons, instead of remaining street-sellers, would soon learn a trade or go to sea if they cared to do regular work. We are largely helping by our foolish gifts to keep them herded together in crowded, dirty, badly-built rooms, among scenes of pauperism, crime, and vice.[40]

A similar point of view was expressed in the 1880s by Josephine Shaw Lowell, the founder of the New York Charity Organization Society:

> Human nature is so constituted that no man can receive as a gift what he should earn by his own labor without a moral deterioration. No human being . . . will work to provide the means of living for himself if he can get a living in any other manner agreeable to himself.[41]

The social philosophy of the Charity Organization movement thus included the following ideas: (1) pauperization is caused by people gaining too easily the means of livelihood that they ought to earn for themselves; (2) indiscriminate charity increases pauperization; (3) pauperization, the degradation of character of the poor man or woman, is the most serious aspect of poverty, which thus needs to be understood more as a moral defect than as a mere insufficiency of livelihood. The cure for poverty, therefore, involves three main elements: (1) putting some order into the way charities work so that they do not simply give out money or food to anybody who comes looking for it, (2) offering the poor true friendship, so they can regain their self-respect and ability to be self-supporting, (3) finding out the facts of the situation that led the particular person into that loss of self-respect that led to the seeking of charity.[42]

This interpretation of poverty and its cure grew out of the social climate of the Victorian period. The emphasis on individualism—an emphasis that did not diminish substantially until the 1930s and 1940s—was extreme. In this view, poverty arises more from individual faults of character than from any problems in the way the larger society is organized. Moral changes in character are more important than social changes and also more important than providing material assistance. At the same time, this outlook took it for granted that people who were financially well off were morally superior to those who were impoverished. If they offered their friendship to the poor, they would not only assist them in regaining their self-respect but would also help to reduce the class divisions in society. The middle class and the well-to-do should offer their friendship by visiting the poor in their homes, finding out the facts, and then offering advice on how to rise from poverty. When the facts warranted, charity might be offered to those deserving of it, that is, those in financial difficulty through no fault of their own. Those who were not deserving (for example, those who were poor because of squandering their money on drink) would be referred to public authorities who would provide minimal relief. Thus the COS viewpoint assumed that it was an easy matter to determine who was deserving and who was not.

The pattern of organization

To carry out its ideas, the Charity Organization movement used a pattern of organization that had actually been tried fifty years earlier but had not caught on at the time. During the years 1819–1823, in a poor parish in Glasgow, Reverend Thomas Chalmers, a minister of the Church of Scotland, had developed an organization that screened all applicants for charity and investigated their financial circumstances. Although his ideas and practices did not gain wide application in his own time, they helped to shape the ideas and practices of the Charity Organization movement fifty years later.[43]

The London COS was governed by a council that included politicians, members of the aristocracy, professional men, leading clergymen, and a few people, such as Octavia Hill, who in retrospect have come to be thought of as social workers, although a formal occupation of that name did not exist at the time. In addition:

> To some extent the C.O.S. always went in for skillful window-dressing. In the second annual report the category of vice-president appears, and includes twenty-four men. . . . Most of the vice-presidents took little active part in the work of the Society beyond lending it the support of their names and purses. . . . Yet the enlisting of great names which appeared in all the Society's publications was part of the Society's method and its strength. It was a propagandist body, and must give all the weight it could to its utterances and its work. Names helped in this, the more influential the better. In the fourth report, the Queen appears as the Society's Patron.[44]

In addition to the council, there was a central office and a secretary (the term today would be executive director). The main work was done through district committees, set up in each of the districts that had been established for public relief purposes by the Poor Law Reform of 1834 (see Chapter 6). Each district committee managed a charity office staffed by a charity agent. The agent's job was to keep in touch with all charities and charity societies of the district, all the clergy, and the Poor Law relieving officer. The agent was supposed to maintain a register of all cases being helped by all the charities in the district. New applications were to be investigated, and referred to the appropriate charity. The agent was to help only very special cases that did not fit any existing charity.

By the end of its second year, the London COS recognized that it had failed to gain the cooperation of the clergy, the heads of the various charities, and the government Poor Law authorities. None of these were willing to grant the COS the central position it was claiming for itself. The COS thus did what many organizations do when they cannot attain their goals: It adjusted its goals to what it was able to do. The district offices became, in effect, the forerunners of the modern family casework agency. The COS became just one charitable society among many, instead of the coordinator of them all that it had hoped to be. It was, however, distinctive in that it had a definite philosophy and it worked toward establishing systematic procedures for dealing with cases.

Each district office was staffed by women volunteers, in addition to the agent, who was paid, and perhaps one or two other paid employees. People in need of help came into the office and were interviewed. Records were kept of the interviews. The applicant's home was visited by the agent or by one of the volunteers. The district committee then decided what kind of help to give, if any. The worker on the case continued to visit the person's home "until it was clear that the family had been restored to independence and self-support (or that it was beyond help."[45]

The Charity Organization movement continued for a long time, though by the turn of the twentieth century its philosophy was increasingly under attack. The idea of abolishing poverty by changing the character of poor people was seen as an insufficient concept for dealing with the problem. (This idea, slightly altered, surfaced again later in the twentieth century.) But while the philosophy was, at least temporarily, discredited, the idea of investigating each applicant to discover the facts of the case and the exact nature of the problem survived and became one of the key procedures of the social work profession (a theme that will be discussed further in Chapter 9).

The transformation of charity organization

The Charity Organization movement's activity of "friendly visiting" brought about a significant and unanticipated change in its point of view. The movement began with the assumption that poverty was caused by defects in character and with the further assumption that simply granting aid for relief of material needs would not cure poverty but would result in pauperization and an unending dependence upon charitable donations. Friendly visiting was undertaken in a spirit of both sympathetic concern and scientific rationality; the goal was to discover, in a friendly way, what the causes of poverty were in each specific case and then, through friendly advice and encouragement, to help needy persons to reform their characters in ways that would enable them to become self-supporting. What happened instead was that through a scrupulous search for "the facts," the friendly visitors discovered that their initial assumptions were incorrect. They discovered that many people were in need not because of defects in their character but because of illness, unemployment, old age, or desertion or death of the breadwinner—in brief, involuntarily. The COS remedies were too simple, and a more complex service was required. This key discovery led to the development of a new modality of social welfare, the modality of social service (discussed in Part IV).

Here again it can be noted that although the five main modalities of social welfare are to some extent competitive with each other, no one of them ever completely supersedes and displaces any other one. They all coexist in changing combinations as circumstances warrant or as new ideas on how to combine modalities are proposed. So philanthropy in the form of the Charity Organization movement gives way to social service, but it does not disappear as a modality.

To sum up, the Charity Organization movement used three key ideas to accomplish its goals: (1) case-by-case investigation of need through friendly visiting, (2) allocation of funds in a planned and systematic way, and (3) use of volunteers to implement its programs. All three of these ideas have survived, even though the Charity Organization societies themselves no longer exist as such. Case-by-case investigation by friendly visitors became, as was noted, a key element in the development of social service. Today the principle of volunteerism is a kind of auxiliary to professional social service. The organized, systematic handling of money, which was a COS idea, but which was resisted by existing charitable societies that did not wish to give up their autonomy to this upstart movement, in fact became an accepted idea after the disappearance of the Charity Organization movement in its original form.

TWENTIETH-CENTURY PHILANTHROPY

Philanthropy in the twentieth century has centered upon two main types of organization: the united fund-raising campaign and the business corporation. From the beginnings of Western history until the sixteenth century, charity had been shaped and motivated by religious ideas and organizations. Beginning in the sixteenth century and gathering momentum from there, business ideas gained greater importance than religious ideas in stimulating and organizing charity. Mercantilists were less concerned with personal salvation than with the stability of society; a stable society was necessary in order to sustain a productive and profitable economy. Ideas of efficiency in the dispensing of charity grew in significance; ideas of Christian love and of salvation were edged from the center of concern to the periphery, although at no time were they completely eliminated.

By the nineteenth century, when individualist ideas were most influential, ideas of efficiency, factualness, good organization, and concern for the effects of charitable acts on the character of the recipients were the dominating concerns. Religious considerations were not totally suspended, but they were reinterpreted to conform with the businesslike outlook that, increasingly, shaped people's views of what was important and correct. As historian Irvin G. Wyllie has observed:

> Throughout the nineteenth century clergymen and laymen alike insisted that business stood high on God's list of approved callings. Matthew H. Smith, writing for *Hunt's Merchants' Magazine* in 1854, asserted that God had ordained business as the great purpose in life. . . . "Adam was created and placed in the Garden of Eden for business purposes; it would have been better for the race if he had attended closely to the occupation for which he was made." . . . If religion blessed business by approving the pursuit of wealth it doubled the blessing by sanctifying all the economic virtues essential to its accumulation. Of the virtues dear to the

business community, religion exalted industry above all others. God required hard, continuous labor of rich and poor alike, not only as punishment for original sin, but as a constructive means of personal discipline.[46]

Satisfied with the moral justice of their position in society, business people nevertheless often felt obligated to engage in philanthropic activity, and when they did not feel so obligated, they were pressed by others to do so. Their philanthropies went to voluntary social welfare agencies and to organizations collecting funds for voluntary agencies.

The Great Depression of the 1930s, a period of ruin for millions of people, undercut the exalted status that businessmen had enjoyed. It was also abundantly clear during this period that voluntary charities were not large enough or strong enough to cope with the needs of people for the elementary means of survival —food, clothing, and housing. After much delay, the state finally became the most significant social welfare institution. Yet voluntary agencies continued to perform an important function.

The persistence of voluntary agencies

A voluntary social welfare agency is an agency "organized by private initiative and usually supported by voluntary contributions."[47] This type of agency (sometimes called a private agency) is in contrast with a public agency, that is, one organized and run by a branch of government and supported from tax monies. However, the distinction is no longer as pure as it once was, since many voluntary agencies now receive some of their support from government funds. "Voluntary institutions are being used by government for public purposes, and they are becoming more dependent on government funding."[48] Nevertheless, they are not absorbed into government, and private funding remains important.

What is the scope of voluntary social agencies? A national directory of private social agencies lists approximately ten thousand agencies, homes, and organizations. "Only such welfare agencies are included that give direct help to individual applicants or refer them to the proper address. Homes listed are bona fide non-profit establishments."[49] The agencies are grouped into twenty-five categories of service, such as Adoption; Foster Home Placement for Children; Elderly Persons, Special Services; Services for Transients; and Volunteer Services Under Professional Guidance. The listing does not include the 3,210 local chapters of the American Red Cross, an organization that helps military personnel and their families and assists wherever a disaster such as a flood, fire, or earthquake has occurred.

Even this national directory's listing of ten thousand agencies does not provide the full picture. Across the United States and Canada, approximately thirty-seven thousand local private, voluntary agencies receive money from unified fund-raising campaigns known as United Way Campaigns in more than twenty-two hundred communities.[50]

Another way to gain a view of the scope of private, voluntary agencies is to compare the volume of funds involved in different types of *transfer payments,* a term whose meaning becomes clear in the following statement:

> Turning to the way in which industrialized societies organize to support their dependent populations, there are essentially three institutions which transfer funds from individuals who work in the market to those who do not: the family, the government, and private philanthropy. The study of these one-way transfers has been called "grants economics" by Kenneth Boulding, and, as he points out, the family is by far the largest donor in the grants system, accounting for $313 billion of transfer in 1970, as compared to $74 billion for the public sector and $20 billion for private charity.[51]

The comparison of the family, the government, and private philanthropy is perhaps misleading here; private charity is in fact no longer used much for transferring money from people who work to people who do not. More commonly, the money raised by private charity pays the costs of running organizations that provide specialized social services—such as helping with adoptions, providing counseling of various kinds, and referring people with disabilities to the appropriate agencies. While the $20 billion donated through private charity in 1970 is small in comparison with the other two figures, the sum is not insignificant. Moreover, it continues to grow. In 1977, about four hundred philanthropists and representatives of the organizations they support met at the twenty-third annual conference of the National Council on Philanthropy "to discuss the $32 billion that Americans will give away this year and how to collect and spend it more creatively."[52] A further indication of the importance of the voluntary agencies is that it is these agencies that employ most of the professionally trained social workers.

United Fund Raising

The founders of the Charity Organization movement were not the only ones concerned with the problem of coordination of funds. The twentieth century has seen the emergence of united fund raising among voluntary agencies. While the modern voluntary agencies are not much more willing to have their welfare activities prescribed by an outside group than were the charitable societies of the nineteenth century, many believe that a single, coordinated fund-raising campaign is more likely to gain public support and be less subject to public apathy and antagonism than numerous individual campaigns.

The Charity Organization movement was concerned with *coordination* of *benefits to recipients;* the members of the movement did not want recipients to receive duplicate benefits from multiple charities just because the charities had no way of keeping track of their beneficiaries. About the same time, another type of coordination—*of fund raising*—began, so that prospective donors would not be approached repeatedly by different charities. The first effort at what became known as federated fund raising was carried out by agencies in Liverpool, England, in 1873. In a pattern of influence similar to what occurred in the Charity Organization movement, the federated fund-raising idea was carried to the United States by migrating English clergymen. The first federated fund-raising campaign in the United Staes was in Denver, Colorado, in 1887.[53] A major impetus to federated fund raising came during World War I; many appeals for helping war victims in Europe led to the organization, in more than four hundred communities, of "war chests" for joint solicitation of funds. The idea was pursued after the war, and hundreds of communities established what were first called Community Chests, and later called United Funds; these evolved into what is today called the United Way.[54] Every year there are United Way campaigns in about 2,400 communities of the United States and Canada, and they collected $1.3 billion in 1979.[55]

As has been noted above, many local agencies have joined in the federated fund drive. But the federated idea has been controversial from the beginning, and some local and national agencies have refused to join it, preferring instead to conduct their own fund-raising campaigns. As F. Emerson Andrews noted, "Chests sometimes do not open their doors soon enough to new causes that capture the interest of givers."[56]

A single campaign on behalf of many groups and agencies may be more efficient, but it also poses problems for dividing the funds collected among the various agencies whose interests are represented. There are no clear, agreed-upon principles for doing so, though there are continued efforts to arrive at more rational and equitable bases for making allocations. In the meantime, there are protests and some of them are recognized as justified. In late 1977, a group of black civic, business, and political leaders charged that the Tri-State United Way (which operates in Connecticut, New Jersey, and New York) was not giving a fair share of the funds collected to the black community. It was reported that officials of the Tri-State United Way "acknowledged that they were not doing as much as they could for either the black or Spanish-speaking community, and agreed to consider the recommendations from the group of about 25 black leaders."[57]

One of the important techniques of fund raising used by the United Way is to arrange with companies to solicit contributions from their employees. Employees can have their contributions deducted from their paychecks. The company, in effect, acts as collector of the funds that its employees agree to contribute, and in addition often makes a contribution from its own treasury. Many employers, including many large corporations, favor the United Way because it limits the amount of charity solicitation that goes on in the company, while at the same time allowing the company to cooperate in charitable endeavors by facilitating employee contributions through this one channel. But in Los Angeles, an organization called Associated In-Group Donors filed a court suit against United Way, charging it with conspiring to eliminate fund-raising competitors. And as was noted above, not all charities participate in the United Way. In recent years, there has been criticism that the United Way was trying to monopolize charitable collections and thus gain increasing control over the policies and programs of individual local charities. Officials of charities such as the American Cancer Association, the American Heart Association, and the National Black United Fund complained of the United Way's alleged efforts to control paycheck donations, complaints that the United Way denied.[58]

It is not within the scope of this book to judge the merits of the conflict between what has been called "the nation's dominant volunteer charity" and those who challenge its dominance. What should be noted is that charitable activity, indeed all social welfare activity, is like all other types of human activity in that it gives rise to conflict—of values and of interests. Every arena of human activity, including social welfare in all its forms, also allows for the development of positions of power and control, and though these are sought in the service of worthy objectives, not everyone agrees on their worthiness or that the means are the right ones for attaining the objectives.

Modern Corporations and Philanthropy

From the early days of the rise of business as a significant factor in postmedieval Western society to the end of the nineteenth century, philanthropy was an activity of businessmen first acting individually and later acting together in associated philanthropy. One of the most notable philanthropists of the nineteenth century was Andrew Carnegie, who began as a poor Scottish immigrant boy and became the multimillionaire head of the United States Steel Corporation. Carnegie, influenced by the Social Darwinist thinking of his time, believed that life was a competitive struggle for survival and that millionaires were superior people who had demonstrated their fitness to survive through their successful business endeavors. This was a secular interpretation of the validity of wealth, as distinguished from the earlier doctrine of the stewardship of wealth, in which wealth was part of God's plan. But millionaires had a social responsibility, as well as a responsibility to safeguard their own interests. Historian Edward Chase Kirkland has observed that "this was a period of widespread discontent; apprehensive observers saw Socialism and Communism marching forward to confiscate wealth and divide it among 'the rabble.' "[59] Carnegie, in a widely noted article, wrote: "The problem of our age is the proper administration of wealth, so that the ties of brotherhood may still bind together the rich and poor in harmonious relationship."[60]

Carnegie's notion that millionaires were the best fitted to decide what was best for the community and to decide how their surplus wealth should be used was termed by an English critic "the gospel of wealth to distinguish it from the gospel of Christianity."[61] Carnegie accepted the label and thus turned the criticism into a slogan he believed in. Like the charity organization reformers, Carnegie was unsympathetic to almsgiving. In another article, "The Best Fields for Philanthropy," he wrote that he favored donating money to institutions that would bring about future improvements in people's lives rather than easing distress deriving from the past. His objectives included libraries, concert halls, universities, public baths, parks, and conservatories "filled with beautiful flowers, orchids, and aquatic plants which they [the workingmen], with their wives and children, can enjoy in their spare hours."[62] Kirkland considers that Carnegie, because of his approach, "transformed 'giving,' consecrated over centuries as charity, into philanthropy. The differences between charity and philanthropy were not merely matters of scale; they were matters of kind."[63] The problem for Carnegie, and for other wealthy contemporaries, was what to do with their personal fortunes. In the twentieth century, the world of business has been dominated by the large corporation. Individual and family fortunes remain weighty and influential with respect to philanthropy, but the impersonal corporation has risen to a position of significance. As already noted, many corporations give to the United Way exclusive fund-raising privileges. But corporations are active in philanthropy in other ways as well, ways that can affect the success of social agencies.

Corporations make philanthropic contributions. The first corporations to do this were the railroads, which supported the YMCAs. The YMCA movement began in London and spread in 1851 to the United States. The railroads were looking for housing for their employees, and contributed to constructing and maintaining YMCA buildings. YMCA secretaries were placed on railroad payrolls.[64] The YMCAs then proceeded to seek support from other industries, becoming the first national organization to engage in skilled, organized fund-raising campaigns.

Corporations that make philanthropic contributions usually do so because they believe that such contributions generate good will and are therefore good for the company's business. They had to fight for the right to make contributions, which they won in 1935 when the U.S. Congress passed a law allowing a company to donate amounts totaling not more than 5 percent of the company's profit.

The largest portion of the funds contributed to charity and philanthropy still comes from individuals, however. For example, in 1970, individuals contributed $14.3 billion, compared to $1 billion contributed by corporations. Corporations make other kinds of contributions to philanthropy. In some companies, personnel on all levels are given paid time off from work and their services are contributed to fund-raising campaigns; and employees doing voluntary charitable work are often allowed to use company equipment for the purpose. Company work time is used for in-plant solicitations of funds.[65]

There is continuing controversy among economists, business executives, and other students of corporations as to whether philanthropy is an appropriate activity for businesses.[66] Nevertheless, many corporations consider it a necessary activity in creating good will, and they expect their management staff to play a prominent role in philanthropic activities as part of their responsibilities to the company.[67] In some situations, a corporation can be powerful enough to influence which social agencies receive support and which do not. Such an exceptionally powerful corporation, whose activities have been documented in this regard, is E. I. du Pont de Nemours & Company ("DuPont"), "which dominates Delaware as does no single company in any other state."[68]

SUMMARY

Charity and philanthropy, although differing from each other at times, together constitute a mode of social welfare that has been in continuous operation from the earliest origins of Western society until our own day. This mode is characterized by the effort to base social welfare on the principle of voluntarism—that is, voluntary concern for people in need. Throughout its long history, this mode has been heavily influenced by religious ideas that have offered rationales for the existence of material inequality and for softening the effects of inequality. Charity and philanthropy have not, for the most part, sought to alter the basic inequalities in society. The continued existence of such categories of people as rich and poor, fortunate and unfortunate, is taken for granted. But the rich and fortunate are perceived as having duties to the poor and unfortunate, duties that derive from religious teachings or from membership in a common community. Businessmen, and their ideas about wealth and poverty, became more influential than religious leaders and ideas.

Voluntarism originated in a time when human communities were small and relatively self-contained. Today the most effective and powerful sociopolitical units are nation-states, not local communities. People do not remain members of the same local unit as long as they once did, and their loyalties to its members are less commanding. In the nineteenth and twentieth centuries, it became clear that voluntary philanthropy was unreliable, unpredictable, and, most important, insufficient to deal with the needs of people in complex, urban, industrialized Western societies. And so voluntarism has given way to principles of public welfare, social insurance, and professionalism.

But it must be noted that the principle of voluntarism has receded, not disappeared. It continues as a component of the complex set of arrangements known as social welfare. Many social welfare organizations continue to receive,

PHILANTHROPY IN A BUSINESS CIVILIZATION

and to require, philanthropic donations, though more of their funding may come from the government. Similarly, while social welfare organizations increasingly utilize professionally trained people, their success is often heavily dependent on the services of volunteers as well. And while some of the trustees who sit on the boards that govern voluntary social agencies are fulfilling corporate responsibilities, many others are volunteers donating their time and effort.

Notes

[1] Sylvia L. Thrupp, *The Merchant Class of Medieval London, 1300—1500* (Chicago: University of Chicago Press, 1948), pp. 4–8.

[2] *Ibid.*, p. 174.

[3] *Ibid.*

[4] *Ibid.*, pp. 179–180.

[5] *Ibid.*, p. 178. See also pp. 150–154.

[6] *Ibid.*, p. 180.

[7] Walter H. Godfrey, *The English Almshouse—With Some Account of Its predecessor, the Medieval Hospital* (London: Faber and Faber, 1955), pp. 15–16.

[8] *Ibid.*, pp. 61ff.

[9] *Ibid.*, p. 15 and *passim.*

[10] John Pound, *Poverty and Vagrancy in Tudor England* (London: Longman, 1971), p. 39.

[11] *Ibid.*, See also Frank Aydelotte, *Elizabethan Rogues and Vagabonds*, Oxford Historical and Literary Studies, Vol. I (Oxford, England: Clarendon Press, 1913).

[12] G. G. Coulton, *The Medieval Scene* (Cambridge: Cambridge University Press, 1930), pp. 81–82; and Geoffrey Baskerville, *English Monks and the Suppression of the Monasteries* (London: Jonathan Cape, 1937), pp. 31–32.

[13] Pound, *Poverty and Vagrancy*, pp. 16–25; and Baskerville, *English Monks.*

[14] See E. M. Leonard, *The Early History of English Poor Relief* (Cambridge: Cambridge University Press, 1900), p. 18; and Wilbur K. Jordan, *Philanthropy in England, 1480–1660* (New York: Russell Sage Foundation, 1959), pp. 58–61.

[15] Jordan, *Philanthropy in England*, p. 108.

[16] *Ibid.*, p. 140.

[17] Karl de Schweinitz, *England's Road to Social Security* (New York: A. S. Barnes, 1972), pp. 25–26. First published in 1943.

[18] The discussion in this section is based on Jordan, *Philanthropy in England*, except as otherwise indicated.

[19] Pound, *Poverty and Vagrancy*, p. 25.

[20] Joel T. Rosenthal, *The Purchase of Paradise* (London: Routledge and Kegan Paul, 1972).

[21] B. Kirkman Gray, *A History of English Philanthropy—From the Dissolution of the Monasteries to the Taking of the First Census* (New York: Augustus M. Kelley, 1967), pp. 37–38. First published in 1905.

[22] Gareth Jones, *History of the Law of Charity, 1532–1827* (Cambridge: Cambridge University Press, 1969), pp. 27, 29, 105. See also Jordan, *Philanthropy in England*, pp. 109–125; and Gray, *A History of English Philanthropy*, pp. 35–63.

[23]David Owen, *English Philanthropy, 1660–1960* (Cambridge: Belknap Press of Harvard University Press, 1964), p. 11.

[24]*Ibid.*, p. 38.

[25]*Ibid.*, p. 53.

[26]*Ibid.*, p. 24.

[27]*Ibid.*, pp. 31–32 and *passim.*

[28]*Ibid.*, pp. 62–63.

[29]Robert H. Bremner, *American Philanthropy* (Chicago: University of Chicago Press, 1960), pp. 7–10.

[30]*Ibid.*, pp. 12–13.

[31]Cotton Mather, in Perry Miller, *The New England Mind: From Colony to Province* (Cambridge: Harvard University Press, 1953), p. 413.

[32]*Ibid.*, p. 401.

[33]Cedric B. Cowing, *The Great Awakening and the American Revolution: Colonial Thought in the 18th Century* (Chicago: Rand McNally, 1971), p. 15.

[34]Bremner, *American Philanthropy*, p. 21.

[35]Bremner, *American Philanthropy*, p. 25; and June Axinn and Herman Levin, *Social Welfare—A History of the American Response to Need* (New York: Dodd, Mead, 1975), p. 14.

[36]Owen, *English Philanthropy*, p. 91.

[37]Robert H. Bremner, *From the Depths—The Discovery of Poverty in the United States* (New York: New York University Press, 1956), p. 9.

[38]Owen, *English Philanthropy*, p. 234.

[39]Walter A. Friedlander and Robert Z. Apte, *Introduction to Social Welfare*, 4th ed. (Englewood Cliffs, N.J.: Prentice-Hall, 1974), p. 83.

[40]Octavia Hill, in de Schweinitz, *England's Road to Social Security*, p. 146.

[41]Josephine Shaw Lowell, in Walter I. Trattner, *From Poor Law to Welfare State—A History of Social Welfare in America* (New York: Free Press, 1974), p. 86.

[42]The discussion in this and following paragraphs draws primarily upon Charles Loch Mowat, *The Charity Organization Society, 1869–1913—Its Ideas and Work* (London: Methuen, 1961).

[43]See de Schweinitz, *England's Road to Social Security*, pp. 100–113; and Owen, *English Philanthropy*, pp. 225–228.

[44]Mowat, *The Charity Organization Society*, pp. 19–20.

[45]*Ibid.*, p. 30.

[46]Irvin G. Wyllie, *The Self-Made Man in America—The Myth of Rags to Riches* (New Brunswick, N.J.: Rutgers University Press, 1954), pp. 61–63.

[47]F. Emerson Andrews, *Philanthropic Giving* (New York: Russell Sage Foundation, 1950), p. 111.

[48]Eleanor L. Brilliant, "Private or Public: A Model of Ambiguities," *Social Service Review*, Vol. 47, No. 3 (September 1973), p. 389.

[49]Helge B. Croner, comp., *National Directory of Private Social Agencies* (Queens Village, N.Y.: Social Service Publications, 1977–1978), p. 1.

[50]Michael J. Murphy, "Financing Social Welfare: Voluntary Organizations," in John H. Turner et al., eds., *Encyclopedia of Social Work*, 17th ed. (New York: National Association of Social Workers, 1977), pp. 479–480.

[51]Heather L. Ross and Isabel V. Sawhill, *Time of Transition—The Growth of Families Headed by Women* (Washington, D.C.: Urban Institute, 1975). The authors use as their sources Kenneth Boulding, "Love, Fear and the Economist," *Challenge*, Vol. 16, No. 3 (July–

August 1973); and Kenneth Boulding, *The Economy of Love and Fear* (Belmont, Calif.: Wadsworth, 1973).

[52]"Philanthropists and Beneficiaries Discuss Use of $32 Billion Gifts," *New York Times,* December 11, 1977, p. 22.

[53]Scott M. Cutlip, in George G. Kirstein, *Better Giving—The New Needs of American Philanthropy* (Boston: Houghton Mifflin, 1975), p. 27.

[54]Andrews, *Philanthropic Giving,* p. 138; and Kirstein, *Better Giving,* pp. 28–29.

[55]*Pocket Data Book, USA 1976* (Washington, D.C.: U.S. Government Printing Office, 1976), Table 303, p. 214; *Statistical Abstract of the United States.* (Washington, D.C.: GPO, 1980.)

[56]Andrews, *Philanthropic Giving,* p. 158.

[57]Charlayne Hunter-Gault, "Tri-State United Way Is Accused of Shortchanging Black Groups," *New York Times,* October 12, 1977, p. 1.

[58]Robert Lindsey, "United Way Accused of Monopoly in Fight over Charitable Funds," *New York Times,* April 3, 1978, p. 1.

[59]Edward Chase Kirkland, *Dream and Thought in the Business Community, 1860–1900* (Ithaca, N.Y.: Cornell University Press, 1956), p. 147.

[60]Andrew Carnegie, in Kirkland, *Dream and Thought in the Business Community* p. 141.

[61]Bremner, *American Philanthropy,* pp. 106–107.

[62]Andrew Carnegie, in Kirkland, *Dream and Thought in the Business Community,* pp. 148–149.

[63]*Ibid.,* p. 148.

[64]F. Emerson Andrews, *Corporation Giving* (New York: Russell Sage Foundation, 1952), pp. 24–25. See also Marion R. Fremont-Smith, *Philanthropy and the Business Corporation* (New York: Russell Sage Foundation, 1972), p. 6.

[65]Fremont-Smith, *Philanthropy and the Business Corporation,* pp. 45, 67–68.

[66]For a concise summary of different views on this issue, see Fremont-Smith, *Philanthropy and the Business Corporation,* pp. 79ff. For an argument against corporate philanthropy, see Deane Carson, "Companies as Heroes? Bah! Humbug!!" *New York Times,* December 25, 1977, p. 10F.

[67]Aileen D. Ross, "Philanthropic Activity and the Business Career," *Social Forces,* Vol. 32, No. 3 (1954), pp. 274–280. Reprinted in Mayer N. Zald, ed., *Social Welfare Institutions—A Sociological Reader* (New York: Wiley, 1965), pp. 341–352.

[68]James Phelan and Robert Pozen, *The Company State—Ralph Nader's Study Group Report on DuPont in Delaware* (New York: Grossman, 1973), Introduction by Ralph Nader, p. ix.

VARIETIES OF SOCIAL WELFARE INSTITUTIONS
Charity and Philanthropy

Almsgiving	Church chests
Almshouses and hospitals	Church dioceses
Associated philanthropy	Community chests (and community funds)
Begging (soliciting alms)	Funeral doles
Bequests	Gleaning of fields
Canon law	Houses of industry
Charitable trusts	Monasteries
Charity organization societies	United Way
Charity schools	Voluntary social agencies

Significant Figures in Charity and Philanthropy

Amos—Ancient Jewish prophet

Augustine—Early church father

Andrew Carnegie—Nineteenth-century Scottish-born American millionaire industrialist, advocated the "gospel of wealth"

Reverend Thomas Chalmers—Nineteenth-century Scottish minister, advocated case by case investigation of need

Chrysostom—Early church father

Gratian—Twelfth-century Italian monk, compiled *Decretum*, which organized church doctrines on charity and poverty

Octavia Hill—Nineteenth-century, preprofessional social worker, one of leaders of London Charity Organization Society

Josephine Shaw Lowell—Leader of New York Charity Organization Society

Cotton Mather—Eighteenth-century American colonial minister, emphasized the importance of doing good

George Whitefield—Eighteenth-century English minister, preached in the American colonies during Great Awakening, broadened the base of do-goodism from the wealthy to the general populace

Significant Dates in Charity and Philanthropy

8th to 6th centuries B.C.—Jewish prophets call for justice to the poor in ancient kingdoms of Israel and Judah

5th century B.C. to 2nd century A.D.—Philanthropy practiced in Greek city-states, Roman Republic, and Roman Empire

1st to 4th centuries A.D.—Early Christians organize individual church charity chests

313—Legalization of Christianity in the Roman Empire stimulates increase in charitable contributions. Diocese-wide administration of charity by bishops replaces individual church chests

4th century—Church fathers teach that wealth can be ennobling and almsgiving can bring salvation

1140—Gratian compiles *Decretum* in attempt to standardize church teaching and law on poverty, charity, and other issues

16th century—Christian religion divides into Protestant and Catholic branches. Protestants repudiate Catholic teaching that almsgiving can bring salvation

1601—Statute of Charitable Uses passed in England during reign of Queen Elizabeth I to correct abuses in administration of funds left in trust for charity

1935—U.S. Congress passes law allowing corporations to make philanthropic contributions

Public
Welfare

III

Emergence of
the Concept of
Public Welfare

5

The major distinction between public welfare and charity is that the concept of public welfare involves the taking on of obligations to the needy by the public authority of the state, whereas charity rests primarily on voluntary donation. Like almost all distinctions in social welfare, the distinction between public welfare and charity is not absolute; public welfare developed gradually out of charity, and for a time during the reign of Queen Elizabeth there was a kind of intermediate stage where charity was no longer purely voluntary but was not yet quite completely public welfare either.

Public welfare is a twentieth-century term. In the nineteenth century, people spoke of public charities and private charities, not of public welfare and charity. Contemporary public welfare descends from ideas that first emerged clearly in the Tudor, and specifically the Elizabethan, period. These ideas took form in the Elizabethan Poor Law. The Elizabethan Poor Law, which reached its final form in 1601, was the model that the English colonists had in mind when they began to settle North America in the 1600s. The Elizabethan Poor Law was supplemented by additional laws in the seventeenth and eighteenth centuries, but it was not changed fundamentally until 1834. Thus the Elizabethan Poor Law is also known as the Old Poor Law, and the law of 1834 is known as the New Poor Law or, sometimes, as the Poor Law Reform. The 1834 law introduced a new harshness in dealing with the poor, and twentieth-century readers of this book will undoubtedly be as divided as were the people of the nineteenth century about the merits of the reform. Some will surely marvel at how the word *reform* can mean such different things to different people.

The most enduring component of public welfare has been the provision of income to people unable to obtain a livelihood by means that enjoy higher social esteem, namely, by work or by inheritance. This income component has at times been broadened to include supplementing the income of "the working poor"—people whose income does not meet a certain prevailing standard of the time. In addition to the income provision—generally known today as public assistance—the concept of public welfare expanded over time to include certain kinds of care for dependent persons. Children who have no parents and no other relatives to care for them have come under the protection of the state; child welfare is thus another component of public welfare. Other categories of dependents also receive assistance from public welfare programs; such categories of people as the mentally retarded, mentally ill, blind, and elderly have come under the umbrella of public welfare.

The central relationship in public welfare is, then, between the government and members of the society who are unable to care for themselves in the ways that are considered "usual." The government assumes responsibility for providing such care and protection, in the form of income and in other forms as well: Instead of providing income directly, the government may provide some of the things income buys (known as income "in kind"), such as shelter, in the form of public housing, or free food. Various kinds of institutions to care for dependent persons have also developed as part of public welfare: Systems of foster care for children who do not have or cannot live with natural parents; special residences for mentally retarded people and for others whose social functioning is impaired. The public welfare system has at times provided jobs for the unemployed and training for employment.

Public assistance, public housing, publicly sponsored jobs and job training, public institutions for persons requiring special forms of care or protection—these are the main forms that public welfare has assumed, the forms of government obligation to those in need of special, noncustomary, care. From its very beginnings, however, government action and attitude directed toward people unable to support themselves have oscillated between punishment and help, for two basic reasons: (1) Government officials—and people in general—have not understood why some people do not or cannot support themselves; their "solutions" to the problem have changed when their explanations of the problem changed; and (2) government officials—and employers—generally want able-bodied people to support themselves through work; government therefore has not wanted public assistance to be too freely available.

This chapter will focus on the development of the enormously influential Elizabethan Poor Law. Chapter 6 will discuss the transformations of public welfare from the New Poor Law to the present.

RESTRAINT AND REPRESSION

Throughout its history, the subject of public assistance has been a thorn in the side of public authorities and of the citizens whose taxes provide the funds for it. The continuously vexing question has been: Of all those people claiming to be in need of public assistance, how many could be and should be earning their own livelihood by working? The question perhaps first arose in its modern form as medieval society was breaking up and the feudal relationship of serfdom was being replaced by free labor. Under serfdom, the laborer had been tied to the land; while he was not a slave, not the absolute property of a master, he had fixed obligations to give service to a lord who, in turn, had fixed obligations to the serf. The lord was as obligated to make land available to the serf to cultivate for himself as the serf was to contribute a certain number of days to working the lord's land. With the revival of trade and town life, the feudal social order gave way to a commercial one. Gradually the serf became an agricultural laborer, working for a cash wage; he became free of his ties to the lord's land, and the lord became free of his obligations to the serf.

Forbidding Charity

Europe was struck by a deadly epidemic, the bubonic plague (also known as the Black Plague or Black Death), during the years 1348–1349. This epidemic had two important effects on the population: (1) Many people fled from their homes and towns in an effort to escape the plague, and (2) between one fourth and one third of Europe's population was killed by the disease.[1]

The consequence of death on such a large scale, plus the departure of many people, was the development of a severe shortage of labor. Farm laborers took this opportunity to charge higher wages for their work. Others took advantage of the increased movement of the times by switching to a livelihood of begging or by otherwise profiting from the life of vagabondage. This situation led to the proclamation by King Edward III in 1349 of a law—the Statute of Laborers—

that is regarded by some social welfare scholars as the first step toward the national control of poor relief. The purpose of the law was to force able-bodied men to work at prevailing wages. To accomplish this goal, the statute forbade donations of alms to able-bodied men. It stated:

> Because that many valiant beggars, as long as they may live of begging, do refuse to labor, giving themselves to idleness and vice, and sometime to theft and other abominations; none upon the said pain of imprisonment, shall under the color of pity or alms, give anything to such, which may labor, or presume to favor them towards their desires, so that thereby they may be compelled to labor for their necessary living.[2]

It is evident that the attitude toward charity in this statute represents a significant departure from the attitude held by the church. St. Augustine's distinction between the deserving and the undeserving, put forward in the fourth century, seemed not to receive much attention. But in the fourteenth century, Edward III's regulation introduced an even sharper note: Being charitable to able-bodied beggars was against the law; they were definitely undeserving of charity. Edward III began to use the powers of government to separate the deserving from the undeserving, an effort that has continued for more than six hundred years down to our own day. This was also the beginning of a new way of thinking in Western society: What is considered to be in the best interests of society, as determined by government authorities, gained ascendance over the church's conception of the obligations of Christian charity.

It should be noted that this first major secular intervention into this sphere was aimed at keeping charity from being given to those who were not "truly needy"—as the modern phrase would put it—and at getting them back to work. Deterrence of idleness has continued to be a recurrent theme in the development of public welfare, and a constant focus of attention in any discussions about developing a program of guaranteed minimal income for everybody. Public welfare, as a mode of social welfare, began, in the modern world, by the taking action against the practice of charity. This was not a total rejection of almsgiving but rather an effort to bring it under control, the control of the national government.

Punishing Begging and Vagrancy

Concern about vagrancy and begging was an intermittent theme in English government and society for more than three hundred years. The problem was at its most intense during the Tudor period (1485–1603), and from time to time over a period of four hundred years, laws were passed that sharply restricted people's freedom to move from one place to another.

Restriction of such movement became one of the lasting ways in which government authorities attempted to maintain control over segments of the population that were regarded as potential troublemakers and in which they also attempted to limit the cost burdens of providing for indigent people. English colonies in America adopted such procedures, and as recently as 1971, the governor of the state of New York attempted to reduce the migration of poor people into the state by proposing that the state not pay public assistance benefits to newcomers who moved into substandard housing. He made this proposal despite the fact that restriction of benefits on a residency basis had already been ruled unconstitutional by the U.S. Supreme Court. He must have known that he could not make his proposal stick (legislative leaders from his own party said it was illegal), but he was nonetheless giving public expression to a long-existing sentiment in Western society. It might be stated as "Go back where you came from, and stay put. Your travels and migrations are making trouble for us."[3]

Note, however, that the group being troubled by such migrations changes. The earliest laws restricting movement did so because the *district being left* suffered from labor shortages and higher wage demands. From the sixteenth century onward, however, after responsibility for the poor was assumed by the government, migration troubled the *district into which* the people were moving because the district might become obligated to provide support for them.

The 1349 Statute of Laborers (and follow-up statutes) engendered evasion; men moved from county to county to escape the laws that required them to work for whoever wanted their services and at no more than the prevailing wage for such work. In 1388, during the reign of King Richard II, Parliament passed a tightening-up measure that provided that no laborer could leave his district without a letter stating the purpose of his trip and the date of his return; the penalty for violation was placement in the stocks. The law also stipulated that beggars "impotent to serve" (that is, disabled) had to stay in the city or town in which they had been living when the law was proclaimed. The only exception was that if the city or town could not support the beggar, he could move elsewhere within the district or return to the town in which he was born; this had to be done within forty days of the announcement of the law. This law of 1388 appears to be the first that recognized that some people could not work and therefore required relief. It gave them the right to beg, in contrast to the able-bodied, who were obligated to work. But neither type of person was free to wander around according to his own preference.[4]

As noted in Chapter 3, the Tudor period had major significance for the development of social welfare. One of the reasons is that "in the sixteenth century the numbers of rogues and vagabonds were larger in proportion to the population than they [had] ever been before or since."[5] This increase in the number of people wandering about the countryside and hanging about the towns —a "rowsey, ragged rabblement of rakehelles," one commentator called them —was caused by the economic, political, and legal changes that had been taking place in English society. People whose forebears had enjoyed relative security as serfs and tenant farmers had been forced off their land. Feudal rules about a person's rights to a piece of land or a portion of what it produced changed as feudal society gave way to a new economic order which no longer recognized traditional economic rights. Henry VII's breaking up of the private bands of fighting men that had been part of the feudal organization of society further increased the number of wanderers. And "all through the Tudor reigns, the 'beggars coming to town' preyed on the fears of the dwellers in lonely farms and hamlets, and exercised the minds of magistrates, Privy Councillors, and Parliaments."[6] They spread rebellious ideas, and rebellions occurred from time to time.[7] These threats to public order prompted increasing efforts to reduce the troublemaking potential of the rogues and vagabonds. In the course of the efforts, the English government was obliged to recognize that some of the people who wandered about were not troublemakers but disabled people who had no way to gain a livelihood except by begging. But from the fourteenth through the sixteenth centuries, before this realization took firm hold, vagabonds were subjected to a variety of brutal punishments, including whipping, placement in the stocks, branding on the forehead or chest with a hot iron, cutting off of an ear, and for repeat offenders, death.[8]

THE DEVELOPMENT OF GOVERNMENT RESPONSIBILITY

The development of government responsibility for the poor took place over a period of seventy years, from 1531, during the reign of Henry VIII, to 1601, near the end of the reign of his daughter, Elizabeth I. This seventy-year period is, in effect, the beginning of public welfare as a mode of social welfare. During this period, various procedures were tried, until a basic pattern was achieved that lasted in England from 1601 until its complete revision in 1834, and that influenced poor relief in America.

From Alms to Taxes

The Tudor efforts began in 1531 with Henry VIII's law that prohibited begging by able-bodied men—sturdy beggars or valiant beggars, as they were known. This revived and extended the policy prescribed in Richard II's law of 1388. The new element in Henry VIII's law was the giving of explicit recognition and support to the right of the disabled and aged poor to beg. Local officials, particularly justices of the peace, were to search out all those in their parishes who had to subsist on alms, issue them each a letter authorizing them to beg, and assign them each to a specific area in which to beg.[9]

This was a significant development despite the fact that the law was designed primarily to limit the number of beggars rather than to provide relief to the deserving poor. In succeeding legislation, the government moved in stages from what might be called government-encouraged voluntarism to the imposition of taxes for the support of the poor, aged, and infirm in 1572. Thus, in 1536, the second Poor Law of Henry VIII's reign provided for greater support of those in need, mainly through prescribing more specific procedures: The churchwardens in each parish and the mayor of each town were charged with collecting alms every Sunday, holy day, and festival day. Casual almsgiving to individual beggars was prohibited; contributions were to be given to the common collection. Contributions were still voluntary, but the law instructed "every preacher, parson, vicar, curate of this realm" to "exhort, move, stir, and provoke people to be liberal and bountifully to extend their good and charitable alms and contributions." The clergy were to do this exhorting in all their activities: when preaching sermons, hearing confessions, and assisting people in writing their wills. Thus the concept of voluntary support of the needy through church-based charity was retained from the waning Middle Ages, but was blended, somewhat awkwardly, with the newly emerging concept of governmentally prescribed and administered provisions for the poor. This law of 1536 is innovative also in that it requires the collectors of church alms to keep records of their collections and disbursements, and specifies that the collectors will receive wages for the time spent in this work. These, then, are the first paid public welfare officials.

During the years 1551–1552, new pressures on the people to make voluntary contributions were added to the law. The collectors were ordered "to gently ask" each householder what he would contribute each week for relief of the poor, and the amount he stated was entered in a book and collected every Sunday. If a householder refused to contribute, he was exhorted by the parson, and if he still refused, the parson certified the man to the bishop, who exhorted him. In 1563, under the reign of Elizabeth, an addition to the law gave the bishop the power to compel the uncharitable householder to appear before the justices of the peace (or, in towns, before the mayor and the churchwardens). These officials were also to ask in a nice way for the householder's contribution, and if he still refused, they had the authority to decide how much he should "contribute" and to assess him for that amount. He could be imprisoned if he refused to pay it. Finally, in 1572, a tax—the poor rate—was imposed on all parishioners, who thereby took on the new role of taxpayer, or ratepayer, as it was called in England. From the first, taxpayers manifested opposition to this requirement. Such opposition between taxpayers and the poor also surfaced at later times, not only in England but in the United States, as taxpayers came to feel that taxes in support of the poor were too high.[10] The opposition from taxpayers created difficulties for the overseers of the poor, officials newly designated by the law of 1572.

Perhaps the complaints about taxes had something to do with the fact that when the Poor Law was rewritten in 1597, a provision was explicitly included that stated that parents were financially responsible for their children and children for their parents, depending upon who was able to work and earn a living and who was not. Another rewriting of the bill in 1601 extended family responsibility to grandparents and grandchildren: Thus an able-bodied grandchild was responsible for the support of an aged or infirm grandparent. Similarly an able-bodied grandparent was responsible for the support of a grandchild if the child's parents could not support him or her. Only if the family was unable to support its dependent members did parish and city poor relief become available. This is a clear example of Wilensky and Lebeaux's residual concept of social welfare: The ordinary and expected ways of gaining a livelihood are by working or, if one cannot work, by receiving aid from one's parents, grandparents, children, or grandchildren, whoever is the able-bodied member of the family. Only if there is no able-bodied family member able to support the dependent members does the social welfare system come into play.

It is noteworthy that the provision in the law requiring family members to support one another involves a recognition of social change on the part of the Parliament: there was an awareness that the traditional feudal relationships, which assured the aged or disabled serf a livelihood, had substantially passed out of existence. The traditional manorial village was being replaced by villages and towns consisting of independent household units—whose members no longer had the support of a manorial lord. Thus these last two rewritings of the Elizabethan Poor Law contain a concept of the family as distinct and separable from the community. The first line of collective responsibility had passed from the manor to the individual family. Historian Lawrence Stone has stated that "the Elizabethan village was a place filled with malice and hatred," and he further noted that "as for pregnant unmarried women, they were treated with a ruthless cruelty which only the fear that the child would become a burden on the local poor-rate can explain."[11]

Paid Welfare Officials

The Tudor Poor Laws marked the beginning of paid public welfare officials. The Statute of 1536, which required mayors and head officers in each city and churchwardens in each parish to collect alms every Sunday, holy day, and festival day, also provided that they be paid for this work.[12] For reasons that are not clear, the later Tudor Poor Laws (1572, 1597, 1601) did not include a provision for paid officials. Instead, they called for the appointment in each parish of unpaid officials known as overseers of the poor. Overseers were appointed for a one-year term by the justices of the peace; they were selected from among the members of the parish, and service in the post was compulsory even though unpaid.[13] In the middle of the seventeenth century, there was criticism of a Poor Law administration carried out by overseers who were necessarily amateurs, had no interest in their work, and were replaced every year.[14] Nevertheless, this system prevailed for a long time. And it is significant that the Poor Laws did create a category of official, the overseer of the poor, whose specific responsibility was to administer poor relief.

Localism

One of the significant features of the Tudor Poor Laws was that they took over the existing units of church organization, local parishes, and made these the units of administration of the Poor Laws. This policy continued and reinforced a longstanding emphasis on localism in English society. From the earliest days of English society,

> Every person was . . . a member of some local community, to which he owed obligations, and from which he was entitled to expect some measure of protection, and, when in need, some undefined support. An unknown person, absent without credentials from the community to which he belonged, was an object of grave suspicion, having, in early times, practically no rights.[15]

With the introduction of a tax to pay for support of the poor, each parish was concerned that it not have to support the poor from some other parishes. This concern led to some absurdities, as will be noted in the discussion of the Law of Settlement and Removal. As already indicated, the intense localism has continued into the present; the example of New York in 1971 is assuredly not an isolated one. In 1981, President Reagan's administration took the first steps toward a major revival of localism.

The Poorhouse

The Tudor Poor Laws may contain the origins of the concept of public housing. The Poor Law of 1597 empowered justices of the peace and town officials to impose a tax on the parish for the purpose of maintaining "convenient houses of habitation" for paupers. The building that served as the "poorhouse" might be an old one or one built specifically for the purpose. It provided housing for a variety of people: the widowed, aged, and sick; mothers of illegitimate children; and tramps and paupers awaiting removal to other parishes. Thousands of poorhouses were in operation from the sixteenth to the nineteenth centuries.[16]

THE NEW IMPORTANCE OF WORK

The dissolution of the feudal system and its replacement by a market economy, and the change in attitude toward indiscriminate almsgiving and *its* replacement by taxes imposed to support the poor, led to a new emphasis on putting the able-bodied poor to work. The number of unemployed idlers had greatly increased, not only because of many men being turned loose from manorial settlements but also because of an enormous increase in population. For reasons that are not fully understood, the population of Europe doubled between 1500 and 1600.[17] The attitudes toward work that developed in the sixteenth century and that were built into the Tudor Poor Laws have, in many important aspects, prevailed into the present.

Work and the Tudor Poor Laws

Before the Tudors themselves began to introduce work provisions into their national laws for dealing with the poor, efforts were made on a local level. In response to the growing number of poor people and the increasing problem of vagrants, the city of London obtained permission to take over an unused royal palace at Bridewell and turn it into a place to put idle people and those of bad character to work in such trades as cap and wire making. This was the first of a series of new institutions known as houses of correction. Its location caught on as a name for the type of institution, and any *house of correction,* in America as well as in England, might be known as "the Bridewell."

Houses of correction sometimes served more than one purpose. Willful idlers were put in them and made to work; but innocent people who were unemployed and seeking work would also be given work in these institutions. In some localities, the poor thought of the house of correction as a prison; in others, they were paid prevailing wages and thus, in effect, were being provided with secure employment in a sheltered place. However, these institutions became increasingly punitive and eventually were scarcely distinguishable from jails.[18]

The London Bridewell was one element of the efforts of the city authorities to deal with poor, sick, and idle people. However, because the effort was local, the system failed. It could not cope with the great flow of people into the city, and its funds for running the system were insufficient.[19] Within a short time, consideration of the problem moved to the national level. The legislation of the latter half of the sixteenth century made use of several approaches.

The obligation to work

An important law passed in 1563, the Statute of Artificers, assumed that employment was available for all and that all able-bodied people had an obligation to work. People between the ages of twelve and sixty who were not employed could be made to work as agricultural laborers.[20] The insistence on the obligation to work represented an important social change—for not only were there people who sought to maintain themselves entirely by begging and vagabondage, but people who did work did not do so with the regularity that later became customary. The sixteenth century was a period of transition between two different types of economy, and the attitudes toward work that were appropriate in an earlier time were becoming outmoded. As historian Christopher Hill has stated:

> To celebrate a hundred or more saints' days in a year was all very well in an agricultural society like that of medieval England. . . . But an industrialized society, such as England was becoming in the sixteenth century, needs regular, disciplined labour. . . . Holy-days, said the Order of 1536 abrogating them, are the occasion of much sloth and idleness, riot and superfluity, and lead to the decay of industrial crafts. Artificers and labourers, the Bishop of Exeter observed in 1539, still needed "spiritual instruction," backed up by punishment, to persuade them to work on saints' days.[21]

In addition to time off for many saints' days, workers had little incentive to work steadily during periods when wages were high. There were few consumer goods that ordinary people could buy. Consequently people worked "short time" when wages were high; that is, they worked only enough to pay for the basic necessities of subsistence, after which they relaxed. The Statute of Artificers of 1563 and the Poor Law of 1597 referred to idleness, drunkenness, and unlawful games as "lewd practices and conditions of life," and the laws construed these as interfering with agricultural and industrial production.[22]

"Setting the poor on work"

The laws of the Tudor period, and especially of the Elizabethan period, reflected the beginnings of a national government taking responsibility to provide work

for the unemployed. As humanitarian Juan Luis Vivès had urged in 1526, and
as the city of London had undertaken in 1555, the English government in 1572
passed a law giving local justices of the peace the authority to put idle rogues
and vagabonds to work. The 1572 law was vague as to how the justices were
to do this, and detailed procedures were written into the law in 1576. The justices
were to obtain "a stock of stuff"—that is, materials such as wool, hemp, and iron
—which they were to make available to all poor people, who were to be paid
for the goods they made from them. The officials would sell the goods, and the
proceeds would be used to buy additional raw materials. Able-bodied people who
refused this work were to be put into a house of correction modeled on the
London Bridewell.[23]

The law of 1572 marked a significant step in thinking about social welfare.
Until that time, people who did not work were divided into two categories—
those who were unable to work (the impotent poor) and those who refused to
work (rogues, idlers, vagabonds). Now a third category was recognized—able-
bodied people who wanted to work and could not obtain a job. It has been seen,
even in the present, that many people who are working and obtaining a satisfactory livelihood do not like to acknowledge that such a third category exists
because such recognition creates complications for these taxpayers, who are
likely to feel reasonably satisfied with the social arrangements that enable them
to sustain themselves. They do not wish to be deeply critical of those arrangements. It is much easier to blame those without work for their own situation than
to blame the society for failure to assure jobs for all. It is not too great an
exaggeration to say that recognition of this third category of people keeps
dropping out of people's understanding of unemployment and reappears from
time to time only with difficulty. As will be discussed more fully later, the
sixteenth and seventeenth centuries have left a heritage of ideas and attitudes that
make it hard to believe that a person who wants to work cannot find work.

Apprenticeship

The purpose of setting the poor on work, as the phrasing of the time put it, was
that idle rogues would no longer have an excuse for not working. The Statute
of 1576 also introduced a *preventive* concept: Setting the poor on work would
not only correct the behavior of adult rogues but also instill in youth the habit
of working and thus reduce the chances that they would grow up to be idle
rogues. The means for assuring this were specified in the 1597 revision of the
Poor Law: Poor children were to be apprenticed to learn a trade. Henry VIII's
law in 1536 had specified apprenticeship for children between the ages of five
and fourteen who were vagrant and begging. The statute in the Elizabethan
period (1597, and rewritten in 1601) went further, in empowering the churchwardens and overseers of the poor in each parish to "bind out" as an apprentice
any child whose parents could not, in the officials' judgment, maintain him or
her. Boys could be kept as apprentices until age twenty-four, girls until age
twenty-one or until they married.

The workhouse

The new emphasis on work that emerged in the Tudor period developed even further in succeeding years, eventuating in the creation of a new institution, the workhouse, which was a feature of social welfare for more than two hundred years. By the nineteenth century, the workhouse had become a horror, though it does not seem to have begun that way. The idea of the workhouse as a place where the able-bodied poor would be gathered to work seems to have originated with the Dutch, who built such a facility in Amsterdam in 1596. This was a combination workhouse for the able-bodied seeking work, house of correction for the able-bodied idle, who had to be confined in order to get them to work, and poorhouse for those too old or too sick to work.

The success of the Dutch merchant class in building up business created some envy among English businessmen, who thought that the Dutch ways of dealing with their poor contributed to their economic success and thought that England should follow the Dutch example. In the late seventeenth century, some English business leaders wrote pamphlets advocating the establishment of workhouses. In addition, setting the poor to work on a piecemeal, individual basis had proved to be rather impractical. A further complication was that providing them with a stock of stuff in their homes sometimes resulted in theft of the materials.[24] The workhouse came to be seen as a way of achieving greater efficiency in carrying out the Poor Law, but it also had other meanings attached to it. These meanings will become clear in the next section.

Social Change and the New Emphasis on Work

Three important changes took place in the sixteenth and seventeenth centuries that gave rise to the increased importance of work. First, the Tudors tried to concentrate more power in the central government in order to establish a firm and stable national rule. As part of that effort, they stopped the nobility from conducting private wars with each other and passed laws to control vagabonds, for example, by making them work.[25] The Tudors were successful, but their successors, the early Stuarts, provoked great antagonism with their authoritarian ways. A revolution and civil war broke out; King Charles I was beheaded in 1649; the country came under the domination of the Puritans, led by Oliver Cromwell, who became the head of state under the title Lord Protector; and when, after Cromwell's death, the monarchy was restored under Charles II in 1660, it had less power than it had had under the Tudors. Men of property— wealthy businessmen and country gentlemen who owned large estates—had much power in their local areas. The pressure to work no longer came from a strong central government trying to maintain "law and order." The pressure continued, however, from two changes that were to have longer-lasting effects, mercantilism and the Protestant Reformation.

Mercantilism and the rise of business

As we noted in Chapter 2, The Commercial Revolution changed the organization of Western society from an agricultural basis to an increasingly commercial
one. These changes in the ways people gained a livelihood led to changes in
ideas, which in turn led to changes in social relationships. The mercantilist
period (which began during the reign of the Tudors) saw the emergence of a
new outlook that has been called *the capitalist spirit*. As business developed, those
making money—the capitalists—became increasingly influential, and their views
helped to push aside earlier medieval ideas:

> The businessman came slowly to look upon his enterprise as merely a means for
> making profits. In fact, his search for profits pushed into the background all
> thoughts of his duty to society, to God, and to his neighbors. There was a growing
> tendency to value all things in terms of money, to believe that success meant the
> heaping up of wealth, to think that riches were the chief end of life and the most
> certain basis of power. In the middle ages, the rich man had been suspected because
> he was rich. In the sixteenth and seventeenth centuries, the rich man came to be
> respected because he was rich.[26]

This new spirit of capitalism had an impact on public welfare, as on everything
else. In the second half of the seventeenth century, businessmen viewed the
unemployed able-bodied poor as an undeveloped source of profits, and they
began to advocate and to organize workhouses that would be economically
advantageous to them, the nation, and the poor as well. One businessman calculated that "even a blind, armless, one-legged man could, in a well-managed
institution, earn sixpence a day."[27]

Business leaders of the last half of the seventeenth century—for example, Sir
Josiah Child, chairman of the East India Company—wrote pamphlets advocating
the establishment of workhouses as a solution to the problems of poverty, destitution, and vagrancy. They considered the parish poor relief authorities to be ineffective. As a philanthropic endeavor, businessman Thomas Firmin put the greater
part of his fortune into building a workhouse. It was devoted to employing the
poor at manufacturing linen, and is reported to have kept 1,700 people at a time
working in various textile activities. Firmin devoted the last twenty-one years of
his life (1676–1697) to running this organization and claimed that he had almost succeeded in getting it to pay its own way (including the costs of educating children
and maintaining aged people). His experience helped strengthen the general belief that employment of the poor could be a paying enterprise. The mayor and
alderman of Bristol, then the second-most important commercial city in England,
requested and, in 1696, received authorization from Parliament to take the administration of poor relief out of the hands of the overseers in the city's nineteen parishes and place it in the hands of a new citywide "Corporation of the Poor,"
which built and administered a workhouse. Other cities followed this same path.

Despite the contagious optimism that spread from city to city, the effort to employ the poor in workhouses and make a profit on their work proved a total failure. Not only were the workers unskilled in their work, but the managers of the workhouses were also incompetent and not very motivated to carry out their assigned responsibilities. It proved more costly to maintain people in workhouses than to give them relief in their own homes.[28]

While the workhouse as a profit-making enterprise was a failure, the spirit that led to its creation lived on after it. The capitalist spirit endures to this day as perhaps the most significant attitude regulating the flow of energy and activity in Western society. The capitalist spirit seems to have received a boost from religion, even though the result was that the capitalist spirit pushed religious ideas and attitudes out of the dominant position they had held during the Middle Ages. Ideas that arose during the Protestant Reformation blended with mercantilist ideas about business to produce an influential set of beliefs concerning the importance of work, beliefs that continued to shape American public welfare practices into the 1960s and 1970s.

Puritanism and the spirit of capitalism

Protestantism had a profound influence on Western society, an influence that was felt in every social institution, including work and social welfare. A brief summary of key points about the Protestant Reformation will help to show the way in which this new attitude toward work came about.

The Reformation's beginning is traceable to the activities of a German monk, Martin Luther, who criticized the Roman Catholic Church in a series of pronouncements and publications beginning in the year 1517. In those days, people whom the Church called sinners could buy their redemption from sin and thus assurance of salvation in the hereafter. Luther denounced this corrupt practice, known as the sale of indulgences. As Luther developed his ideas about returning to the purity of early Christianity, he attracted many followers but was denounced by both the Church authorities and secular political authorities. Although he had initially wanted to purify the Roman Catholic Church, it became apparent by the 1530s that no reconciliation between him and the Church was possible. Separate Protestant churches—Lutheran churches—began to form. The religion of Lutheranism gained legal recognition in Germany in 1555.[29]

Luther's most important religious idea, from the standpoint of the present discussion, was that people could be assured of salvation from eternal torment through their faith in God. Those who had such faith were saved by God's grace, the freely given, unmerited favor and love that God bestowed on the believer. Salvation could not be bought. It could not even be earned by good works such as giving money to the church for charity. Nevertheless, people had to fulfill the obligations imposed on them by their position in the world; every person had a "calling," an occupation and social position to which he or she had been summoned by God.[30]

Luther's ideas of salvation through faith and of the importance of a person's calling received a somewhat changed interpretation from John Calvin, a Frenchman living in Switzerland. He and Luther were the two most influential originators of Protestantism. Calvinism became the most influential form of Protestantism outside Germany.[31] Calvin's followers in England became known as Puritans—they were people who were dissatisfied with both Henry VIII and Elizabeth I for retaining too much of Catholicism in the Church of England. Eventually, some Puritans left England to establish colonies in the New World, one group settling at Plymouth, Massachusetts, in 1620 and another establishing the Massachusetts Bay Colony in 1630.

According to Calvinism, God is all-powerful, and the purpose of all human activity is not to attain salvation but to glorify God. Since God is all-powerful, humans can do nothing to influence God, who, by his own will, predestined some people for salvation and consigned the rest to eternal damnation. Nevertheless, every Christian must work for the glory of God. Individuals must not merely accept their calling but, with self-discipline and zeal, carry out their tasks, the tasks set by God.[32] The true Christian must be industrious, thrifty, frugal, and ascetic, turning away from frivolity, sentiment, and interest in comfort and luxury.

Thus a new meaning of work was developed in the teachings of the English Puritans. As stated by historian R. H. Tawney, the Puritans idealized work and saw it as

> not simply a requirement imposed by nature, or a punishment for the sin of Adam. It is itself a kind of ascetic discipline, more rigorous than that demanded of any order of mendicants—a discipline imposed by the will of God, and to be undergone, not in solitude, but in the punctual discharge of secular duties. It is not merely an economic means, to be laid aside when physical needs have been satisfied. It is a spiritual end, for in it alone can the soul find health, and it must be continued as an ethical duty long after it has ceased to be a material necessity. Work thus conceived stands at the very opposite pole from "good works," as they were understood, or misunderstood by Protestants. They, it was thought, had been a series of single transactions, performed as compensation for particular sins, or out of anxiety to acquire merit. What is required of the Puritans is not individual meritorious acts, but a holy life—a system in which every element is grouped round a central idea, the service of God, from which all disturbing irrelevances have been pruned, and to which all minor interests are subordinated.[33]

This religious doctrine supported several social changes taking place in England during the late sixteenth and seventeenth centuries. Conscientious attention to business came to be seen as a fulfillment of the highest religious and moral virtue. The personal virtues stressed by Puritanism—industriousness, punctuality, frugality—fit well with the mercantilist emphasis on production (rather than consumption) as the main purpose of economic activity. Puritan religious writers and preachers joined with businessmen in emphasizing the dangers of pampering poverty. Economic success came to be regarded as evidence that the prosperous person was one of God's elect, predestined for salvation. The prosperous found it easy to believe that the poor—and even the entire wage-earning class—were predestined to eternal damnation.[34]

These principles of Puritanism have come to be known as "the Protestant ethic," or sometimes simply as "the work ethic." There has been much scholarly discussion concerning how important this ethic was in the development of capitalism. Some writers have pointed out that capitalism had clear beginnings and even flourished in certain Catholic countries before the rise of Protestantism. This issue is beyond the scope of this book. There is little disagreement, however, that Puritanism was influential in changing the basic attitude toward work in the Western countries in which it was followed, including the Netherlands as well as England and the United States.[35]

Before the Protestant Reformation, Christians viewed work as God's punishment for human sinfulness. It was an unwelcome burden, necessary in order to obtain a livelihood, but not virtuous in itself. Protestantism, and particularly the Calvinist branches of it (the Puritans had various disagreements among themselves and eventually divided into the Presbyterian, Congregational, Quaker, and Baptist churches, among others), saw working hard as a way of serving God, of being a moral person, of carrying out their responsibility to the community. Not less important, strictly disciplined work was a means of controlling the ever present threat of disorder in society.[36] Idleness thus became a multiple threat— to the order of the state, to the productivity that was so important to developing business, and to the carrying out of God's will, which demanded energetic labor in a calling. Political, economic, and religious ideas combined to generate a conception of work that dominated the consciousness of Western humanity until the middle of the twentieth century, when it began to lose its hold.

THE LAW OF SETTLEMENT AND REMOVAL

One of the important features of English society, as noted earlier in this chapter, was the notion that everyone belonged to a particular local community. From the middle of the fourteenth century on, as we also noted, laws were passed from time to time to keep various categories of people in their home districts or towns.

During the development of the Tudor Poor Law in the sixteenth and seventeenth centuries, towns began to adopt various measures to keep out newcomers. Some towns, for example, adopted a procedure of making monthly searches for newcomers who seemed poor enough that they might become "chargeable"—that is, might become public charges who would have to be supported from the poor rates—and expelled them.[37]

The practices of a few towns, concerned with keeping poor strangers out, were made nationwide and applicable to almost everybody in a sweeping law passed in 1662, during the reign of King Charles II. The Law of Settlement and Removal was not a radical piece of legislation, since it only put into law what had in many places already been a matter of local custom. Nevertheless, it has been called by some the worst law ever passed in England.[38] The enforcement of the law resulted in enormous hardship to poor people and led to endless legal proceedings that enriched lawyers. And it put enormous obstacles in the way of people who were trying to overcome their poverty or improve their economic position by moving to an area that offered better opportunity.

The community to which a person belonged was his "settlement." The 1662 law empowered local authorities to removed *any* person who came into a parish or borough (district of a town) unless he could prove that he would *never* become chargeable. If he could not prove this, he could be removed to the place that was considered his legal settlement. Good character and conduct were not sufficient, nor did it matter that the person had not applied for relief from the poor rates. The mere possibility that the person might at some time become a pauper was sufficient reason for ejection—unless the required proof to refute this possibility could be offered. The procedure was as follows: Newcomers had to demonstrate that they were able to rent property worth £10 per year. They had forty days to establish this level of financial ability. Since the average laborer's cottage was valued at no more than a fourth of that amount, the level of financial ability required was not attainable by most agricultural laborers, manual workers, and craftsmen. A neighbor's complaint to the churchwarden or overseer of the poor was sufficient basis for the official to remove a newcomer.

But the law had a loophole, since people might slip into a parish and remain out of sight until forty days were up. Apparently some parish officers had been bribing their own poor to go into another parish and stay hidden for forty days, thus making the new parish thereafter responsible for their relief. So the law was amended to require that the forty days be counted from the time the overseer of the poor was notified of the person's arrival. This safeguard proved insufficient, so a few years later the law was amended again to start the counting of the forty days' residence from the time of a public announcement in church of the newcomer's arrival. Not until 1795 was the law changed so that people could not be removed from a parish until they actually applied for relief. The 1795 amendment did not, however, apply to pregnant, unmarried women "who were potentially the most expensive, and hence the most unpopular, of all paupers." Even in the early twentieth century, some removals were still being carried out.[39]

Since the parish officials and the taxpayers were responsible for the poor, they looked for ways to meet the responsibility at the lowest possible cost. The Law of Settlement and Removal provided the officials some legal means by which to keep costs down. For example, the law required the overseers of the poor to bind out young boys and girls as apprentices, but the overseers seldom took the trouble to look for a master craftsman who would train the youngster; in order to save money, the overseers would put the children out "to any sorry masters that [would] take them, without any concern for their education and welfare, on account of the little money that [was] given with them."[40] The law stipulated that apprentices be given a settlement from whatever parish they were placed in. Consequently, overseers tried to find masters in other parishes who would take their apprentices. This would relieve the original parish of any future responsibility for the boy, the woman he would later marry, and the children they would have. Since all parishes were resorting to the same tactics, it is doubtful that any parish actually reduced its costs for supporting the poor. This practice only guaranteed that there was not even the little supervision over the parish apprentices that the churchwardens and overseers would have exercised if the apprenticing had been done in the home parish.[41]

All in all, the Law of Settlement and Removal resulted in the compulsory moving around of thousands of people annually for more than two hundred years. A parish receiving a person removed from another parish would often dispute the claim that it was in fact the person's legal settlement. It would go to court against the removing parish and sometimes get the removed person sent back. The person had no right of appeal and might be shuttled back and forth several times while the courts decided the case. A Parliamentary report in 1837 gave this summary of the situation:

> . . . a perpetual transplantation was going forward, which set the whole country alive with the movements of vagrant carts, and filled the coaches and the inns with burly overseers and fat constables, traveling from all points between the Thames and the Tweed, from Berkshire to Leicestershire, and from Sussex to Cornwall, with laborers and laborers' wives, and astonished children. All this was managed to the great satisfaction of the vestry and overseers, and the lawyers; under whose auspices it was generally arranged that the laborers, and the wives, and the children, or some of them with many of their friends and fellow-laborers, should make a journey to the county sessions [court] as witnesses, and after the most solemn inquiry, travel back again to the place whence they came and from whence they had been "illegally" removed.[42]

The intense localism, traditional for centuries, but further intensified by the sixteenth-century Poor Laws and the seventeenth-century Law of Settlement and Removal, was carried by English settlers to the American colonies and remained a powerful element in social welfare in England and in the United States until well into the twentieth century.

THE POOR LAWS IN
THE AMERICAN COLONIES

The English people who began establishing colonies in North America, beginning with Jamestown, Virginia, in 1607, brought to the new land much of their
English culture, including their concepts for dealing with dependency. As early
as 1646, legislation passed in Virginia called for avoiding the sloth and idleness
with which children are corrupted and gave local officials the authority to put
poor children to work by binding them out as apprentices. Additional legislation
in later years was prompted by concern about increasing numbers of idle and
dissolute vagabonds who abandoned their wives and children.[43]

The basic principles of English poor relief became the basic principles of the
colonies. The most important of these were: (1) *public responsibility* for the poor
and dependent classes; (2) *taxation* of those with property to pay for support of
the poor and dependent; (3) *localism*—geographic restriction of eligibility for aid
to those who had established a settlement.[44] The colonists were willing to assist
their neighbors who fell upon hard times. But they were as resistant as their
compatriots in England to providing assistance to strangers. An example of this
intense localism is the Rhode Island law of 1702, which made shipmasters
responsible for chargeable passengers that they transported to the colony. The
shipmaster was obliged to remove any passenger not accepted by a town, and
he could be jailed if he refused or did not put up a substantial sum of money as
security for the care of the person.[45]

The extreme localism broke down in many places during the Revolutionary
War. The task of providing relief to refugees from war-torn areas was too great
to be handled by the local system, and so, for example, New York's way of
arranging emergency relief for such people was to create a category known as
"the state poor," who were not chargeable to a specific local unit.[46]

A major theme in the development of public welfare from the eighteenth to
the twentieth century, both in America and in England, has been the progressive
shifting of responsibilities for public welfare from small local units to larger units
of local government and eventually to the national government. Most of these
shifts have come about because the particular local units handling public welfare
at the time found their resources inadequate for coping with new problems
thrust upon them by changing circumstances such as wars or major economic
upheavals. Most generally, the states took over important responsibilities in the
nineteenth century, and the federal government in the twentieth.

A word should be said about colonial methods of caring for the poor.[47] The
dominant practice throughout the colonial period was to support the person in
his or her own home; when this was not possible, a neighbor would take respon-

sibility for caring for the person and would be reimbursed for the expenses by the parish (in the southern colonies, which followed the Church of England) or by the town (in the New England colonies, which, being Puritan, did not follow the Church of England). Poor relief in colonial times was essentially assistance to one's neighbors, and was thought of in this way. The settlement laws, of course, helped to keep it this way. Strangers coming into a town were "warned out," and townspeople who had out-of-town visitors had to give assurance to town officials that the visitors were of "good substance" and would not become chargeable.[48]

Although poor relief in colonial times had a neighborly aspect, it had a harsher side as well. As a way of minimizing the cost of poor relief, many towns adopted the practice of auctioning the poor to the lowest bidder. At the auction,

> . . . the qualities of each pauper were detailed with the same callousness as that shown in discussing the merits of a horse—or a slave. . . . To add to the festivity of the occasion (and to stimulate bidding) liquor was furnished at the expense of the town in some places.[49]

This procedure originated in New England and spread to other colonies and later to various states. It began to be outlawed in the 1830s; the last state to make the practice illegal was North Carolina, in 1877.[50] The binding out of children as apprentices was the practice used with orphans, illegitimate children, and children whose parents were considered dissolute and unfit to bring them up properly.

SUMMARY

Public welfare—the assumption of responsibility by the government for meeting the dependency needs of people unable to support themselves through the usual institutions of market and family—originated during the Tudor period in sixteenth-century England. The state's concern for public dependency can be found even earlier, in fourteenth-century measures to curtail almsgiving and punish begging and vagrancy. During the Tudor reigns, the state's responsibility was at first confined to requiring localities to take care of their own poor. This requirement strengthened an already existing tradition of localism and led to an intense concern about having to support "somebody else's poor." The concept of local responsibility has persisted for centuries, even though the concept of locality has broadened as times have changed—from parish to union of parishes (in England and from parish or township to county and state in the United

States. The legal concept of settlement did not disappear in the United States until 1969, when the Supreme Court ruled that the individual states could not require a certain period of residence in the particular state before public assistance could be received.

The Elizabethan Poor Law introduced several new concepts into public welfare that have remained influential to this day. Reliance upon voluntary charity to support the poor was replaced by taxation to provide the necessary funds. The government undertook to provide work for able-bodied people unable to find work, and it accepted responsibility for finding training situations for children deemed likely to grow up without skills to earn a living. The Poor Law made parents and grandparents responsible for children and grandchildren who could not support themselves, and able-bodied children and grandchildren responsible for parents and grandparents in need of support.

During the Tudor period, work assumed a new importance under the impact of political, economic, and religious changes. The newly strong central government of the Tudors saw idleness and vagrancy as threats to its stability and to the public order. The growing mercantilist spirit of this period led to a new emphasis on hard work and disciplined, systematic pursuit of profit. Finally, the Protestant Reformation, occurring first on the European continent and spreading to England, introduced the idea that work was a way of serving God, not a punishment for original sin as the Roman Catholic Church had taught.

All of these new ideas stressing the importance of work also called into question the traditional Christian belief that giving charity was always beneficial to the recipients. The idea began to take hold that giving help could be damaging, both to the person who received it and to the society, which suffered the loss of good workers who lapsed into sluggish dependency when sustained by alms. This idea became dominant in the nineteenth century, and has not entirely lost influence in the twentieth.

The English colonists who began establishing permanent settlements in America four years after the death of Queen Elizabeth brought the Elizabethan Poor Law with them. The principles of public responsibility for the poor and dependent classes when family responsibility failed, taxation, and localism became the foundation of American public welfare.

Notes

[1]The estimate of one fourth killed is given by Norman Cantor, *Medieval History,* 2nd ed. (New York: Macmillan, 1969), p. 533. The estimate of one third killed is given by Henri Pirenne, *Economic and Social History of Medieval Europe,* trans. I. E. Clegg (New York: Harcourt, Brace & World, 1937), p. 193.

[2]*Statutes of the Realm,* in Karl de Schweinitz, *England's Road to Social Security* (New York: A. S. Barnes, 1972), p. 1. First published in 1943. De Schweinitz agrees with an earlier scholar, E. M. Leonard, that this statute can be regarded as the beginning of English government efforts to deal with poverty. See Leonard's *Early History of English Poor Relief* (Cambridge: Cambridge University Press, 1900), p. 3.

[3]"Governor Weighs Drastic Changes to Curb Welfare," *New York Times,* March 10, 1971, p. 1; "City and State Officials Are Wary on the Governor's Reported Ideas on Curbing Welfare," *New York Times,* March 11, 1971, p. 27; "Welfare's Bankruptcy," editorial, *New York Times,* March 12, 1971, p. 36.

[4]Leonard, *Early History,* pp. 3–6; de Schweinitz, *England's Road,* pp. 3–8.

[5]Frank Aydelotte, *Elizabethan Rogues and Vagabonds* (Oxford: Clarendon Press, 1913), p. 3.

[6]G. M. Trevelyan, *English Social History—A Survey of Six Centuries, Chaucer to Queen Victoria* (Harmondsworth, England: Penguin Books, 1967), p. 128. First published in 1942.

[7]*Ibid.,* p. 133; Aydelotte, *Elizabethan Rogues,* pp. 52–53.

[8]Sidney Webb and Beatrice Webb, *English Poor Law History—Part I: The Old Poor Law* (Hamden, Conn.: Archon Books, 1963), pp. 23–24 and *passim.* First published in 1927.

[9]The discussion in this section of the development of the poor laws draws mainly on three sources: de Schweinitz, *England's Road;* Leonard, *Early History;* and Webb and Webb, *English Poor Law History.*

[10]Leonard, *Early History,* pp. 167–171.

[11]Lawrence Stone, *The Family, Sex and Marriage in England, 1500–1800* (New York: Harper & Row, 1977), p. 98.

[12]de Schweinitz, *England's Road,* pp. 24–26.

[13]Leonard, *Early History,* p. 76.

[14]Margaret James, *Social Problems and Policy During the Puritan Revolution, 1640–1660* (London: Routledge, 1930), p. 278.

[15]Webb and Webb, *English Poor Law History,* p. 315.

[16]*Ibid.,* pp. 212–214; de Schweinitz, *England's Road,* p. 27; Leonard, *Early History,* p. 77.

[17]John A. Garraty, *Unemployment in History—Economic Thought and Public Policy.* (New York: Harper & Row, 1978), pp. 32–33.

[18]Webb and Webb, *English Poor Law History,* pp. 49–53, 83–86.

[19]Leonard, *Early History,* pp. 39–40, 45–46.

[20]Garraty, *Unemployment in History,* p. 30. See also Richard B. Morris, *Government and Labor in Early America* (New York: Harper Torchbooks, 1965), pp. 3–4.

[21]Christopher Hill, *Society and Puritanism in Pre-Revolutionary England* (New York: Schocken, 1964), pp. 146–149.

[22]*Ibid.,* pp. 124–125.

[23]Webb and Webb, *English Poor Law History,* pp. 52–59.

[24]Garraty, *Unemployment in History,* p. 44; Leonard, *Early History,* p. 225; Samuel Mencher, *Poor Law to Poverty Program—Economic Security Policy in Britain and the United States* (Pittsburgh: University of Pittsburgh Press, 1967), p. 32.

[25]Christopher Hill, *Reformation to Industrial Revolution—The Making of Modern English Society,* Vol. I, 1530–1780 (New York: Pantheon, 1967), pp. 19–20; Trevelyan, *English Social History,* pp. 74–75.

[26]Shepard Bancroft Clough and Charles Woolsey Cole, *Economic History of Europe* (Boston: D. C. Heath, 1941), p. 151.

[27]Garraty, *Unemployment in History,* p. 46.

[28]Webb and Webb, *English Poor Law History,* pp. 101–125, 215–240.

[29]Hans J. Hillerbrand, *The World of the Reformation* (New York: Scribner's, 1973), pp. 95ff.

[30]Max Weber, *The Protestant Ethic and the Spirit of Capitalism*, trans. Talcott Parsons (New York: Scribner's, 1930), pp. 80ff.

[31]Hillerbrand, *World of the Reformation*, p. 151; R. H. Tawney, *Religion and the Rise of Capitalism* (London: John Murray, 1936), p. 102.

[32]Weber, *The Protestant Ethic*, p. 85. Tawney, *Religion*, pp. 109, 240.

[33]Tawney, *Religion*, p. 242.

[34]*Ibid.*, pp. 241, 251, 262–273.

[35]Garraty, *Unemployment in History*, pp. 39–40. For discussions on issues surrounding the importance of the Protestant Ethic, see S. N. Eisenstadt, ed., *The Protestant Ethic and Modernization—A Comparative View* (New York: Basic Books, 1968); and R. W. Green, ed., *Protestantism and Capitalism—The Weber Thesis and Its Critics* (Boston: D. C. Heath, 1959).

[36]Michael Walzer, "Puritanism as a Revolutionary Ideology," in S. N. Eisenstadt, *Protestant Ethic and Modernization*, pp. 109–134.

[37]Leonard, *Early History*, pp. 107–109.

[38]Norman Longmate, *The Workhouse* (New York: St. Martin's Press, 1974), p. 17.

[39]de Schweinitz, *England's Road*, pp. 41–42; Longmate, *The Workhouse*, p. 18.

[40]From a report written in 1732, in Webb and Webb, *English Poor Law History*, p. 198.

[41]*Ibid.*, pp. 199–200.

[42]in de Schweinitz, *England's Road*, p. 45.

[43]Marcus Wilson Jernegan, *Laboring and Dependent Classes in Colonial America, 1607–1783* (Chicago: University of Chicago Press, 1931), pp. 179–180.

[44]This summary of principles is adapted from Jernegan, *Laboring and Dependent Classes*, p. 208; Elizabeth Wisner, *Social Welfare in the South* (Baton Rouge, La.: Louisiana State University Press, 1970), pp. 3–4; and David J. Rothman, *The Discovery of the Asylum* (Boston: Little, Brown, 1971), pp. 20ff.

[45]Margaret Creech, *Three Centuries of Poor Law Administration* (Chicago: University of Chicago Press, 1936), p. 47.

[46]David M. Schneider and Albert Deutsch, *The History of Public Welfare in New York State, 1867–1940* (Chicago: University of Chicago Press, 1941), pp. 4–5.

[47]Rothman, *Discovery of the Asylum*, p. 4.

[48]*Ibid.*, pp. 20–35; Creech, *Three Centuries*, pp. 22–23.

[49]Benjamin J. Klebaner, "Pauper Auctions: The 'New England Method' of Public Poor Relief," *Historical Collections of the Essex Institute*, Vol. 91, No. 3 (July 1955), p. 1.

[50]*Ibid.*, p. 10. See also Benjamin J. Klebaner, "Some Aspects of North Carolina Public Poor Relief, 1700–1860," *North Carolina Historical Review*, Vol. 31, No. 4 (October 1954), p. 480.

From the
New Poor Law
to the Present

6

Neighborliness as a component of public poor relief was gradually washed away in the nineteenth century in the wake of increasing urbanization and industrialization both in the United States and in England. As Western countries began their decisive transformation from farm and village-based societies to factory- and city-based societies, new concepts of what to do about the poor emerged. In England, the debate over the new and the old ideas was sharper and more dramatic than in the United States.

INDOOR VERSUS INDOOR RELIEF: THE GREAT DEBATE IN ENGLAND

For social welfare, the nineteenth century was, above all else, the century in which efforts were made to prevent poverty by discouraging the poor from seeking help. The basic and dominating idea seemed to be that if help were made difficult to obtain, the poor would be discouraged from seeking it and would try harder to support themselves, and if they tried harder, they would succeed. Therefore, poverty would eventually disappear. This scenario did not unfold as expected. The nineteenth century ended and the twentieth century began, and one thing had certainly not changed: "The poor ye have always with you," Jesus had said, and it was still true. But it is important to understand how the people in the nineteenth century came to hold their beliefs, what the beliefs were that enabled them to think they could abolish poverty, and how they attempted to put their beliefs into specific social welfare practices. Their efforts resulted in the Poor Law Amendment Act of 1834 (the New Poor Law). It is the development of this law that will be explained here. A brief review of the fundamental changes that were taking place in the eighteenth century will be useful first.

If the Commercial Revolution of the fifteenth through the seventeenth centuries can be regarded as the first major step toward a modern economic and social organization, then the second, and even more dramatic, step was the Industrial Revolution, which began around the middle of the eighteenth century. Business was already powerful, and as businessmen sought new markets and larger profits, they encouraged the invention and use of machinery that could produce goods more rapidly and more cheaply. Manufacturing thus gained in importance. Efficiency in manufacturing was accomplished first by concentrating workers in cities and then by having them leave their dwellings to go to a specialized workplace, the factory. This social change began with the manufacture of cotton:

> Whoever says Industrial Revolution says cotton. When we think of it we see, like the contemporary foreign visitors to England, the new and revolutionary city of Manchester, which multiplied tenfold in size between 1760 and 1830 (from 17,000 to 180,000 inhabitants), where "we observe hundreds of five- and six-storied factories, each with a towering chimney by its side, which exhales black coal vapour. . . .[1]

This transformation of Manchester from a small town to a densely populated, factory-choked city is typical of the transformations that occurred in many locations in England during the nineteenth century (and that occurred in the United States, with a lag of about fifty years).

The introduction of the factory system coincided with the enclosure movements in the farming areas. These were the acts of powerful landowners to acquire more land (driving tenant farmers out) and then to enclose their property with hedges and use it for sheep raising instead of for raising crops; sheep raising required fewer workers and was more profitable. Periods of enclosure had begun in Tudor times, and some of the people driven off the land became the vagrants so feared then. In the eighteenth century, the small tenant farmers who lost their rights to farm in new spurts of enclosure became part of the growing propertyless working class whose only way of earning a living was by working in the new factories.

In the eighteenth century, the Elizabethan Poor Law and the Law of Settlement and Removal were still the basic public welfare laws. It is obvious that the Law of Settlement was incompatible with the newly developing industrial system. Enclosures were depriving rural people of their farmland, thereby forcing them to seek work elsewhere, that is, in the factory districts. The Law of Settlement, on the other hand, required people to stay in the location in which they could claim a legal settlement. Thus their free and easy movement to factory towns was hindered, which also caused problems for factory owners, who needed workers.

The Law of Settlement was criticized as being obsolete. It had originated in the heyday of mercantilism, and after a hundred years of it, eighteenth-century businessmen found it increasingly unacceptable. Whereas businessmen had, in the mercantilist period, turned to the state for help in maintaining their business advantage—such as calling for the passage of laws to limit competition from imports—now they wanted the state to let them do business without restrictions. A new economic, political, and social philosophy had been developing throughout the eighteenth century and became influential in the nineteenth. This philosophy—liberalism—dominated social welfare in England and the United States until almost the middle of the twentieth century.

The Rise of Liberalism

In an increasingly commercialized society, liberalism spread quickly among businessmen. The organizing concept in this doctrine was that society consisted of isolated individuals. Influenced by the significant discoveries of the natural sciences during this same period, social thinkers (business leaders as well as political and economic philosophers) thought of society as having a "natural order" and as being governed by "natural law." In 1690, John Locke had argued that individuals have a "natural right" to own property. According to Locke, people live in society only for their own mutual convenience, and society and government exist in part to protect private property.[2] Locke also argued for freedom of thought and of religious belief. His ideas influenced those demanding their freedom in the American Revolution in 1776 and in the French Revolution in 1789.

Although a full account of the development of liberalism is beyond the scope of this book, mention must be made of Adam Smith, whose book *The Wealth of Nations*, published in 1776, is often regarded as the first work of modern economics. The idea of Smith's that most captured the imagination of his contemporaries (and of many people since his day) is that people are most strongly motivated by their own self-interest and are the best judges of what these interests are. Although Smith recognized that people also had benevolent feelings toward others, he believed these were less powerful motivators than self-interest. Thus, in Smith's view, a *laissez-faire* philosophy should be adopted in which people were free to pursue their own interests, unhampered by the government, unless someone else's interests were unjustly infringed upon. They should be free to acquire property and wealth, and to enjoy the use of the wealth they have acquired. The government should not busy itself laying down rules about what can and cannot be done either in acquiring property or in the use made of it. Such, at least, has been the common interpretation of Adam Smith's doctrine. However, Smith was more concerned with justice than was recognized by most of the people inspired by his ideas. They preferred to focus on what he had to say about pursuing one's own interests without interference. Besides, Smith also said that when a person pursues his own interests, he is

> led by an invisible hand to promote an end which was no part of his intention. Nor is it always the worse for the society that it was no part of it. By pursuing his own interest he frequently promotes that of the society more effectually than when he really intends to promote it.[3]

Here, then, was a philosophy that pleased the rising business class. The growing prestige of scientific ideas had contributed to an appreciation of rational thinking (as opposed to unquestioned acceptance of traditional beliefs). Social thinkers were also trying to think more rationally about society and human behavior. Liberalism was a philosophy that emphasized freedom in all spheres of activity, but freedom in the acquisition and use of wealth and property was the theme that attracted the widest attention. The idea that most interested businessmen was the apparent claim that selfishness—pursuit of one's own interests—was rational because it accomplished the most both for the selfish individual and for the society. Liberalism was on a collision course with the ideas that underlay the Elizabethan Poor Law—that society was an organic whole in which the community was obligated to care for its poor, and that government regulation was right and necessary. The collision came in 1834, leaving the Elizabethan concept battered.

The Road to the New Poor Law

Although the Poor Law of 1601 had specified that money was to be given to the disabled poor, while the able-bodied poor were to be put to work, the overseers of the poor found it difficult to organize such work, and putting people into institutions was also neither easy to arrange nor administer. Consequently the most widespread method of poor relief for the able-bodied, as well as for the disabled, poor was to provide them with money, "outdoor relief," that is, financial relief given to people without requiring them to be in a public institution. This was both the easiest and the cheapest way for the parish to provide relief.[4]

Outdoor relief was criticized on and off throughout the eighteenth century and early in the nineteenth. A key event was the discovery in the early eighteenth century of a new use for the workhouse. Although the workhouse was failing as a method of getting the poor to pay their own way, some Poor Law administrators discovered that it could be used as a deterrent to applications for relief. Some parishes therefore began turning down the applications of the able-bodied for outdoor relief and insisted instead that they enter the workhouse if their situations were as dire as they claimed. Only those who truly had no other means of support were willing to give up their freedom and enter such an unpleasant institution. An act of Parliament in 1723 made this procedure legal, although not mandatory. Local parishes could decide whether they wanted to use this method, which came to be known as "indoor relief," or to provide outdoor relief.[5] A substantial minority did use it.

The workhouses into which those applicants for relief who had no other means of subsistence were driven usually became general mixed workhouses

> in which were heaped, pell-mell, men, women and children, the senile and the infants, healthy and sick, sane and insane, without classification, privacy or order, subjected to arbitrary tasks of work, spasmodically enforced by the capricious tyranny of venal and occasionally cruel masters or contractors. On first application this "Workhouse Test" always achieved the success of driving off a number of the paupers, and therefore reducing the local Poor Rates. But what became of those whom it "deterred"? Whilst it may have made some of the idlers seek and obtain employment at wages, others, it is clear, and apparently the great majority, simply reverted to the vagrancy and mendicancy, with incidental crime and disorder, the prevention of which had been the very object of the establishment of a public provision for the destitute. So far as these persons were concerned, the Workhouse Test . . . defeated the very purpose of the system of which it formed a part. On the other hand, those who "passed the test"—those who proved the extremity of their destitution, and its involuntary character, by their acceptance of the intensely disagreeable "General Mixed Workhouse" of the period—found themselves subjected, it might be for the rest of their lives, to conditions not essentially differing from, and in some respects positively worse than, those of the contemporary prisons.[6]

After sixty years of use of the deterrent concept of the workhouse, the pendulum swung back to outdoor relief. In 1782, Thomas Gilbert, an influential member of Parliament, succeeded in having a law passed that provided that: (1) indoor relief be given only to the impotent poor—the aged, sick, infirm, and orphaned, and young children and their mothers; (2) parishes could combine into unions and pool their funds to build and run an institution for indoor relief; (3) unions were allowed to replace unsalaried overseers of the poor with paid guardians of the poor; (4) able-bodied people who wanted to work but could not find employment had to be given paid employment by the guardians; and (5) the guardians had to pay for the support—outside the workhouse—of these able-bodied people until they could find work for them.

The provisions of Gilbert's act were not mandatory. The act was applicable only to parishes whose propertied members voted to form unions. By 1830, almost fifty years later, fewer than a thousand of the fifteen thousand parishes in Britain had formed Gilbert Act unions. Altogether, about four thousand workhouses existed. Thus both outdoor and indoor relief of the able-bodied were legal.[7] Many parishes preferred to continue to use the workhouse test—that is, to refuse relief to those who failed to prove their absolute destitution by entering the workhouse. Still others simply continued to give relief to disabled and able-bodied alike, without requiring the workhouse test or making efforts to find employment for the able-bodied.

The allowance system

The practice of outdoor relief took a new turn in 1795 that eventually led to enormous dissatisfaction with it and, finally, to decisive repudiation of it in the Poor Law Amendment Act of 1834 (the New Poor Law). An insufficient harvest in 1794 brought a rapid increase in food prices the following year. There were similar shortages in the next few years, made worse by the fact that England was at war with France in an effort to stop Napoleon's conquests. The scarcity of food and consequent high prices led to widespread distress and widespread discussion of ways to alleviate these problems.

A key event at this time that has achieved a special place in the history of social welfare was a meeting of justices of the peace in 1795 in the village of Speenhamland. At this meeting, the justices of the peace (the top local officials in the administration of the Poor Law, above the churchwardens and overseers of the poor) decided against recommending a minimum wage as a way of assuring workers in their counties a minimally adequate income. Instead, they recommended that when the price of bread rose, and wages did not keep up, workers should receive supplementary income from the poor rates. How much they would receive depended upon the number of children they had, as well as upon the price of bread. Thus not only were the able-bodied unemployed to receive relief out of tax funds, so also were employed workers whose wages were not keeping up with rising prices. This system of "allowance in aid of wages" became known as the Speenhamland system, although such a system had been in occasional use in some parishes even before the famous meeting at Speenhamland.

The allowance system, which became more widespread after the Speenhamland meeting, has been regarded as a significant development because it seemed to create a right to live. A worker who did not earn enough to support his family was entitled to a supplement to bring his income in line with the bread scale. (The bread scale was a rough equivalent of today's consumer price index. Both measure cost of living.) The Speenhamland system was a last-ditch effort to prevent workers from becoming totally dependent on the ups and downs of the market during the emergence of industrial capitalism. When the Speenhamland system was eliminated by the New Poor Law of 1834, with it went all suggestion of a "right to live." Thereafter, workers were entitled only to the income they could earn through their work, whether or not the income was enough for them and their family to live on, which it often was not.[8]

The attitude incorporated into the New Poor Law (which is discussed below) was vastly different from the one that underlay the allowance system. The New Poor Law said, in effect: "Nobody owes you a living." But this began to be questioned, and in more recent times, there have been revivals of the Speenhamland concept (which will be discussed later in this chapter).

The years 1795–1830 saw three developments that led to the final turning from the Elizabethan Poor Law: (1) The cost of poor relief escalated enormously. (2) The number of people receiving relief increased greatly. (3) The cost of relief and the number of people receiving it remained very high even though the wars ended with Napoleon's defeat in 1815 and there were plentiful harvests in the years following, so that food prices came down.[9] Many believed that the Poor Law was causing pauperism. In other words, so many people were receiving public help, even people who were employed, that employed and unemployed alike were becoming dependent on it (twentieth-century scholars believe that those people were misguided in their analysis who took that view). Thus a strong effort was launched to get rid of the Poor Law altogether. The effort failed. What came about was a "reform" that abolished outdoor relief and established indoor relief—confinement in the workhouse—as the obligatory method of providing relief.

The New Poor Law

After many years of debate in Parliament and throughout the country, a Royal Commission—a group of nine prominent people not holding office in the government—was appointed to investigate the functioning of the Poor Law and to recommend changes. From 1832 to 1834, the commission gathered evidence throughout the country, and issued its findings and recommendations in 1834 in a lengthy report that became the basis of the Poor Law Amendment Act, passed later that year. A social welfare historian who has studied the report and the events leading up to it has observed:

The Commissioners found the evils they expected to find, and documented them at great length. They were concerned above all to make a case against the allowance system as a form of relief for the able-bodied, and were themselves surprised and shocked to find allowances so widespread, even in manufacturing districts.[10]

In its report, the commission made a distinction between "indigence" and "poverty." Poverty was the condition of a person who was forced by his situation to work in order to obtain a mere subsistence. Indigence was a condition in which a person was unable to work to obtain even the minimal necessities of life due to total or partial disablement. Government had an obligation to relieve indigence, but not poverty. The independence of the working person would be undermined if government tried to relieve poverty. Thus the allowance system and indeed the entire concept of the Elizabethan Poor Law as it applied to the able-bodied were now considered to be mistaken.[11]

The New Poor Law introduced a new system of poor relief, according to which (1) all relief to able-bodied persons or their families was illegal, except in workhouses. And (2) in place of the autonomous parishes, each with its own interpretation of and approach to the Poor Law, a National Board of Poor Law Commissioners was established. This central board would develop national standards and regulations for the workhouses, including determining how much relief was to be given and how much work was to be required of the inmates.

The harsh provision of requiring the able-bodied and their families to enter the workhouse if they wanted relief had many opponents. Benjamin Disraeli, a young politician who later became prime minister, said in a famous speech that the Poor Law Amendment "announces to the world that in England poverty is a crime."[12]

The main purpose of this law was to deter people from seeking relief by making the acquisition of it terribly unpleasant—and thus to encourage responsibility for maintaining oneself and one's family through working for a living. In the view of the Poor Law commissioners, the pauper's situation should be less desirable than the lowest-paid laborer's situation; otherwise laborers would be tempted to quit work and to subsist on public relief. (In the language of the time, it was said that the pauper's situation should be "less eligible" than that of the laborer. This expression should be understood to mean "less eligible for reward from society." Any kind of work at any pay made a person more eligible for reward than did idleness, regardless of size of family or any other consideration.)

Deterring people from seeking public relief was in line with the new, prevailing laissez-faire philosophy. Self-reliance was the watchword of the time. Thus, with the enactment of the Poor Law Amendment:

(1) Public assistance was no longer a right. Indeed, needing and expecting such help were considered virtually antisocial behavior.[13]

(2) The government no longer took responsibility for providing work for

the unemployed. "The last vestiges of mercantilist paternalism had been cleared away by the poor law reforms of 1834."[14]

In the introduction to a modern reprinting of *The Poor Law Report of 1834*, two economic historians summed up a significant dimension of the new social outlook and the poor law that it produced:

> With the rise of the new individualism many of the insights into human need upon which the fathers of the church and the schoolmen had insisted were weakened and even abandoned. At the very time when society was imposing unprecedented strains on the mass of its members, the concept of the need of the individual for group support was being lost, at least by a large part of society, especially the most active and innovatory. For the notion of a society based upon the operation of enlightened self-interest led to a loss of appreciation of the need of the individual to locate himself within a group and to assimilate himself to it; psychological support was being withdrawn when it was most needed.[15]

There was considerable opposition to the Poor Law Amendment and many districts refused to build workhouses. Some local authorities resented the New Poor Law's implied criticism of their administration of the Old Poor Law. Some districts did not want to pay the cost. Some local authorities in industrialized areas resisted the amendment because they did not want to put into the workhouse factory workers temporarily out of work because their employer's business was in a slump. The 1834 amendment had been written with agricultural areas in mind; little thought had been given to problems in industrial areas. The National Board of Poor Law Commissioners had not been given strong enough enforcement powers to make local areas comply with the provisions of the New Poor Law. It is useful to recall here the earlier discussion that social welfare consists of ideas about how to help people and organizations for carrying out the ideas. Ideas can be put into practice only if an effective organization is established to carry them out. The Poor Law Amendment Act of 1834 contained the concept of a national social welfare program, but the organization for putting it into practice was not effective.

In 1854, twenty years after the enactment of the new law, 84 percent of paupers were still on outdoor relief.[16] Nevertheless, the number of people in workhouses was substantial, particularly after the relief policy was toughened around 1870. An 1898 census showed that 216,000 people were in workhouses on the day of the census, and it was estimated that about three times that number spent some time in them in the course of a year.[17] Early in the twentieth century, during a new period of reform, the term *workhouse* was abandoned and the institution was thereafter officially called a "poor-law institution," but it continued to be popularly referred to as a workhouse. The 1834 Poor Law remained in force until 1929; only then did the workhouses disappear.[18] Also in 1929, the Poor Law Boards of Guardians were abolished and their functions turned over to the county government, and the term *poor law* disappeared, and was replaced by the term *public assistance.*[19]

INDOOR RELIEF IN
THE UNITED STATES

Indoor relief began to grow in importance in the United States early in the nineteenth century. Later in that century, it became the dominant method of relief, and it was still the basic legal method of providing for paupers at the beginning of the Great Depression in 1929.[20] Well before the decisive *Poor Law Report of 1834,* American public officials, clergy, and other concerned citizens were familiar with the issues in the debate over indoor versus outdoor relief that had been going on in England, but in the United States, it was somewhat different considerations that led to indoor relief. The seemingly unlimited amount of land in the United States, the great amount of work that needed to be done in the still new country, the relative scarcity of labor—all these seemed to promise a good livelihood for all. There seemed to be no good reason for poverty; yet it existed. In the early 1800s, people began to pay more attention to poverty and to try to understand its causes in a way that they never had attempted during the colonial period.[21]

The new thinking was prompted by other important changes that were taking place. After gaining its independence, the United States changed from a set of separate colonies to a unified nation whose state boundaries were easily crossed. Geographic movement and social mobility became more common. As cities grew, it became more difficult to keep strangers out and to enforce the settlement laws. The formerly clear distinction between neighbors and strangers became blurred, as neighbors moved elsewhere and strangers moved in next door. In a while, the sense of a well-ordered society gave way to growing tension, uncertainty, and fear of social breakdown. It was in this context that the poor began to be considered a social problem. Concerned citizens formed societies— such as the New York Society for the Prevention of Pauperism—that studied the causes of poverty, and especially the degree of poverty that led to dependency or pauperism. State legislatures set up committees to conduct official investigations into poverty and its causes.

Two major types of explanations for poverty emerged from the discussions and investigations. Most prominent was the idea that the poor were to blame for their own condition. They were thought of as depraved, and vicious, and generally as moral failures. It was widely believed that they fell into this disreputable condition because of excessive drinking. Instead of working hard and saving for a rainy day, they squandered their money—or so it was believed—on liquor. Efforts were sometimes made to distinguish between the "poor"—people who were unable to work, such as widows, orphans, and the aged, sick, and disabled, and who deserved aid—and "paupers"—able-bodied people who were unworthy of aid because they were lazy and vicious. However, commentators on the subject failed to keep even this distinction clearly in mind:

> Invariably, within a few minutes into the speech or after a few pages of the pamphlet, the distinction fell away, and the poor became synonymous with the idle and the degenerate. The dangers of indulging the vagrant and the shiftless, not the plight of orphans and widows, now captured the greater attention.[22]

This "confusion" has continued to the present day.

Some, however, advanced a second explanation of the problem, one that supplemented the first. These observers recognized that poverty—and even pauperism—often occurred because of circumstances beyond the victims' control. The author of the first American treatise on political economy considered pauperism to be due to the unequal distribution of property, which led to an unequal division of the products of labor. Others recognized that there was considerable involuntary unemployment; this point of view gained additional adherents during periods of economic depression, such as the winter of 1837–1838.[23] Economic slowdowns and crises also resulted in the reduction of wages below subsistence level. Still others blamed society for the "viciousness" of the pauper, because vice—in the form of taverns, gambling places, and houses of prostitution—was available in the community.

Finally, two influential legislative committee reports put forth the belief, similar to the one that had been gaining ground in England, that the Poor Laws themselves were contributing to pauperism. In 1821, the Massachusetts legislature appointed a committee, headed by Josiah Quincy, to investigate poverty and poor relief throughout the state; in 1824, the New York State legislature appointed a similar committee, headed by John Yates. After conducting detailed investigations, both committees came to substantially the same conclusion. Of the four principal methods of relief—the auction system, the contract system, home relief, and relief in an almshouse—the first three were considered harmful. The auction and the contract systems were harsh and cruel; both placed the poor in the hands of people determined to carry out the task of relief at the lowest possible cost. Home relief (outdoor relief) was perceived as encouraging people to become idle and dependent. Well-regulated, orderly almshouses were regarded as the best antidote to the social disorder that was seen as tempting poor people into a surrender of all honor and dignity.

The reports issued by the Quincy and Yates committees became the guides to action in their respective states. The building of almshouses began. (In New

York and the Midwest these institutions were called poorhouses. In New England and some other eastern states, the term almshouse was most frequently used. There were local variations: Indiana called its institutions county asylums; Ohio, county infirmaries; California, county hospitals.[24]) Responsibility for the poor was shifted from the towns to the counties, and almost every county built an almshouse. Throughout the nineteenth century, other states followed the examples of Massachusetts and New York. Although outdoor relief did not disappear completely, it became less prevalent than indoor relief. Occasionally individual cities attempted to require total adherence to indoor relief. Philadelphia tried this in 1827, Chicago in 1848. Both cities found the policy unworkable and went back to selective granting of outdoor relief.

Advocates of the almshouse thought it was ideally suited to provide care and rehabilitation of the poor. The aged and infirm would have "a refuge from the evils and miseries of life." The able-bodied would have a regimen of "order, regularity, industry and temperance." They would learn "constancy and diligence" as well as "to obey and respect." These institutions failed to realize the goals of those who had hoped so much for them. The goal of rehabilitation was undermined primarily by the goal of saving money—by terrorizing the poor and thus deterring them from seeking relief, which was somewhat the same purpose as the English workhouse. Even so, some of the institutions became enormously overcrowded; people with all kinds of problems were mixed together, making an orderly operation impossible; and work for the able-bodied was often not provided. Almshouses in less densely populated areas were somewhat more successful, according to reports by Dorothea Dix, an energetic reformer in the mid-nineteenth century who inspected these institutions all over the country, in her efforts to promote more humane treatment of the poor (and of the insane).

The almshouse remained the preferred form of public relief throughout the nineteenth century. The heavy immigration, increased urban crowding, and high unemployment of the late nineteenth century strengthened the widely held belief that compelling dependent people to enter these residential institutions was the best way to deal with them. The institution appealed both to those who saw it as an avenue to rehabilitation and to those who saw it as a way of saving money by deterring would-be applicants for relief.

Child Saving

The use of almshouses was one aspect of a more general trend during the nineteenth century—the use of large institutions for confining all kinds of dependent and disorderly persons. During this period, the punishment of criminals changed from whipping, placement in the stocks, and other bodily punishments to incarceration in a penitentiary. Home care of the insane was increasingly shifted from their own homes or homes of relatives to care in insane asylums. And two new types of public institutions for children became widespread—the reformatory (sometimes called a house of refuge) and the orphan asylum (sometimes called a home for the friendless), which took in not only orphans but also neglected and abandoned children. There had been a few orphan asylums earlier, but they had not caught on as a way of caring for dependent children.

A new concern with "saving" children developed in the nineteenth century, a concern that grew out of the same fear of the consequences of social disorder that had given rise to the poorhouse. Historian David Rothman has noted:

> The founders of orphan asylums and houses of refuge shared fully with the proponents of other caretaker institutions a fear that anyone not carefully and diligently trained to cope with the open, free-wheeling, and disordered life of the community would fall victim to vice and crime. The orphan, robbed of his natural guardians, desperately needed protection against these dangers. Many children of the poor were in no better position, since their parents—at best too busy trying to eke out a living and at worst intemperate—provided no defense against corruption. The vagrant, by definition lacking in supervision, would certainly come under the sway of taverns, gambling halls, and theaters, the crowd of drunks, gamblers, thieves, and prostitutes. The nightmare come true, of course, was the juvenile delinquent, his behavior ample testimony to the speed and predictability of moral decline.[25]

Development of children's asylums was stimulated by the realization that the almshouse was an unfit place for children. The almshouses were not as well regulated as their early promoters had anticipated, and later observers saw them as destructive to children. The specialized institution for children was regarded as a necessity as of 1857, when a New York legislative investigating committee first took note of the situation.[26] These institutions were seen as rescuing children from the dangers of the slums and as rehabilitating them through teaching them discipline and obedience to authority, which training would enable them to resist the dangerous and immoral temptations that they would encounter in the community, which would, in turn, enable them to avoid becoming paupers or criminals. To carry out this discipline program, asylum officials sought and gained the power to isolate the children from contact with outsiders. Some asylums required parents who were institutionalizing their child to sign a pledge that they would not interfere with the way the institution conducted its work.

Although this chapter focuses primarily on the ideas and organizations that developed in public welfare, it is appropriate to take note of an alternative concept of child saving that gained influence under private auspices during the nineteenth century. A Protestant minister named Charles Loring Brace founded an organization in New York City in 1853 called the Children's Aid Society. This organization, which he led for more than thirty years, was strongly opposed to putting children into institutions regulated with a military or prisonlike discipline. He developed the idea of placing out, that is, putting children into private homes. This idea has survived to the present day and is known as foster-home placement.

Brace did share one of the views of those who favored institutional care: He believed that New York City was a dangerous place. (He later wrote a book called *The Dangerous Classes of New York and Twenty Years' Work Among Them.*) He too believed that poor children had to be removed from this community and be placed in a totally different environment in order to save them. Brace was alarmed that so many poor, homeless, neglected city children grew up to become threats to public order and safety. They had to be saved because they were dangerous classes making the city an unsafe place. He conceived the idea of sending children out west to be placed in the homes of farmers, away from the corrupting influence of city slums. Every two weeks an agent of the Children's Aid Society would lead a group of from one to four dozen children to a particular locality in the West. Their prospective arrival would be advertised in advance. When they arrived, a meeting would be held in a church or hall. The children were displayed on the platform and the citizens would take their pick. Both farmer and Society thought the arrangement good: The child was rescued from the slums and at the same time helped the farmer and his wife with their work and helped in the building of the pioneer West. Over a period of twenty-five years, nearly fifty thousand children were transported west. In time, the practice fell into disfavor. Westerners felt most of the children were already delinquent and were turning out badly: the "tainted products of New York's saloons." At the same time, reports of brutal treatment of the children reached the Children's Aid Society. Placement declined from about four thousand per year in the 1870s to about five hundred in 1892.[27]

The Increase of Control by State Governments

The tradition of localism that the colonists brought from England continued for a time after the colonies became a nation, but it underwent substantial modification during the nineteenth century. State governments had appropriated funds for the many types of welfare institutions that had been developing, but had not established effective procedures for supervising them. In addition to almshouses, insane asylums, orphanages and reformatories, the century saw the establishment of separate institutions for the feeble-minded, the blind, the deaf, and the epileptic. "The mixed almshouse was gradually transformed as group after group was withdrawn from its confines and placed in separate institutions."[28]

In addition to expansion of the number and types of institutions resulting from more careful classification of types of cases, the numbers of institutions grew for other reasons as well. The Civil War (1861–1865) left a great number of war orphans, which prompted the building of additional orphanages. The various institutions served wider areas of a state than a single township or county. The increase in numbers, the development of many different types of institutions, and the fact that they each served more than one local area made local control in its original form inappropriate. Control had to move to the level of the state government, if the activities of the various institutions were to be coordinated. Within the American system of federal government, state control is seen as contrasting with federal control and is thus regarded as a form of local government control. But it obviously represents some modification of the original small-scale localism that left authority in the parishes, townships and (later) counties. It began in 1863, when Massachusetts became the first state to establish a State Board of Charities to supervise the institutions within the state. Most other states followed, although by 1931, almost seventy years later, five states still had not.

Eventually the concept of public charities was superseded by the concept of public welfare. For example, state boards of charities were renamed departments of public welfare. After the rise of social service (discussed in Chapter 9), some states emphasized this aspect of their work as a way of putting the pauper concept further out of sight and again renamed their departments. Table 1 presents a listing of the fifty states with the names (as of 1977) of their departments devoted to public assistance and social services. It can be seen that the linking of other kinds of services to public assistance in the same department varies considerably from one state to another.

The Return to Outdoor Relief

The State Boards of Charities gained varying degrees of supervisory authority over the institutions that provided indoor relief, but outdoor relief was left in the hands of local authorities. As noted above, early in the nineteenth century, Philadelphia and Chicago had tried to abolish outdoor relief but had not succeeded. In the late nineteenth century, several of the largest cities in the country (Baltimore, Brooklyn, Kansas City, New York, Philadelphia, St. Louis, and San Francisco) abolished it. Most of these did not resume it until the Great Depression struck in 1929. The rationales for abolishing outdoor relief were familiar: Giving relief to people in their own homes encouraged dependence, broke their spirit, corrupted their character, and made them feel entitled to a free livelihood from the state. In addition, public relief departments in the cities were subject to thievery by politicians; in the 1870s and 1880s, several cities had financial scandals, and this corruption in public relief departments led to the stopping of outdoor relief. The shutdowns in Brooklyn and Philadelphia were not accompanied by an increase in requests to private agencies for assistance, which

MAJOR STATE SERVICES

Reorganization of Human Services Programs

State	Agency	Reorganization date (a)	Programs (b) PA&SS	H	MH	MR	Corr.	YI	VR	ES
Alabama	Dept. of Pensions & Security	....	★							
Alaska	Dept. of Health & Social Services	1939	★	★	★	★	★	★	★	
Arizona	Dept. of Economic Security	1973	★			★			★	★
Arkansas	Dept. of Social & Rehabilitative Services	1970	★		★	★		★	★	
California	Health & Welfare Agency	1968	★	★	★	★	★	★	★	★
Colorado	Dept. of Social Services	....	★						★	
Connecticut	Dept. of Social Services	....	★ (c)							
Delaware	Dept. of Health & Social Services	1969	★	★	★	★		★	★	
Florida	Dept. of Health & Rehabilitative Services	1975	★	★	★	★		★	★	
Georgia	Dept. of Human Resources	1972	★	★	★	★	★			
Hawaii	Dept. of Social Services & Housing	1959	★	★	★	★	★	★	★	
Idaho	Dept. of Health & Welfare	1973	★ (d)	★	★	★		★		
Illinois	Dept. of Public Aid	....	★							
Indiana	Dept. of Public Welfare	....	★					★		
Iowa	Dept. of Social Services	1967	★		★	★	★			
Kansas	Dept. of Social & Rehabilitation Services	....	★	★	★	★		★	★	
Kentucky	Dept. for Human Resources	1972	★	★	★	★		★		★
Louisiana	Health & Human Resources Administration	1972	★	★						
Maine	Dept. of Human Services	1931	★						★	
Maryland	Dept. of Employment & Social Services	1970	★							★

Reorganization of Human Services Programs

State	Agency	Reorganization date (a)	Programs (b)							
			PA&SS	H	MH	MR	Corr.	YI	VR	ES
Massachusetts	Executive Office of Human Services	1971	★	★	★	★	★	★	★	:
Michigan	Dept. of Social Services	1965	★	:	★	★	:	★	:	:
Minnesota	Dept. of Public Welfare	1939	★	:	★	★	:	:	:	:
Mississippi	Dept. of Public Welfare	: :	★	:	:	:	:	:	:	:
Missouri	Dept. of Social Services	1974	★	★	★	★	★	★	★	:
Montana	Dept. of Social & Rehabilitation Services	1972	★	:	:	:	:	:	:	:
Nebraska	Dept. of Public Welfare	: :	★	:	:	:	:	:	:	:
Nevada	Dept. of Human Resources	1963	★	★	★	★	:	★	★	:
New Hampshire	Dept. of Health & Welfare	1961	★	★	★	★	:	:	:	:
New Jersey	Dept. of Institutions & Agencies	1948	★	:	★	★	★	:	:	:
New Mexico	Health & Social Services Dept.	1969	★	★	★	★	:	:	★	:
New York	Dept. of Social Services	: :	★	:	:	:	:	:	:	:
North Carolina	Dept. of Human Resources	1971	★	★	★	★	:	:	★	:
North Dakota	Social Services Board	1973	★	:	:	:	:	:	:	:
Ohio	Dept. of Public Welfare	: :	★	:	:	:	:	:	:	:
Oklahoma	Dept. of Institutions, Social & Rehabilitative Services	: :	★	:	★	★	:	★	★	:
Oregon	Dept. of Human Resources	1971	★	★	★	★	★	★	★	:
Pennsylvania	Dept. of Public Welfare	1958	★	:	★	★	:	★	★	★
Rhode Island	Dept. of Social & Rehabilitative Services	1972	★	:	:	:	:	:	★	:
South Carolina	Dept. of Social Services	: :	★	:	:	:	:	:	:	:

Reorganization of Human Services Programs

State	Agency	Reorganization date (a)	Programs (b)							
			PA&SS	H	MH	MR	Corr.	YI	VR	ES
South Dakota	Dept. of Social Services	1972	★	····	★	★	★	····	★	····
Tennessee	Dept. of Human Services	····	★	····	····	····	★	····	····	····
Texas	Dept. of Public Welfare	····	★	★	★	★	★	★	····	····
Utah	Dept. of Social Services	1969	★	★	★	★	★	★	★	····
Vermont	Agency of Human Services	1970	★	★	★	★	★	★	★	····
Virginia	Office of Human Affairs	1972	★	★	★	★	····	★	★	····
Washington	Dept. of Social & Health Services	1970	★	★	★	★	★	★	★	····
West Virginia	Dept. of Welfare	····	★	····	····	····	····	····	····	····
Wisconsin	Dept. of Health & Social Services	1967	★	★	★	★	★	★	★	····
Wyoming	Dept. of Health & Social Services	1969	★	★	★	★	····	····	★	····

Source: The Council of State Governments' Project on Human Services Integration, 1975.
(a) Although some of the agencies may have changed their names since the reorganization date listed, the programs covered have remained essentially the same.
(b) *Symbols:* PA & SS—Public Assistance and Social Services (Includes medical assistance); H—Health; MH—Mental Health; MR—Mental Retardation; Corr.—Corrections; YI—Youth Institutions; VR—Vocational Rehabilitation; ES—Employment Security.
(c) Social services for children are administered by the Dept. of Children and Youth Services.
(d) Social services are administered by the Dept. of Children and Family Services.
Source: The Book of the States, Vol. XXI (Lexington, Ky.: Council of State Governments, 1976–77).

confirmed the belief of prominent charity leaders such as Josephine Shaw Lowell that outdoor relief was wasteful.[29]

Thus, in the last quarter of the nineteenth century, the great debate over indoor and outdoor relief had shifted to a debate over public charity (in the form of outdoor relief) and private charity. The almshouses had become largely custodial institutions for the aged, sick, and infirm—people who could not work. They were no longer seriously viewed as places for rehabilitating able-bodied paupers. Leaders of private charity argued its superiority over public relief. They were opposed by other groups, particularly members and supporters of the trade union movement, who accused private charity leaders of being out of touch with the conditions of industrial society, which sometimes resulted in people of good character being thrown out of work because the economy was in a slump. Unemployed workers needed income maintenance, not character improvement, they said. This issue remained unresolved until the private charities were overwhelmed by the Great Depression, at which time public assistance on a large scale became a significant component of American social welfare.

Categorical Assistance

While the Great Depression of 1929 brought outdoor relief back on a sweeping scale, the pendulum had been swinging back to it even earlier, but only for certain categories of problems. The first category to receive special attention was the blind. Around the turn of the century, several states, beginning with Ohio in 1898, passed laws permitting direct outdoor assistance to be given to the blind by counties that wished to tax its residents for the purpose. When Illinois passed a law in 1915 *requiring* its counties to grant a benefit of $365 to any blind person with an income of less than $465 per year, the law was opposed by many social workers. They opposed it for three reasons: (1) The flat grant did not take into account degrees of need. (2) The law discouraged industriousness in those blind persons whose income was slightly less than $465 a year. (3) The law made no provision for rehabilitating the blind.[30] The concept of case-by-case investigation of individual need, passed down from the Charity Organization Society movement to the more professional social work movement around the turn of the century, remained blended with the centuries-old concept of the importance of industriousness, and together the two concepts were the basis of opposition to an assured income for blind people outside of institutions.

Social workers advanced essentially the same argument against outdoor relief for widowed mothers. In 1909, President Theodore Roosevelt held a White House Conference on the Care of Dependent Children. The conference recommended that children of widowed mothers no longer be taken from their mothers and put into institutions simply because they were poor. Instead, mothers should care for their children in their own homes. Efforts to pass legislation to provide public funds to widowed mothers to enable them to keep their children at home were opposed by many social workers, particularly, but not only, leaders of the COS, on the grounds that the legislation was a step backward to outdoor relief. Nevertheless, beginning in 1911, many states passed legislation enabling counties to provide "widows' pensions" or "mothers' pensions," as these funds came to be known. As two students of this trend noted, the term "pension" was a misnomer, since the money was to be paid on the basis of need and was a relief measure. Nevertheless, it was an effort to remove the stigma of "poor relief" from a selected category of recipients of aid. For the same reason, some states created special boards of child welfare, to remove the program from the existing poor-relief organizations. This step was also an effort to remove the program from political influence.[31] These events illustrate the point made in Chapter 1 concerning the different amounts of honor that are attached to income from different sources. They further illustrate the fact that a change of name is sufficient to be thought of as a change of source. Calling a grant of aid a "pension" instead of "relief" generates much wider social acceptance, both among those receiving the money and among those whose taxes provide the money.

Beginning in 1923, some states added a third category of outdoor relief: old-age assistance. By 1934, twenty-seven of the forty-eight states had some type of old-age assistance plan, a development that represented a reaction against the poor food, decrepit buildings, filthy conditions, and general disorder of the almshouses. These state plans, like the plans for assistance to the blind and to widowed mothers, were permissive rather than mandatory. Each state allowed such a program to be put into practice by counties that wished to tax their residents for the purpose; the state did not require the counties to do so, and many did not. The states that adopted such plans imposed restrictions: They required that assistance go only to citizens (above age 65 or 70) who were deserving or of good character.

> Persons who deserted their husbands or wives, who failed to support their families, who had been convicted of a crime, or who had been tramps or beggars were ineligible. . . . Some states required continuous residence of fifteen years prior to application.[32]

There was also an income ceiling and a limit on the amount of property a recipient could own. The amount of money given in assistance later became a lien on the recipient's property, collected after the recipient's or the spouse's death.

After more than a hundred years in which indoor relief had been considered the best solution to dependency, individual states began a hesitant, step-by-step, category-by-category return to outdoor relief.

THE GREAT DEPRESSION AND THE PARTIAL FEDERALIZATION OF PUBLIC WELFARE

In October 1929, the stock market crashed, thus initiating the most severe economic depression the United States had ever experienced. The value of the stock in major American corporations, traded on the New York Stock Exchange, decreased so enormously in a few days that the share documents were transformed from certificates of wealth to almost worthless paper. "The great crash" cost rich investors their wealth and modest investors their hard-earned savings. This sudden loss was only the beginning of a series of losses that brought great suffering to millions of people and made a mockery of all they had believed about the importance of being thrifty and of assuring their financial independence by saving for a rainy day.

The Great Depression

Apart from war, the Great Depression that began in 1929 and continued, with only moderate alleviation, for ten years, was the most catastrophic event ever to befall the country. Some indication of the impact can be given by the extent of unemployment: In the spring of 1929, before the depression began, there were 2.86 million unemployed people in the country. By spring 1933, the number had reached 15 million.[33] As people competed for the jobs that remained, wages and salaries fell. Banks and other financial institutions were in great difficulty and many eventually collapsed; depositors lost their savings. Companies went bankrupt. The scope of the economic decline was unprecedented, and many "solid citizens" joined the ranks of the dependent. Many people were close to starvation.

The First Responses

Although the use of public relief in the form of categorical relief had been growing for some years before the depression hit, private charities had long been speaking out about the superiority of private charity over public relief. For the first two years of the depression (1929–1931), ". . . the private family agencies made a valiant attempt to carry staggering loads and, under the greatest pressure, to justify the faith of their leaders in the superiority of their methods over those of the public 'dole' system."[34] Pressure was building for federal action, but President Herbert Hoover was a firm believer in private charity supplemented by local government action as the appropriate method for dealing with what he and many others still believed was a temporary emergency.

Hoover was a humanitarian, and he had gained a great reputation as administrator of a food relief program in Belgium during World War I. But he believed it was not appropriate for the federal government to take major responsibility for alleviating distress. He did take some actions, however: He met with business leaders and urged them to continue production and not to make steep wage cuts. He asked Congress to appropriate $150 million to provide jobs in various federal government departments to carry out projects that had already been authorized.

He also established an Emergency Committee for Employment, whose function was to cooperate with local organizations, encouraging them in their efforts to see that no one went hungry and cold. The committee

> became, in effect, a huge correspondence mill turning out endless letters of encouragement, advice, requests for information, pamphlets, and books. Letters went off to the magazine of social work, *Survey*, asking for copies of its special numbers on unemployment; a request to the director of the Charity Organization Department of the Russell Sage Foundation for copies of Mary Richmond's "Emergency Relief," and "On the Coming Winter"; letters to chairmen of unemployment committees asking a series of questions on local conditions, and ending with: "Will your county be able to handle the situation?" Words of cheer and advice went to trade associations, industrial institutes, and college professors. Then the committee summarized its findings in numerous pamphlets of its own, and urged mayors, governors and chairmen to incorporate the ideas in their localities. It was, in truth, a gigantic clearing house. But, in addition, it was an organ of exhortation for the American way.[35]

With this approach, it is not surprising that "when governors asked for the committee's plan, they were told that the committee had none, and the governors received instead a pamphlet on what others were doing."[36]

Not until late 1931 did Hoover recognize the gravity of the situation and abandon his old assumptions.[37] He helped create a new federal agency, the Reconstruction Finance Corporation, which lent money to businesses to keep them from going bankrupt. However, since Hoover never allowed the federal government to become directly involved in helping individuals in distress, his actions to overcome the depression were widely seen as favoring the upper classes and their financial interests. People did not believe his prediction that prosperity was just around the corner; they lost confidence in him and in the business leadership. In the election of November 1932, Hoover was defeated by Democrat Franklin Delano Roosevelt, governor of New York and a distant cousin of Theodore Roosevelt.

The New Deal

In his presidential-nomination acceptance speech to the Democratic convention, Roosevelt said, "I pledge you, I pledge myself, to a new deal for the American people."[38] The phrase caught on, and Roosevelt's administration, the longest in American history (1933–1945), became known as the New Deal. (Specialists in the study of government consider the term applicable only to the earlier years of his period in office when he was heavily occupied with creating new government programs for alleviating hardship and for preventing future hardship. The later years were occupied with World War II.)

The New Deal was one of the most significant periods in the history of American social welfare because of two major concepts that it introduced: the concept that the federal government has a necessary role in public welfare and the concept of federal responsibility for social insurance. The major discussion of social insurance appears in Part IV. Here the focus is on the measures the New Deal took to combat the hardships besetting the American people.

When Roosevelt took office on March 4, 1933, the American people were so frightened and desperate that the new president had unprecedented power to take whatever measures he thought necessary to save the country. He acted quickly and the first hundred days of his administration were a period of remarkably rapid government accomplishment. Many laws were passed to strengthen the country's banking system and business institutions; Roosevelt and Hoover did not differ much in their view that strong business institutions were the basis for assuring work and livelihood to people. But a difference between them was evident in the Federal Emergency Relief Act of May 1933, which made available half a billion dollars for immediate, direct relief to starving individuals; never before had the national government provided direct relief.

In addition to immediate relief to prevent starvation, the federal government initiated several types of work relief. The most novel was the Civilian Conservation Corps (CCC), whose purpose was to save both human and natural resources. Young men between the ages of eighteen and twenty-five from families who were on relief were enrolled and sent to camps in the countryside where they worked on soil conservation, flood control, and reforestation projects. They received subsistence plus a cash wage of $30 per month, $25 of which was sent to their families. By the time the CCC was terminated in 1942, more than 2.75 million young men had participated in the program.

The New Deal created so many new agencies in such a short time that they became known primarily by their initials and as a group were called "the alphabet agencies." In November 1933, Roosevelt created the Civil Works Administration (CWA) to build bridges, roads, post offices, and other public works of various kinds.

Within thirty days the CWA was a thriving concern and a means of living for 4,000,000 men and their families. It seemed for a time that Roosevelt's approval of the CWA signified capitulation to what were then considered to be radical doctrines—that every man was entitled to a job, not merely a dole, and that it was the federal government's duty to provide work if private industry did not.[39]

Political attack by opponents forced Roosevelt to drop the CWA a few months later, and many men who had been working went back to receiving a dole from the Federal Emergency Relief Administration (FERA).

The elections of 1934 sent many additional Roosevelt supporters to Congress. With this new support, Roosevelt became the leader of a coalition of farmers, workers, lower-middle-class people, unemployed people, and disadvantaged minorities. He began a trend in social welfare that remained dominant in the United States until the election of Richard Nixon as president in 1968. Roosevelt took steps to provide more security and better incomes for the great masses of the American people. He interpreted the election results as a mandate from the people to carry out a program of social justice in which business profits would be of secondary importance to the general welfare.

Early in 1935, the FERA was ended and replaced by perhaps the most famous of the New Deal agencies, the Works Progress Administration (WPA). Between 1935 and 1941, an average of more than 2 million men per month were on WPA payrolls, with a peak of about 3.25 million in November 1938. More than $11 billion was spent on "some 250,000 projects ranging in size from large airports to stone walls on university campuses." In addition to public construction work, money also went to unemployed artists, actors, writers, and musicians to support them in various artistic projects.[40] The WPA was sometimes criticized for paying people who either did no work or worked at projects that were unnecessary or too costly. However justifiable some of this criticism may have been, the buildings, parks, and other public facilities constructed during the WPA years added significantly to the country's level of functioning, and the artists created some important work.

Another important agency was the National Youth Administration (NYA), which provided jobs to high school and college students. The dual purpose of the program was to keep students off the labor market and to enable them to improve their skills and knowledge for future employment. The head of the NYA in Texas was a young man named Lyndon Johnson (who became president in 1963 and himself embarked on a significant social welfare program).

Permanent federal welfare

The New Deal agencies and programs discussed so far were all temporary— aimed at the immediate depression hardship. In addition to these programs, the

New Deal established a permanent public welfare program. In one history-making law, the Social Security Act, passed in August 1935, two significant social welfare programs were launched. The federal government began both a social insurance system and a federal public welfare system that was not a response to a temporary emergency situation but was to be an ongoing part of the national government as long as it was needed. The tradition of completely local financial responsibility for the poor that had begun in Tudor England and that had continued not only in the British colonies but into the American nation was terminated after four hundred years with the passage of this act in 1935.

The public assistance program required the cooperation of the federal government and the states. Each state was obliged to submit for approval of the new Social Security Board a plan for operating a public assistance program for three categories of people in need of income: old people, blind people, and dependent children. If the state's plan was approved by the board, the federal government would pay half the state's cost for old-age assistance and aid to the blind, and one third of the state's cost for aid to dependent children.[41]

General assistance

People in need of income who did not fit one of the three categories provided for in the Social Security Act and who were unable to get employment through the federal work programs (WPA, CCC, NYA) remained the responsibility of state and local governments, and they remain so to this day. Single adults and childless couples who are poor and who do not qualify for federal financial support (they are neither blind, nor old, nor permanently and totally disabled) must depend on help from their local or state government under the General Assistance Program.

There is very little systematic knowledge about General Assistance for two reasons: (1) The individual programs vary tremendously not only from one state to another but also from one county to another within a single state; and (2) almost no systematic research on General Assistance has been done. One of the few studies, done in California in 1962, showed that one county might give help only in the form of surplus food distribution, while another might give small amounts of cash for very short periods.

General Assistance payments are almost always lower than benefits under federally assisted programs, because the states and counties set higher benefit levels when part of the cost is paid by the federal government. The California study provided a vivid example of this: A woman, whose husband was in jail, and her three children received $215 per month from the aid to families with dependent children (AFDC). When her husband returned from jail, he was unable to find work. The family was no longer eligible for AFDC; both parents and the three children received $177 per month under the General Assistance Program.[42]

What emerged, then, from the New Deal period and has continued into the present was a complex system of public assistance in which the three major levels of government were involved in complex interrelationships. The aged, the blind, and dependent children were recognized as appropriate categories for a permanent program of federal help. (Unemployed able-bodied workers were to be helped by federal work relief programs only as long as the depression lasted. No federal work program was permanent.) Two more categories were later added to the original three: aid to the permanently and totally disabled (APTD) in 1950, and aid to the medically indigent in 1960. Aid to dependent children (ADC), which became later aid to families with dependent children (AFDC), was for a long time restricted to families in which there was no father in the home due to his death or desertion. In 1961, Congress for the first time permitted states to receive federal funds for families with dependent children in which the father was still in the home but was unemployed (AFDC-UP).

Federal funds are given to states that agree to share the costs of aid to one or more of the specified categories and that submit a satisfactory plan to the federal government. A federally approved plan must meet certain standards— for example, every part of the state must be included in the plan; state officials are not allowed to exclude some portion of the population they do not like; and none of the localities has the option of not participating in the plan. In deference to the diversity of local traditions, each state is allowed to decide whether part of the state's share of the costs will be passed on to the towns and counties or whether the costs will be assumed entirely at the state level. States and their local subdivisions remain fully responsible for people in need of income who do not fall into one of the five categories.

It is important to note that categorical assistance was and continues to be based on a *means test,* that is, demonstrated proof by the applicants that they have no other sufficient means of livelihood. The means test has long been considered an obvious necessity. Not until the 1960s were some serious efforts begun to assure everyone of at least a minimally adequate income without requiring a means test. The nineteenth-century COS worker would have thought the means test a good thing, but some people saw it as costing the very poor their human dignity. Harry L. Hopkins, a social worker who became President Roosevelt's major advisor on and administrator of New Deal social welfare programs, wrote in 1935:

> Then there is the humiliation of relief, a humiliation that we cannot help inflicting, for the "means test" is our one way of keeping panhandlers off the rolls. It calls for the most detailed prying into the lives and habits of every applicant for relief. We butt into their homes, digging around to find out if they have any hidden resources, or some relative who is able to aid.[43]

The means test, with its humiliation of the applicant, is still used today.[44]

THE WELFARE CRISIS
OF THE 1960s

During the 1960s, both government officials and the American public became concerned about the rising cost of public assistance. Many felt that the country was suffering a "welfare crisis" and that "the welfare system was a mess." The number of people receiving public assistance increased dramatically throughout the decade, and the cost climbed rapidly as well. The atmosphere was thick with public outcries, newspaper editorials, government investigations, and proposals for reform—and with hostility to people on welfare. The 1960s were turbulent years in American society; a full analysis of the events of the time and their effect on public attitudes toward the public welfare system would take a volume in itself, but certain of the main factors can be summarized.

The Withering-Away Fallacy

Federal public assistance—which still required, of course, a substantial part of the cost to be borne by each participating state—was introduced as part of the same law that introduced social insurance. Payments under social insurance (social security) were to be made to elderly people after they retired. In the case of workers who died before retirement, payments would be made to their widows and dependent children. The old-age assistance (OAA) and aid to dependent children provisions (ADC) of the 1935 act were seen as temporary. They would lose importance once the depression was over and most people went back to work and became eligible for future social security payments. Public assistance would virtually "wither away," continuing to be needed only by a relatively small number of people who were not connected with the work force. Elderly retired people would no longer need OAA because they would be entitled to old-age insurance (OAI). There was, in fact, a slow decrease in the number of people receiving OAA from 2.8 million in 1950 to about 2.2 million in 1965, so this aspect of public assistance seemed to be conforming to the predictions of the mid-1930s. But the number of dependent children did not decrease as expected. The number of AFDC recipients (dependent children and their adult caretakers, usually in female-headed households) increased from 2.2 million in 1950, when the adult caretaker provision was first introduced, to 4.3 million in 1964, and to 11.1 million in 1975.[45]

Poverty Amid Affluence

The increase in the number of AFDC cases was baffling to officials and ordinary citizens alike because it occurred during a generally prosperous period.

> By the summer of 1955 the American economy was again booming. . . . Employment went up to an all-time high. . . . Consumers, enjoying a higher living standard than ever before, went on the biggest buying spree in history. They used their large incomes to buy without restraint, and borrowed to buy still more.[46]

With so many people enjoying prosperity, there was little sympathy for or understanding of those who were not participating in it. At the end of the 1950s, there was a widespread belief that the country had attained a permanent affluence and that everyone had become middle class. But then a number of events led to "the rediscovery of poverty." While campaigning for the Democratic presidential nomination in spring 1960, John F. Kennedy discovered in West Virginia that poor schoolchildren receiving a free lunch from surplus food distributed by the federal government would save part of it to bring home to other undernourished family members. In addition to the impact of newspaper stories about this discovery, Michael Harrington's *The Other America*, Dwight Macdonald's magazine article about Harrington's book, and other writings that gained wider readership at this time contributed to greater public awareness of the continued existence of poverty.

Nevertheless this awareness did not spread rapidly or deeply enough to overcome the anger of the public nor the anxiety of politicians who had to make decisions about rising AFDC costs. So far as the public was concerned, the major reason for the rise in AFDC cases was the increase in the number of black illegitimate children. The proportion of AFDC families that were black increased from 36 percent in 1953, to 43 percent in 1961, and to 47 percent by the end of the 1960s.[47]

> Black recipients still accounted for less than half of those in the program, but they were much more visible. While over half of white welfare families were still scattered in small towns and outside of metropolitan areas, two-thirds of black welfare families were living in the central cities of the metropolitan areas.[48]

Harry M. Caudill, in a classic study of the mountaineers of eastern Kentucky, mostly descendants of early English settlers, reported that the history and social conditions in that area had led to "the growth of 'welfarism' on a scale unequaled elsewhere in North America and scarcely surpassed anywhere in the world."[49] But the residents of that area were largely invisible to the wider public because their hamlets, villages, and towns were in remote mountain areas.

The overall increase in AFDC recipients led government authorities to attempt new approaches to public welfare.

Rehabilitation

When the Kennedy administration took office in 1961, it began the first major effort in twenty-five years to develop a new concept of public welfare. The goal was not simply to give money to dependent people but to prevent dependency in the first place and, where that failed, to rehabilitate the dependent. The principal welfare population had changed. For centuries, the major concern had been the cost of supporting unemployed able-bodied men; now it was dependent children living with mothers who had either been deserted or had not been married to the father of their children. Measures to strengthen the family were seen as the solution to the problem. One measure was to provide aid to families with dependent children and unemployed parents (AFDC-UP). Federal funds would be given to states that included this category in their state plan. By the end of the decade, however, only about half the states had taken this step.[50]

Greater emphasis was placed on rehabilitation. The public assistance section of the Social Security Act was amended in 1962 to require a social service plan for every AFDC family. Employees of local public welfare departments, called caseworkers, were to spend time with the families on their "caseload" and to help them to understand and overcome the problems that were keeping them from participating fully in family and community life. The caseworkers were to counsel each family and, where necessary, refer families to other social service agencies for specialized help. The caseworker was to visit each family's home at least once every six months to check whether the family was still eligible for AFDC.[51] The activities of the caseworkers came to be regarded as the key to solving one of the country's major problems, as the public thought of it: getting people off the AFDC rolls and thereby saving the taxpayers' money. The expectation proved unrealistic, and attention shifted to other ideas.

The program of the 1962 amendment to the Social Security Act, which proposed to reduce public dependency through providing social services to AFDC clients, was based on wishful thinking rather than on reality. It was bound to fail because (1) the services to be provided were diverse, vague, and of uncertain value in accomplishing the task for which they were intended; and (2) even assuming the effectiveness of the types of services proposed, not enough money was appropriated and not enough qualified staff were ever hired to carry out the program.

The vagueness of the law is illustrated in the statement of services to be performed for unmarried mothers and their children:

> ... arranging for prenatal, confinement, and postnatal medical care for the mother and child; planning with mother for her future and that of her child; help to mother in child care and training if child remains with mother or planning for placement elsewhere; help to mother with respect to legal problems affecting the rights of mother and child; work to change environmental conditions seriously

contributing to illegitimacy; use of available specialized agency and community resources for serious problems or needs.[52]

In addition to the vagueness, it was not apparent how provision of these services would result in freeing recipients from dependency on AFDC.

The second major problem was the lack of qualified staff. The 1962 amendment required the states to limit each caseworker's caseload to sixty cases in order to assure quality service to each case. However, this limit was often exceeded. In addition, caseworkers were expected to do work for which they were not trained. Only about 4 percent of caseworkers doing public assistance work had Master of Social Work degrees. (The Bachelor of Social Work degree did not exist at that time.) Caseworkers generally had to be college graduates, but their degree could be in any subject. Trained social workers tended to avoid public assistance work, preferring instead to work for the voluntary social welfare agencies, which offered greater prestige and somewhat greater autonomy. Moreover, there was a high and rapid turnover among public assistance caseworkers. Although it might be argued that the social service approach to reducing dependency on public assistance was never given an adequate test, the judgment of social welfare leaders as well as Congress in 1967 was that the attempt of the preceding five years had failed.[53]

Food Stamps

The Kennedy administration revived a program for improving nourishment among the poor. As noted above, Kennedy had learned personally of inadequate nourishment among some Americans during his campaign. To remedy this situation, he introduced "food stamps," which could be purchased by a poor person for a modest price and exchanged at grocery stores for food worth more than their purchase price.

The food stamp idea had first been introduced during the New Deal. The original purpose was as much to aid farmers with food surpluses as to help people with not enough to eat. Beginning in 1933, the federal government bought and distributed to poor people food that farmers had produced and been unable to sell. The use of stamps as an alternative procedure for distributing food was tried between 1939 and 1943. The plan enabled people to obtain their food in ordinary grocery stores instead of in special distribution centers, but the stamps were good only for surplus food items.[54]

The distribution of surplus food items, at no cost to poor people, continued after the New Deal. John Kennedy's first official act as president was to increase the amount and kinds of food distributed. But he regarded free food distribution as a temporary measure. Distribution of free surplus foods had three drawbacks:

(1) It was stigmatizing because most people did not obtain their food in this way, and the difference was fairly visible. (2) Surplus foods may not necessarily be the foods that people want or need most for their diet. (3) The procedure was wasteful. Food was distributed only once a month, so people would receive impractically large amounts of certain items at one time, such as twenty pounds of cheese.[55]

The food stamp concept allows people to obtain their food at ordinary grocery stores, and with only a few restrictions, enables them to purchase whatever food items they wish, instead of limiting them to surplus commodities. The plan was introduced on an experimental basis in 1961 and later expanded nationwide. The very poorest family obtained stamps without charge; those somewhat better off were required to buy the stamps, which could then be exchanged for food whose cost was greater than what they had paid for the stamps.

Studies done in the late 1960s revealed that many poor families were not taking advantage of the stamp program. A principal factor was the need to buy the stamps; these families could not assemble sufficient cash at one time to buy, say, $60 worth of stamps, even though the stamps might yield $80 worth of groceries at the store. The result was that fewer people were participating in the stamp program than had been receiving food under the surplus commodities program.[56]

Participation in the food stamp program did eventually expand, after various adjustments were made in the operation of the program. From the four hundred thousand people using food stamps in 1965, the number increased to more than 19 million in 1975, and then declined to 16.7 million in 1977.[57]

The food stamp program was revised in late 1977, with these provisions: (1) Stamps were given free to all those eligible for them. (2) Eligibility was restricted to those whose incomes fell below a government-defined "poverty line"; previously, some people of moderate income had been allowed to purchase stamps. (3) Recipients were required to accept public service jobs, where available, to help pay for their stamps. The changes in the law made stamps available only to those officially defined as poor, but they were able to obtain the stamps more easily than before.[58]

Since 1971, the food stamp program has been administered nationwide. The amount of additional purchasing power provided by the stamps varies with the person's or family's income. Thus, to some extent, food stamps help to even out differences in AFDC benefits among the states. An AFDC family in a state that pays low AFDC benefits receives more stamps than a family in a state that pays high benefits.[59] The *schedule of benefits* is, however, the same nationwide. That is, same-income and same-size families qualify for the same amount of food stamps in all parts of the country. The food stamp program is the only public welfare (means-tested) program that provides a national standard of benefits. Whether the food stamp program is to be the forerunner of a general national standard in public welfare remains to be seen. At this time, such a development is unlikely.

The War on Poverty

In 1964, President Lyndon Johnson, who only a few months earlier had taken over the presidency following the assassination of John F. Kennedy, declared a "total war on poverty," as part of his effort to enable the United States to become a "Great Society." Congress approved his administration's Economic Opportunity Act that year, thereby launching the broadest and most diverse federal social welfare effort since the New Deal. New public welfare programs that grew out of the act focused on jobs, job training, and work for AFDC mothers. (Community action, the best-known concept in this program, is discussed in Chapter 11. New social service ideas contained in the program are discussed in Chapter 9.)

Neighborhood Youth Corps

The Neighborhood Youth Corps (NYC) was somewhat similar to the New Deal's National Youth Administration in that it too provided part-time employment to poor high school youths. In addition, it provided summer jobs for high school students. The in-school and the summer programs were intended to diminish the need of poor youths to drop out of school, thereby enabling them to continue to acquire the education necessary for adequate functioning in a society with increasingly complex technology.[60]

Job Corps

The Economic Opportunity Act established a Job Corps to prepare out-of-school young people, ages sixteen to twenty-one, "for the responsibility of citizenship and to increase their employability" by placing them in rural and urban residential centers for education, useful work, and "other appropriate activities." The Job Corps bore a superficial resemblance to the CCC, but was significantly different in that its target was people with severe educational deficiencies that made them unequipped for employment. The program's underlying assumption was that "many youths from impoverished homes must be removed from their home environment before they could be rehabilitated through training and education."[61]

Work Incentive Program

This program, adopted in 1967 (after the 1962 amendment to the public assistance section of the Social Security Act was judged a failure), changed the nature of AFDC. From its beginning in 1935, the ADC program had been based on the concept that a mother's place was in the home, taking care of her children.

However, if a mother did happen to earn any money from a job, the ADC grant she received was reduced by an equivalent amount. This procedure, which had seemed logical in the 1930s, was considered a poor idea in the 1960s for two main reasons. First, it functioned as a tax of 100 percent on earnings because 100 percent of the woman's earnings were subtracted from the benefits to which she would otherwise have been entitled. No other individuals were subject to such a high rate of tax on any of their income. There was a new understanding that a tax that takes away a person's entire earnings is a disincentive for the person to work: Why not subsist totally on AFDC if nothing is gained by working? Second, there was a growing recognition that more and more mothers were working, even mothers whose families had adequate incomes. The idea that a mother's place was in the home was becoming obsolete. The Work Incentive Program (WIN) was therefore adopted to encourage mothers to work. It allowed them to retain part of the money they earned without losing any of the AFDC money to which they were entitled.

The effort to get additional AFDC mothers to work was not successful. Most of the mothers had low skills, and there were few jobs for people with low skills. In addition, there were not enough day-care centers to take care of the mothers' children while they worked. However, allowing working mothers to retain part of their earnings did help those families improve their standard of living. In addition, some mothers whose earnings had previously made them ineligible for AFDC now became eligible. Political scientist Gilbert Steiner has observed: "To disregard a portion of earned income means to accept the principle of aid to the working poor."[62] This was a major change, but the program did not result in a reduction in the number of people receiving, or the cost of, AFDC. Whether this outcome should be considered a failure or a success depends, however, on one's values. Steiner, reviewing the various reform efforts of the 1960s, has concluded that "cost increases are precisely what the reformers sought to avoid," but, he continued:

> It is also a mistake to conclude that failure to meet the stated goals of the various reform efforts means that there has been no welfare reform. Admitting more of the needy poor to the relief rolls, no matter how reluctantly, rather than keeping them off, no matter how ingeniously, is the quintessence of welfare reform.[63]

WELFARE REFORM

From the early 1960s through the 1970s, political leaders, social welfare specialists, and the American public engaged in a continuing struggle to reform the welfare system that had been established during the New Deal. This period of debate, with one proposal after another being offered and rejected, in some ways resembled the post-Speenhamland period in England—and for basically the same reason: The cost of public welfare had reached a level that was unacceptable to the taxpayers.

There are also important differences between the 1960–1980 period in the United States and the post-Speenhamland period in Great Britain. One important one is that the earlier period resulted in a decisive "reform"—the New Poor Law of 1834. In contrast, no decisive change in the American public assistance system has yet occurred (at least, not as of the completion of this book). Another important difference is that the problem of reform has become more complex. Between 1815 and 1834, the main issue was whether traditional community obligations toward the needy (as established in the Elizabethan Poor Law and further elaborated in the allowance system) were to continue or, in the name of individualism, be abolished. The main issue in the United States today is how much public responsibility for people in need should be expanded. This issue, however, is complicated by other issues that did not exist in Great Britain one hundred fifty years ago. Two are of major importance:

(1) Although, as pointed out earlier, more whites than blacks receive welfare (which, in this context, refers mainly to AFDC), a much larger proportion of blacks than of whites are recipients. Welfare in the late twentieth century thus is not only an economic, political, and philosophical issue, it is also an issue of race relations. Providing welfare is not merely a question of what to do about poor people; it is widely understood as a question of what whites are doing about blacks (and to some extent about Hispanic people).

(2) The concept of need has itself become a major issue. In brief, it is being redefined by more and more reformers as a *need for equality rather than simply a need for subsistence.* The debate today is not simply between those who want government to assure everybody subsistence and those who do not. There is a third position: that government should assure every citizen *a decent income,* one in keeping with the high consumption standards of an affluent society. This would mean reducing the extent of inequality in American society, so that those with the lowest incomes would not be as far below the general standard of living as were low-income people in earlier times.

All public assistance plans involve some *redistribution of income.* That is, the government collects income taxes from people (and companies), and it pays out some of that money as benefits to those who do not have income from work or ownership of property (or who have insufficient income from those sources). The question today is how far that redistribution should go. Who should receive benefits? How much should be collected in taxes to pay for the benefits? What income level should people be brought up to?

The United States does not yet have a national minimum income standard for everybody. Each state has its own schedule of AFDC payments, although the schedule must be approved by the federal government. Each state computes its own estimate of what families of each size require. For example, in 1976, Texas estimated that a family of four required $187 per month, while Wisconsin estimated $456 a month, and Hawaii $497. But most states' benefits do not match their own estimates of need. "Texas, for example, provides only $140.25 to a penniless family of four rather than $187."[64] *Average* family benefits under AFDC in January 1976 ranged from a low of $48.53 per month in Mississippi to a high of $367.19 per month in New York. It is certain that such variations reflect differences among the states in ability to pay for public assistance, but they also reflect differences in *willingness* to pay.

Since the Supreme Court in 1969 prohibited states from imposing a duration-of-residence requirement for AFDC, people have been free to move from low-benefit states to higher-benefit states. And it is widely believed that such moves occur frequently. There is evidence, however, that this belief may be exaggerated. A study found that 75 percent of AFDC mothers in New York City were born outside of New York State, but that only 14 percent of them had received assistance within twenty-three months of moving to the city. The inference to be drawn here is that if the great proportion of migrant mothers on AFDC had moved to the city in order to obtain higher benefits, they would have begun receiving those benefits much sooner. The maximum estimate of those who moved for the specific purpose of obtaining higher benefits would be 14 percent; that is, it cannot even be said with certainty that these 14 percent moved for that reason. The others must have moved for other reasons and only later found that they had to apply for AFDC benefits.[65] The evidence seems to indicate that while there is some basis for the popular belief, migration in search of higher AFDC benefits may not be as prevalent as is popularly believed.

The variation in benefits among states can be looked at from another angle: Why should equally needy people receive differential treatment because they live in different states? (Cost of living differences among the states are not as large as differences in benefits.) Is the long-established principle of state responsibility for its poor more important than the principle that people who are citizens of the same country should receive equal treatment? At the beginning of the 1980s, the issue rests there, unresolved. Since 1969, efforts to assure a national minimum income have been unsuccessful. The effort continues. We turn now to new concepts of reform and recent actual attempts at reform.

New Concepts for Providing Income

During the 1960s and 1970s, two major ideas for replacing welfare received attention. One was known as family allowances (or children's allowances); the other was a guaranteed minimum income.

Family allowances

Family allowances are regular payments made to families in order to promote the welfare of the children. More than sixty countries, including all the countries of Europe, have systems of payment to families with children. The United States is the only major industrial nation that does not have such a system. The idea originated in France in 1870 when some branches of the government and one private employer began supplementing the salaries of workers who had families to support. In the late 1920s and the early 1930s, several other countries adopted family allowance plans that covered almost all families with young children. Canada adopted an allowance plan in 1945.

Although the basic concept of all family allowance plans is the same—to assure that parents have adequate funds to meet the expenses of raising children —the provisions vary from one country to another. In some countries, the plan is employment-related; people who work in industries that are not covered or who do not work at all receive no benefits for their children. In other countries, eligibility does not depend on employment. Most countries pay benefits beginning with the first child, but some being with the second. Some pay only up to a specified number of children. The plans pay benefits until the child reaches the age of fourteen, fifteen, or sixteen, depending on the country.

Children's or family allowances are seen as desirable by the advocates of this system because children represent a substantial proportion of those who need financial assistance. Further, this system "corrects for" the fact that modern industrial society pays wages on the basis of how much a worker's labor is worth, not on the basis of how many people must be supported by that wage. And in countries where the plan is not based on employment, all families receive benefits, regardless of income. This helps the poor as well as those whose standard of living is only modestly above the poverty level. People in the latter category in the United States have been financially hard-pressed, and, according to many observers, have also felt left out of government assistance programs. Furthermore, since benefits are paid to all parents with children of eligible age, there is not a stigmatized recipient group and a respectable non-recipient group. Thus an important source of social conflict in the United States would be diminished with such a plan. Advocates also argue that payments to parents with high incomes would, in effect, be recovered in their payment of income taxes.[66]

Although there are supporters of a family allowances program in the United States, they do not seem very numerous or persuasive. The idea of a guaranteed income has received more attention. One reason for this may be that family allowances by their very nature do not offer anything to single people, childless couples, and people with grown children, all of whom may also need income support. A guaranteed income program would be applicable to all people who require income support.

Guaranteed annual minimum income

Under a plan of guaranteed income, the government would make certain that every person had at least a certain minimum income. An Advisory Council on Public Welfare has stated: "The very concept of a guarantee requires that it be available to all it is intended to protect, be adequate to their needs, consistent with the standards of the society in which they live, and available on a dignified basis as a matter of legal right."[67]

Numerous versions of the guaranteed income idea have been proposed. The two best-known are the (1) negative income tax, which would make use of the existing income tax system and pay benefits to persons reporting low incomes on income tax returns, and (2) the demogrant, or universal payment, of which Senator McGovern's proposal was one example (see Chapter 2). In whatever version, the guaranteed income is intended to replace the existing welfare system (that is, AFDC, SSI, and General Assistance. SSI is discussed in Chapter 8 for reasons that that context makes clear.) Three main benefits would be anticipated from such a change: (1) A minimum income for everybody would be a matter of legal right. (2) Minimum subsistence would be assured to everyone without the requirement of a humiliating means test. (3) The scale of benefits would be nationwide, thus eliminating differences in benefits among people in different states and people in different age and family-status categories. Two presidents (Nixon in the years 1969 to 1971 and Carter in 1977) have included a guaranteed income provision in their proposals for welfare reform.

Nixon's Family Assistance Plan (FAP)

When Richard Nixon took office in 1969, there was considerable clamor for welfare reform. As noted earlier, the WIN program had not reduced the number of people on AFDC. At the beginning of 1962, there were about 3.5 million AFDC recipients; by the middle of 1967, there were 5 million, and the number was still increasing. (It reached 11.3 million in 1976.)[68] It was the growing number of these recipients that provided the strongest impetus to reform. But it was not the only one. Other ideas were also being discussed, such as the variations in benefits from state to state, with southern states generally paying lower benefits than northern ones. Half the states did not pay benefits to a family with an unemployed, able-bodied father, while half did. Families with a father who worked full time but earned an inadequate wage received no benefits at all; thus families with a full-time worker might have a lower income than a family receiving AFDC. "Less eligibility" was not part of the American system. This tempted at least some low-paid workers to quit their jobs and desert their families, since the families would receive more income from AFDC benefits than they were receiving from the workers' wages.

Here, then, were at least four major problems that called for reform:

(1) The excessive number of people receiving welfare.
(2) The unequal benefits paid by different states.
(3) The lack of benefits in half the states for families with an able-bodied unemployed father.
(4) The possibility of gaining better income from welfare than from a low-paying job.

What kind of welfare program would solve all these problems and not produce major new ones? Could any? If not, which problems were the most urgent? As happens with any complex social issue, the president's advisors were divided on which major problems were the most important targets of reform, and they engaged in much discussion and controversy before Nixon decided what he would recommend to Congress.[69]

Nixon's Family Assistance Plan (FAP), which he announced in August 1969, had these main provisions:

Income Provisions

(1) An income floor (assured minimum income) for every family with at least one child under eighteen (under twenty-one if in school). Example: $1,600 per year for a family of four with no earned income.
(2) Benefits to an employed worker earning a low income. Example: A family of five in which the worker earned $2,000 per year would receive $1,260, resulting in a total income of $3,260.
(3) Benefits to a family with an unemployed male head.
(4) An earnings disregard in determining eligibility for benefits. That is, benefits would not be reduced for the first $60 earned monthly. The worker would also keep 50 percent of benefits as earnings rose above $60 a month.

Work Provisions

(1) Able-bodied adults (male and female) had to accept work or training, provided suitable jobs were available.
(2) Mothers of preschool children would be excused from work (as were disabled people).
(3) Mothers of preschool children could work if they wished; major expansion of day-care facilities would be provided to make this possible.

Training Provisions

(1) Adults on welfare would receive a bonus of $30 per month if they entered a job training program.
(2) For heads of families on welfare, one hundred fifty thousand new training slots would be created.[70]

The most striking aspect of the FAP was its adoption of the guaranteed income idea. Nixon claimed that the income floor was not a guaranteed income because it did not assure benefits to an able-bodied adult who refused to work. But Nixon was overestimating the importance of the work rule, according to one analysis:

> He exaggerated the force of the work rule, failing to concede what the eventual draft of the legislation made clear: that if an ablebodied parent refused to accept work or training, only the parent's payment would be withheld. Thus, for all children the federal floor of FAP would be an unconditional guaranteed income, standard across the nation.[71]

Nixon did not want to *call* his proposal a guaranteed income, because he knew that would arouse opposition, but he made the guaranteed income a main element of his proposal because it was a way of providing greater equality of benefits for residents of different states and of providing benefits for low-income working people. Thus his proposal would have helped to solve three of the four major problems listed above. It would not have solved the problem of excessive numbers receiving welfare. On the contrary, it would have added many low-income working people to the rolls. To supporters of the proposal, this was a virtue; to opponents, it was its most serious flaw. Opponents attacked it as a revival of the Speenhamland allowance system.

The Nixon FAP passed the House of Representatives but was defeated in the Senate. A revised version in 1971 met the same fate.

Carter's Program for Better Jobs and Income (PBJI)

President Carter came into office determined to succeed in reforming welfare. He recognized, as had Nixon before him, that getting welfare recipients to work had to be a prominent feature of any reform that Congress would pass and that the country would accept as a genuine reform. Thus the very title he gave to the proposal emphasized jobs.

Carter's proposal was intended to replace not only AFDC but also the food stamp program and SSI. It therefore had to take account of the fact that not everybody could work. His plan made a distinction between people expected to work and people not expected to work. Those *not expected to work* were: the aged, blind, and disabled; single parents with children under age seven; single parents with children between seven and thirteen if a job and day care were not available; and two-parent families in which one parent was incapacitated. People *expected to work* were: two-parent families with children; single parents whose youngest child was over thirteen; and single persons and childless couples unable to find full-time work without the help of PBJI.

The main provisions of Carter's 1977 proposal were:

Income Provisions for those not expected to work

(1) An assured minimum income. Examples: Aged, blind, or disabled: $2,500 per year for an individual; $3,750 per year for a couple; $4,200 per year for a family of four.
(2) Earnings disregard (of varying amounts) for persons who chose to work even though they were not required to. Example: Single parent with child between seven and thirteen could keep first $3,800 in earnings with no reduction in benefits; above $3,800, benefits reduced $.50 for each $1.00 earned.

Income Provisions for those expected to work

(1) Assured minimum income. Example: $2,300 per year for a family of four.
(2) Assured minimum increased to $4,200 if principal wage earner could not find job after eight weeks of searching.
(3) Assured minimum back to $2,300 when job found or refused.
(4) Disregard of first $3,800 of earnings; reduction of benefits of $.50 for each $1.00 earned above $3,800.
(5) Cash assistance to family of four until its earned income reached $8,400 per year.

Work and Training Provisions

(1) Federal money to state and local governments to create 1.4 million public service jobs and training slots paying the federal minimum wage.
(2) Public service jobs to provide training in skills useful in jobs in the private sector.
(3) Unemployment and at least a five-week job search in the private sector for eligibility for a public service job.
(4) After one year in a public service job, another five-week job search in the private sector required for continued eligibility for a public job.
(5) Private jobs to be more rewarding than public ones: a worker would get a government check equal to 10 percent of his earnings, up to a maximum of $400 on earnings of $4,000, as a bonus for working in a private job.

Benefits of less than 10 percent would be payable on earnings above $4,000.[72]

Like the Nixon proposals, the Carter plan would have created greater equality of benefits for residents of the different states by setting national minimums. It would have facilitated the finding of work by overseeing the creation of jobs, and it would have made work in the private sector financially more attractive than work in the specially created public sector. However, like the Nixon proposal, it would have increased the number of people receiving benefits. Approximately 30 million people were receiving AFDC, SSI, and food stamp benefits in 1977; it was estimated that Carter's proposal would have provided benefits to about 32 million people.[73]

Congress was unreceptive to Carter's proposal, and it got nowhere. In 1979, Carter proposed a less ambitious, less costly plan in the form of two bills entitled Social Welfare Reform Amendments of 1979 and Work and Training Opportunities Act of 1979.[74] They were not adopted by the time Carter left office. His successor, Ronald Reagan, is opposed to national minimum income, as is much of the Congress elected with him.[75]

WELFARE REFORM, WORK, AND POVERTY

The public assistance programs in the United States in the early 1980s satisfy very few people. In his 1979 message to Congress on welfare reform, President Carter stated:

> For too many years we have lived with a welfare system universally recognized to be inadequate and ineffective. It is a crazy-quilt patchwork system stitched together over decades without direction or design. It should offer opportunity, but often breeds dependency. It should encourage and reward useful work, but often penalizes those who find jobs. . . . I recognize that welfare reform is a difficult undertaking. No legislative struggle in the past decade has provided so much hopeful rhetoric or so much disappointment and frustration. . . . I urge the Congress to cap a decade of debate on welfare reform with action.[76]

There are different reasons for the dissatisfaction, some of which Carter mentioned in his message: (1) The existing system is inadequate. Nowhere do welfare benefits equal the poverty level. (2) The existing system is unfair, because benefits to families in the same situation differ depending only on which state they live in. (3) The system is unnecessarily complicated both for applicants and for the government. (4) The system does not do enough to help people move from welfare to adequate-paying jobs. But Carter did not mention what is probably the most widely felt reason for dissatisfaction—the cost.

There are some who believe that eliminating poverty through a guaranteed income is impossible, at least under current circumstances. Martin Anderson, a conservative economist who worked in the Nixon administration (and who opposed Nixon's FAP) and now an important official in the Reagan administration, has argued that a welfare reform plan must accomplish three goals at the same time. It must (1) provide a decent level of support, (2) contain strong incentives to work, and (3) have a reasonable cost. A plan that would accomplish this would be a radical reform. Yet he states that such a plan is impossible:

> Radical welfare reform or any variety of a guaranteed income is politically impossible. No radical welfare reform plan can be devised that will simultaneously yield [adequate] minimum levels of welfare benefits, financial incentives to work, and an overall cost to the taxpayers that are politically acceptable.[77]

The political impossibility of eliminating poverty through welfare reform is argued by Sheldon Danziger and Robert Plotnick, two analysts of Carter's plan:

> PBJI would have reformed welfare, but it would not have eliminated poverty. To do so . . . would have required an expansion in welfare beyond the bounds of political feasibility. . . . The elimination of poverty is a goal that could be achieved only at the expense of Carter's first principle of welfare reform—holding down costs. The two most direct ways to expand PBJI from a welfare reform proposal to an antipoverty one as well would have been to raise income guarantees to the poverty line for those not expected to work and to provide a public job to all those who wanted one.[78]

These authors look to reducing poverty through improving the economy so that more jobs are available, and by expanding social insurance. (Social insurance is discussed in Part IV.) These alternatives still lie in the future. Welfare has not yet been reformed, not enough work and training opportunities exist to enable all able-bodied people to be self-supporting, and poverty, though somewhat reduced since the 1960s, has not been abolished.

SUMMARY

Dissatisfaction in England with the rising cost of outdoor relief led to the adoption of the New Poor Law in 1834. The growing influence of liberalism in the social context of industrialization made the Elizabethan Poor Law and the allowance system, with their emphasis on community responsibility for support of the poor, seem inappropriate and out-of-date. The New Poor Law, which stressed less eligibility, required applicants for relief to live in a workhouse. This form of indoor relief was intended to deter all but the most desperate from applying for public support.

Indoor relief became the dominant form of public welfare in the United States during the nineteenth century. A variety of asylums were built—poorhouses, orphanages, and more or less specialized asylums for the blind, the mentally retarded, the insane, and the juvenile delinquent. After more than a hundred years in which indoor relief was considered the ideal form of public welfare, ideas changed, and the period from the 1930s to the 1970s saw the gradual disappearance of the nineteenth-century institutions.

The tradition in England of local responsibility for the poor, traceable to Henry VIII's law of 1536, began to be altered after three hundred years, when the New Poor Law prescribed a role for the national government. That same tradition in the United States dominated public welfare from the first colony in 1607 until the advent of the New Deal in 1933. The federal government then took action to supply emergency relief to millions of starving and unemployed Americans during the Great Depression, which had been debilitating the country for four years. A partially federalized system of public assistance was introduced in 1935 as part of the Social Security Act passed in that year. That system has remained, with some modifications, until the present time. Rising costs and various inequities have stimulated efforts to reform the system, the most recent having been President Carter's in 1979. None have yet succeeded. The major features of the American public welfare system today are essentially those that were introduced during the New Deal.

Notes

[1] E. J. Hobsbawm, *Industry and Empire—The Pelican Economic History of Britain, Volume 3, From 1750 to the Present Day* (Harmondsworth, England: Penguin Books, 1969), p. 56.

[2] Harold J. Laski, *The Rise of Liberalism* (New York: Harper & Brothers, 1936), p. 126; George H. Sabine, *A History of Political Theory* (New York: Henry Holt, 1937), p. 528.

[3] Adam Smith, *An Inquiry into the Nature and Causes of the Wealth of Nations,* ed. and intro. Edwin Cannan (New York: Modern Library, 1937), p. 423. First published in 1776.

[4] J. R. Poynter, *Society and Pauperism—English Ideas on Poor Relief, 1795–1834* (London: Routledge & Kegan Paul, 1969), p. 14.

[5] Sidney Webb and Beatrice Webb, *English Poor Law History—Part I: The Poor Law* (Hamden, Conn.: Archon Books, 1963), pp. 243–245, 414–417. First published in 1927.

[6] *Ibid.,* p. 415.

[7]*Ibid.*, pp. 272–276. Poynter, *Society and Pauperism,* p. 15.

[8]Karl Polanyi, *The Great Transformation* (New York: Rinehart, 1944), pp. 77–85.

[9]J. D. Marshall, *The Old Poor Law, 1795–1834* (London: Macmillan, 1968), p. 25.

[10]Poynter, *Society and Pauperism,* p. 318.

[11]Mencher, *Poor Law to Poverty Program,* pp. 93–94.

[12]Benjamin Disraeli, in de Schweinitz, *England's Road to Social Security,* p. 124.

[13]Mencher, *Poor Law to Poverty Program,* pp. 119, 213.

[14]*Ibid.*, pp. 213, 227.

[15]*The Poor Law Report of 1834,* ed. and intro. S. G. Checkland and E. O. A. Checkland (Harmondsworth, England: Penguin Books, 1974), p. 21.

[16]Derek Fraser, *The Evolution of the British Welfare State* (New York: Barnes & Noble, 1973), pp. 45–50.

[17]Norman Longmate, *The Workhouse* (New York: St. Martin's Press, 1974), p. 263.

[18]*Ibid.*, pp. 276ff; Maurice Bruce, *The Coming of the Welfare State* (London: B. T. Batsford, 1961), p. 180.

[19]Bruce, *Coming of the Welfare State,* pp. 225–226.

[20]Josephine Chapin Brown, *Public Relief, 1929–1939* (New York: Henry Holt, 1940), p. 9.

[21]The discussion of indoor relief in the United States is drawn from David Rothman, *Discovery of the Asylum* (Boston: Little, Brown, 1971), except as otherwise indicated.

[22]*Ibid.*, p. 164.

[23]Benjamin J. Klebaner, "Poverty and Its Relief in American Thought, 1815–61," *Social Service Review,* Vol. 38, No. 4 (December 1964), pp. 382–399; Rothman, *Discovery of the Asylum,* pp. 165ff.

[24]Alexander Johnson, *The Almshouse* (New York: Russell Sage Foundation, 1911), p. 8.

[25]Rothman, *Discovery of the Asylum,* p. 210.

[26]David M. Schneider and Albert Deutsch, *The History of Public Welfare in New York State, 1867–1940* (Chicago: University of Chicago Press, 1941), p. 60.

[27]*Ibid.*, pp. 72–77.

[28]*Ibid.*, p. 105.

[29]Brown, *Public Relief,* pp. 40ff; Trattner, *From Poor Law To Welfare State* (New York: Free Press, 1974), p. 82.

[30]Arthur P. Miles, *An Introduction to Public Welfare* (Boston: D. C. Heath, 1949), p. 191.

[31]*Ibid.*, pp. 202–205; Schneider and Deutsch, *History of Public Welfare,* p. 189.

[32]Miles, *Introduction to Public Welfare,* p. 198.

[33]Brown, *Public Relief,* pp. 64–65.

[34]*Ibid.*, p. 63.

[35]Albert U. Romasco, *The Poverty of Abundance—Hoover, the Nation, the Depression* (New York: Oxford University Press, 1965), p. 147.

[36]*Ibid.*, p. 148.

[37]Arthur S. Link, with the collaboration of William B. Catton, *American Epoch—A History of the United States Since the 1890s,* Vol. II, 3rd ed. (New York: Knopf, 1967), pp. 377–383; Brown, *Public Relief,* pp. 69–71.

[38]Franklin D. Roosevelt, in Link, *American Epoch,* p. 385.

[39]*Ibid.*, p. 403.

[40]*Ibid.*, p. 412.

[41]Brown, *Public Relief,* p. 328.

[42]Joel Handler, *Reforming the Poor* (New York: Basic Books, 1972), pp. 22–24.

[43]Harry L. Hopkins, in Brown, *Public Relief,* p. 396.

[44]Journalist Richard M. Elman offers examples of the many indignities inflicted upon appli-

cants for public assistance in *The Poorhouse State—The American Way of Life on Public Assistance* (New York: Pantheon, 1966).

[45]Dorothy K. Newman et al., *Protest, Politics, and Prosperity—Black Americans and White Institutions, 1940–1975* (New York: Pantheon, 1978), Table 7-15, p. 280; Gilbert Y. Steiner, *Social Insecurity: The Politics of Welfare* (Chicago: Rand McNally, 1966), p. 31.

[46]Frank Freidel, *America in the Twentieth Century*, 3rd ed. (New York: Knopf, 1970), p. 523.

[47]Newman et al., *Protest, Politics, Prosperity*, pp. 260–262.

[48]*Ibid.*

[49]Harry M. Caudill, *Night Comes to the Cumberlands* (Boston: Little, Brown, 1963), p. 273.

[50]Gilbert Y. Steiner, *The State of Welfare* (Washington, D.C.: Brookings Institution, 1971), p. 35.

[51]Joel F. Handler, *Reforming the Poor*, pp. 48–51.

[52]In Steiner, *State of Welfare*, p. 37; Handler, *Reforming the Poor*, p. 55.

[53]Steiner, *State of Welfare*, pp. 37–40. See also James Leiby, *A History of Social Welfare and Social Work in the United States* (New York: Columbia University Press, 1978), pp. 303–304, 328–330. A detailed account of the 1962 amendment is given in Steiner, *Social Insecurity*, Chapters 1–3.

[54]Steiner, *State of Welfare*, pp. 199–200.

[55]*Ibid.*, p. 216.

[56]*Ibid.*, pp. 215–225. See also Sar A. Levitan, *Programs in Aid of the Poor for the 1970's* (Baltimore: Johns Hopkins Press, 1969), p. 99.

[57]Harrell R. Rodgers, Jr., *Poverty amid Plenty* (Reading, Mass.: Addison-Wesley, 1979), p. 103.

[58]*Ibid.*, pp. 103–108.

[59]*Ibid.*, p. 106.

[60]Levitan, *Programs in Aid of the Poor*, p. 58.

[61]Sar A. Levitan, *The Great Society's Poor Law* (Baltimore: Johns Hopkins Press, 1969), p. 273.

[62]Gilbert Y. Steiner, "Reform Follows Reality: The Growth of Welfare," in Eli Ginzberg and Robert M. Solow, eds., *The Great Society* (New York: Basic Books, 1974), pp. 60–62.

[63]*Ibid.*, p. 48.

[64]Rodgers, *Poverty amid Plenty*, p. 95.

[65]Lawrence Podell, in Steiner, *State of Welfare*, p. 87.

[66]The discussion of family allowances is based primarily on James C. Vadakin, *Children, Poverty and Family Allowances* (New York: Basic Books, 1968).

[67]Advisory Council on Public Welfare, *"Having the Power, We Have the Duty,"* Report to the Secretary of Health, Education, and Welfare, in Theodore R. Marmor, ed., *Poverty Policy* (Chicago: Aldine-Atherton, 1971), p. 58.

[68]The 1962 and 1967 figures are from Steiner, *State of Welfare*, pp. 40–41; the 1976 figure is from Rodgers, *Poverty amid Plenty*, p. 94.

[69]Readers who are interested in how government officials get welfare reform ideas proposed can find three somewhat different accounts of how the Nixon plan was fought out in Martin Anderson, *Welfare* (Stanford, Calif.: Hoover Institution Press of Stanford University, 1978); Vincent J. Burke and Vee Burke, *Nixon's Good Deed* (New York: Columbia University Press, 1974); and Daniel P. Moynihan, *The Politics of a Guaranteed Income* (New York: Random House, 1973).

[70]"Transcript of Nixon's Address to Nation Outlining Proposals for Welfare Reform," *New York Times*, August 9, 1969, p. 10; "Nixon Administration's Welfare Reform: The Family Assistance Plan," in Marmor, *Poverty Policy*, pp. 77–87.

[71]Burke and Burke, *Nixon's Good Deed*, p. 112.

[72]"Carter, Congress and Welfare: A Long Road," *1977 CQ Almanac* (Washington, D.C.: Congressional Quarterly, 1978), pp. 471–478.

[73]*Ibid.,* p. 471.

[74]President Carter's special message on Welfare Reform, *U.S. Code Congressional and Administrative News,* No. 5, July 1979.

[75]The uncertainty over whether they ever had a chance of passage was reflected in two newspaper accounts published only two weeks apart in the same newspaper: David E. Rosenbaum, "Congress Hasn't the Will to Update Social Policy," *New York Times,* October 21, 1979, p. E5; and Steven V. Roberts, "Modest Welfare Reforms Given a Chance This Time," *New York Times,* November 4, 1979, p. E3.

[76]*U.S. Code Congressional and Administrative News,* No. 5, July 1979, pp. 1026–1028.

[77]Anderson, *Welfare,* pp. 133–135.

[78]Sheldon Danziger and Robert Plotnick, "Can Welfare Reform Eliminate Poverty?" *Social Service Review* (June 1979), pp. 244–260.

VARIETIES OF SOCIAL WELFARE INSTITUTIONS
Public Welfare

Allowance system (also called rate-in-aid-of-wages or Speenhamland system)
Apprenticeship
Asylums (indoor Relief)
    Almshouse (or poorhouse)
    Insane asylum
    Orphan asylum
Categorical assistance
    Aid to the blind (AB)
    Aid to families with dependent children (AFDC and AFDC-UP)
    Aid to the permanently and totally disabled (APTD)
    Old-age assistance (OAA)
Dole (outdoor relief)
House of Correction (Bridewell)
House of Refuge (reformatory)
New Deal Agencies
    Civilian Conservation Corps (CCC)
    Civil Works Administration (CWA)
    Federal Emergency Relief Administration (FERA)
    National Youth Administration (NYA)
    Works Progress Administration (WPA)
Parish responsibility (poor rate, overseers of the poor, and churchwardens)
Pauper auctions
Poorhouse
Public housing
Regulated begging
War on Poverty (Great Society) agencies
    Job Corps
    Neighborhood Youth Corps (NYC)
    Work Incentive Program (WIN)
Workhouse

Diverse Goals of Public Welfare Programs

Deterrence from dependency
Rehabilitation
Relief
Work

Significant Figures in Public Welfare

Government heads

King Edward III (reign, 1327–1377)—Curtailed charity; used powers of government to
    try to separate "deserving" from "undeserving" poor

King Henry VIII (reign, 1509–1547)—Made the church parish a unit of government and
    made parishes responsible for supporting their own poor; also licensed aged and
    impotent beggars

Queen Elizabeth I (reign, 1558–1603)—Daughter of Henry VIII; introduced first system
    of taxes to raise money for support of the poor, as part of a comprehensive Poor Law

President Franklin D. Roosevelt (1933–1945)—First president to say that federal govern-
    ment was responsible for relief of poverty and for employing the unemployed

President Lyndon B. Johnson (1963–1969)—Announced a "total war on poverty" as duty
    and responsibility of federal government

Influential thinkers

Charles Loring Brace—Nineteenth-century reformer who promoted foster-home place-
    ment instead of institutional asylums for dependent children

John Calvin—One of major founders of Protestantism whose teachings led to a new
    dominant conception of work as an obligation to God

Dorothea Dix—Nineteenth-century reformer who advocated federal government re-
    sponsibility in public welfare, an idea that was rejected until the New Deal

John Locke—Late seventeenth-century philosopher whose concept of the individual's
    "natural right" to own property helped lay the basis for individualism

Mercantilists—Sixteenth- and seventeenth-century businessmen who, before economics
    became a separate profession, wrote pamphlets on economic problems and recom-
    mended workhouses as the solution to the problem of the unemployed able-bodied
    poor, and whose disciplined and systematic pursuit of profit led them to emphasize
    the importance of dependable, steady work

Adam Smith—Eighteenth-century philosopher, considered the founder of the field of
    economics, whose concept of the free market led to further development of the ideas
    of individualism and the limitation of government regulation of economic affairs

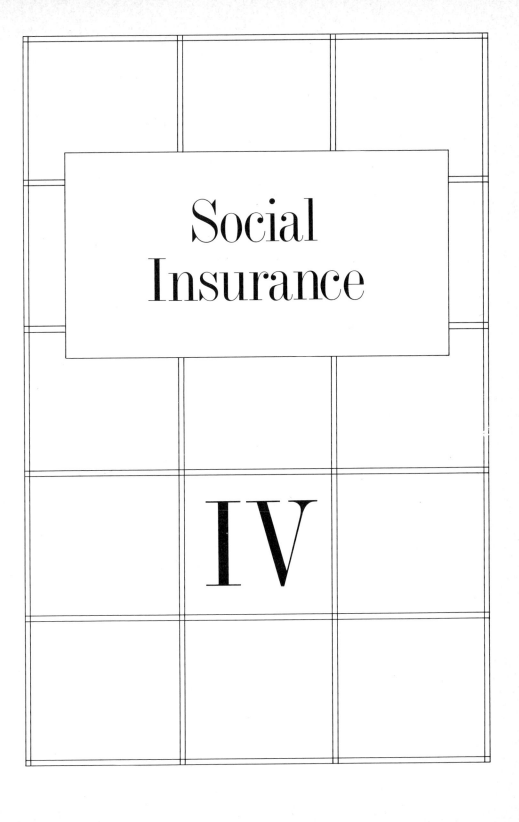

Social Insurance

IV

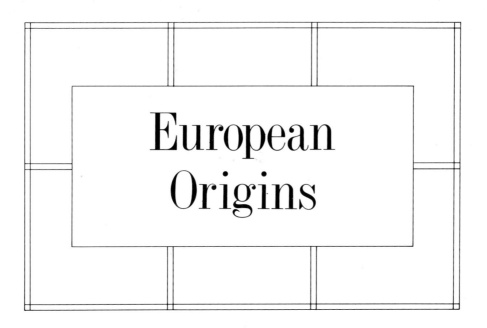

European Origins

7

Charity and public welfare, the two major ideas that for centuries had guided efforts to keep the poor from starving and from rebelling against the prevailing social order, had two major limitations that became important in the nineteenth century and even more so in the twentieth. First, charity and public welfare were both unpredictable. The benefits from charity fluctuated according to people's ability and willingness to give, which might have little correspondence to other people's needs. The benefits of public welfare also fluctuated not only in the amount but also in the form they took—for example, indoor relief at one time, outdoor relief at another. Second, both charity and public welfare were stigmatizing; they deprived the recipients of the honor and dignity enjoyed by other members of society.

In the nineteenth century, pressures began building for greater certainty of assistance in time of need, assistance based on a principle of entitlement to predictable benefits. The predictability would reduce insecurity; the principle of entitlement would lend dignity to the receipt of income because the income would be owed rather than given as a favor, and it would be provided without subjecting recipients to a character evaluation and without attempting to deter them from seeking the income. The concept that developed came to be known as social insurance.

Social insurance has taken many forms and been known by different names. *Social security* is the term used in the United States for the system that provides income in old age to retired people, to workers who become totally disabled before reaching retirement age, and to surviving family members of workers who die before reaching retirement. Workers who are temporarily unemployed receive another form of social insurance known as *unemployment compensation*. Injuries received on the job entitle a worker to payments known as *workmen's compensation*. Most industrialized countries (except the United States) have some form of nationally sponsored medical insurance program that pays at least part of the medical costs of *all* citizens; the United States has such programs only for the poor (Medicaid) and for the elderly (Medicare).

THE CONCEPT OF INSURANCE

Social insurance is modeled on private or voluntary insurance. Private insurance originated in the ancient world to protect people against losses of income due to shipwreck, and it has evolved to protect against many varieties of loss, such as loss of property by fire or theft, and loss of income by death. Private insurance is based on certain key concepts: (1) *peril* or *hazard*—the source of a loss (fire, death from illness, death from accident), (2) *risk*—the chance of loss (the risk of being killed by lightning, for example, is far lower than the risk of being killed in battle during a war), and (3) sharing or *pooling risk* by advance payment into a common fund.

Insurance is provided by private businesses organized for that purpose. An insurance company may decide that it will insure against certain perils (for example, some companies specialize in hazards to life and sell life insurance, others may specialize in hazards to property and sell property insurance). By using specialized methods of applied mathematics (known as actuarial methods), insurance companies can calculate the chances that particular hazards will occur. On the basis of these risk calculations, the companies can decide on the premium (the charge) for protection against loss from each particular hazard. The premium for insurance against loss of a house by fire is larger for one built of wood than for one built of brick, since the risk of fire is greater for a wooden house.

Private insurance is based on the voluntary, individual purchase of an insurance contract. (Today there are group insurance policies also, but this type of insurance is not relevant to the current discussion.) A man insures his house against loss by fire in order to protect the money he has invested in it. The size of the premium he pays depends upon how much he insures it for, the material it is built of, and various other factors that affect the size of the risk. Or a woman purchases life insurance to protect her family against the loss of income that would result from her death. An important feature of private insurance is that once the terms of the insurance policy (the contract between company and purchaser) are agreed to by the insurance company and the purchaser, the policy is in effect as soon as the purchaser pays the first premium. Thus, if a life insurance policy specifies that the purchaser is to pay a premium of $500 a year for the rest of his life, in exchange for which the company will pay $20,000 to his survivors when he dies, the company must pay the proceeds—the full $20,000 —if the man dies the day after he pays his first premium. (However, most policies specify that the proceeds are payable in the case of suicide only if the suicide occurs after the policy has been in effect for at least two years.)

Social insurance differs from private insurance in three important ways that concern us here. First, private insurance companies can insure against many kinds of perils, depending to a large extent on their wish, and individuals can decide which perils they want to buy insurance against. Lloyds of London is a company that is famous for its willingness to insure against many kinds of perils that other companies will not insure against. For example, a highly paid singer can insure her voice against loss of its commercial value. Social insurance in any country at any given time insures only against certain specified perils. And the creation of social insurance for each of those perils has been accomplished only through great political struggles, struggles which continue even while this book is being written and will continue long after it is in print. In the sections that follow, we shall attempt to clarify the nature of those struggles. A second difference between private insurance and social insurance is that benefits in social insurance tend to be proportional to payments made, so that a single payment does not elicit a large benefit, such as is possible under private insurance. Third, benefits in social insurance often do not fully reflect payments made (an aspect of social insurance that will be explained in Chapter 8.) The fact that the principles of social insurance do not strictly follow principles of private insurance in figuring benefits is a source of controversy.

As the nineteenth century wore on, industrialization resulted in many people being thrown out of work, due to the ups and downs of business. People recognized that this unemployment resulted not from character defects in the workers but from outside economic forces. The old laissez-faire ideas did not explain the situation of these individuals, and they refused to submit to the indignities of the Poor Law.

The developers of social insurance were aware that the public assistance concept expressed in the Poor Law was no longer acceptable. Social insurance created a new relationship between the state and its citizens: In place of the grudging aid and the punishing and deterrent practices of the Poor Law, it offered protection on the basis of citizenship. Under certain conditions of loss of income, citizens became entitled to have at least a portion of their income maintained by the state as guarantor of its citizens' well-being. With social insurance, the laissez-faire concept of self-interest and individual responsibility was partially replaced by the concept of membership in society entitling those who suffer losses due to events beyond their control to the protection of that society.

The concept of social insurance did not take hold easily nor all at once. The first social insurance programs went into effect in Germany in the 1880s. Other countries soon followed, with Great Britain adopting some social insurance programs shortly before the beginning of World War I. In the United States, as mentioned in Chapter 6, the concept of social insurance was accepted at the national level only in 1935, under the stresses of the Great Depression.

The experiences of the British during World War II led to the emergence, toward the end of the war in 1945, of the concept of the "welfare state," in which all citizens are assured an income and services such as education, health care, housing, and social service counseling—essentially an enlargement of the social insurance concept in that more services are considered necessary to a citizen's well-being and are provided by the state. It has been debated both whether any society actually deserves to be called a welfare state, and whether a welfare state, if it exists, is good or bad for its citizens. Sweden, it is generally agreed, more closely approaches such a state than any other country.

The concept of social insurance in the form of a guaranteed minimum annual income for every citizen, whether needed or not, has not yet gained acceptance. Whether and when this will happen remain to be seen; the issues involved will be discussed later in this chapter. The more immediate task is to understand the issues involved in the emergence of social insurance as a concept. And for this, a brief review of the social consequences of the Industrial Revolution and a discussion of the development of the concept of citizenship will be useful.

THE NEW SOCIAL CLASSES

Social insurance developed as a response to the recognition that industrialization was changing society. The changes began in Great Britain, the first country to become industrialized. The growth of business and industry created two significant new segments in society, a middle class of business men and an industrial working class. For this new middle class:

> The ideal of an individualist society, a private family unit supplying all its material and moral needs on the basis of a private business suited them, because they were

men who no longer needed traditions. Their efforts had raised them out of the rut. They [the efforts] were in a sense their own reward, the content of life, and if that was not enough, there was always the money, the comfortable house increasingly removed from the smoke of mill and counting-house, the devoted and modest wife, the family circle, the enjoyment of travel, art, science and literature. They were successful and respected. . . . Only the nightmare shadow of bankruptcy or debt sometimes lay over their lives, and we can still recognize it in the novels of the period: the trust in an unreliable partner, the commercial crisis, the loss of middle-class comfort, the womenfolk reduced to genteel penury, perhaps even emigration to the dustbin of the unwanted and the unsuccessful, the colonies.[1]

While the emerging middle class benefited substantially from industrialization, the working class did not. The rural way of life of the new working class families was destroyed, and their lives otherwise disrupted, as they moved from agricultural areas to increasingly congested cities and manufacturing districts. The allowance system, which had supplemented rural workers' wages from local taxes, did not carry over into the industrial setting. In the new situation, workers had only their wages to support themselves and their families whether or not these wages were sufficient—and they usually were not. One consequence of this was that wives and children also worked in the factories. All family members had also worked in the preindustrial period, but they had worked together on the family's own modest plot of land and supplemented their farming income with handicraft work done at home. Although the work was hard, the pace was more leisurely and more under the family's own control. Local custom allowed various work interruptions. In contrast, factory work required strict punctuality and submission to someone else's rules. Machines were set to run at a certain pace, and machine operators had to adjust to it. The difficulty in getting workers to accept the rigid work discipline led to the passage of laws that permitted the jailing of workers who violated their work contract, which, in theory, they had freely agreed to (but imposed only fines on employers who did so).

For the new industrial workers, there was a fundamental conflict between their traditional view of gaining a livelihood and the business class's view, which was being forced upon them:

> The traditional view, which still survived in a distorted way in all classes of rural society and in the internal relations of working-class groups, was that a man had a right to earn a living, and if unable to do so, a right to be kept alive by his community. The view of middle-class liberal economists was that men must take such jobs as the market offered, wherever and at whatever rate it offered, and that the rational man would, by individual or voluntary collective saving and insurance make provision for accident, illness and old age.[2]

A very significant impact of industrialization was that many traditional skills became obsolete. The manual skills necessary for, say, making a chair or a pair of shoes became useless with the introduction of machines that could be run by unskilled or semiskilled operatives and that could rapidly produce many chairs or pairs of shoes that could be sold more cheaply than the handmade items. As industrialization progressed, more and more manual skills were replaced by machines; independent craftsmen, owning their tools and making their products by hand, were replaced by the factory system, in which low-paid wage earners worked at machines that each accomplished only one operation in the manufacture of a product, machines owned not by the worker but by the industrialist. Industrial workers, and sympathetic observers, perceived industrialization as destructive and dehumanizing, robbing workers of their human dignity and subjecting them to the impersonal requirements of the machine and the arbitrary authority of industrial capitalists.

Scholars of the Industrial Revolution argue that the negative effects have been overemphasized and give an incomplete picture. Whether or not this is so, the fact remains that the negative effects were widely perceived and that reactions to them led, eventually, to the development of social insurance.

Throughout the nineteenth century, workers expressed their dissatisfactions in various ways—in rebellions, in organizing trade unions, in agitating for political change that would accord them a say in regulating work activities and a larger measure of protection against industrial ups and downs. An important new set of ideas was introduced by Karl Marx in his theories of revolutionary socialism, which called for and predicted workers' revolutions that would result in the transfer of political and economic power from capitalists to workers. In 1848, a number of revolutions did break out—in France, Germany, Switzerland, and elsewhere. The revolutions were all unsuccessful, but they generated a widespread concern in Europe (a concern that spread to the United States a generation or so later) about the dangers to existing governments of working-class radicalism. Social insurance, when eventually adopted, partly in response to rising discontent, conferred new rights upon workers, and these rights were founded upon an enlarged conception of citizenship.

THE DEVELOPING CONCEPT
OF CITIZENSHIP

In Chapter 1, the following question was posed: On what basis does anyone deserve anything from society? The answers to this question vary from one society to another, and from one historical period to another. Here is a quick sketch of a developmental sequence of answers to this question in Western society: In the period after the fall of the Roman Empire, people deserved what they could take by force. As feudalism developed, the most powerful people continued to be entitled to what they could take and hold by force; less powerful people were entitled to what they were given by the more powerful in exchange for services to them. Rights of entitlement were also regarded as hereditary, but kings often disregarded customary rights and took what they wanted. In response to their arbitrariness, limitations were placed on the power of rulers. Rights of citizenship began to be proclaimed.

The rights of citizenship developed gradually in modern Western society (and here the focus is on England, the earliest society to develop these rights). Sociologist T. H. Marshall has classified the rights of citizenship into three types: civil rights, political rights, and social rights. *Civil rights* are those that are basic to individual freedom: freedom from arbitrary arrest; freedom of thought, speech, and religion; the right to own property; and the right to enter into contracts. These rights gained acceptance during the eighteenth century as part of the larger process that established individualism and laissez-faire as dominant ideas in society. A crucial and even earlier link in the chain of development of the rights of citizenship was the abolition of hereditary servile status (serfdom), which had lingered after feudal times into Elizabeth's time, when it was abolished. People became free to work wherever they could get work, and they were entitled to receive a wage in exchange for their work.[3] (It must be noted, however, that the Law of Settlement and Removal hampered this right by restricting freedom of movement.)

Political rights are rights to participate in the exercise of political power, either as a member of a decision-making body such as Parliament or any legislature, or as a voter in political elections. The expanding middle class gained increased political rights from the Reform Bill of 1832, which shifted some of the voting power from the rural aristocracy to the growing numbers of urban businessmen. The bill, however, included a financial qualification for voting. Wage earners were thus largely excluded until their political activity generated enough pressure to produce the Reform Bill of 1867 and the Reform Bill of 1884, which removed all financial qualifications for voting. All men (but not yet women) thus had the right to vote.

The *social rights* of citizenship range from the right to a moderate amount of economic welfare and security to "the right to share to the full in the social heritage and to live the life of a civilized being according to the standards prevailing in the society."[4] Social rights derived originally from membership in a local community; the serf had a right to basic economic welfare and security. The Speenhamland system of the late eighteenth century also sought to assure a basic level of support. The New Poor Law of 1834 attacked those traditional social rights.

> [It] treated the claims of the poor, not as an integral part of the rights of the citizen,
> but as an alternative to them—as claims which could be met only if the claimants

ceased to be citizens in any true sense of the word. For paupers forfeited in practice the civil right of personal liberty, by internment in the workhouse, and they forfeited by law any political rights they might possess. This disability of defranchisement remained in being until 1918. . . . The stigma which clung to poor relief expressed the deep feelings of a people who understood that those who accepted relief must cross the road that separated the community of citizens from the outcast company of the destitute.[5]

The introduction in the nineteenth century of free, compulsory education for children was a step toward reestablishing the social rights of citizenship:

The right to education is a genuine social right of citizenship, because the aim of education during childhood is to shape the future adult. Fundamentally it should be regarded, not as the right of the child to go to school, but as the right of the adult citizen to have been educated.[6]

Social rights differ from civil and political rights in an important respect. Civil and political rights are bestowed on citizens through the restraint of government. Governments grant civil and political rights when they agree (or are compelled) to not interfere in the lives of citizens who are pursuing their own interests. As T. H. Marshall has noted:

. . . civil rights . . . confer the legal capacity to strive for the things one would like to possess but do not guarantee the possession of any of them. A property right is not a right to possess property, but a right to acquire it, if you can, and to protect it, if you can get it. But if you use these arguments to explain to a pauper that his property rights are the same as those of a millionaire, he will probably accuse you of quibbling.[7]

Civil rights, in short, protect people from arbitrary actions of their own government. The government—or some greedy ruler—is restrained from taking property away from its lawful owner, as used to happen before property rights were securely established. All those who enjoy full civil rights are *legally* equal; someone born in an impoverished family has as much legal right as anyone else to own lawfully acquired property. But the legal equality of a pauper and a millionaire may not have much practical economic value for the pauper whose income is scarcely enough to live on. Social rights, in contrast, involve providing something, assuring citizens that they will receive support from the government when they need it. The development of social rights—in the form of social insurance—obviously meant moving away from the strict individualism that dominated thinking in early nineteenth-century England (and the United States) and that led to the New Poor Law. A series of developments throughout the nineteenth century prepared the way for the eventual acceptance of the concept of social insurance.

THE MODIFICATION OF
THE DOCTRINE OF
LAISSEZ-FAIRE

The absolute individualism of the laissez-faire doctrine, which holds that people have the right to pursue their own interests with minimal interference from government and that people are entirely responsible for their situations, was modified in England in the nineteenth century by three significant developments: (1) the factory acts, (2) the development of public health programs, and (3) the beginning of large-scale social research. All of these helped to prepare the way for a new understanding of poverty and for new measures for dealing with it that led eventually to the overthrow of the workhouse concept and to the movement toward social insurance. These modifications ultimately affected the United States as well.

The Factory Acts

Before the Industrial Revolution, young children worked on farms and as apprentices to craftsmen. Furthermore, children were long abused by their employers; we have noted the abuses that occurred when apprenticeship was used as a subterfuge by parish authorities enforcing the Law of Settlement and Removal. But the working conditions brought on by industrialization stimulated a sense of outrage that led to government protection of working children. The first major factory act, limiting the hours of child labor in factories, was passed in 1833.

The factory system altered the working conditions of children in at least three important ways. First, children were concentrated in one place. Abuses that could be hidden when children worked in small numbers in countless scattered homes and workshops of their masters could not be overlooked when large numbers of children were assembled in factory buildings whose size, smoke, and noise dominated their localities. Second, factory discipline was extremely severe. Children as young as eight years old were obliged to work twelve and fourteen hours a day. Foremen beat children with straps, partly to keep them awake at their machines. Third, the factories were dangerous. Moving machinery parts were unshielded, and many children were maimed in accidents that occurred while they were working. In addition, factories and mines (in which children also worked) proved morally corrupting, as children were drawn into licentious activity of adult co-workers.

Outraged by these conditions, various groups of people in England coalesced into a reform movement to get Parliament to pass a law making it illegal for children below the age of ten to work more than ten hours a day. One of the many arguments offered in opposition to such a step was that it would reduce the income of working-class families who needed all the income they could obtain just to avoid starvation. After several years of building political support, the reformers' cause was won with the passage of the Factory Act of 1833, which (1) forbade the employment of children below the age of nine in all textile mills except those making silk and lace, (2) set a maximum of an eight-hour workday for children between the ages of nine and thirteen, (3) set a maximum of a twelve-hour workday for children between the ages of thirteen and eighteen, (4) required that two hours per day be set aside for education, and (5) provided for four factory inspectors to enforce the act. In including these provisions, the authors of the act acknowledged that children could not protect themselves and that therefore the concept of free workers negotiating on their own for the best possible terms of employment was not applicable to children. The state, therefore, had a right to intervene in their behalf. This departure from the principle of laissez-faire was achieved only after a hard fight.[8]

The battle was fought all over again in the United States about eighty-five years later. Although some states had adopted child labor laws near the end of the nineteenth century, it was not until 1938, during the New Deal, that an effective national law, the Fair Labor Standards Act, was passed. Even today, however, not all children are protected by legislation, much less by effective implementation of the laws that do exist. Child labor on farms continues to be unregulated, and many (some estimate as many as three hundred thousand) do farm work that requires them to stoop and crawl in the heat for ten hours per day.[9]

The Concept of Public Health

Industrialization drew people from the countryside into the new industrial cities, which became congested as people crowded into dark, ramshackle, closely built housing. Water supply and sewerage were inadequate. In many cities, the nearby river served both as a source of drinking water and as a sewer. Epidemics were frequent; death rates in urban areas were higher than in rural areas.

Over a period of about sixty years—from the 1770s to the 1830s—British doctors began to develop the idea that environmental conditions contribute to disease. In 1839, the government ordered an investigation of the sanitary conditions in working-class housing areas. Edwin Chadwick, an author of the *Poor*

Law Commission Report of 1834 who had since been serving as secretary to the Poor Law Commission that administered the New Poor Law, directed the investigation. Chadwick's "Report on the Sanitary Condition of the Labouring Population of Great Britain," published in 1842, made a strong case that inadequate sewerage and water supply, as well as unsanitary housing, were related to disease, high death rates, and shortened life expectancy.

Nevertheless, there was strong opposition to taking public action to remedy these conditions. Important among the grounds for opposition was property owners' resistance to being taxed to pay for sewer pipelines and water pipelines that would benefit the working class. They paid for a private water supply and for their own sanitary needs; they did not want to be taxed to pay for the sanitary needs of others. In addition, regulations to enforce the installation of sewerage were seen by many as an unacceptable interference with property rights. Further, there were companies that supplied water to those who could pay for it, and their businesses would be hurt by the introduction of a publicly financed water supply.

Despite opposition, the concept of public health—government action to prevent disease—slowly took hold. Individual cities built public water supply and sewage systems. A national law was passed in 1848, but because of continuing opposition, it was a permissive rather than a mandatory law. That is, in cities in which the death rate from all causes was below twenty-three per thousand, local health boards could choose whether or not to undertake sanitary reforms; in cities where the death rate was higher, local boards were required to take action.[10]

The adoption of a permissive law rather than a mandatory one has been a frequent occurrence in the history of social welfare. Such a law often represents a compromise between strong advocates and equally strong opponents of a particular course of action. It has the effect of slowing the pace of social change. Even when a principle, policy, or practice has outlived its usefulness for the majority, there are always traditionalists who oppose its change. When such a change is unavoidable, perhaps because even the traditionalists see that it has merit, or because its proponents are simply too strong, the traditionalists eventually concede to the new measures, but if they still retain some political strength, they often seek to modify or "water down" the new measures and to arrive at some kind of compromise. The first factory act, which regulated children's working hours, was in fact just such a watering down. At the time, efforts were also being made to limit the working hours of adult males. Limiting children's hours was a compromise, a partial response to the reform efforts then being made. Laws limiting the hours an employer could require adult males to work were not passed until much later.

Similarly, the permissive public health law in Great Britain represented a compromise between those who wanted countrywide, government-enforced sanitary standards and those who opposed a strong central government that could impose and enforce nationwide standards. Thus the public health law of

1848 was a compromise, but it was nevertheless a step away from pure individualism and toward collective responsibility for social welfare. The spread of disease was not understandable in terms of individualism; it had to be thought of as affecting collectivities of people. Whereas Chadwick's individualist ideas put forth in the Poor Law of 1834 had been in tune with wide popular sentiment at the time, his public health ideas in 1842 were radical and original. He had learned a great deal about the impact of disease on poverty; he had seen that disease could lead to poverty by leaving men too sick to work or by killing them, leaving their widows and children to be supported. He regarded sanitation measures as making economic sense: Prevention of disease would reduce the costs of supporting people whose poverty was a consequence of disease. By 1872, after Chadwick was gone, thinking moved in the direction he had advocated, and Great Britain passed a mandatory public health law; local authorities in all parts of the country had to take measures to provide sanitation.[11]

American efforts to establish and implement the concept of public health gained strength only after the Civil War ended, in 1865. Opposition to the concept was similar to that in Great Britain: People did not want to pay higher taxes and they were resistant to interference with private property. However, when the germ theory of disease was discovered in the late nineteenth century, people's new understanding of contagion facilitated acceptance of the concept of public health. And by the beginning of the twentieth century, individualist arguments against public health had lost some of their influence.[12] The U.S. government established a Public Health Service; the individual states and localities began to establish health departments.

But while the concept of public health has gained acceptance, and organizations for implementing this concept have become well established, the potential scope of the concept remains a controversial issue. For example, as new industrial processes are developed, new forms of environmental pollution are produced, and the right of the government to take action continues to be weighed against the rights of individuals to make free choices (such as in the widely disputed issue of smoking in public places) or the rights of corporations to conduct their businesses with minimal government interference (as in matters of chemical waste disposal, for example). The right of the U.S. government to protect the health of its citizens is not absolute; it is offset by the constitutional rights of individuals and corporations to carry on their day-to-day activities. The implementation of the concept of public health is a continuously shifting battleground. New knowledge leads to the discovery of new hazards to public health; each hazard must be evaluated, and the size of the risk weighed against the rights that will be abridged if public health measures to reduce the hazard are adopted. The responsibility and right of the state to protect its citizens against diseases caused by microorganisms has been widely recognized and accepted. The responsibility and right of the state to protect its citizens against diseases caused by toxic chemicals has not been fully accepted; it is a conflict on the late twentieth-century battleground between the concept of the state as protector of the public against health hazards and the concept of the free individual and free enterprise.

The Growing Awareness of Poverty

A third development that helped to prepare the way for social insurance in Great Britain was the growth in awareness of poverty. This awareness undermined the belief that individual responsibility caused pauperism. Until the late 1880s, few people had a clear idea of how widespread poverty was. It was widely believed that all hardship could be handled by the Poor Law and by private charity.[13] Although various writers and speakers tried to stimulate greater concern, a fundamental change in public outlook did not come about until the publication of a monumental study conducted by Charles Booth.

Booth was a wealthy businessman who had encountered a report in 1885 by a Marxist group in London that claimed that 25 percent of the working class lived in dire poverty. Convinced that this was erroneous, he set out to learn the facts about working-class life.[14] Using his own money, he hired a group of assistants and launched a detailed investigation that occupied him for seventeen years—from 1886 to 1903. The seventeen-volume report of his work, entitled *The Life and Labour of the People in London,* was the largest-scale project of social science research undertaken up to that date. Although it was begun with the hypothesis that the extent of poverty claimed by the Socialists was exaggerated, Booth did not allow his conservative political views to distort the findings of his study. He was committed to a belief in the value of objective statistics:

> In intensity of feeling and not in statistics lies the power to move the world. But by statistics must this power be guided if it would move the world right.[15]

Booth's study concluded that the 25 percent figure of poverty among the working class was an underestimate and that the correct figure was about 30 percent.

In order to distinguish the poor from the nonpoor, Booth formulated the concept of the "poverty line," an income level that could separate those who earned barely enough to obtain the necessities of life from those who had "regular standard earnings" or better.[16] (The concept of the poverty line gained new prominence in the late 1960s when, in the atmosphere of Lyndon Johnson's War on Poverty in the United States, efforts were renewed to measure poverty with ever greater precision.)

The Charity Organization Society in Britain did not want to believe that Booth's findings applied to the country as a whole; they believed London's distinctive characteristics contributed to the size of the segment living in poverty. Booth's work stimulated another businessman, B. Seebohm Rowntree, a chocolate manufacturer in the north of England, to undertake a study in York, a small northern city. Using slightly different methods, Rowntree concluded that 28 percent of the people of York were living in poverty, a figure that was considered close enough to Booth's to suggest that about a third of the urban population across the nation was living in poverty. The statistical evidence provided by these two businessmen helped create greater receptivity to new approaches to social welfare by the state.[17]

THE BEGINNINGS OF SOCIAL INSURANCE

Although Britain was moving away from the concept of individualism, the change in outlook was slow in coming. And, in fact, social insurance came to Great Britain after being adopted in Germany, the first Western country to initiate such a program. The reasons for this lie partly in some special aspects of German society at the time.

Germany had been a collection of separate states (Prussia, Bavaria, and others) that were united into one country in 1871 under the leadership of the Prussian chancellor Otto von Bismarck, who became chancellor of the new German government. Bismarck was worried about the growing strength of the Socialists, who were gaining support among the German working class. Bismarck's goal was to strengthen the loyalty of the workers to the new German state. In a speech made early in his career in Prussia, he had said: "Factories make a few individuals wealthy . . . but they generate the mass of proletarians, of ill-fed workers whose insecurity of existence makes them dangerous to the state."[18] German industrialization, which had started later than British industrialization, proceeded more rapidly in the nineteenth century and was producing more insecure workers, whom Bismarck saw as a threat to the new German state. He felt he had to strengthen their loyalty by offering them benefits that would reduce the appeal of socialism.

Since the individualistic ideas of liberalism had never taken as firm a hold in Germany as they had in Great Britain, Bismarck's goal was made easier to achieve. People were still accustomed to looking to those of higher status and higher authority for protection; the conservative, landed aristocracy, in turn, continued to accept this paternalistic role, as part of their effort to retain power against the challenge of the rapidly rising industrialists. As a result: "After generations of patriarchal tutelage by the state and social superiors, the German workman was not prepared for the gospel of self-help, whether it was preached by liberals, conservatives, or Christian social reformers."[19] As the political conflicts among the working class, industrialists, and landed aristocracy took shape, there was not much possibility that the German government would tell industrial workers to sink or swim on their own or else face the punishing indignities of the workhouse. The only likely options were revolution, by which the workers would gain control of the state, or a social insurance program that would ease the insecurity of the workers. Social insurance was Bismarck's tool for preserving the traditional political inequality in Germany. He was willing to grant new social rights—in the form of assured income under certain conditions—in order to blunt the demand for new political rights by workers.

As is clear from this discussion, social insurance benefits not only those who may suffer from loss of income. It also benefits those who have the power to decide how to deal with worker unrest. The method chosen for paying for social insurance can also serve those in power as well as those who will make use of the insurance. For example, in regard to compensating workers who lose wages while they are recovering from a job-related injury, Bismarck considered having employers pay the major part of the cost, with workers contributing a portion of the premium from their wages. Further, some of Bismarck's advisors recommended that the premiums be paid to private insurance companies. Bismarck decided against most of these recommendations because he wanted injured employees to look to the state rather than to private institutions for help. However, political opposition to Bismarck's proposals resulted in a compromise: the Accident Insurance Law, passed in 1884, had employers paying a large part of the cost, as well as running the program under the supervision of a government Imperial Insurance Office.

The first social insurance law, passed a year earlier, in 1883, was a health insurance law. Bismarck's approach to this was different from his approach to accident insurance, which he had first tried to get passed in 1881. Many occupational groups, factories, and industrial associations already provided sickness benefits. Bismarck decided to stay with this existing system. His health insurance law provided sickness benefits for workers in industries that did not already have their own plan, and also provided coverage to people who did not fit into established categories. Workers paid two thirds of the premium, employers one third.

The third major piece of German social insurance legislation was enacted in 1889 and provided old-age and invalid insurance. Bismarck saw the provision of old-age pensions as a way of increasing workers' loyalty to the state; the more people drawing such pensions, the more people there would be who would fear losing their pension in the event of a worker revolution. Bismarck's opponents in government succeeded in limiting the state subsidy, with the larger portion of the pensions coming from equal contributions by employers and employees to a government-run fund.

Socialists contended that these social insurance programs were just another form of Poor Law, with one major difference: Workers now had to pay part of the cost instead of the wealthy and well-to-do carrying the whole cost as had formerly been the case. Socialists also argued that benefits financed out of workers' wages could not possibly be adequate to needs. In contrast, the political leaders who succeeded in getting worker contributions made part of the law argued that such contributions were necessary to maintain the worker's sense of self-respect and individual responsibility; they wanted to prevent workers from feeling that they were receiving a gift from the state and from becoming dependent on the state.[20]

The social insurance programs of the Germans provided an example to the British, but not until twenty to twenty-five years later. For decades, there had been growing dissatisfaction with the 1834 Poor Law. Steady and conscientious industrial workers had suffered frequent periods of unemployment as a result of changing business conditions. They shared the middle-class antipathy for pauperism and were not about to let themselves be put into the workhouse. On the other hand, even if the authorities had wanted to strictly enforce the 1834 law, the workhouses could not possibly have accommodated the sudden increases of unemployment; they were not large enough. But the fact is that many officials did not want to enforce it; they could see that involuntary industrial unemployment was a problem that that harsh law could not solve. Evasions of it became widespread. The British government itself began to introduce new ideas to handle various aspects of poverty outside the framework of "less eligibility" and the workhouse "means test." The concept of deterring lazy, drunken paupers from seeking help made no sense when the people in need were steady workers who had been thrown out of work against their will.

Recognizing a long-term threat from socialist ideas taking hold among the working classes, British political leaders borrowed some of Bismarck's ideas. A. J. Balfour, a Conservative party politician who later became prime minister, said in 1895:

> Social legislation, as I conceive it, is not merely to be distinguished from Socialist legislation but it is its most effective antidote. Socialism will never get possession of the great body of public opinion . . . among the working class or any other class if those who wield the collective forces of the community show themselves desirous to ameliorate every legitimate grievance and to put Society upon a proper and more solid basis.[21]

Balfour became prime minister in 1902. He appointed a Royal Commission on the Poor Laws in 1905. The commission of twenty people included business and labor leaders, such as Charles Booth, who wanted to move in new directions, and government officials, such as J. S. Davy, who was in charge of administering the Poor Law, and who wanted a vigorous return to the principles of 1834. The commission remained split, and instead of producing a joint report when it finished its work in 1909, it issued a majority report and a minority report. Partly because of this split and partly because Balfour's Conservative administration had since been replaced by an administration of the Liberals, the opposition party, the government was already at work on new measures that ignored the Poor Law.[22]

In 1908, Parliament passed an old-age pension act, the first major piece of social insurance in Britain. Unlike the German system, the British old-age pensions were noncontributory; they were paid for out of general tax revenues. The pension law provided for payment of a modest five shillings a week to people aged seventy and older whose income was less than eight shillings a week. The size of pensions was determined on the basis of a sliding scale of incomes, with a maximum income above which no pension was paid. Thus pensions were generally tied to need.

But a fundamental organizational aspect of the program gave it special importance. People had to apply for their pensions, but they applied to the Post Office, not to the Poor Law authorities. The government designed the program in this way because it recognized the widespread opposition to the Poor Law. More people applied for pensions than had been anticipated, indicating that there were many poor who had refused to apply for help under the Poor Law. The social legislation of this period, which was just prior to World War I, was "thoroughly permeated by the desire to provide decent treatment and social incentives to the respectable, and to separate them from the residuum,"[23] the drunken, lazy, habitually improvident people who were regarded as beyond hope. And in fact, old-age pensions were denied to people considered drunkards, malingerers, or criminals; this distinction between "deserving" and "undeserving" elderly poor was discarded only in 1919.

Despite the fact that some critics attacked the new pensions as just a new, barely disguised form of outdoor relief, the placing of the administration of the pension program in an ordinary branch of government, the Post Office, which served all the people, instead of in the hands of the Poor Law administrators was a significant factor in endowing pensions with a meaning very different from that of aid under the Poor Law:

> To the grateful recipient, pensions could never be a form of outdoor relief; it was
> a new birthright of an Englishman, a part of his citizenship, not a deprivation of
> it. State pensions paid as of right and financed out of taxation set the Liberals firmly
> on a course which was to involve basic departures in social policy.[24]

The old-age pensions in Great Britain have been referred to here as that country's first program of social insurance. It should be noted that some scholars in the social welfare field consider as social insurance only those benefits that are based at least partly on contributions by, or on behalf of, those who are to benefit. In this terminology, while noncontributory government pensions provide social security (a socially planned income provided as a right), they are not social insurance.

The issue of who pays is obviously significant in any socially planned program for providing income, and the unexpectedly high cost of the British old-age pensions led to changes in the method of paying for new social security measures. The National Insurance Act of 1911, which introduced both health insurance and unemployment compensation, was contributory. The health part of the law provided for compulsory health insurance, supervised by the state, and paid for by specified contributions from employee, employer, and the state into a special fund. When an employee was sick, the fund paid both sick pay and medical expenses. The unemployment part of the law provided for a similar sharing of contributions by employee, employer, and the state. The plan was compulsory for certain specified industries that were particularly subject to business fluctuations; other industries were covered in later years through changes in the law. Great Britain had the first national unemployment insurance law; Germany did not adopt this form of social insurance until 1925; the United States, not until 1935.

SUMMARY

The concept of social insurance took hold slowly in nineteenth-century Europe in response to pressures from the new industrial working class. Social insurance is modeled roughly on the concept of private, voluntary insurance. Voluntary insurance involves the payment of a contractually specified fee or premium in exchange for a specified return if peril insured against should befall the insured person. Social insurance involves the provision by the state of protection against certain perils. Social insurance is usually compulsory for the categories of people who are covered.

Social insurance was first offered in Germany by Bismarck in the 1880s in the hope of generating loyalty of workers to the German state and of lessening their attraction to revolutionary socialism. Programs of health insurance, industrial accident insurance, and pensions for retirees and disabled workers were instituted in the 1880s.

Great Britain followed Germany and introduced social insurance in the early twentieth century. Germany was more favorably disposed than Great Britain to programs of social insurance because Germany had an established tradition of paternalism, whereas in Great Britain individualism and self-reliance had been emphasized. Several developments in the nineteenth century modified the dominant British belief in individualism and the doctrine of laissez-faire. The adoption of legislation limiting child labor in factories, the acceptance of public health measures, and the research studies of poverty by Booth and Rowntree contributed to the idea that much poverty was beyond the control of the individual and that the society had some responsibility for counteracting it. The developing concept of citizenship enlarged the ideas of which benefits people were entitled to from their society; increasing civil, political, and social rights were gained by wider segments of the population. Thus the right to a retirement pension and to insurance against illness and against unemployment became established in Great Britain early in the twentieth century.

Notes

[1]E. J. Hobsbawm, *Industry and Empire—The Pelican Economic History of Britain, Volume 3, from 1750 to the Present Day* (Harmondsworth, England: Penguin Books, 1969), p. 84. This section draws heavily on Chapter 4 of this work.

[2]*Ibid.,* p. 88.

[3]T. H. Marshall, *Class, Citizenship and Social Development* (Garden City, N.Y.: Doubleday Anchor Books, 1965), p. 84.

[4]*Ibid.,* p. 78.

[5]*Ibid.,* p. 88.

[6]*Ibid.,* p. 89.

[7]*Ibid.,* pp. 96–97.

[8]Derek Fraser, *The Evolution of the British Welfare State* (New York: Barnes & Noble, 1973), Chapter 1.

[9]Lela B. Costin, *Child Welfare: Policies and Practices* (New York: McGraw-Hill, 1972), pp. 68–78.

[10]The discussion of public health to this point draws primarily on Fraser, *British Welfare State,* Chapter 3.

[11]*Ibid.*

[12]Walter I. Trattner, *From Poor Law to Welfare State—A History of Social Welfare in America* (New York: Free Press, 1974), Chapter 7.

[13]*Ibid.,* p. 126.

[14]Sidney E. Zimbalist, *Historic Themes and Landmarks in Social Welfare Research* (New York: Harper & Row, 1977), p. 74.

[15]Charles Booth, in Fraser, *British Welfare State,* p. 127.

[16]Zimbalist, *Historic Themes,* p. 78.

[17]Fraser, *British Welfare State,* p. 127.

[18]Otto von Bismarck, in Gaston V. Rimlinger, *Welfare Policy and Industrialization in Europe, America, and Russia* (New York: Wiley, 1971), p. 100.

[19]*Ibid.,* p. 104.

[20]*Ibid.,* Chapter 4.

[21]A. J. Balfour, in Fraser, *British Welfare State,* p. 129.

[22]Michael E. Rose, *The Relief of Poverty, 1834–1914* (London: Macmillan, 1972), pp. 41–48.

[23]J. R. Hay, *The Origin of the Liberal Welfare Reforms, 1906–1914* (London: Macmillan, 1975), pp. 34–35; Fraser, *British Welfare State,* pp. 142–143.

[24]Fraser, *op. cit.,* p. 34.

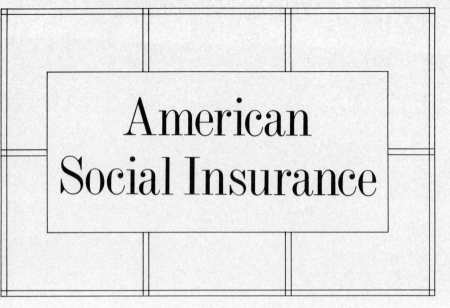

American Social Insurance

8

Although American government officials, at both the state and federal levels, began studying European social insurance programs in the early 1890s, there was little movement toward adopting such programs in the United States until after the turn of the century.[1] The values and beliefs that had developed in the United States made the nation less receptive to the social insurance concept. Individualism in America was stronger than in Great Britain for at least two important reasons. First, the United States had no feudal tradition, a tradition of aristocratic "superiors" being responsible for the wellbeing of people who had a legally recognized status as social inferiors; second, the expansiveness of the American continent made for a more open society and a stronger belief in self-reliance, self-help, and individual achievement. This "colonial and frontier philosophy" emphasized the ability of the ambitious to acquire property sufficient to provide for themselves and their families in bad times as well as good.[2] The American ideas of individual achievement and responsibility also differed from the German emphasis on the duty of the state to protect individuals for reasons of national and public interest, including an open interest in maintaining the existing inequalities of social classes.[3]

There were also economic and organizational differences that slowed American acceptance of social insurance. First, American workers were economically somewhat better off than European workers, even though they too were subject to poor working conditions, periods of unemployment, and low wages. Second, private individual insurance was more fully developed in the United States than in Europe. A third factor was the U.S. system of government. Until the Great Depression that began in 1929, American officials and most of the American people believed that the federal government did not have the power to offer social insurance. If any level of government had such authority, it was the state level, but even the first social insurance laws passed by the states were declared unconstitutional.[4] Eventually, state laws concerning workmen's compensation were held to be constitutional.

In the following sections, a brief account of the major American social insurance programs will be presented, with indications of the issues involved in adopting and developing each type of insurance. It is not possible to provide detailed accounts of these programs, since each represents a specialized area and volumes would be required to present all the details.

WORKMEN'S COMPENSATION

Compensation of workers for injuries received on the job was the first item of social insurance provided in the United States. Workmen's compensation began and remains entirely under the jurisdiction of the state governments, rather than the federal government. States began passing workmen's compensation laws in 1910; all states have such laws now, though they vary considerably from one state to another.

Workmen's compensation insurance developed in the context of increasing numbers of industrial accidents. Until the early twentieth century, accidents were considered to result from employees' own carelessness. An extensive social survey in Pittsburgh in 1906–1907 (modeled on Booth's London survey) included a study of industrial accidents and established that employees were not always to blame for the accidents they suffered. The blame for some accidents could be attributed to supervisors; for others, to the employers; and for others, to the inexperience of new workers. But even this attribution of responsibility needed to be understood in the context of the unrelenting pressure for speed, efficiency, and productivity built into the industrial system. Fatigue and boredom were to be expected from the high levels of noise, the speed of the machinery, the monotony of the tasks to be performed, and the long working hours.[5] Fatigue and boredom increased the risk of accidents.

As state legislatures took account of these conditions, they began to revise the concepts governing compensation of work-related injuries. At the time, injured workers had to sue their employers for compensation; they had to prove that their injuries were not caused by their own carelessness. The laws were heavily weighted in favor of employers, whose defense was that the workers knew the risks of the job when they accepted it.[6] It was eventually recognized by the state legislatures that allowing employers this defense gave them no incentive to improve safety conditions in their plants. Legislatures began to produce laws that replaced the concept of worker responsibility with the concept of "liability without fault." This meant that injured workers (or their families in the event of the workers' deaths) would be compensated without regard to whose fault the accident was. Workers were *entitled* to compensation by virtue of their status as employees. This concept gained acceptance at least in part because employers saw the new approach as a way of lowering their costs of compensation. Many had been buying insurance from private companies against the risk of lawsuits by injured employees, and their insurance costs were rising.[7] Employers anticipated that a standardized schedule of payments for specified types of injury would cost them less than the awards that might be granted to workers whose lawsuits were successful. Social reformers, on the other hand, supported no-fault workmen's compensation laws in the hope that all job injuries would receive adequate compensation; under the existing arrangements, many injured workers received nothing and thus suffered the entire cost of their injuries, on top of suffering the injuries.

The hopes of the reformers have not been fully realized, but workers are more adequately compensated now than before. The following sections summarize the main features of workmen's compensation programs.

Coverage

The first workmen's compensation laws applied only to employees in a few high-risk industries such as mining, railroading, steel making. Gradually more and more industries became covered. Nevertheless, many workers in the United States are still not protected by workmen's compensation laws. Employers who have fewer than a certain specified number of employees are often exempt from complying with the law; thus employees in small firms may not be insured in many states. Certain occupations are not protected by workmen's compensation laws: agriculture and domestic service, most commonly. The trend has been toward amending the laws to include more and more categories of employees, but the principle of universal coverage has not yet been established.[8] In no state are all of the workers covered. In addition, state laws vary, so that employees in the same industry or occupation do not enjoy the same protection in all states.

Benefits

The amount of money paid to an injured worker depends upon the type of injury and the duration of the recovery period (i.e., how long a worker must stay out of work). Payments made in compensation are always lower than regular earned wages. Payments are computed as a percentage of the worker's wages, up to a fixed maximum payment. For example, compensation may be fixed at 60 percent of regular earned wages, up to a maximum payment of $60 per week. Those who earn $100 per week or less will receive compensatory payments of 60 percent of their wages, but those whose weekly earnings exceed $100 will be compensated at a lower rate, because $60, the maximum weekly compensatory payment, would not equal 60 percent of their regular pay. Percentages and maximum payments vary from state to state, and change as laws are amended, but the fact remains that injury requiring an employee to stay out of work invariably results in reduced income, and higher-paid workers experience a greater reduction in income than do lower-paid workers. Some states set limits on the total amount that may be paid or the total number of weeks for which payments can be made. Some states provide for payment for life in cases of total, permanent disability. When injury results in the worker's death, payments to survivors are also calculated as a percentage of the worker's wage, and the benefit period usually has a maximum number of years, often from seven to ten years.[9] All states now provide for medical care payments to injured workers. Some states also provide rehabilitation or retraining programs.

Financing

In all industries covered by workmen's compensation, in all states, virtually the entire cost is borne by employers. Employers pay premiums to private insurance companies or into a state-operated fund for workmen's compensation in order to create a source of money from which compensation will be paid when injuries occur. (In most states, however, the laws allow employers to buy insurance from private insurance companies, but, they are required by law to buy such insurance from one or another company.[10]

Effectiveness

Workmen's compensation provides many workers a measure of protection against the risks of lost income due to injury on the job. These programs do not, however, meet the hopes of the early advocates who wanted a comprehensive government-run program of coverage that would transfer the economic burden of work injury from the injured workers to the society as a whole. As the actual programs operate, workers still bear a high portion of the cost of injury, since they lose a significant portion of their wages and may also have to pay part of the medical costs as well.[11] However, the need to pay workmen's compensation has provided some incentive to employers to improve safety conditions in their plants, since their premiums are often reduced when the number of accidents goes down. Overall, there appears to have been some decrease in accidents since the introduction of workmen's compensation, though many authorities believe the number of accidents would be reduced even further if employers were obliged to pay more adequate benefits than they now pay.[12]

UNEMPLOYMENT COMPENSATION

Before it was possible for the concept of unemployment insurance to develop, it was necessary to change the traditional understanding of the causes of unemployment. In the late nineteenth and early twentieth centuries, businessmen, political leaders, economists, political scientists, and others came to understand that the able-bodied could be out of work through no fault of their own (an idea exemplified in the title of a book by the English economist William Beveridge, published in 1908, called *Unemployment—a Problem of Industry*). The problem thus was due to industry and not to "poor moral character," a viewpoint still being promulgated by the Charity Organization movement and still influential both in England and in the United States. Beveridge's book helped to change official and popular thinking in both countries, and he became one of the most influential figures in the field of social insurance until his death in 1963.

Social welfare ideas are usually closely bound up with the general values of a society. Thus early efforts in the United States to awaken and establish industry's responsibility to its unemployed were aimed at connecting the welfare of workers to the profit motive. The most prominent American idea in the early twentieth century was that employers could stabilize production and sales and thus keep stable their number of employees, instead of discharging them when business was slow. The notion was that instead of unemployment insurance, a plan should be developed for preventing unemployment. One of the provisions of a law passed in Wisconsin in 1932 was seen as encouraging prevention. This law compelled each employer of ten or more workers to put money into a state-operated account—a separate account for each company— until each employer had deposited $75 for each employee. This was a reserve fund for compensating employees who lost their jobs. (Employees had to meet certain qualifications of length of employment and length of residence in the state; and benefits were limited to ten weeks.) As money was paid out, employers would have to contribute to their accounts again to bring the amount back to $75 in reserve for each employee. It was thought that this would prompt employers to spread out the work among their employees so they would not have to let any go.[13]

The Wisconsin plan failed as the Great Depression wore on and employers, like employees, were swept up by events beyond their control. In a failing economy, employers were not able to retain all their employees. The federal government eventually acted by passing the Social Security Act of 1935, which provided an approach to unemployment insurance, to old-age insurance, and (as discussed in Chapter 6) to public assistance.

As noted earlier, the Social Security Act marked the first involvement of the federal government in social welfare on a permanent basis. However, concern that the Supreme Court would rule unconstitutional any national system of unemployment insurance led to the inclusion in the law of an ingenious procedure to prevent such a possibility. The law established a national tax on payrolls; this was constitutional. Employers' payroll taxes could be offset, however, by an amount equal to what they paid into a state unemployment insurance fund—if the state had such an insurance fund. The result was that all the states set up such funds.[14]

Coverage

State plans differ in their coverage, with domestic and agricultural workers often not covered. For many years, employees in firms of fewer than four employees were not covered in many states, but a change in the federal law in 1972 required the plans in all states to cover all employees in business and industry.[15]

Benefits

As with workmen's compensation, unemployment benefits are provided as a proportion of the worker's earnings, generally about 50 percent of regular earnings. Again, there is a maximum amount payable, so that the highest-paid workers, when unemployed, often receive a benefit lower than 50 percent of what they were earning. Only a few states also provide an additional allowance for dependents.

All states limit the number of weeks that benefits can be paid—usually twenty-six weeks. Sometimes, when unemployment is especially high, laws go into effect for a limited time that extend benefits for another thirteen weeks. But unemployment of longer than twenty-six or thirty-nine weeks generally leaves the worker unprotected, as this finding suggests:

In 1970 about 1¼ million beneficiaries, equal in number to a quarter of all who had received benefit at some time during the year, were still unemployed when they had exhausted their claim to benefit. The unemployed in this position were not covered by any national follow-up programme. . . . Some states and a large number of local authorities denied public assistance to unemployed but employable workers. The economic position of the long-term unemployed in the U.S.A. was in general much worse than that in any other country of this study.[16]

Financing

State unemployment compensation programs are financed by employers, who may contribute to the state unemployment fund 90 percent of the amount they owe the federal government for the payroll tax. This complicated way of paying for unemployment compensation, put into the law in 1935 to ensure the law's constitutionality, is still in effect today, and has resulted in the failure of unemployment benefits to keep up with rising wages and the rising cost of living. The reason for this is that originally the federal law gave employers a tax credit of up to 3 percent of wages of $3,000, so that is what state plans required of employers in the state. That is, the employer could keep from the federal government $90 for each employee, provided the employer paid it into the state's unemployment fund. Most workers in 1935 earned $3,000 per year or less, so using that amount as a basis for deciding how much money should be set aside to pay unemployment benefits was reasonable. However, since 1935, wages have gone up considerably, but the basis for crediting employer payments has risen much less—only to $4,200 in 1972. Thus the percentage increase in money set aside for unemployment benefits is much lower than the percentage increase in wages and cost of living. Therefore, unemployment benefits have lagged behind the rising cost of living.[17]

Effectiveness

The benefits paid to unemployed workers are obviously helpful, and their underlying principle is superior to that of the grudgingly given "outdoor relief." Yet approximately 20 percent of all employees are not covered by unemployment compensation.[18] And long-term unemployment exhausts the benefits of those who are covered. Labor unions in a few major industries, such as steel and automobiles, have won for their members supplementary unemployment benefits, paid by the employers. These benefits extend the coverage beyond what is provided in state plans, but as of 1969, fewer than 4 percent of all employees in private industry were covered by supplementary unemployment benefits.[19]

Finally, unemployment benefits are paid only to those who have worked a certain length of time and are now out of a job. They are not paid to people who are looking for their first job and are unable to land it. It is estimated that millions of teenagers and people in their early twenties have been looking for their first job for years and have found no more than temporary employment, if that. Unemployment benefits are not paid to people who have had only brief employment or to those who have been unable to break into the labor market.[20] According to a recent study, "Four out of ten black teenagers who seek jobs cannot find them."[21] The percentage of white teenagers who cannot find jobs is not as high, but it is nonetheless substantial. Those who cannot break into the labor market are deprived of both employment and compensation for unemployment.

SOCIAL SECURITY

The program popularly known as social security was voted into being as part of the Social Security Act of 1935. It began as a program of old-age insurance and is often referred to in the literature as OA. In 1939, coverage was added for the dependent survivors of a worker who died before retirement, so the official name of social security became Old-Age and Survivors Insurance (OASI). Insuring workers against loss of income due to total disablement was added in 1956; health insurance for people aged sixty-five and over was added in 1965. So OASI became first OASDI and now OASDHI. People, however, tend to think of the income-providing insurance program and the medical-cost insurance program as two separate entities and refer to them by their popular names, social security and Medicare, respectively. For convenience here, this distinction will be maintained and Medicare will be discussed in a separate section from social security.

The idea of old-age insurance had been proposed by some American thinkers in the early twentieth century, but it was rejected for a long time as a foreign idea.[22] Only the severe effects of the Great Depression began to make the concept more appealing. Unemployment in cities and industrial towns not only deprived workers, spouses, and children of income but also affected aged parents who were being supported by their adult children. Bank failures wiped out the savings of many, including retired people whose bank savings were their only financial resource. Many who had followed the ideals of self-help and thrift found themselves wiped out.

It was in the context of these events that a California dentist named Francis Townsend began advocating in 1933 the idea that the government should pay every person aged sixty and over a pension of $200 per month, with the stipulation that the person must spend the whole amount during the month. He saw this as a way of providing income to destitute old people and of reviving the economy through consumer spending that would stimulate business activity. His idea gained wide appeal; Townsend clubs to promote the idea were set up in all states. This was the first mass movement in American history organized for the goal of social protection.[23] The pressure on government to enact a program that would prevent destitution in old age was enormous. Members of Congress received millions of postcards. An especially effective one had two scenes on it:

> [One depicted] a forlorn old couple trudging up a snowy road with their few belongings. Underneath was the title, "Over the Hill to the Poorhouse." The other picture showed the same couple seated before a cheery fire, the old lady knitting and the old man smoking his pipe. Its title was "Comfort in Old Age." Across the bottom of the card was the clear-cut message, "Vote for the Townsend Plan."[24]

Although the Townsend Plan was itself considered impractical, an alternative old-age insurance plan was prepared at the direction of President Franklin Roosevelt, who in June 1934 was the first American president to state that the Constitution implied a citizen's right to economic security: "If, as our Constitution tells us . . . our Federal Government was established among other things 'to promote the general welfare,' it is our plain duty to provide for that security upon which welfare depends."[25] One of the economists who helped develop the plan wrote in later years:

> Social security has now become a common and comforting *expression* in the American language. More important, it has become a meaningful *factor* in meeting the contingencies of life for nine out of ten Americans. In 1934, this vast enterprise in preventing hardship and dependency was but a tenuous idea in the minds of a few deeply concerned individuals. Seldom in modern times has an idea, hammered out by a small group of planners, become in a single generation such a pervasive and practical part of the way of life of a people. "Social security" is now taken for granted. In September 1934, even the term was unknown.[26]

The planners' idea, of course, had to be approved by Congress and the president in order to become law.

The old-age insurance program of the Social Security Act contains the following requirements: (1) Coverage is compulsory, except for certain specified categories of people. (2) The program is contributory; it is not paid for out of general tax revenues. (3) The program is national. (4) Benefits are paid as a right to those who qualify. (5) Benefits are related to earnings. The provision of compulsory coverage marked the first time in the history of American social welfare that a program was not geared to specific need. It was the beginning of an effort toward universality, the inclusion of all workers and their dependents. The fact that benefits are earnings-related, however, means that people who do not work are not covered.

Coverage

To be covered by the Social Security Act, a person must work in a job that is included in the category of "covered employment." In the early days, various types of work were not included—agricultural labor, domestic service, self-employment, employment in government (which, however, provided its own retirement plans for its employees). Subsequent amendments to the law have given coverage to more and more occupations, so that more than 90 percent of workers are now covered.[27]

Workers become insured under the plan when they have accumulated a certain number of quarters of employment. Until 1978, a quarter of employment was defined as a calendar quarter, that is, any three-month period ending March 31, June 30, September 30, or December 31 in which the worker earned at least $50 in wages or salary. Thus, if a person earned, say, $750 between January 1 and March 31, but was unemployed the rest of the year, that worker was credited with one quarter of employment. In 1978, the method of defining quarters was changed from a calendar basis to an earnings basis. Now workers are credited with a quarter of employment for each $250 that they earn.[28] Thus a person who earned $500 each week for two weeks and was unemployed the rest of the year would be credited with four quarters of employment.

Benefits are paid to persons who gain what is called "insured status." There are several categories of insured status. Workers with forty quarters of coverage are *fully insured* for life; they and their families are then eligible for most benefits based on the workers' social security earnings record. Survivors of a worker who dies before retirement or dependents of a worker disabled before retirement are entitled to benefits if the worker is *currently insured*. Workers gain this status if they have at least six quarters of coverage out of the thirteen quarters before death or disablement. Other rules specify insured status for disability benefits for the worker who becomes disabled.

Financing

Social security is financed by contributions from employees and employers. Both pay a special tax into a federal fund that is kept separate from general tax revenues. The tax is paid on a certain amount of earnings, called the wage base or earnings base. When the payment of the social security tax began in 1937, employees paid a tax of 1 percent of the first $3,000 of their wages and employers paid the same tax of 1 percent of the same wage base (the first $3,000) for each of their employees. An employee who earned, say, $4,000 per year paid tax on the first $3,000 only. Amendments to the law over the years have raised the tax to 6.65 percent for both employees and employers of the first $29,700 of workers' earnings; both the tax rate and the earnings base are expected to be raised in future years.

When financing for old-age insurance was being discussed in the government, it was decided to have the program financed on a fifty-fifty basis by employer and employee, with no contribution from the government out of general tax revenues. The importance of employee contributions was emphasized as being in line with the American tradition of self-help. Thus workers could feel that they were entitled to the benefits they received in old age because they had earned them and paid for them. As one of the economists who worked out the program later wrote: "We wanted our government to provide a mechanism whereby the individual could prevent dependency through his own efforts."[29]

In recent years, there has been a growing concern over the fact that the social security system is not taking in enough money to pay for all the benefits that it must pay out.[30] One of the proposals being discussed for remedying this situation is to have the government add money from general tax revenues to the Social Security Trust Fund. In 1977, President Jimmy Carter proposed trying this for a five-year experimental period. Changing from a self-financing approach to one involving partial financing from general tax revenues aroused opposition from many sources, including Al Ullman, chairman of the Ways and Means Committee of the House of Representatives, which originates all tax and spending proposals. Ullman said, "We don't want to make a welfare program out of the Social Security system. That's always the danger."[31] (Note that the Ways and Means chairman in 1977 thought of the relationship between "social security" and "welfare" in a very different way from President Franklin D. Roosevelt in 1934–1935. The chairman was talking about "welfare" in its restricted, modern sense of income without honor, donated by the government, whereas the president was speaking of welfare in its original sense of personal and community well-being.) In fact, the social security program already is, in certain respects, a welfare program in the sense that the House Ways and Means chairman said he did not want it to be. The sharp distinction between social insurance and "welfare" is not maintained in the American social security program, which blends aspects of both ideas, as will become clear below.

Benefits

As passed in 1935, social security old-age insurance was to be an earnings-replacement program. That is, benefits would be paid to a worker at age sixty-five, provided the worker retired from employment. The worker had to meet this "retirement test" in order to receive benefits. In later years, the retirement test was relaxed to enable a person to earn a modest amount of money and still receive OA benefits. At age seventy-two, the retirement test is withdrawn; a person may earn any amount of money at that age and thereafter and receive full OA benefits.

The imposition of a retirement test at age sixty-five and its removal at age seventy-two were the result of a compromise between two conflicting ideas that are built into the American social security system, those of *individual equity* and *social adequacy.* Equity means fairness; it is also one's share of a large asset that has many owners. (For example, if two people buy a sailboat, and one of them puts up $500 and the other $1,000, the second has twice as much equity as the first. If they later sell the boat for $1,650, the equitable division of the *profit* would yield $50 to the first investor and $100 to the second one.)

People who have paid taxes into the social security system for at least forty quarters—and whose employers have paid matching amounts on their behalf— have a certain amount of equity in the social security system and are entitled to some return from it. Privately purchased insurance works entirely on the basis of equity. Why then cannot a fully insured worker collect full benefits at age sixty-five without retiring? Because the principle of individual equity is balanced by the principle of social adequacy. The social security program compels workers (and their employers) to put money away so that the workers will have an income when their earnings cease at retirement. The program also assures all insured workers of at least a minimum amount of income at retirement (a "socially adequate" amount), no matter how low their earnings have been. For example, a person who worked at the lowest qualifying wage for as long as it took to become fully insured would receive a pitifully small retirement income if benefits were paid entirely on the basis of individual equity. To achieve the goal of social adequacy, the schedule of benefits provides for a higher minimum benefit than would be payable on a strict equity basis. Some of the money to pay more adequate benefits to the lowest-wage retired workers comes from not having to pay benefits to people who continue working between ages sixty-five and seventy-two, as many do.

Providing a socially adequate minimum income to the low-wage worker is not the only application of the principle of social adequacy. Suppose two individuals of the same age earn the same income at the same kind of work. One is unmarried and remains so until retirement at sixty-five. The other marries, say, at age forty, and has several children. When he retires at sixty-five, he has a wife and one or more children below the age of eighteen as dependents. Both men apply for old-age retirement benefits. The married man with dependents receives a monthly retirement benefit considerably higher than the unmarried man, though both have paid into the social security system the same amounts of taxes over their working lives. A socially adequate income for a family must be higher than a socially adequate income for a single person. It can be said that one person is receiving more benefits than he paid for and that the other is receiving fewer than he paid for, and both statements might be true. But what is happening is that individual equity is being modified by the principle of social adequacy. At the same time, the principle of individual equity is also operative because both individuals would be receiving greater benefits than two other men—one married and with a family, and the other single—who had earned less money and paid less into social security during their working lives (and fewer benefits than men with higher earnings).

The principle of equity is also evidenced by the lifting of the retirement test at age seventy-two. If the retirement test were continued at that age, people who continued to work might never receive any benefits, even though they had paid the social security tax for their entire working lives.[32]

Effectiveness

The social security system in America made its first payment on January 31, 1940, to a retired unmarried woman who died thirty-five years later at the age of one hundred. Like many of the first people to receive benefits, her benefits were far greater than her contributions. Her own case was spectacular, because in exchange for total tax contributions of about $22, she received more than $20,000 over the thirty-five-year period. In 1940, her monthly social security check was $22.54; in 1974, it was $109.20; and over the years it nearly paid her living expenses in the dwelling she shared with a niece.[33]

By 1976, the social security system was paying out more than $55 billion a year in retirement benefits and another $28 billion in benefits to disabled workers, dependents, and survivors. There can be little question that the social security system has placed an income floor under many workers that has eased the retirement years of many and provided replacement income for many families of workers who died or were disabled before retirement. However, there are many problems with the system as it now exists. The relationship between the contributions made and the benefits ultimately received is complex, and some observers feel it is unfair to many people. In addition, the concept of social adequacy does not in fact assure an adequate retirement income to all retirees. It must be said that OA was never intended to be a person's or a family's total retirement income; it was expected that individuals would have taken steps on their own to supplement their OA benefits, or else would receive a pension through their places of employment. However, as of 1974, fewer than 45 percent of workers were covered under any private pension plan; many of these plans are mismanaged; and in many of them, employees lose all pension rights when they lose or change their jobs.[34]

Other problems involve the financing of the program. In 1976, there were thirty beneficiaries for every one hundred workers. It is estimated that in the year 2050, as the American population ages (with life expectancies increasing) and fewer children are born, there will be fifty-one beneficiaries for every one hundred workers.[35] Changes in financing or benefits, or both, will be necessary in order to pay the cost of benefits to a higher proportion of elderly in the population. Workers are likely to be encouraged to retire at later ages, so that taxes continue to be paid into social security and benefits can begin later. In the late 1970s the federal government raised the compulsory retirement age from sixty-five to seventy. Coming years are likely to see considerable debate and discussion over reforming the social security system.

SUPPLEMENTAL SECURITY INCOME

The reader who has come this far in the book is well familiar by now with the fact that social welfare is a field of activity in which certain ideas are sharply distinguished from each other but in which the ideas become blended and blurred in actual social welfare programs. Certainly the social welfare field recognizes a sharp distinction between public assistance and social insurance. In a public assistance program, people must pass a "means test," that is, they must prove that they are without adequate means of support. In a social insurance program, people are entitled to the benefits they receive as a matter of earned right. Consider two unemployed people, one who has never been able to get a job and the other who has been laid off. The first receives public assistance by proving he has no other way to live; the second receives unemployment insurance payments, to which he is entitled as a worker who has lost his job. But after the latter has been out of work for twenty-six or thirty-nine weeks (and the longer he remains out of work), his distinctive social status fades and he will come to have more nearly the same social status as the first man.

A planned blurring of this kind took place with the adoption in 1972 (taking effect January 1, 1974) of the Supplemental Security Income program (SSI). This program placed three of the federally aided state-administered public assistance categories into a single, federally administered program. The three categories are: old-age assistance (OAA); aid to the blind (AB); and aid to the permanently and totally disabled (APTD). In place of the varying state programs for each of these categories of need:

> . . . benefit levels, eligibility conditions, and means tests are uniform nationwide. States have the option of supplementing SSI payments and are required to do so for those current recipients who would receive less under SSI than under the former federal-state-local system.[36]

The adoption of SSI to replace three categorical programs places a "welfare" program under the Social Security Administration, a "social insurance" agency. The effect of this change is to increase the honorableness of the income received. This income does not come from social insurance based on earnings; it comes from general tax revenues. But the income is now called supplemental *security* income instead of *aid* or *assistance*. In short, the poor elderly, blind, and disabled who receive this income have been destigmatized, and their benefits have been brought under a set of nationwide, uniform standards. Most observers would consider that this is a significant improvement in concept and in practice. But alongside this improvement is an omission: AFDC was not taken over entirely by the federal government. It continues to be a state-administered program, though it is federally assisted with grants-in-aid.

It is something of an anomaly that Congress was willing to adopt a completely federally supported "welfare" program for three categories of needy persons and to remove them as much as possible from the stigma of receiving welfare by calling the benefits security income and by administering the program under social security, but unwilling to take the same action with regard to AFDC. One possible explanation is that AFDC is not only the costliest "welfare" program but also the most unpopular. It is unpopular because a substantial proportion of AFDC recipients are unmarried mothers and their children, two categories of people who have been stigmatized for centuries and who continue to be even in modern times. In addition, AFDC is widely thought of as a program for blacks. In fact, whites have always made up the majority of recipients of AFDC, but since blacks make up a substantial minority—larger than their proportion in the population—and since black recipients are concentrated in large cities while white recipients are widely dispersed geographically, there has been an impression of black predominance in the program,[37] and needless to say, blacks are a population that have been and continue to be discriminated against. Federal decision makers apparently are not ready to remove the stigma that adheres to unmarried motherhood nor, especially, to black unmarried motherhood.

MEDICARE

In 1914, three years after health insurance was adopted in Great Britain, efforts were begun in the United States to develop support for health insurance. Between 1915 and 1920, health insurance was one of the most controversial social issues in the country.[38] Advocates presented six arguments in favor of compulsory health insurance: (1) Sickness and death rates among American wage earners were high. (2) Low-income groups received inadequate medical care. (3) Illness led to widespread poverty. (4) Prevention of illness was essential; compulsory health insurance would prompt both employers and employees to try to reduce the incidence of occupational diseases. (5) Existing social welfare agencies lacked both the resources and the willingness to handle the medical problems of low-income people. Therefore ⑥ "compulsory health insurance was the only effective solution to the medical problems of the wage-earner."[39]

Compulsory health insurance was fought by various organized interests in American society—employers, druggists, some labor unions, insurance companies, fraternal organizations. But the most vigorous opposition came from physicians who feared that the American system of medical practice, based on individuals choosing their own physician and paying a fee for each medical service, would be transformed into a system in which doctors would be required to practice in groups and would be paid a salary from funds prepaid into a common fund. The doctor would be transformed from an independent professional into a salaried subordinate of an organization, subject to government control. The doctor would lose freedom, income, and status in the community. But the physicians' main argument against compulsory health insurance was not that they would lose out but that patients would receive incompetent medical service under such a system. Social welfare historian Roy Lubove has observed:

> The economic and status fears of the physician were translated into a concern for high standards of service, and particularly the need to protect the physician-patient relationship. No legislation should be allowed to disturb the feeling of "confidence, trust and personal relationship between doctor and patient." Compulsory health insurance . . . would allow non-medical agencies to "dictate the terms of . . . services, thus placing them on a purely commercial or business basis." The personal element, a "most important factor in the treatment of the sick," would be destroyed. This line of reasoning ignored certain questions raised by advocates of health insurance. Could the poorer population afford a physician with whom to establish a personal relationship? Did such stress on the personal relationship make sense in an era of specialization, hospitals, and advancing medical science? Were high standards of medical practice so uniquely dependent upon one financing mechanism (fee-for-service) and one method of organization (entrepreneurial, solo practice)?[40]

Efforts were made to get several state legislatures to pass compulsory health insurance laws, but all were defeated.

Brief consideration was given to the issue of national compulsory health insurance when the Social Security Act was being prepared, but the idea was dropped in response to the great opposition from physicians for fear that the entire Social Security Act might be defeated. Additional efforts to institute national health insurance were made during the late forties and fifties by Roosevelt's successor, President Harry Truman, again without success. (Since Truman, no president has seriously tried to get it adopted, although some Senators and Representatives have made the attempt.) Repeated failures led social welfare planners to attempt a more modest goal: obtaining national health insurance for people over age sixty-five.[41]

It took thirteen years from the time the idea of medical insurance for the elderly was proposed in 1952 until Medicare was enacted into law, in 1965, during President Lyndon Johnson's "great society" administration.

Coverage

Medicare provides health insurance for people over age sixty-five who have gained fully insured status under social security. Certain categories of people over sixty-five, who do not have this status, are also eligible.

Benefits and financing

Medicare has two parts. Part A provides insurance for hospitalization. The program pays for the first sixty days of a hospital stay, after the patient pays the deductible of the first $144 of the cost. (Since a day's stay in a hospital costs about $200 or more, the patient pays less than one day's cost before Medicare takes over.) If the hospital stay extends more than sixty days, Medicare pays part of the cost for the next thirty days. The hospitalization benefits come from funds collected from the social security payroll tax.

Part B of Medicare pays 80 percent of the physicians' charges. Unlike Part A, which is provided to all insured over age sixty-five, Part B is voluntary. The insured person must choose to be covered, and those who do so pay a premium for the coverage. It was $3 per month in 1965 and rose to $11 in 1981.

Effectiveness

Medicare has eased the burden of medical costs for the elderly, but the burden remains heavy. A person who spent ninety days in the hospital would have to pay over $1,000 in hospital bills plus 20 percent of the physician's bills if covered by Part B of Medicare, or 100 percent if not covered. Medicaid would pay some of these costs for some of the elderly (those who are medically indigent). However, Medicare, Medicaid, and privately purchased health insurance together pay only 71 percent of the health expenses of the aged.[42]

Medicare and Medicaid were adopted as compromises between those who wanted a national health insurance system that would provide universal coverage for the American people and those who wanted no social insurance program of health coverage. The United States and the Republic of South Africa are the only two industrialized countries that have neither a national health system (government-operated hospitals and clinics) nor a national health insurance system.[43] The high cost of medical care, especially in the case of long-term illness, and the continuing belief on the part of many citizens that the government should deal with social problems, make it likely that national health protection will continue to be a major social welfare issue for some years to come.

THE WELFARE STATE

Toward the middle of the twentieth century, social thinkers and political leaders in Great Britain began to talk about a concept of government that acquired the label "the welfare state."[44] The term gained currency in other countries as well, and many industrial countries are now widely referred to as welfare states. "The essence of the welfare state is government-protected minimum standards of income, nutrition, health, housing, and education, assured to every citizen as a political right, not as charity."[45] The welfare state thus takes the concept of social insurance and applies it to all major perils to the general well-being of the individual. This vision of a more humane society and government developed most clearly in Great Britain in the 1940s during World War II.

World War II was the first war in which there was large-scale aerial bombing of civilian populations. German bombing of British cities affected rich and poor alike, and as they huddled together in air-raid shelters, traditional social distances diminished. There was a sense of everybody being "in it together." Further, as a safety measure, enormous numbers of city children were sent away from home to less vulnerable rural areas. The evacuation of the children from the cities had a profound social effect: "Evacuation was part of the process by which British society came to know itself, as the unkempt, ill-clothed, undernourished and often incontinent children of bombed cities acted as messengers carrying the evidence of deprivation of urban working-class life into rural homes."[46] Sentiment grew for more sharing of social rewards after the war, just as there was a wide sharing of the hazards during the war. William Beveridge was called upon to draft proposals for postwar social welfare. The famed Beveridge Report of 1942 proposed "cradle-to-grave" provision of social benefits, and with modifications, it eventually became law. The British Labour party, which came to power in 1945, adopted many new measures based on the Beveridge Report and considered basic components of a welfare state, most important among them: (1) a system of family allowances, providing each family with a regular monthly allowance toward the cost of bringing up children, for second and subsequent children, regardless of parents' means, (2) a National Health Service, which pays a large share of the costs of medical care for all citizens, (3) a National Insurance Act (described below), (4) a National Assistance Act, to provide income to people not covered by family allowances or National Insurance.

Beveridge was in the mainstream of British thinking about social insurance in insisting that government benefits be tied to citizens' contributions. In this way, citizens would not be receiving a gift from the state but benefits they would be entitled to on the basis of their contributions. Thus the National Insurance Act of 1946 provided workers and their families with seven forms of benefits in return for a single weekly contribution by the workers. These were: (1) sickness benefits, (2) unemployment benefits, (3) a retirement pension, (4) maternity benefits, (5) widow's benefits, (6) a guardian's allowance should the children become orphaned, and (7) a death benefit to cover funeral expenses.[47]

The cost of the benefits and their adequacy are matters of continuing debate, and the programs are modified from time to time in response to changing conditions. But the fundamental concept that the state has a responsibility for the social welfare of all of its citizens appears to have gained widespread acceptance, even within the Conservative party, the other major political party in Great Britain. The laissez-faire concept of the state, associated with Adam Smith's work in 1776 and the 1834 Poor Law concept of "less eligibility" were decisively replaced in Great Britain by the welfare state concept that emerged in the Beveridge Report and the social welfare programs instituted in 1946–1948. What they accomplished has been summarized as follows:

> Four Acts had constructed a social security network which protected everyone against destitution or want: these were the 1945 Family Allowance Act, the 1946 National Insurance and Industrial Injuries Acts, and the 1948 National Assistance Act. . . . the social security system was to be seen in the context of a full employment policy which equally attacked want. Under this universal system the whole population was provided for in times of loss or interruptions of earnings (sickness, unemployment, retirement and industrial injuries benefits), in times of exceptional family expenditure (maternity benefits, child allowances and death grants), and on the death of the breadwinner (widows' and orphans' benefits). Underpinning the social security system, national assistance provided a last-ditch relief agency to guarantee every member of society against destitution. It required a massive administrative exercise to launch the new scheme, for some 25 million people had to be classified, recorded and issued with national insurance numbers. Thousands of staff had to be recruited. . . . Enormous publicity was required to explain the new system to the nation. . . . By the appointed day in July 1948 when the whole scheme was to start the nation had to be administratively and psychologically prepared for the new system which of course included . . . a national health service.[48]

Criticism of the Welfare State

The concept of the welfare state has been attacked from opposing viewpoints. Some conservatives believe that the welfare state is just another name for socialism and therefore an intrusion into people's lives. Radical thinkers believe that "the welfare state" is little more than an empty slogan because the state that goes by that label does not in fact produce a very high level of well-being for many citizens. As noted, most conservatives today accept at least a moderate version of the welfare state. Relatively few conservatives wish to abolish it and return to the laissez-faire, noninterventionist state. The radical criticism—that the welfare state does not intervene enough to create well-being throughout the society —is understandable in terms of two alternate concepts of what the welfare state should be. One of these concepts emphasizes assuring a *minimum* to everybody. The other focuses on *reducing inequality;* it therefore emphasizes not merely an assured minimum of income, housing, health care, and so on for all, but goes beyond to call for greater *redistribution* of income. In the radical view, too little redistribution perpetuates too much unjust inequality in the welfare state.

The United States as a Welfare State

While conservatives in the United States believe that the country has deviated too far from its original laissez-faire principles and leans too far toward socialism now in the extent to which it insures people against perils to income, a comparative perspective shows that the United States is less of a welfare state than many other industrial countries. As mentioned above, the United States is one of the few industrial countries that has neither a national health service nor a national health insurance plan. A family with even a moderately high income can be financially devastated by a long-term illness in one of its members. Group insurance plans (such as Blue Cross and Blue Shield) do much to reduce this possibility, but they do not cover everybody, and even for those who are covered, the benefits may be exhausted before all the major costs are paid for.

The United States is the only developed country that has no universal family allowance program.[49] Other industrial countries provide families with a monthly cash allowance for each child, or for each child after the first or second, in recognition of the costs to the family of rearing children. Such allowances seem similar, at first glance, to the Speenhamland system, but there is an important difference. Whereas the allowance system of Speenhamland days made payments to the poor earning a low wage, modern family allowance systems make payments to all families with specified numbers of children regardless of income. This means that payments go to some families who do not need the money; but the government presumably recovers these payments through the income tax system, at least in countries where progressively higher taxes are collected from progressively higher incomes. The coordination of social welfare benefits with the tax system is one way in which the welfare state can reconcile two goals: providing benefits to all persons in a certain category as a matter of citizenship right (thus avoiding the humiliation of a means test), and collecting tax revenues according to ability to pay.

The most elementary conception of the welfare state would assure a minimum income to every member of the society. The United States does not have a program that assures a minimum income to every member. As mentioned in Chapter 2, Senator George McGovern proposed such a program during the presidential election campaign of 1972, but his idea received little support.

Nixon's FAP and Carter's PBJI (see Chapter 6) were guaranteed minimum income plans, and both were rejected. There are many other proposals for assuring a minimum income to everyone, but none of these *transfer* proposals (so-called because they would transfer money, through taxation, from those who have ample income to those with inadequate income) has much immediate prospect for adoption in the United States, although it is widely believed that they would prove advantageous—less costly, more efficient, and fairer than existing public assistance programs, which they would replace.[50]

The introduction of social insurance into the United States led to a change in political terminology that should be noted, if confusion is to be avoided. From New Deal times on, those who have favored the expansion of social insurance and other social welfare measures by the national government have come to be known as liberals. As applied to such people, liberal means being in favor of reform, in favor of government action to ameliorate poverty and hardship. Since social insurance and national welfare measures are a form of government involvement in economic and social affairs, the term liberal is therefore now used in the U.S. in a sense exactly opposite to its original meaning. Adam Smith and his immediate successors are sometimes referred to as "classical liberals" to distinguish them from the newer kind. (See Chapter 6.) The people who today emphasize pursuit of self-interest unhampered by government interference (and taxation for social welfare is regarded as a form of government interference) have come to be known as "conservatives," since they favor going back to the older type of relationship between government and society that existed before the Great Depression. Thus, according to this terminology, the Lyndon Johnson administration of the 1960s was considered liberal and the Reagan administration elected in 1980, conservative.

SUMMARY

Although American government officials began studying European social insurance programs in the 1890s, the strong American belief in individualism caused slow acceptance of the concept. Beginning in 1910, individual states began adopting workmen's compensation laws for injuries suffered on the job. These were the first social insurance laws in the United States, but they remain entirely under state jurisdiction, and coverage and benefits vary from state to state. Their adoption was facilitated by a significant change in thinking: The idea that individual workers were entirely responsible for their safety was replaced by the idea that employers have a responsibility to maintain safe working conditions for their employees.

Unemployment insurance became a component of American social welfare with the passage of the Social Security Act of 1935, which provided for federally regulated, but state-administered, programs. Adoption of unemployment insurance represented a change in traditional ideas about unemployment. The long-prevailing view that failure to work was due to poor moral character was replaced by the realization that unemployment was often involuntary and was frequently due to poor business conditions.

Social security, which provides some retirement income to workers based on contributions by them and their employers to the Social Security Trust Fund, was the first federally administered social insurance program. It still does not cover all employees, but it covers more people than any other social welfare program in the United States. Although social security has some features of an insurance program, the very complex and uneven relationship of benefits received to contributions paid in leads many to question whether it is a genuine social insurance program. One complexity results from the blending of the principles of individual equity and social adequacy. The result of this blending is that those who pay in the most and those who pay in the least do not receive benefits proportional to their contributions. Those who pay in the most receive less than strict individual equity would justify; those who pay in the least receive more than equity would justify, in order that their benefits may approach social adequecy. The social security program is experiencing some financial difficulties. Revisions in how the program is paid for and in the benefits provided are predicted.

In 1974, three public assistance programs—aid to the blind, aid to the permanently and totally disabled, and old-age assistance—were combined into one program called Supplemental Security Income (SSI). Because this program is paid for out of general taxes and is means-tested, it remains a public assistance program, not a social insurance program. But because it is now called a "security," rather than an "aid," program, and because it is administered by the same agency that administers the social security program, the stigma suffered by welfare recipients has been removed from the blind, the disabled, and the elderly poor. AFDC was not included in this reshuffle.

Efforts to introduce a national health insurance system in the United States have been unsuccessful. Because of the sharply increasing costs of health care and because elderly people usually experience reduced income upon retirement, a compromise health insurance plan (Medicare) for people aged sixty-five and older did gain acceptance in 1965. Health insurance for the entire population remains a politically controversial issue.

The idea of a welfare state, a state that would insure its citizens against all significant hazards to income and that would assure to all certain services essential to their well-being, developed in Great Britain during World War II. The welfare state concept is attacked by conservatives as "socialism in disguise" and by radicals as an empty slogan. Whether any country is a true welfare state is open to debate. However, many industrial countries do provide their citizens with a wider range of income maintenance supports and services than does the

United States, one of the few industrial countries to offer neither family allowances nor a national plan for health care.

Notes

[1]Roy Lubove, *The Struggle for Social Security, 1900–1935* (Cambridge: Harvard University
Press, 1968), Chapter 2.

[2]Daniel Nelson, *Unemployment Insurance—The American Experience, 1915–1935* (Madison,
Wisc.: University of Wisconsin Press, 1969), p. 3.

[3]Albert H. Mowbray, Ralph H. Blanchard, C. Arthur Williams, Jr., *Insurance: Its Theory and
Practice in the United States,* 6th ed. (New York: McGraw-Hill, 1969), p. 570.

[4]*Ibid.;* Lubove, *Struggle,* p. 53.

[5]Lubove, *Struggle,* pp. 46–48; Sidney E. Zimbalist, *Historic Themes and Landmarks in Social
Welfare Research* (Harper & Row, 1977), pp. 127–128.

[6]Charles I. Schottland, *The Social Security Program in the United States,* 2nd ed. (New York:
Appleton-Century-Crofts, 1970), p. 126.

[7]Domenico Gagliardo, *American Social Insurance,* rev. ed. (New York: Harper & Brothers,
1955), pp. 389–390; Lubove, *Struggle,* pp. 61ff.

[8]Schottland, *Social Security,* p. 129.

[9]*Ibid.,* pp. 129–131.

[10]Gagliardo, *American Social Insurance,* pp. 404–410.

[11]*Ibid.,* pp. 393–404; Schottland, *Social Security,* p. 131; Lubove, *Struggle,* pp. 59–62.

[12]Lubove, *Struggle,* pp. 64–65.

[13]John Garraty, *Unemployment in History* (New York: Harper & Row, 1978), p. 213.

[14]*Ibid.,* p. 214.

[15]P. R. Kaim-Caudle, *Comparative Social Policy and Social Security—A Ten-Country Study*
(New York: Dunellen, 1973), p. 229.

[16]*Ibid.,* pp. 230–231.

[17]*Ibid.,* p. 231.

[18]*Ibid.,* p. 229. See also Dorothy K. Newman et al., *Protest, Politics, Prosperity* (New York:
Pantheon, 1978), p. 244.

[19]Kaim-Caudle, *Comparative Social Policy,* p. 232.

[20]Philip Booth, *Social Security in America* (Ann Arbor, Mich.: University of Michigan/Wayne
State University Institute of Labor and Industrial Relations, 1973), pp. 83–84.

[21]Garth L. Mangum and Stephen F. Seninger, *Coming of Age in the Ghetto—A Dilemma of
Youth Unemployment* (Baltimore: Johns Hopkins University Press, 1978), p. 1.

[22]J. Douglas Brown, *An American Philosophy of Social Security* (Princeton, N.J.: Princeton
University Press, 1972), p. 8.

[23]Gaston V. Rimlinger, *Welfare Policy and Industrialization in Europe, America, and Russia*
(New York: Wiley, 1971), p. 203.

[24]Brown, *An American Philosophy,* p. 7.

[25]Franklin D. Roosevelt, in Rimlinger, *Welfare Policy,* p. 221.

[26]Brown, *An American Philosophy,* p. 3.

[27]Alicia H. Munnell, *The Future of Social Security* (Washington, D.C.: Brookings Institution,
1977), p. 1.

[28]*Social Security Handbook,* 6th ed. (Washington, D.C.: U.S. Government Printing Office, 1978).

[29]J. Douglas Brown, in Rimlinger, *Welfare Policy,* p. 229.

[30]Edward Cowan, "Congress Told Social Security Fund Needs New Money," *New York Times,* August 6, 1979, p. D6.

[31]Al Ullman, in Edward Cowan, "Califano Says Shift on Social Security Could Be Permanent —Backs Use of Treasury Funds: Comments from Congressmen and Criticism from Business Hint Long Fight on Carter Plan," *New York Times,* May 11, 1977, p. 1.

[32]The discussion of benefits under Social Security is based on Munnell, *Future of Social Security.*

[33]"Ida Fuller, 100, Who in '40 Got First Social Security Check, Dies" *New York Times,* January 28, 1975, p. 36.

[34]Munnell, *Future of Social Security,* pp. 19–20.

[35]*Ibid.,* p. 4.

[36]*Ibid.,* p. 9.

[37]Newman et al., *Protest, Politics, Prosperity,* pp. 261–262, Table 7–16, p. 281. For a description of the use of AFDC by rural whites living in Appalachia, see Harry M. Caudill, *Night Comes to the Cumberlands—A Biography of a Depressed Area* (Boston: Little, Brown, 1963), Chapter 18.

[38]Lubove, *Struggle,* pp. 66–67.

[39]*Ibid.,* pp. 71–75.

[40]*Ibid.,* p. 82.

[41]Theodore R. Marmor, with the assistance of Jan S. Marmor, *The Politics of Medicare* (Chicago: Aldine, 1973), pp. 7–20.

[42]Harrell R. Rodgers, Jr., *Poverty and Plenty* (Reading, Mass.: Addison-Wesley, 1979), p. 132.

[43]*Ibid.,* p. 137.

[44]Charles I. Schottland, ed., *The Welfare State* (New York: Harper Torchbooks, 1967).

[45]Harold L. Wilensky, *The Welfare State and Equality* (Berkeley, Calif.: University of California Press, 1975), p. 1.

[46]Fraser, *British Welfare State,* p. 195.

[47]*Ibid.,* p. 212.

[48]*Ibid.,* pp. 214–215.

[49]Kaim-Caudle, *Comparative Social Policy,* p. 278.

[50]Theodore R. Marmor, ed., *Poverty Policy* (Chicago: Aldine-Atherton, 1971), Chapters 2 and 3.

VARIETIES OF SOCIAL WELFARE INSTITUTIONS
Social Insurance

Children's allowances (also called family allowances)	Social security (old age, survivors, disability, health insurance—OASDHI)
Guaranteed annual income	Supplemental Security Income (SSI)
Medicare	Unemployment compensation
National health insurance	Workmen's compensation
Old-age pension	Welfare state

Significant Figures in Social Insurance

William Beveridge—Analyzed unemployment as a problem of industry rather than of individual character defect, helping to pave the way for unemployment compensation; later produced report advocating comprehensive system of social insurance for all contingencies that interrupt earned income, leading to Great Britain's tending toward a welfare state

Otto von Bismarck—Chancellor of Germany, first to introduce social insurance

Charles Booth—English businessman who conducted a survey revealing poverty in London to be widespread, a finding that helped to undermine pure laissez-faire explanations of poverty

Edwin Chadwick—English reformer, whose report on sanitary conditions helped people to understand that disease was one of the causes of poverty and thus contributed to the development of a public health concept

President Franklin D. Roosevelt—Led the effort to establish social insurance institutions in the United States

Significant Dates in the Development of Social Insurance

1833—First Factory Act (Great Britain), restricted employment of children

1842—Chadwick's *Report on the Sanitary Condition of the Labouring Population of Great Britain*

1848—National law (Great Britain) *allowed* local health boards to enforce sanitary measures in sewage and water supply systems

1872—National law (Great Britain) *required* local health authorities to enforce sanitary measures

1879—United States established a National Board of Health

1883—Health insurance introduced in Germany; the first social insurance program

1884—Industrial accident insurance introduced in Germany

1889—Old-age and disability insurance introduced in Germany

1886–1903—Charles Booth's survey of poverty in London

1908—Old-age pension system introduced in Great Britain, administered by Post Office Department, not by Poor Law authorities

1908—William Beveridge's book *Unemployment—A Problem of Industry* published

1911—National Insurance Act (Great Britain) introduced health insurance and unemployment insurance

1906–1907—Pittsburgh Survey revealed many aspects of industrial work, and not workers alone, were responsible for on-the-job accidents

1911—Workmen's compensation insurance for industrial accidents adopted in ten American states

1935—Social Security Act passed in the United States, establishing an old-age retirement income system; later expanded to include disability and survivors insurance; act also encouraged all states to adopt unemployment insurance

1942—Beveridge Report published during World War II laid out plan for Great Britain to become a welfare state after the war

1965—United States adopted Medicare as part of the social security system, extending health insurance to all persons over age sixty-five

1974—Three categorical public welfare programs—AB, APTD, and OAA—combined into one program called Supplemental Security Income (SSI), administered by the Social Security Administration, thereby removing the public assistance stigma from recipients; AFDC did not receive this social upgrading

1969–1979—President Nixon, presidential candidate McGovern, President Carter, and numerous social scientists and social welfare specialists proposed plans for guaranteed minimum annual income, none of which were adopted

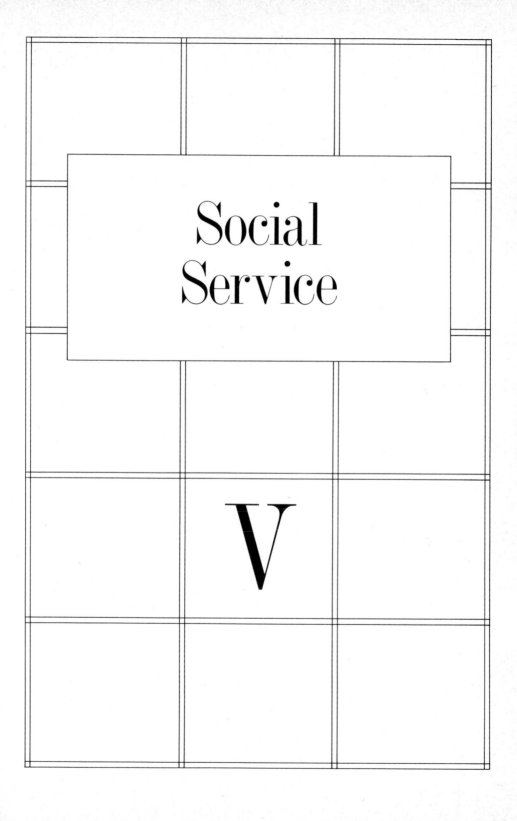

Social Service

V

From Charity to Social Service

9

Social service is a concept that embodies and builds upon the idea that human interaction is a fundamental way of giving help. Human interaction leading to personal and social change is the central idea of social service. This differs from the concepts of help discussed so far, since they all were focused on providing money, or the objects and services that money buys.

The social welfare field can be roughly divided into two categories of assistance: the provision of money and the provision of social services. Historically, social services developed as an alternative to the provision of money. There has been a fairly continuous conflict in the field over the relative importance of providing services versus providing money. It has been recognized, however, that at times poor people require both income support and social services. This has led to the question of whether provision of income and provision of service should be handled by the same worker or by different workers. In view of the ongoing conflict and the issues surrounding it, it seems useful to maintain a distinction between these two general concepts of help. They do represent two fundamentally different ideas about what kinds of help people need. But it must be kept in mind that while at times these two ideas have been considered to be completely opposed to each other, at other times they have been considered not just complementary but inseparable in terms of helping people in need to function better in society.

What, then, are the kinds of interaction that are thought to be helpful to people in need? At one time or another, they have taken such diverse forms as offering friendship, giving advice, leading groups in recreational and artistic activities, organizing groups to engage in political activity, teaching, exploring and treating the personality, providing information and referrals for more specialized forms of help, providing a safe environment for people in need of supervision (for example, day-care centers for very young children, sheltered workshops for the blind).

Although help in the form of human contact is as old as the human race—any society depends on it—it was not until the nineteenth century that such help became the focus of systematic attention and thought. Only then did people begin to organize and sharpen their ideas about how human contact could be helpful. Their efforts led to the emergence of the occupation of social work, devoted to the provision of social service. Today some social services are provided by persons in still newer occupations. Day-care services for young children are provided by day-care workers. Legal services for poor people are provided by legal aides and legal aid lawyers. Various counseling occupations exist—marriage counseling, vocational counseling, school counseling, rehabilitation counseling.

Social work today is, then, one of the occupations that provide social service, one of a grouping that social workers often refer to as "the helping professions." This chapter will focus primarily on social work because it was the first of these new social service occupations and because it developed specifically in the context of the long Western tradition of concern with poverty. Social service occupations that originated in other contexts lie outside the scope of this book.

DISCONTENTED RESPONSES TO INDUSTRIALIZATION

Social work originated in late nineteenth-century England when there was growing discontent with the kind of society that had been created by industrialization and by the political and economic practices of laissez-faire capitalism. The early ideas from which social work grew soon traveled to the United States, where they developed more vigorously and more rapidly. Thus, although the germinating ideas for the new helping activities were of British origin, their fullest development took place in the United States, which became the leading center of social work and ultimately the leading exporter of social work ideas.

Modern social work has two main roots, the Charity Organization movement and the Settlement House (see page 216) movement. Both roots took hold in England and then in the United States as part of a growing recognition that industrial society was not working for many people. The scientific knowledge and engineering know-how that produced ever more sophisticated manufacturing techniques had not produced the widespread contentment that many people expected to result virtually automatically from the rational workings of the human mind. It had been thought in nineteenth-century England—Victorian England—that the use of scientific facts and technology had set the country on an unswerving course of "progress." But the growing gap between the social classes could not be ignored, even by the many who believed that the social order was fundamentally correct and just.[1]

Discontent within a society that was shaped by the values and institutions of laissez-faire capitalism, a society whose industries and urban concentrations were destructive of many people, led to diverse ideas for change. Three main currents of thought were particularly important.

Socialism

Socialism is a term that covers not only Marx's ideas but other collectivist ideas as well. Despite important differences in the several varieties of socialist thought, they have in common the belief that the rewards of labor belong collectively to those who have contributed to production rather than to those who simply own the means of production. Instead of the individualist doctrine of self-interest, and the pursuit of individual gain, socialism emphasizes the sharing of rewards among all.

Marxist socialism is revolutionary; Marxists anticipate one day coming to power and changing the social system by violent uprising. Other varieties of socialist thinking call for coming to power through peaceful use of the existing political system, such as by winning elections. Revolutionary socialism had some appeal in England in the 1840s, but it lost appeal thereafter. Nevertheless, some British people continued to be concerned about an uprising of the poorer laboring classes.[2] As the nineteenth century wore on, many members of the laboring classes became better off economically. Labor unions (called trade unions in England) had been formed (they had been illegal until 1824) in some industries, and the workers in those industries sought agreements with employers for higher wages, with some success.[3] A distinctively British form of socialism took shape in the 1880s with the establishment of the Fabian Society, a group of intellectuals who regarded society as "an organic whole" and advocated collective ownership of the means of production. They lectured and wrote pamphlets, seeking peaceful and gradual change toward a socialist society. Their ideas contributed to the development of the British welfare state.

Socialism was less influential in the United States. A Socialist political party was established and its candidate polled almost a million votes in the presidential election of 1912; this was its peak.[4] Activities toward reform of American industrial society gathered strength in the period 1890–1912, but they were under the influence of other currents of thought, not socialism.

Romanticism

Another type of discontented response to industrialization and capitalism was romanticism. Romanticism was concerned not with the distribution of the financial rewards of work but with what it regarded as an overemphasis on material gain. The romantic writers and thinkers took a stand against the basic laissez-faire idea of the pursuit of self-interest. In their view, as a result of laissez-faire values:

> The individual and society had been perverted by concern with selfish economic gain. Individual satisfactions and social good had not proved to be congruent, as the laissez-faire political economists had maintained. Instead there were gross disparities between the sensual luxury of the rich and the degrading poverty of the poor.[5]

The Romantics argued that a human being could not be defined solely in terms of rational self-interest but instead had to be defined in terms of the whole person, his sense of self, growing spiritually, morally, and esthetically.

> The goal of the Romantic was the improvement of man's inner nature. Only through man's free will morally directed could man and, consequently, society, progress. . . . social reform must begin with the individual.[6]

Both the Charity Organization movement and the Social Settlement House movement were heavily influenced by romanticism's idealistic emphasis on the moral and spiritual improvement of the individual.

Social Christianity

The second half of the nineteenth century saw the development of a new impulse in Christianity, particularly in Protestantism. As noted in the discussion of the

Protestant Reformation in Chapter 5, Protestantism placed major emphasis on individual believers and their obligation to serve God. In the late nineteenth century, some Protestant ministers and lay people both in England and in the United States became aware of the social problems developing in urban, industrial society. In England, there was a new idea: People's self-sacrificing service was transferred from God to other people. Good Christians were to dedicate themselves to the service of their fellow human beings.[7]

At about the same time in the United States, Protestant clergy were turning their attention to social reform. Their emphasis was on saving society, and this new emphasis, so at odds with traditional Protestantism, came to be known as the *social gospel*. The practitioners of the social gospel concerned themselves with basic questions of the economic and political organization of society; they conceived of these concerns as growing directly out of Christian ethics. From about 1870 to 1900, the Social Gospel movement challenged the dominant values and beliefs of the doctrine of laissez-faire. One movement leader proclaimed: "The 'let alone theory of society' . . . bears the mark of Cain. Its theological definition is hell," while another called laissez-faire "the science of extortion, the gentle art of grinding the faces of the poor."[8] In short, the social gospel advocates judged that laissez-faire was incompatible with Christian principles.

Social Christianity, both in England and in the United States, contributed significantly to the decisions of comfortably well-off men and women to take up residence in poor neighborhoods, where they established new institutions known as social settlements or settlement houses. These settlements, along with the friendly visiting and organized charity concepts of the Charity Organization movement, became the nucleus of modern social work. As social work developed, it fashioned three principal methods of helping people: (1) casework, (2) group work, and (3) community organization. Casework is an outgrowth of friendly visiting. Group work developed out of the Social Settlement movement. Community organization blends ideas both from "organized charity" and from the emphasis on community that was central to the thinking of the settlement house workers.

FROM CHARITY TO CASEWORK

The goal of the Charity Organization movement was to reduce dependency, or pauperism, which it regarded as the principal cause of poverty. It mobilized volunteers, organized them into geographical districts, and sent them out to engage in friendly visiting—that is, to investigate the specific circumstances of a person's or family's situation and to report back to the district committee, which would decide what assistance, if any, to give. Careful records were kept of each visit. Keeping these records, and attempting to standardize the techniques of friendly visiting, reflected the growing faith in science of the late nineteenth century, including a growing faith in what was increasingly being referred to as social science.[9] The careful examination of facts was part of the spirit of the age, an example of the growing rationalism discussed in Chapter 2.

Questions about the suitability of volunteers for doing this scientific job were raised in the Charity Organization movements both in England and in the United States. There was increasing recognition that the work required skill and that volunteers should, therefore, be trained. At the end of the nineteenth century, the London and New York charity organization societies instituted training programs. In London, a brief course of lectures and supervised work was given. In New York, the COS established a Summer School of Philanthropy in 1898. The London program became the School of Sociology and then, in 1912, the Department of Social Science and Administration of the London School of Economics. These training programs eventually developed into professional schools of social work, affiliated with universities.[10]

The process of transforming social work from the offering of moral encouragement and advice—motivated in part by the rich's sense of the obligation to the poor and in part by a fear that the poor would be a threat to the social order if they were not morally improved—into a more systematic set of professional skills was greatly enhanced by the work of Mary Richmond. Richmond had worked for many years in the Charity Organization movement, first as general secretary of the Baltimore COS, then as general secretary of the Philadelphia COS. She then moved to the Russell Sage Foundation, where she worked to improve casework practice. Her first book, *Social Diagnosis,* published in 1917, has been considered the first successful major presentation of the general concepts and principles underlying social casework.

Richmond distinguished four phases of the social worker's task in helping a *client,* a term used by the professional social worker to replace the earlier term *applicant.*[11]

(1) The first phase of activity was *investigation,* in which the worker gathered social evidence. Social evidence was "any and all facts as to personal or family history which, taken together, indicate the nature of a given client's social difficulties and the means to their solution."[12]

(2) Next, the caseworker made a *social diagnosis,* which Richmond defined as "the attempt to make as exact a definition as possible of the situation and personality of a human being in some social need—of his situation and personality, that is, in relation to other human beings upon whom he in any way depends or who depend upon him, and in relation also to the social institutions of his community."[13]

(3) The third phase was to *cooperate with all the possible sources of assistance*

that might be able to help with the problem. These included the client's family, relatives, employer, teachers, neighbors, sources of financial aid, and relevant philanthropic institutions. The social worker's task was to make use of these diverse sources in an organized way in the interests of the client.

(4) The fourth phase was *treatment*. In a later work, Richmond indicated that there were four main types of treatment, two of which she called "insights" and two, "acts." Insights were "an understanding of individuality" and "an understanding of environment." The two types of acts were "direct action of mind upon mind" and "indirect action through the social environment."[14] In other words, social workers accomplished their goals of being helpful by understanding the personality of each person they dealt with, by understanding the person's environment, by influencing the person they wanted to help ("mind upon mind"), and by working with other social agencies such as hospitals, schools, churches, and government agencies ("indirect action") to help the person.

Richmond was aware of the relationship between people and their environment, and she recognized the effect of social institutions on the lives of people in difficulty. Her concept of help was thus far more sophisticated than the original COS concept out of which it grew, which had considered the individual entirely responsible for his or her own situation. Still, Richmond's ideas and goals remained significantly individualistic. She sought to establish a profession that helped individuals, as was clear from her definition of social casework: *"Social case work consists of those processes which develop personality through adjustments consciously effected, individual by individual, between men and their social environment."*[15]

There were contributions to the launching of social casework other than those made by the COS. A physician in charge of the outpatient department at Massachusetts General Hospital around the turn of the century felt that many of the patients' illnesses could be partially due to their poverty, overcrowded living conditions, and working in sweatshops. In 1905, he instituted a department of medical social service, with medical social workers responsible for investigating how the patients' social situations affected their illnesses. The innovation was resisted by other physicians; only his power and prestige as department chief enabled him to install the medical social service. The women appointed to medical social service positions worked to define the contribution they could make in the hospital setting. Ida Cannon, an early leader in the field, identified the contribution as "an enlarged understanding of any psychic or social conditions which may cause the patient distress of mind or body. Character, human relationships, and community life are the fields of [their] study and effort."[16]

Schools were another arena for casework. In the early twentieth century, several eastern cities instituted the practice of the "visiting teacher" who undertook to visit children's homes to find out whether problems at home were affecting the child's adjustment to school. The impetus to this development came from the Settlement House movement rather than from within the school systems themselves. The activity came to be known as school social work.[17]

SETTLING AMONG
THE URBAN POOR

The Charity Organization movement and the Social Settlement movement originated at approximately the same time—the last third of the nineteenth century. These movements were similar in that both emphasized the giving of service, but charity organization thinking was a set of ideas concerning what to do about individuals, and social settlement thinking was a set of ideas concerning what to do about communities. Both movements focused on the same problem —improving the lives of individuals—but practitioners went at their task from opposite ends: Caseworkers gave their attention to the individual; social settlement workers sought first to understand the community. Casework was a method of changing individuals; social settlement work was a way of changing communities. Both movements also were concerned with increasing and improving the contact between rich and poor.

The Social Settlement movement began as an expression of both romanticism and social Christianity, an effort to establish a more humane society than the individualistic one brought into existence during the Industrial Revolution. The basic ideas of the Settlement movement are attributed to an Anglican clergyman, Samuel Barnett, pastor of "the worst parish in London."[18] Barnett's idea for bridging the gulf between rich and poor was to have university men live in a slum area and bring education and culture to the poor. Barnett, a graduate of Oxford University who maintained his university ties, was aware that some of the students, influenced by professors and writers at the forefront of the Romantic movement, were looking for ways to become active in changing society. Barnett wrote:

> They were conscious of something wrong underneath modern progress. . . .
> they realized that free trade, reform bills, philanthropic activity and missions had
> made neither health nor wealth. They were drawn to do something for the
> poor.[19]

Barnett established the first settlement house in 1884: Toynbee Hall occupied a new structure built for the purpose in the slum area, a building that resembled an Oxford University building. A number of students came down from Oxford to live in it and became "residents," as settlement workers thereafter were called.

A historian of the Settlement movement has summarized Barnett's general goals (and the activities of the residents) at Toynbee Hall:

> . . . it was spiritual poverty that concerned him more than economic want. "The poor," he wrote, "need more than food; they need also the knowledge, the character, the happiness which are the gifts of God to this Age." The settlement movement was part of the larger Romantic revolt against the vulgarization of society, and its ultimate goal was the spiritual awakening of the whole man—and not just the laborer, but the university man also. Barnett hoped that the settlement resident would obtain an "education by permeation." He also hoped that the settlement would become a rallying point for the neighborhood and that laborers and intellectuals would cooperate in promoting social reform. Though they did not enter politics directly, the settlement workers did try to make politicians aware of the people's needs. They got a library for their district. They promoted parks, playgrounds and cleaner streets; and several of the residents served on the school board.
> . . . the emphasis at Toynbee Hall was on education, for he believed that the greatest need was to bring some of the advantages of college to the workingmen. He sought to restore communication between classes and to revive the humanistic and aesthetic aspects of life. The settlement promoted picture exhibitions, university extension classes, and special lectures.[20]

Although there were skeptics who thought it foolish to try to reform slums through art and education, and Octavia Hill, the London COS leader, thought that permanent residence in a slum would be too much of a strain for educated men, the settlement idea caught on. By 1911, a quarter century after the founding of Toynbee Hall, there were forty-six settlements in Great Britain.[21] The settlement idea also took hold in the United States.

The American Transformation of the Settlement

The Settlement movement grew rapidly in the United States. Independently of one another, a number of Americans, impressed with Toynbee Hall and what it was trying to do, started settlements in the United States. The first settlement was the Neighborhood Guild, established in 1886 on the Lower East Side of New York City by Stanton Coit. A group of seven women, graduates of prestigious eastern women's colleges, established the College Settlement in the same neighborhood in 1889. At almost the same time, Jane Addams and Ellen Starr founded Hull House in Chicago, probably the most famous of all the settlements. By 1910, there were more than four hundred settlement houses in the United States.[22]

The American social settlements, particularly those in Chicago and New York City, were in at least one way significantly different from the English settlements. The American settlements became centers of vigorous participation in the numerous movements for social reform in the years between 1890 and 1914 that have become known as the Progressive Era. From the first, the American settlements focused more sharply on the neighborhood as a community rather than on the individual. The leaders of the movement were concerned with solving the problems of urban life, and they considered the reconstruction of the neighborhoods as their first order of business. Urban life in America was markedly different from urban life in Great Britain because American cities had become home to millions of European immigrants. Thus, in addition to their poverty, there were the many problems of adjusting to a new land and a new culture. The settlements became important agencies for facilitating immigrants' adaptation to American society.

Spearheads for reform

The settlements began with general goals but (unlike the Charity Organization movement) without focused methods. The settlement workers were open-minded, trying various approaches, some of which were discarded, others of which became more or less permanent features of their program. Art exhibits and lectures attracted some interest in the neighborhoods, but did not have the impact anticipated. Kindergartens and child-care activities for children of working mothers were more effective. Classes in homemaking, cooking, sewing, and shopping were often helpful to immigrant women living near the settlements. In short, the settlements offered many direct services to the people of their neighborhoods. In this respect, they were not significantly different from the English settlements.

The distinctiveness of the American settlements was in their broadening of horizons beyond the provision of direct services in their immediate neighborhoods, so that they became, in the words of a social welfare historian, spearheads for reform.[23] In company with other reformers, the settlement workers undertook battles to establish playgrounds for children, as part of a larger struggle to "convince the nation that creative play was important to the development of better citizens." Drawing on their close knowledge of their neighborhoods, settlement workers became leaders in efforts to improve housing. They investigated conditions and then argued for new housing laws before city councils and state legislatures. They organized protests to block government measures that they believed would make a neighborhood or city less livable. They helped immigrants in their dealings with diverse organizations. In 1909, in recognition of the problems faced by blacks migrating from rural areas to cities, three settlement workers founded the National Association for the Advancement of Colored People (NAACP).

Settlement workers, particularly in Boston, Chicago, and New York City, were active in support of organized labor; after investigating and publicizing working conditions in a number of industries, they fought for legislation to help workers. They were in the forefront of efforts to obtain legislation that would make child labor illegal and that would improve working conditions for women. They fought against corrupt politicians and for the reform of municipal government in order to obtain better municipal services for poor neighborhoods. When former President Theodore Roosevelt left the Republican party and ran for president in 1912 as head of the new Progressive party, numerous settlement workers were active in the campaign. Jane Addams spoke and wrote tirelessly for the cause. By 1912, she had become the most famous woman in the United States.[24]

The Settlement movement, particularly in the United States, was begun at least partly in opposition to the charity organization concept of how to deal with the social problems of the day. In the early days, the charity organization leaders criticized the settlement workers for the vagueness of their ideas, the trial-and-error searching for some way to have an impact. The settlement workers criticized the charity organization people for their heavy emphasis on the individual and their failure to appreciate the significance of social factors in the causation of poverty and dependency. After some years, the antagonism was reduced and workers from both movements began to cooperate more, eventually joining together from 1904 on in the same association, the National Conference of Charities and Correction.[25]

Despite the increased collaboration and the eventual mutual acceptance of each other as all being social workers, the Charity Organization movement and the Settlement movement left a legacy of two distinct conceptions of social work. One was the concept of the scientific, methodical, restrained professional, dealing with individual clients one by one, as does the physician or lawyer. The other was the concept of the spirited advocate, gathering systematic information about social evils and joining in or leading campaigns for reform—through protest marches, public speeches, testifying before congressional committees, lobbying in city councils and state legislatures, and joining forces with like-minded people from other segments of society—in addition to the many activities that took place in the settlement houses themselves. The professional concept of social service eventually won out; the concept of the social worker as neighbor to the poor, sharing their life in their neighborhood and also advocating solutions to their problems in political campaigns and legislative forums declined in popularity after World War I and remained dormant for about forty years, until it sprang to life again during the turbulent years of Lyndon Johnson's War on Poverty, only to fade once again in the 1970s. The concept of social worker as activist, front-line reformer lost out to the concept of social worker as technically skilled professional.

SOCIAL WORK'S REACH FOR PROFESSIONALIZATION

With the gradual realization by COS workers that human kindness and a desire to serve humanity were insufficient bases for carrying out "scientific charity," social service workers sought to professionalize their work. The effort began with the inauguration of training courses shortly before the turn of the century. Here we want to consider the ideas and the circumstances that led social work leaders to move in the direction of becoming professional.

A Growing Sense of Skill

The people doing charity organization work increasingly came to recognize that their tasks required skill. They further recognized that some procedures were more effective than others. As their awareness grew, certain issues surfaced that had to be resolved.

Volunteer versus paid work

In the COS philosophy, volunteer workers were the major figures. They were people who wanted to be of service by bringing superior moral understanding into the homes of the poor through friendly visiting. Paid district workers carried out investigations of the poor and kept records of all visits and aid given. Paid workers were seen as aiding the volunteers; the visiting was the main work.

As the idea of social casework skill took hold, the traditional relationship between paid workers and volunteers was challenged. The paid workers saw themselves as the truly knowledgeable workers in the charitable organizations, and they fought against the established idea that "[a] willingness to work for nothing . . . was the hall-mark of a sincere charity worker." There was considerable resistance among COS leaders to the idea of paid work, but in many communities there were not enough well-to-do people with the time and desire to do all the friendly visiting that was needed. Little by little, casework was taken over by paid workers. Volunteers moved into the background as members of advisory and fund-raising committees and as members of the boards of directors of the organizations employing the paid workers. Those who still wished to participate directly in the human contact aspect of the work had to be accepted and trained by the paid caseworkers.[26]

Moralism versus objectivity

The effort to become professional also required social workers to give up the sense of moral superiority that the preprofessional friendly visitors carried into their contacts with the people they wanted to help. The notion of morally superior upper and middle classes enlightening and uplifting a depraved lower class was now seen as an obstacle to effective casework. The professional social worker had to see clients objectively, without judging their moral character. Early leaders in establishing medical and psychiatric social work insisted that moralistic evaluations of patients interfered with helping them regain their health. (For example, they challenged the prevailing idea that venereal disease was a sign of immorality.)[27]

Reform versus professional service

Professionalization meant the replacement of sentiment with skill. By the end of World War I in 1918, much of the steam had gone out of the Settlement movement. Social reform was not an activity that could easily be fitted into the idea of a profession. The Russian Revolution that brought the Communists to power in 1917 was followed soon after by a "red scare" in the United States; people with nonconforming ideas were suspect and often hounded by the police and by the U.S. Justice Department. The settlement houses, where expression of all kinds of political and economic ideas was accepted, came to be regarded, particularly in Boston, Chicago, and New York City, as radical institutions. Settlement leaders became more hesitant to speak out on controversial issues. The settlements depended more and more upon paid staff workers, specializing in casework, physical education, arts and crafts, leadership, or recreation; settlement workers were increasingly known by their work titles rather than by the designation of "neighbor." Further, the second generation of settlement workers did not want to live in the settlement houses; some of them had grown up in slum neighborhoods and were now willing to work, but not to live, in them. The relationship of "friend and neighbor" was replaced by that of "social worker and client."[28]

Medicine as a Model

The developing field of social work was influenced by the field of medicine and patterned itself on that profession. For example, Charles Loch, for more than thirty years the head of the London COS, said in 1895 that charity was "the work of the social physician."[29] Mary Richmond, who is credited with having done more than any other person to establish social work as a scientific rather than a sentimental activity, took her concept of science from medicine. During her years as general secretary of the Baltimore COS, two of her closest advisors were leading physicians at The Johns Hopkins University Medical School, then the leading medical school in the country. Some of the friendly visitors in Baltimore were Hopkins medical students. Richmond even adopted medical language.

> It was during the Baltimore years that she wrote, for example, of pauperism as "a disease" and of the friendly visitor as a "social physician or general practitioner of charity" who is called upon to "heal" complex conditions. Although her writings contain references to what the teacher does with pupils and to how the lawyer uses forms of evidence, it was the medical or disease metaphor which was ultimately selected, developed, and refined by Mary Richmond and by later generations of casework theorists.[30]

As the medical model gained in influence over social work thinking, Mary Richmond's four phases of casework were reduced to three: study, diagnosis, and treatment. Her third phase, "cooperate with all possible sources of assistance," dropped out of the official definition of casework, though caseworkers continued to carry out this activity.

The Influence of Psychiatry

The medical model on which social casework fashioned itself became even more dominant as a result of the influence of psychiatry, and particularly psychoanalysis, which became the leading theory in American psychiatry after World War I.

Psychoanalysis was developed in the late 1890s by Sigmund Freud, a Viennese neurologist and psychiatrist. He had collaborators, and they had numerous followers, many of whom contributed to the theory, but Freud remained the dominant figure until his death in 1939. He is regarded as one of the towering figures of modern thought because of the far-reaching impact of his discoveries about human nature and human behavior.

Freud showed that humans were not the completely logical, rational beings they had credited themselves with being. Rather, they are beset by many desires and impulses that are irrational or simply have nothing to do with rationality. Some of these impulses originate in infancy and early childhood. As the person develops toward maturity, shaped by the socializing influences of his or her society, these desires become considered immature or otherwise unacceptable, both to the individual who has them and to others. The desires and impulses are not, however, always abandoned. For various reasons, the individuals may not want to give up the impulse or desire. They are then faced with a dilemma: wanting to do something that is unacceptable to others and that they would also feel guilty about or ashamed of if they actually acted on the desire. In brief, the individuals experience a *conflict* between the desire to do something and the desire not to do it. The conflict gives rise to *anxiety*. To protect themselves against the anxiety, the individuals develop a *defense*. There are many types of defenses, but the most common is *repression:* the individuals simply become unaware of having the particular desire; the desire becomes *unconscious*. The continued existence of the desire, despite the individuals' unawareness of it, shows up in indirect ways, such as in slips of the tongue (which Freud called "the psychopathology of everyday life"), in dreams, in nervous mannerisms, or in various kinds of symptoms that may be serious enough to hamper the in-dividuals' functioning.

This brief summary can scarcely do justice to the scope and depth of Freud's ideas, which influenced numerous fields, such as psychiatry, education, political science, literary criticism and literature itself, and perhaps most of all social work.

The influence of psychiatry on social work began to be felt even before Freudian thought gained prominence after World War I. As psychiatry began to move away from the custodial insane asylum, psychiatric clinics were set up for dealing with psychiatric problems on an outpatient basis. In the early twentieth century, these new clinics, as well as some of the older asylums, began hiring social workers. As with medical social workers and school social workers, these psychi-atric social workers were assigned the work of visiting the homes of patients in order to find out what aspects of the home situation might be affecting the pa-tients' behavior and giving rise to the patients' problems. Some of the early psychi-atric social workers found work for mental patients, and provided other rehabilita-tive services. The new type of psychiatry that found social work helpful was known as social psychiatry; its approach, developed during the Progressive Era, was based on the belief that the patients' difficulties were the outcomes of their struggles to adapt to the pressures of their environment.

Freudian ideas began to gain ground after World War I and became more influential than social psychiatry. Psychoanalysis offered a more comprehensive theory, it was more exciting, and appeared to be more penetrating in its explana-tions. More and more psychiatrists adopted the psychoanalytic view. They began to pass on their view to social workers in a new type of organization that appeared in the 1920s, the child guidance clinic.[31] Child guidance clinics were first set up to deal with the problem of delinquency, but their scope of activity widened to include other types of problems.

Child guidance clinics typically established a team of workers from three professions—psychiatry, social work, and psychology. The psychologist administered intelligence and other types of tests; the psychiatrist treated the patient, the child; and the social worker established and maintained a relationship with the parents, since their cooperation was necessary in helping the child. The social workers helped the parents to deal with any fears that they had in relation to their child's problems. The psychiatrists, supervising these transactions, transmitted psychoanalytic ideas and techniques to the psychiatric social workers. The psychiatric social workers came to regard traditional casework, with its focus on the client's social environment, as superficial, in comparison to probing into the client's emotional life. Some psychiatric social workers left child guidance clinics to work in other types of social work agencies such as the family welfare agencies that had evolved from the old Charity Organization societies. Thus they carried the psychoanalytic point of view into new contexts. Perhaps not surprisingly, family welfare agencies began to regard many of their clients as being emotionally disturbed and in need of psychoanalytic treatment.

Between 1920 and 1940, social casework underwent a profound transformation. Concern with the client's social environment receded into the background, although it was usually not totally disregarded. The focus of interpretation was nonetheless the client's emotional life, not his or her social situation. Some leaders in the field asserted that all good casework was essentially psychiatric in nature. But while casework became less sociological in its methods and more psychological, the change had a sociological consequence: It gave casework a basis for dealing with people who were not poor. Everybody has emotional problems; therefore, social casework no longer needed to be thought of as a profession that dealt only with poor people. It became a generalized helping profession. Economic dependency was just one of the problems it might deal with, and economic dependency was often interpreted as a manifestation of emotional dependency, an inability of the client to stand on his own feet.[32] With "the rediscovery of poverty" in the United States in the 1960s, the psychiatric emphasis in social work was destined to come under attack; the War on Poverty (see Chapters 6 and 11) focused attention on countering unemployment and on strengthening communities.

The Other Methods

Casework is the most widely practiced method in social work. Without casework, there would be no profession of social work. The vast majority of students who graduate from schools of social work come out as caseworkers. But there are two other core social work methods: group work and community organization.

Group work

Group work (sometimes called social group work) developed out of settlement work, although the beginnings of the idea can be found earlier. The discussion of associated philanthropy in Chapter 3 touched briefly upon the many charitable associations that were established in Great Britain from the seventeenth to the nineteenth centuries. Some of them were directed toward making young people "virtuous." Thus, in the late nineteenth century, Samuel Barnett's wife

> exhorted the lady visitors of the Metropolitan Association for Befriending Young Servants to counsel the girls on behaviour and dress and to direct their minds from lovers to the wholesome reading of monthly periodicals. "It is not like the girls of our own class whose ignorance about sin we foster for fear of losing their innocence," she explained. "The girls, alas! many of them with naturally coarse minds . . . are conversant already with all the terrible facts of life."[33]

The beginnings of group work are to be found, then, like those of casework, in what has been called "the Lady Bountiful tradition" of Victorian society: well-to-do women bringing gifts of moral superiority to their moral inferiors. Samuel Barnett was perhaps a key figure in introducing groups into social work, for although he accepted the COS idea that poor and distressed people had to be helped on an individual basis, he also recognized that a person could often more readily be helped to improve by being part of a group with a common purpose, a group whose members cooperated with and supported one another. In the clubs and classes he established at Toynbee Hall, he tried to make all participants feel that they could contribute to the group.[34]

The nineteenth-century groups and associations, out of which social group work developed, were a response to the sense of isolation, anonymity, and demoralization that had spread in the industrial cities. The closeness of village life had been lost, and the new groups, each organized with a specific interest or purpose, were efforts to compensate for the loss.[35]

The early groups and associations used the concept of the group in a conscious, purposeful way; the group was its own reason for being. But groups also were formed for other purposes. As early as 1909, Jane Addams reported on "how Hull House used the gang spirit in a group of young drug addicts to help them overcome their addiction."[36] It was not until the 1920s that social group work was formally incorporated into social work, when it was first taught at the School of Applied Social Sciences of Western Reserve University in Cleveland. The first theoretical work on the method, considered as significant for group work as Richmond's first book was for casework, was by Professor Grace Coyle of that university; her book *Social Process in Organized Groups* appeared in 1930.[37]

Group work today uses groups in relation to purposes originating both inside and outside the group. It can be defined as "a method of interpersonal helping developed within the profession of social work which uses the small group as both means and context for achieving individual and group objectives."[38] The focus on individual objectives within group work was a later development; Coyle envisioned working with groups in order to encourage growth of responsibility to the larger society and to thereby enable "socially intelligent citizens" to accomplish social change in a democratic way.[39] Today group workers still consider that they have an "enabling role," but they are more concerned with enabling individuals to develop their personalities and potentials through participation in a group than in enabling the group to bring about changes in the larger society.

The use of group work spread beyond the social settlements that were its first locale and the community centers that are modern-day successors to settlement houses (though a few settlements still retain that designation). Group work processes are utilized in such agencies as summer camps and recreation programs, mental health programs, and agencies specializing in the problems of particular populations—delinquents, the elderly, unmarried mothers, and so on.

Community organization

Community organization was the last of the three major social work methods to be explicitly recognized as a method. Nevertheless, it was, "like social group work, . . . practiced long before it was defined."[40] Community organization can perhaps be traced back to the seventeenth century when merchant philanthropists began to shift from individual philanthropy to associated philanthropy (see Chapter 4). The more immediate origin, however, was the Charity Organization movement, which was concerned with coordinating services in order to save money. The COS undertook various measures to achieve their goals:

> They established social service indexes or exchanges listing individuals or "cases" known to cooperating agencies. They evolved the "case conference," in which workers from different agencies interested in the same "case" or the same family —workers from the settlement house, the relief-giving agencies, the child-placing agencies, the agencies established to protect children from cruelty, the visiting nurse association, and others—would meet to plan a constructive course of action in behalf of the "case." In some instances, too, the charity organization societies made broad studies of social and economic problems and recommended specific remedial measures.[41]

Just as businessmen played a large role in the social welfare field in the fourteenth century with their founding of hospitals and almshouses, in the seventeenth century with their development of associated philanthropy, and in the nineteenth century with their gospel of wealth, in the twentieth century it was businessmen who supplied the major impetus in initiating community organization in its modern form. In the early 1900s, business organizations in several cities began evaluating social agencies on the basis of efficiency and whether there was a need for the particular agency; only agencies that met their requirements received their endorsement and, consequently, monetary contributions. Social workers did not like business organizations being the evaluators of social agencies, but they accepted the necessity of this form of coordination of agency work rather than letting each social agency go its own way.

The coordination of financing efforts was accelerated during World War I, when many communities organized "war chests" to raise money for problems arising out of the war. After the war, the idea of combined fund raising was continued in the establishment of "community chests." (The term derives from the actual church chests of the early Christian period.) Experience in several cities had revealed that a relatively small proportion of citizens were donors to charitable agencies; the agencies engaged in fierce competition to raise money. Joining together in raising funds—federated fund-raising—was seen as helping the agencies in their work by increasing the number of donors, eliminating the time and effort wasted in competing for funds, and increasing the effectiveness of all the agencies through their working cooperatively.

Planning of welfare activities became part of the community chest activities, along with fund raising. The federations—or associated charities, as they were called in some cities—became increasingly independent and gradually gained some control over the agencies by gaining the power to examine the agencies' budgets, their plans for obtaining money to run their programs, and their plans for spending the money. The federation's power to examine the budgets of the agencies to which it channeled the funds it raised presumably exerted pressure on the agencies to improve both their efficiency in the use of the monies and their standards of practice; since there was usually less money to go around than the agencies felt they needed for their programs, the federation tended to give money to those that were judged to be doing the best work. Fund raising became systematic, carried out in widely publicized "campaigns" adapted from the public relations and advertising techniques used in business.

Federated fund raising, largely instigated by businessmen, was the major impetus toward the development of the community organization method in social work. A second impetus came from social work leaders themselves, also in the early years of the twentieth century. In some cities, local social work leaders organized a Council of Social Agencies to study community problems and coordinate the work of their agencies in dealing with the problems. Later, the federations and councils of social agencies in the cities fused into unified organizations.[42] Today most of these organizations are known as the United Way (see Chapter 4).

Community chest and council planning have been the core of community organization practice, which was officially recognized as a social work specialty by the Council on Social Work Education only in 1962.[43] The community organization social worker who does planning and fund raising works mostly with executive and staff members of social agencies, rather than with individual clients or groups. In recent years, two other concepts of community organization have emerged. One has been called *community development;* it focuses on the economic and social progress of a whole community based on as active participation by the members as the community development worker can elicit. Community development is most actively pursued in underdeveloped countries rather than in the United States; however, the work of the settlement houses in neighborhoods can be considered an example of community development.

The second of the newer concepts of community organization is *community action,* which focuses usually on mobilizing neighborhoods to obtain a larger share of power and benefits from the larger community or city of which they are a part.[44] Social workers who work with such community segments (usually just called communities) make an effort to have the community members act together for their own welfare. For this reason, community action will be discussed under the general concept of mutual aid, in Part VI. The social worker who works in community action is usually referred to as a community organizer, whereas the social worker who works in the more traditional setting of the welfare council and fund raising organization may be referred to as a welfare planner.

PROFESSION AND AGENCY

The preceding section dealt with social work's transformation from an activity based primarily on religious and humanitarian sentiments to an activity based on skills and formal concepts. Although humanitarian sentiment is not absent from the practice of contemporary social work, it is modified by more technical considerations. This transformation is generally regarded as the professionalization of social work.

Social work has been referred to as a profession, though the term *profession* has not yet been defined. This section offers an examination of the concept of profession and of the respects in which social work does or does not conform to the concept. Social work is first considered in relation to the general category of professions, and second in relation to the typical setting in which it is practiced, the social agency.

What is a Profession?

The work a person does to gain a livelihood is generally known as an occupation. An occupation is a more or less standard grouping of activities in an economic organization; most occupations have names—farmer, letter carrier, salesperson, manager, physician, and so on. The U.S. government publishes the *Dictionary of Occupational Titles,* which lists more than twenty-five thousand occupations. Only a small number—perhaps between forty and a hundred —of these occupations are known as professions.[45] (The need to give such a broad range is indicative of the uncertainty that exists about which occupations merit being called professions.) For many years, students of occupations sought to identify specific characteristics that distinguish professions from other occupations. Recently, they have come to the conclusion that a profession is an occupation that claims to be a profession *and* that has its claim recognized by the wider society. This definition is based on observations that reveal that (1) the label of "profession" is valuable to the occupation that has it and to the people who work in it; (2) not all of the occupations that refer to themselves as professions have their claim recognized by the public and by government agencies that regulate certain aspects of professional activity; (3) the characteristics of occupations may change over time, so that occupations that once were not considered professions can acquire that status; their claims may be recognized.

The designation of profession is valued by people in an occupation because it brings them one or more of the following rewards: (1) prestige, (2) higher income, (3) autonomy in doing their work. With such rewards, it is not surprising that people in many occupations claim that their line of work is a profession. Thus a cleaning firm may announce that it does "professional carpet cleaning." The public may accept such a claim, because the adjective "professional" has two somewhat different opposites, "nonprofessional" and "amateur." If the owners mean that the service is professional and not amateurish, they are saying they know their work well and are not dabbling in it. But if the owners say they are in "the carpet cleaning profession" instead of in "the carpet cleaning business," people are likely to think they are trying to inflate their status, claiming more prestige for their work than it is entitled to.

Which occupations claiming to be professions are likely to have their claim recognized by the wider society? A clue to the answer is suggested by the fact that professions were once referred to as "the learned professions." Law, medicine, the ministry, and university teaching were the first occupations to be recognized as professions, recognition that goes back several centuries. In modern times, many more occupations have gained inclusion in this category. Examination of these newer professions, along with the older ones, suggests that they have two main characteristics in common: (1) Each occupation is based upon *a body of abstract thought and knowledge,* which takes a prolonged period of study to acquire; and (2) each occupation is governed by a moral norm that is known as the *ideal of service.*

Most lines of work require that the worker know something in order to do the work. Some lines of work require considerable skill and a good deal of technical information—the work of laboratory technicians, television repairers, and automobile mechanics, for example. However, the workers in these lines do not necessarily have broad knowledge of the theoretical principles upon which their particular specialties are based. The period of study required to become a technician or a skilled craftsperson is shorter than that required to become a physician, an electronics engineer, or an industrial engineer. The latter, professionals, need to consider theoretical principles in order to solve the problems they encounter in their work. Technicians or skilled craftspersons may have some knowledge of the principles of physiology or electronics or physics underlying their work, but the ability to do the work depends much more on know-how than on "know-why."

The service ideal specifies that "the technical solutions which the professional arrives at should be based on the client's needs, not necessarily the best material interest or needs of the professional himself or, for that matter, those of society."[46]

The occupations that are based on theoretical knowledge and a service ideal are usually able to convince the wider society in which they function that (1) they have a monopoly of knowledge in their field and that (2) people who are not workers in the profession should not be allowed to do that kind of work, both because they do not have sufficient knowledge and because they cannot be counted on to be dedicated to the client's best interests. When society accepts a profession's claim to a monopoly, it grants the profession's exclusive right to take certain kinds of actions or offer certain kinds of advice. Only physicians and dentists can prescribe controlled drugs; only lawyers can offer legal advice for a fee. (There is no legal restriction on friends or relatives offering legal advice or advice on medical remedies that can be bought without prescription; advice given within such personal relationships is not part of an occupation.)[47]

Is social work a profession?

People within social work and observers outside the field tend to disagree in their answer to this question. The answers offered are not merely "Yes" and "No" but also "Partly" and "Almost."

There is no dispute that social work is governed by a service ideal as much as is any recognized profession. The major disagreements in answering the question revolve around the body of knowledge on which social work is based ("the knowledge base"). In the early days, when the Settlement movement was at its most active, with its leaders campaigning for social reform of health conditions, working conditions, housing conditions, and urban life generally, while the social caseworkers were making their early claims to professionalization, various outside experts said that it was impossible to construct a profession based on reform. Many people were fighting for reform—lawyers, labor leaders, professors, teachers, some business people, citizens in all lines of work. Fighting for reform is the activity of citizens, not an occupation and certainly not a profession. This viewpoint was generally accepted at the time.

In the 1960s, there was some discussion claiming that reform activities had in fact become professionalized, in the sense that the War on Poverty had been developed not directly out of protests by the poor but out of pressures applied by social workers, teachers, doctors, psychotherapists, counselors, and administrators, all drawing upon their specialized knowledge to put pressure on Congress to act.[48] But this argument still did not define social work in terms of reform as its central activity. It acknowledged only that some social workers, in company with some professionals in other fields, had become knowledgeable and skillful in working for social reform. Only later, after the War on Poverty had collapsed, and reform-minded social workers were returning to traditional behind-the-desk practice, were there calls for a "new breed of professional"—a professional social worker with the knowledge of how to bring about reform or, as it is now called, "social change."[49] However, this viewpoint—that the social worker is a professional whose knowledge base is the knowledge of how to bring about social change—is not the dominant one in the field.

What, then, is social work's knowledge base? By widespread agreement, social work is built on knowledge borrowed from the social sciences and from psychiatry, and on knowledge built up out of its own practice. An official view of the knowledge base divides it into three areas: social services, social work practice, and human growth and behavior. Commenting on these three areas, one analyst noted:

> The largest knowledge components in the social service and practice areas have been developed by social work for social work. These have been supplemented by borrowing from medicine, political science, economics, sociology, law and so forth. In the area of human growth and behavior the situation is reversed. Here we depend to the greatest extent on borrowed knowledge, principally from psychoanalytic psychology.[50]

A more recent analysis, pointing to new tasks that social work is being called upon to perform, such as community organizations lobbying for new services and income maintenance programs, points to the necessity of additional borrowing:

> Clearly, as the scope of social work broadens, social workers are required to call on resources beyond and outside their traditional knowledge base. Economics, political science, macrosociology, and communications theory, in addition to new developments in those social and behavioral sciences previously utilized by social

work, such as psychology, psychiatry, social psychology, anthropology, and microsociology, are becoming increasingly important.[51]

To be sure, other professions also borrow knowledge, but to a lesser extent than does social work. As one professor of social work has noted:

> . . . one of the facts about social work is that it is a borrower of knowledge from social and behavioral sciences: it does not ordinarily embark on basic research; instead, it puts together this borrowed knowledge in very particular ways for very particular uses. The way in which social work utilizes basic knowledge of human behavior and social systems is what gives social work its stamp. . . . The kind, scope, and depth of knowledge sought for and needed in social work practice makes imperative the borrowing we have mentioned, and differentiates the social worker from other professional practitioners.[52]

Because most of social work's theoretical knowledge is borrowed from other fields, some students of occupations and professions conclude that social work is among the occupations that should be classified as a semiprofession. In a recent study, Nina Toren came to this conclusion:

> To be granted the rights and rewards of an established profession—autonomous control, high prestige, and high income—social work will have to demonstrate that its members command esoteric knowledge and skills which enable them to accomplish their task more efficiently and with better results than "any other enthusiastic amateur," as is clearly the case, for example, in the medical profession.
> The general conclusion which can be drawn from our discussion at this point is that to claim and to be awarded an "established" position (particularly in the sense of professional autonomy), the profession must demonstrate a certain congruence between the two core elements—systematic knowledge and professional norms. If a profession ranks high only on one of these dimensions and low on the other, it will not be accredited full professional status either by the public or by social scientists. A profession may be based on a great amount of systematic knowledge but lack a collectivity-oriented code of ethics, as in the case of engineering specialists and other kinds of technicians. Or, it may be committed to a service ideal but lack a theoretical knowledge base, as in the case of social work, nursing, and librarianship.[53]

Toren noted that some subdivisions of social work have a more systematic body of knowledge than others and thus are closer to professionalization. Professionalization is not an "either-or" classification; rather, there are degrees of professionalization.

William Goode, another student of occupations, offers these predictions:

> These semi-professions will achieve professionalism over the next generation: social work, marital counseling, and perhaps city planning. . . . The following occupations will not become professional: . . . Pharmacy will not change its status

much. Next, school-teaching will not achieve professionalism, nor will librarianship. Many articles and speeches have argued that business management, public relations, and advertising are, or should be, professions, but none of these will achieve it.[54]

Social workers today are moving in opposite directions. On the one hand, an increasing number are establishing themselves in private practice as psychotherapists. They do not work for any social agency; rather, they maintain private offices and charge fees for their services, as do psychiatrists. The number who do so is not yet very large, but it is growing. These social workers clearly have great autonomy in their work. Their work is largely unregulated, except by the willingness of colleagues and lay people to refer patients to them, and by professional supervisory relationships. In fact, some social workers in private practice have abandoned the social work term *client* to designate the person they help and have adopted the medical term *patient.*[55] These social workers in private practice are perhaps "spearheads for professionalization"; more than any other grouping within the occupation, they are claiming and pushing for the degrees of status, income, and autonomy that the established professions have long enjoyed.

On the other hand, as noted above, some social workers are calling for social work to emphasize social change. Among these, some think of working for social change as a new concept of professionalization, while others say that it is a call for deprofessionalization. In the 1950s, a prominent social work educator wrote an article entitled "How Social Will Social Work Be?" in which he argued that the drive for prestige and professional status was coming to social work at too high a price. He argued that social work was de-emphasizing controversial social action that might be necessary in order for social work to achieve its goals of helping people, and that social work was conforming too much to the dominant ideas in the society rather than taking on a critical role.[56] Criticisms of social work in this vein reached a peak during the years of the War on Poverty, when social work was accused of having turned its back on the poor.[57] From this point of view, private practice of social work for a fee might be considered an even greater turning away from the traditional problems that gave rise to social work as an occupation.

These two opposite concepts of how to do social work represent minority positions within the field. Most social workers argue neither for private practice of psychotherapy nor for working toward social change as the main function of social work. Most social workers deliver services as employees of social agencies, either government departments or voluntary agencies. It appears likely that most will continue to work as employees, whether as direct service practitioners, supervisors, welfare planners, or managers and executive directors. Within the framework of social welfare agencies, it can be expected that social work will look for ways to enlarge its autonomy.[58]

The diverse ideas and opinions about social work's purpose, main activities, and operating style are important. The concepts that win out determine the courses that will be taught in social work programs, the skills and values social workers will acquire, and the kinds of contributions they will make to the social welfare field after they complete their schooling—in short, what kind of occupation social work will be.

Social Agencies

Social work is carried out in a variety of organizations. In some, social work is ancillary to the larger purpose of the organization; this is the case, for example, in hospitals, schools, and prisons. In other organizations, social work is the central activity of the organization; the family service agency is the best example. The differences between these two types of organization are important, but the similarity between them is more important for the present task. Both types are part of a larger trend toward the growth of bureaucracy in modern Western society. All kinds of small organizations have been replaced by large, impersonal ones. In social work, the settlement house, a residence for "neighbors" of the poor who looked for any way to be helpful, has been replaced by the social agency, with its formal programs.

The most usual way of distinguishing between the types of organization in which social work is done is to divide them into voluntary and public agencies. *Voluntary social agencies* are organizations that are run by boards of directors that are generally dominated by successful business people, although in recent years agency boards have been including representatives of the groups being helped by that agency. The board of directors has the ultimate authority and responsibility for running the organization; it is responsible for raising the money and hiring the executive director. The board sets the policy, that is, decides what areas of work the agency will engage in, what categories of problems will be handled. The board may itself be constrained by the United Way or another coordinating group that collects and allocates money for all the agencies that are affiliated with it.

Social workers, as employees of their agencies, may find that the outlook they acquired in the course of training is compatible with their agencies' policies and rules. On the other hand, social workers may find themselves subject to two conflicting sources of authority: professional and bureaucratic.

Professional control is characterized by being exercised from "within" by an internalized code of ethics and special knowledge acquired during a long period of training, and by a group of peers, which is alone qualified to make professional judgments. This type of authority differs greatly from bureaucratic authority which emanates from a hierarchical position.[59]

Social workers may reach conclusions based on professional judgment that may differ from the policies and rules handed down to them by higher authorities in their agencies; the higher authorities will generally prevail. They have the power to govern the agency.

However, social workers are not without recourse in this type of situation. There are strategies that they can use to change the agencies' policies or rules. Two general strategies for doing so have been identified. Social workers can adopt a *collaborative strategy* when they feel the management is open to new ideas, will listen to proposals for alternative ways of doing things, will establish committees within the agency to review policies, rules, problems, and sources of disagreement. When they feel such a collaborative strategy will not work, they can undertake an *adversary strategy* and attempt to accomplish changes through petitions, public criticism of the agency, encouraging noncompliance with existing policy or procedure, engaging in strikes, picketing, formal bargaining, or lawsuits. Thus social workers can use their own knowledge of organizations to attempt to bring about change in their employing organization when they believe that the organization is in some respect not functioning in accord with appropriate professional standards.[60]

Public social agencies are units of government. They are elaborately interconnected and elaborately subdivided. But there are two organizational facts of central importance: (1) Each state in the United States is free to decide what social services it wishes to offer: (2) If a state chooses to offer certain services in accord with federal laws, the federal government will pay a substantial part of the state's cost in providing them.[61] These two features of public social service have been true since the Social Security Act of 1935. (An amendment to that act, known as Title XX, that went into effect in 1975, has introduced some potentially important new developments. Title XX will be discussed later in the chapter.)

Only a small minority of professional social workers have gone to work for public agencies. The principal reason for this may lie in the tradition growing out of the New Deal period. Public agencies took over the task of giving financial relief; social workers who wanted to practice the skills they had learned in social work school found their fullest opportunity to do this in voluntary agencies, and this has remained more or less the case since the days of the New Deal. According to Burton Gummer, a professor of social work who has studied this relationship (or lack of it), graduate schools of social work have generally not prepared students to work in public welfare, and most of those studying for the Master of Social Work degree do not want to work in public agencies. He contends that public welfare departments are staffed by people who are less sympathetic to clients than social workers would be. He believes that in the period of increasingly scarce resources that the United States has recently entered, there is a greater need for social workers who can work to protect client interests in organizations that are focused on saving money. He concludes:

> While the social work profession continues its intramural battles over the defini-
> tion of its goals and purposes, the one function of social work that has the strongest
> claim to legitimacy in the public domain is the care of the dependent, deprived,
> debilitated and demoralized citizens of this society. And it is through the public
> social services—and only through them—that social workers can exercise this
> function. If professional social work rejects that role, its claim to legitimacy and
> status in American society will be greatly weakened.[62]

The relationship between social work and public social agencies thus may be at
a turning point. The recognition by many public agencies of the Bachelor of
Social Work degree as qualifying a person to practice social work—a change that
occurred in the 1970s—may bring about a closer association of social work
education, social work practice, and public welfare agencies than existed in the
period between the New Deal and the War on Poverty.

THE SCOPE OF SOCIAL SERVICE

The social services in modern Western society include a large array of activities
that are carried out by people in a number of occupations, including social work,
clinical psychology, vocational counseling, family and marriage counseling, day-
care work, and legal aid. Scholar Paul Halmos has argued that the social services
(or "personal social services," as they are known in Great Britain) have gained
such importance that their ideology—the basic values and beliefs—is coming to
be the dominant moral force in Western society:

> Instead of the barons, the warriors, and later the industrial and commercial mag-
> nates, it is now the university trained, academically and professionally licensed
> intellectuals who rise to positions of leadership. And now, indeed, I will try to
> show that the personal service professionals are beginning to lead these intellectu-
> als either in fact or through the influence of their ideas.[63]

This view that personal service professionals are on their way to being the leaders
of other influential intellectuals in Western society seems unduly optimistic.[64]
    Nicholas Kittrie has also noted the growing influence of the social service
idea, but he focuses particularly on the psychotherapeutic version of this idea.
As a legal scholar, he is concerned with the fact that psychotherapy is being used
in more and more situations, in such a way as to make it a form of punishment
of the people supposedly being helped. He notes that several categories of social
difficulty that were formerly handled by the American legal system as crimes

requiring punishment are now defined by it as psychiatric conditions requiring psychotherapy. These difficulties include alcoholism, drug addiction, juvenile delinquency, and psychopathic behavior. While acknowledging the meritorious achievements of social welfare overall, Kittrie says that the legal system often imposes psychotherapy upon persons it judges to be suffering from one of these types of difficulty, with the result that they are often incarcerated involuntarily in treatment institutions for longer periods of time than they would have been put in jail had they been convicted of crimes under the older laws. He thus sees a danger in the rise of "the therapeutic state," the state that uses the powers of government to impose psychotherapy on more and more categories of "deviant" citizens.[65]

The social services in the United States expanded considerably in the early 1960s when for the first time, during the administration of President John F. Kennedy, social services were adopted as part of a federal strategy to cope with the rising number of people receiving public assistance under the AFDC program. The idea was that economic growth in the United States was successfully redistributing income; therefore, those who remained poor had personal problems that were preventing them from taking advantage of the economic abundance that was available. This explanation was only moderately different from the explanation of dependency that led to the New Poor Law in England in 1834. The American response in 1962 was, however, different from the British response in 1834. Instead of imposing a workhouse test, the 1962 amendments to the Social Security Act permitted state governments to offer rehabilitation services to AFDC recipients. The federal government would pay for 75 percent of the costs of these services, such as counseling to unmarried mothers in the use of medical care and child-care services, counseling about illegitimacy, referral for legal service when needed, and referral to other specialized agencies that might be helpful.

Social work leaders had advocated the combining of social service with public assistance payments; in other words, the same workers would provide both services. The program undertaken in 1962 was not successful, however; one reason may have been that the services were not administered by trained social workers but by public assistance caseworkers, more than 95 percent of whom were not professionally trained. The 1962 program was withdrawn in 1967, and was replaced by an emphasis on work incentives for AFDC recipients.[66] (Some state and local welfare departments now specify the Bachelor of Social Work degree, recognized as a professional degree by the National Association of Social Workers in 1970, as a requirement for social welfare positions, whereas in the past a college degree in any field would have sufficed.[67])

The scope of social services today can perhaps be appreciated by a consideration of their variety as enumerated in three broad categories by Alfred J. Kahn, a leading contemporary scholar in the field. Kahn suggests that social services can usefully be classified by their *function*, that is, the kind of contribution they make to the person being helped. *Social services for socialization and development* are those that carry out educational, child-rearing, value-imparting, and social affiliation activities. "The goal is socialization into communal values, transmittal of goals and motivation, and enhancement of personal development."[68] Examples include Head-Start day-care programs, youth centers, summer camps, senior citizens centers, home-delivered hot meals, family vacation programs. These social services take over some responsibilities that were once handled entirely by family, relatives, and neighborhood (or by no one at all).

Social services for therapy, help, rehabilitation, and social protection are those that

> seek to help individuals with problems by supplementing or substituting for the primary group supports. . . . Often the focus is on brief or intensive personal help. . . . Frequently the goal is restoration of as much normal functioning as possible. . . . Often the assignment is that of assuming societal control over "dangerous" or unacceptable deviance while help is rendered.[69]

Services of this type include family casework services, child welfare programs, protective services for the aged, group therapy, juvenile probation and parole, school social work, and medical social work.

Because of the great proliferation of services in modern Western society, *access services* have become necessary. These are services of information and referral. The sheer number and variety of social services means that great numbers of people do not know about the many services that may be helpful to them. One of the social worker's important tasks is "liaison," putting people in touch with service organizations that can help them. Access services take such forms as neighborhood information centers, neighborhood legal services, telephone "hot lines," and services for receiving and evaluating complaints (against adverse bureaucratic decisions, for example).[70]

Legal Service as a Social Service

The War on Poverty, initiated under the Economic Opportunity Act of 1964 and administered by the Office of Economic Opportunity (OEO), introduced many new services into the American social welfare field. One of the most innovative was the Legal Services program, begun in 1965, the first major effort by the federal government to provide and pay for legal assistance in civil matters for a large client community. The program operated out of neighborhood offices in poor communities.

Like any profession, the legal profession has an obligation to give some service to clients who cannot pay. Although it is not known how well lawyers meet this obligation overall, the obligation is written into the rules of the bar associations. In addition, the legal profession's image of itself includes the idea that lawyers are "by training and work experience particularly suited to grapple with complex social problems." Moreover, lawyers had been active for many years in organizations working for broader social justice. The rise of the civil rights movement in the late 1950s and early 1960s drew lawyers into reform activities.[71] Thus the way was prepared for this new concept of service to the poor.

The Legal Services program engaged in two main types of activity: individual cases and law reform. Individual cases are those that help solve the legal problem of the individual client. Law reform might involve legislative lobbying for changes in laws as well as taking on *class action* suits, cases in which the court's decision affects a large group of people in a similar situation. An examination of the 282,000 cases handled in 1968 by 850 neighborhood law offices showed that about 40 percent of the Legal Services program caseload in that year dealt with family problems.

> The high percentage of family problems handled by legal services projects, especially divorce and annulment, has been a subject of wide criticism. Critics seemed surprised to discover that in a society where one out of every four marriages ends in divorce, marital life among the poor is not all bliss. Some were hostile to the idea of using poverty funds for such "frivolous" activities. The Legal Services program has taken the position that the poor are entitled to the same rights as the rich and that the same scope of legal services should be offered them.[72]

There were, nevertheless, arguments about setting priorities for the use of limited funds. Legal Services lawyers were active in working for reform of laws dealing with welfare, housing, and consumer affairs. One of the important changes in welfare law achieved by the program was the abolition of state residence requirements for eligibility for public assistance.[73]

Even in the social reform movement that Legal Services was part of, ancient attitudes occasionally reappeared: "Too often legal services . . . attorneys believe they are dispensing charity to the undeserving rather than serving clients with a right to representation."[74] In the rendering of services, creeping condescension is a constant hazard. But this should not be the last word. The Legal Services program introduced a new concept and a new level of effort in safeguarding the legal rights of people unable to pay for legal service. It astonished many that this federally funded program even filed lawsuits against other federal government agencies to obtain satisfactory safeguarding and enforcement of legal rights to the extent possible within the agency's budget.

Title XX

Title XX, an amendment to the Social Security Act of 1935, was passed in 1974 and went into effect in 1975. According to some, it represents a significant new policy of the federal government regarding the social services. The law provides that the federal government will reimburse states up to a certain amount for services provided. In order to receive such reimbursement, the state must prepare a Comprehensive Annual Social Services Program (CASSP), setting forth what services it proposes to offer, how many people it expects to help with each service, and how much money it expects to spend for each service. The state can decide what services it plans to offer its residents, but all must be directed to at least one of the five goals specified in the amendment:

(1) Achieving or maintaining economic self-support to prevent, reduce or eliminate dependency;

(2) Achieving or maintaining self-sufficiency, including a reduction or prevention of dependency;

(3) Preventing or remedying neglect, abuse, or exploitation of children and adults unable to protect their own interest or preserving, rehabilitating or reuniting families;

(4) Preventing or reducing inappropriate institutional care by providing for community-based care, home-based care or other forms of less intensive care; or

(5) Securing referral or admission for institutional care when other forms of care are not appropriate or providing services to individuals in institutions.[75]

Title XX has been seen by one prominent scholar as significant for the following reasons:

(1) The federal government will reimburse states for some services that it offers to everybody in the state, not just to people receiving public assistance or otherwise having low incomes. This is a step toward *universalism* and away from categorical selectivity in social services. It means that certain services, at least, are considered for everybody, not just for the stigmatized poor.[76] Thus they are, in Wilensky and Lebeaux's terms, "institutional" rather than "residual" (see Chapter 1).

(2) The federal government does not place restrictions on the services it will pay for, provided each service fits one of the five goals. In the 1962 amendments (see Chapter 6), "federal grants for social service went mainly to pay the salaries of caseworkers. . . . Under Title XX, each state is free to support whatever social services are deemed appropriate for its communities" in keeping with the five goals.[77] These include what have come to be known as "hard" services such as providing homemaker service and transportation, as well as counseling, which is coming to be referred to in government circles as a "soft" service.

(3) States are allowed to purchase more services from voluntary agencies than formerly and still receive federal reimbursement. "The limited evidence that is available . . . suggests that private agencies receiving government funds continue to maintain their identity and considerable independence of purpose and style."[78]

(4) State planning for the CASSP must include participation by the citizens of the state in the planning process.

Although under Title XX, the federal government reimburses states primarily for social services provided to people on public assistance and SSI, and to other low-income people, the fact that it offers reimbursement for even a few services available to all people without regard to income is a step in the direction of considering social service as one of the social rights of citizenship, as in the right to a public education or to an uncontaminated water supply. Whether this step is to be the beginning of a new trend in social welfare for all remains to be seen.

SUMMARY

The social services employ human interaction and contact as resources for giving help. In the Charity Organization movement, contact was conceived of as the offering of encouragement and moral advice in the form of friendly visiting by people who defined themselves as morally superior to people they defined as morally deficient. In the Settlement movement, contact took the form of residing in the midst of the poor, learning from them as well as advising them, offering instructional and recreational programs, and acting as their spokespeople in social and political struggles for reform.

Modern social work focuses upon the concept of the relationship between professional and client. Social workers attempt to create relationships with their clients that will enable the clients to feel comfortable enough to confront difficult problems, discover new strengths in themselves for dealing with these problems, and deal with them. The group worker makes use of a similar, though necessarily modified, concept of the leader's role in relation to the group.

The nature of social workers' contact with clients is a source of controversy within social work. Some seek to reduce the distance between worker and client(s) and to restore the advocacy role that characterized the Settlement movement; the worker would clearly be identified with the client(s)' beliefs, values, and emotions. Workers and clients would be united against interests in society seen as thwarting clients from full participation in the opportunities society offers. Moving in the opposite direction are those who maintain the distance between professional and client by emphasizing the expertise that the social worker claims as a professional.

An important type of interaction in modern social service is the provision of information. This is part of the social worker's liaison function—knowing the many sources of help that are available for the variety of problems that are presented and being able to help the client gain access to the appropriate source.

As social services become more diversified, new types of contact are introduced. Legal representation of the poor is one of the more recent and significant forms of contact introduced into the social services.

With the passage of Title XX, an amendment to the 1935 Social Security Act that went into effect in 1975, the United States may be at the beginning of a new era in the field of social welfare, in which the federal government encourages increased availability of social services to its citizens.

Notes

[1] Kathleen Woodroofe, *From Charity to Social Work* (Toronto: University of Toronto Press, 1962), pp. 3–8.

[2] *Ibid.*, pp. 48–49.

[3] E. J. Hobsbawm, *Industry and Empire—The Pelican Economic History of Britain, Volume 3, From 1750 to the Present Day* (Harmondsworth, England: Penguin Books, 1969), pp. 117–126; Samuel Mencher, *From Poor Law to Poverty Program* (Pittsburgh: University of Pittsburgh Press, 1965), pp. 184–185.

[4] Mencher, *From Poor Law to Poverty Program*, p. 256.

[5] *Ibid.*, p. 193

[6] *Ibid.*, p 196.

[7] Woodroofe, *From Charity to Social Work*, pp. 21–22.

[8] In Sidney Fine, *Laissez Faire and the General-Welfare State* (Ann Arbor, Mich.: University of Michigan Press, 1964), p. 173.

[9] Woodroofe, *From Charity to Social Work*, p. 48.

[10] *Ibid.*, p. 54; Roy Lubove, *The Professional Altruist—The Emergence of Social Work as a Career, 1880–1930* (Cambridge: Harvard University Press, 1965), p. 19.

[11] Mary E. Richmond, *What Is Social Case Work?* (New York: Arno Press and New York Times, 1971), p. 27. Originally published by the Russell Sage Foundation in 1922.

[12] Mary Richmond, in Woodroofe, *From Charity to Social Work*, p. 108.

[13] *Ibid.*

[14] Richmond, *What Is Social Casework?* pp. 101–102.

[15] *Ibid.*, pp. 98–99. Italics in original.

[16] In Lubove, *Professional Altruist*, p. 33.

[17] The beginnings of the visiting teacher movement are described in Murray A. Levine and Adeline Levine, *A Social History of Helping Services* (New York: Appleton-Century-Crofts, 1970), Chapter 6.

[18] Davis, *op. cit.*, p. 6.

[19] Samuel Barnett, in Woodroofe, *From Charity to Social Work*, p. 66. See also Allen F. Davis, *Spearheads for Reform: The Social Settlements and the Progressive Movement, 1890–1914* (New York: Oxford University Press, 1967), pp. 6–7.

[20] *Ibid.*

[21] *Ibid.*, p. 8.

[22]*Ibid.*, p. 12.

[23]*Ibid.*, p. 25.

[24]*Ibid.*, pp. 65, 74, 101, 105, 123, 170–193, 204.

[25]*Ibid.*, pp. 16–22.

[26]Woodroofe, *From Charity to Social Work*, pp. 97–98; Lubove, *Professional Altruist*, pp. 49–52.

[27]*Ibid.*, pp. 35, 78.

[28]Clarke A. Chambers, *Seedtime of Reform—American Social Service and Social Action, 1918–1933* (Minneapolis, Minn.: University of Minnesota Press, 1963), pp. 117–124; Davis, *Spearheads for Reform*, pp. 231–232. Historian Judith Ann Trolander attributes the settlements' loss of the reform impulse to their coming under the control of the Community Chests, which supplied their funds; see Judith Ann Trolander, *Settlement Houses and the Great Depression* (Detroit: Wayne State University Press, 1975).

[29]Charles Loch, in Woodroofe, *From Charity to Social Work*, p. 53.

[30]Carel Germain, "Casework and Science: A Historical Encounter," in Robert W. Roberts and Robert H. Nee, eds., *Theories of Social Casework* (Chicago: University of Chicago Press, 1970), p. 13.

[31]The development of child guidance clinics is described in Levine and Levine, *Social History of Helping*, Chapter 10.

[32]The section on the influence of psychiatry on social work draws largely on Lubove, *Professional Altruist*, Chapter 4; and Woodroofe, *From Charity to Social Work*, Chapter 6.

[33]Woodroofe, *From Charity to Social Work*, p. 62.

[34]*Ibid.*, pp. 70–73.

[35]*Ibid.*, pp. 73–74.

[36]*Ibid.*, p. 186.

[37]*Ibid.*, pp. 187–188.

[38]James K. Whittaker, *Social Treatment—An Approach to Interpersonal Helping* (Chicago: Aldine, 1974), p. 242.

[39]Woodroofe, *From Charity to Social Work*, p. 189.

[40]*Ibid.*, p. 191.

[41]Campbell G. Murphy, in Fred M. Cox and Charles Garvin, "Community Organization Practice: 1865–1973," in Fred M. Cox et al., eds., *Strategies of Community Organization* (Itasca, Ill.: F. E. Peacock, 1974), p. 42.

[42]The preceding paragraphs draw upon Lubove, *Professional Altruist*, Chapters 6 and 7; and Cox and Garvin, "Community Organization Practice."

[43]Cox and Garvin, p. 57.

[44]This threefold categorization comes from Jack Rothman, "Three Models of Community Organization Practice," in Cox et al., *Strategies*. However, Rothman uses the term *social action* for reasons relevant to his analysis, whereas the more widely used but narrower concept of community action is the one I propose to examine.

[45]William J. Goode, "The Theoretical Limits of Professionalization," in Amitai Etzioni, ed., *The Semi-Professions and Their Organization* (New York: Free Press, 1969), pp. 272, 276.

[46]*Ibid.*, p. 278.

[47]The discussion of professions draws most directly on Goode, "Theoretical Limits"; and somewhat less directly on Wilensky and Lebeaux, *Industrial Society and Social Welfare* (New York: Free Press, 1965), pp. 284–285. It departs from the approach of Ernest Greenwood, "The Attributes of a Profession," in Paul E. Weinberger, ed., *Perspectives on Social Welfare*, 2nd ed. (New York: Macmillan, 1974).

[48]Daniel Patrick Moynihan, "The Professionalization of Reform," *The Public Interest*, No. 1 (Fall 1965), pp. 6–16.

[49]Willard C. Richan and Allan R. Mendelsohn, *Social Work—The Unloved Profession* (New York: New Viewpoints, 1973).

[50]Alfred Kadushin, "The Knowledge Base of Social Work," in Alfred J. Kahn, ed., *Issues in American Social Work* (New York: Columbia University Press, 1959), p. 43.

[51]Sheila B. Kamerman et al., "Knowledge for Practice: Social Science in Social Work," in Alfred J. Kahn, ed., *Shaping the New Social Work* (New York: Columbia University Press, 1973), p. 101.

[52]Carol H. Meyer, *Social Work Practice: A Response to the Urban Crisis* (New York: Free Press, 1970), pp. 26–27.

[53]Nina Toren, *Social Work: The Case of a Semi-Profession* (Beverly Hills, Calif.: Sage, 1972), p. 42.

[54]Goode, "Theoretical Limits," pp. 280–281.

[55]This statement is based partly on personal observation. The use of "patient" by private practitioners is also noted by Bertram Beck, "Professional Associations: National Association of Social Workers," *Encyclopedia of Social Work*, Vol. 2, 17th ed. (Washington, D.C.: National Association of Social Workers, 1977), p. 1088.

[56]Herbert Bisno, "How Social Will Social Work Be?" *Social* Work, Vol. 2, No. 2(April 1956).

[57]Richard A. Cloward and Irwin Epstein, "Private Social Welfare's Disengagement from the Poor: The Case of Family Adjustment Agencies," in George A. Brager and Francis P. Purcell, *Community Action Against Poverty* (New Haven, Conn: College and University Press, 1967).

[58]For a discussion of these issues, see Willard C. Richan, "The Social Work Profession and Organized Social Welfare," in Kahn, ed., *Shaping the New Social Work*, especially pp. 161–163; see also, Kahn's Epilogue to the volume, pp. 199–205.

[59]Toren, *Social Work*, p. 51

[60]Rino J. Patti and Herman Resnick, "Changing the Agency from Within," *Social Work*, Vol. 17, No. 4 (July 1972), pp. 48–57. Reprinted in Ralph M. Kramer and Harry Specht, eds., *Readings in Community Organization Practice*, 2nd ed. (Englewood Cliffs, N. J.: Prentice-Hall, 1975), pp. 65–74.

[61]Arthur Spindler, *Public Welfare* (New York: Human Sciences Press, 1979), pp. 35, 40–41.

[62]Burton Gummer, "Is the Social Worker in Public Welfare an Endangered Species?" *Public Welfare*, Vol. 37, No. 4, (Fall 1979), p. 20.

[63]Paul Halmos, *The Personal Service Society* (New York: Schocken Books, 1970), p. 28.

[64]Gerald Handel, review of Halmos, "The Personal Service Society," *American Sociological Review*, Vol. 36, No. 5 (October 1971), pp. 958–959.

[65]Nicholas N. Kittrie, *The Right to Be Different—Deviance and Enforced Therapy* (Baltimore: Johns Hopkins Press, 1971). A brief synopsis of the book is given in the review by Gerald Handel in *Social Casework*, Vol. 54, No. 7 (July 1973), pp. 429–430.

[66]The preceding two paragraphs draw on Joel F. Handler, *The Coercive Social Worker* (Chicago: Rand McNally/Markham, 1973), Chapter 6; and Martin Rein, *Social Policy: Issues of Change and Choice* (New York: Random House, 1970), Chapter 17.

[67]L. Diane Bernard, "Education for Social Work," *Encyclopedia of Social Work*, Vol. 1, 17th ed. (Washington, D.C.: National Association of Social Workers, 1977), p. 292.

[68]Alfred J. Kahn, *Social Policy and Social Services*, 2nd ed. (New York: Random House, 1979), p. 28.

[69]*Ibid.*

[70]*Ibid.*, pp. 29–30.

[71]Ellen Jane Hollingsworth, "Ten Years of Legal Services for the Poor," in Robert H. Haveman, ed., *A Decade of Federal Antipoverty Programs* (New York: Academic Press, 1977), pp. 290–295.

[72]Sar A. Levitan, *The Great Society's Poor Law* (Baltimore: Johns Hopkins University Press, 1971), pp. 184–185.

[73]Earl Johnson, Jr., in Haveman, *Decade,* p. 316.

[74]Levitan, *Great Society's Poor Law,* p. 189.

[75]*Comprehensive Annual Social Services Program Plan for New York State, October 1, 1978 to September 30, 1979* (Albany, N.Y.: Department of Social Services, October 1978), p. 5.

[76]Neil Gilbert, "The Transformation of Social Services," *Social Service Review* (December 1977), pp. 624–641.

[77]*Ibid.,* p. 630.

[78]*Ibid.,* p. 634.

Contemporary Social Work

10

This chapter will present an overview of contemporary social work activities in order to convey what social workers do, what kinds of problems they work on, what methods and techniques they use. It is not possible to cover the entire field of social work. As one scholar in the field has noted, "social work has not developed a literature that deals with the methods of social work practice within the total range of social work roles."[1] Nevertheless, within the limits of a single chapter, the fundamental aspects of the broad range of activity can be presented from the literature that does exist.

Contemporary social work will be discussed from several vantage points, beginning with *social work methods.* In the 1970s, the traditional division of social work methods into casework, group work, and community organization was challenged. Efforts were made to reconceptualize methods and to forge new ways of working to train social workers to be equally competent in working with individuals, groups, and communities. Nevertheless, in any given instance, a social worker is likely to begin with an individual or with a group or with a community. In the course of working with that individual, group, or community, the social worker may find it necessary or desirable to work with other units as well. For example, an interview with an alcoholic may lead to working with the alcoholic's whole family or with an association of employers to plan job programs for rehabilitated alcoholics. A social worker helping residents of a community organize to strengthen their community may provide individual service to a particular resident who has problems in addition to services to the whole community.

Thus the particular activities that a social worker engages in may vary with the case or situation and may change as the social worker proceeds. There is, however, a general model of how to proceed, an *activity sequence* that applies to many different kinds of cases. The second approach to contemporary social work will be in terms of activity sequence.

Finally, social work deals with many kinds of problems or problem areas—known as *fields of practice*. A field of practice is characterized by one or more of the following: (1) the type of problem being dealt with, (2) the type of agency in which the work is done, (3) the category of the population whose problems are being dealt with. Thus work with the aging is a field of practice defined in terms of a category of the population. The field encompasses all problems of the aging, and the work may be done in various kinds of agencies. School social work is a field of practice based on the agency in which the work is done. Social work with the blind and social work with the mentally retarded are fields of practice defined on the basis of the type of problem.

Before turning to these ways of examining the work of contemporary social workers, it is necessary to note that the term *social worker* has acquired a new ambiguity since 1970. Before that time, the effort to transform social work from a "do-good" activity into a profession led to the development of university-based graduate programs leading to the Master of Social Work degree (M.S.W.). The master's degree became the basic credential for membership in the profession, although the organized profession never succeeded in having the designation "social worker" restricted to those who had earned this degree. In the mid-1970s, however, the Council on Social Work Education, the organization that accredits schools of social work, granted official recognition to social work programs at the bachelor's degree level, provided they met certain standards. Official social work organizations now recognize both the Bachelor of Social Work and the Master of Social Work as professional degrees. The distinction between the competencies of social workers with these two different levels of preparation remains to be clarified.[2] It is likely that there is considerable variation in different parts of the United States and Canada regarding activities restricted to persons with the M.S.W. and activities that may be performed by a person with either an M.S.W. or a B.S.W. Since the competencies are not standardized, the discussion in this chapter makes no effort to distinguish these levels of practice, for any attempt would be either misleadingly oversimplified or overburdened with detailed qualifications.

NEW DIRECTIONS IN
SOCIAL WORK METHOD

As social work was crystallizing three major methods, it was simultaneously becoming dissatisfied with the way those methods had developed. There were two major sources of dissatisfaction. One was the fact that social casework had become predominantly psychological in its orientation. Helen Harris Perlman, a leading thinker in the field of casework, revealed this dissatisfaction when she said:

> Periodically, we ask one another "What is 'social' about social casework?" as if to reassure ourselves of our identity, . . . [because of our] absorbed interest in the inner world of the personality and some loss of perspective about the outer world in which that personality lives.[3]

Social casework tended either to define all client problems as basically psychological or to deal primarily with those client problems that could be handled in psychological terms. The caseworker focused on the individual client, helping him or her to become psychologically stronger but not probing very far to discover whether there were elements in the person's larger social situation that were more in need of change than the client was.

A second reason for dissatisfaction was that the three major methods of social work did not seem to be very clearly connected with one another. Casework, group work, and community organization were all methods of doing social work, but they seemed to have little else in common. Casework dealt with individuals, group work with groups, and community organization with the councils of social agencies and the community chests (now the United Way organizations) concerned with raising money and planning for direct services.

Scholars in the field began to rethink the methods, to find what was characteristic of, or *generic* to, all of them, rather than specific to each. The field had faced a somewhat similar problem in an earlier period. In the first decades of the twentieth century, social *caseworkers* identified themselves on the basis of the type of problem they worked on or the type of organization they worked in. Thus medical social workers, school social workers, psychiatric social workers, each thought of themselves as a somewhat distinct occupational group. They eventually concluded that they were all practicing casework and that there were basic casework principles applicable to all settings in which casework was practiced. Now social workers were looking for the conceptual foundations to unify the three more disparate methods.

These efforts go back at least to the 1950s, but they gathered momentum during the 1960s and 1970s.[4] They signify a growing reassociation of social work with the social sciences, after its longtime dominant (but never exclusive) focus on psychiatry. The need for a more thorough understanding of the interrelationships of individuals, social groups, and social segments (such as social classes, ethnic and religious communities, age categories, and sex categories) was stimulated by the wave of social movements that swept the United States in the 1960s—the civil rights movement, the War on Poverty, the anti-Vietnam War movement,and the women's movement, and as well. The War on Poverty's emphasis on job training and job creation has already been noted in (Chapter 6). (Community action is discussed in Chapter 11.) Another important War on poverty program was Head Start, which was designed to prepare impoverished preschool children for elementary school.[5] In effect, the War on Poverty was a federally sponsored set of community organization efforts. It concentrated on creating new organizations; the goal was to help individuals change through their participation in these organizations. Even though casework activities were built into many of them, the emphasis on new forms of organization had an impact in directing social work thinking more intensively toward revising its methods.

The fundamental idea that has emerged thus far is that individuals are not as separate as traditional casework had been regarding them. They have complex involvements in groups and social categories of all kinds, including their membership in a social class, an ethnic group, a sex, an age category, a religion. Thus it has increasingly come to be recognized that individual, group, and community are so interrelated that social work methods had to be altered to take account of the interrelationships.

There is as yet no single, agreed-upon reconceptualization and new terminology of social work methods. Some writers on method offer the idea of *systems* (borrowed from biology and engineering), which emphasizes the interrelationships of many elements, so that the social worker is alerted to trace out the many possible connections among factors in people's lives that could be causing their problems.[6] For example, a client may need (1) counseling about a housing problem and (2) help in forming a group with other tenants that would (3) bring pressure on city agencies to enforce housing laws.[7]

Another proposed way of redefining social work methods is to distinguish between two main methods, *social treatment* and *social development*. "Social treatment focuses on the social relationships of the individual to other individuals and groups in various situations—family, school, work, neighborhood, corrections, health care, recreation, etc."[8] In contrast, "Social development practice focuses on the institutions of community and society and their social impact on the individual."[9] The social development worker is concerned with creating "effective institutions of social provision, social protection, social control, social rehabilitation, and social problem prevention."[10]

Still another way of thinking about social work methods today is to distinguish between micropractice and macropractice (sometimes just called "micro" and "macro" for short). *Micropractice includes all direct work with individuals, families, small groups, and communities.*[11] *Macropractice* is work at the city, state, regional, federal, or any large-system level. It includes planning for providing services and income, analyzing strengths and weaknesses of existing ways of providing services and income, and developing better ways of making these provisions. The macropractitioner must have "a greater recognition of the interrelationship of the economic, political, and social systems in society, and the awareness that social problems, programs, and issues rarely occur in isolation but are almost inevitably intertwined with political and economic factors."[12] While this is true, it is probably also correct to say that the micropractitioner must have much more of the same kind of awareness and understanding than the caseworker, group worker, or community organizer of twenty or thirty years ago. In fact, it is just such an awareness that has been leading organized social work to reconceptualize its methods.

Change in social work—or in any other area—does not come easily. Thus a recent textbook on social work methods, which does not even include the term *casework* in the index, nevertheless states:

> Skill in working with individuals is perhaps the first skill which every social work student must learn, no matter whether he will ultimately specialize in practice with individuals, groups, or communities. . . . The social worker who cannot help an individual cannot help a larger collectivity.[13]

Even though this text does not write about "casework," it still considers the activities that have gone by that name as the foundation of social work. This textbook is not alone in its emphasis on working with the individual. Many social workers believe that this is indeed what social work does best and ought to concentrate on; others believe that social work should become a more important force in changing social norms and social institutions.

Thus the concepts of social work methods are in a state of flux, as reflected by the lack of agreed-upon new terminology. There is, however, a core of agreement on what social workers do. At the very least, whether working with individuals, groups, communities, or government departments, social workers have to:

(1) Respond to problems presented to them, and identify problems they believe exist even if unnoticed by anyone else;
(2) Assemble a variety of information bearing on the problem;
(3) Think about the information in order to understand and define the problem(s) to be solved;
(4) Formulate a course of action or strategy of intervention based upon the understanding that has been reached;
(5) Maintain contact (relationship) with the people who have the problem(s) and with other people who can help solve the problem(s);

(6) Give support in various forms—such as giving practical advice, referring a client to a specialized facility, working for (advocating) changes in how an organization deals with people who use its services; and

(7) Organize or coordinate the activities of people in various organizations whose decisions all have a bearing on the problem.

This listing is a very basic statement of what social workers do. It says nothing, for example, about how to give advice, and when or when not to give it, or about how to coordinate activities in different situations. Those are the specifics that are taught in social work methods courses—regardless of the names given to the methods.

ACTIVITY SEQUENCES

The methods of social work are ways of intervening in clients' situations to bring about changes in the clients or in their situations. The methods are embedded in a sequence of activities that the social worker and client participate in to establish and carry out a relationship. This sequence of activities will be described and then illustrated.[14]

Intake

A person or group that is to be helped by a social worker must come into contact with the worker and be accepted for help by the agency. This initial step in the activity sequence is called intake. The term designates the activities by which the client enters into the prospective helping relationship (or, alternatively, is screened out). The client comes to the agency and makes known his or her (or their) problems. The worker gathers information by interviewing the client, listening to what the client says, eliciting additional information by further questioning. The worker compares this information with the array of services the agency offers in order to determine whether the client's problems fall within its scope. Social agencies are specialized in ways that clients often do not know about, so it may be that they have come to the wrong agency for their kind of problem, in which case the client will be referred to another, more appropriate agency.

Intake thus involves an exchange of information between prospective client and social worker. The prospective client states a problem, need, or concern; the worker explains the possible ways the agency can be of help. If the two kinds of information "match up," the client will be accepted for service and will be assigned to a social worker who may or may not be the same worker as the one who conducted the intake interview. Sometimes, the intake decision is made by a committee that reviews the intake information. If the agency is a very busy one, the client may be put on a waiting list for service.

Some agencies are geared to more rapid intake. Thus, in recent years, a type of service known as a telephone "hot line" provides immediate acceptance for a person who calls for help. The intake procedure and the service offered are condensed into one operation. The client is accepted by the worker's answering the telephone call; help is offered over the phone. Immediate intake and help are especially suited to (1) crises, such as when a person feels suicidal and wants help with these impulses, and (2) when anonymity is desired. Another type of immediate intake is found in agencies that offer "walk-in" service. Certain agencies that serve adolescents have this procedure and also may not require that the person's name be given.[15]

Intake, as just described, assumes a client seeking help and an agency social worker accepting or not accepting the client's request. There is another somewhat less frequently used approach: The agency and its social workers actively seek out clients in order to help them. This version of the intake process is called *outreach*. The agency reaches out to offer services to people who either do not know about the agency or would not be inclined to approach the agency on their own initiative. In this case, it is the agency that takes the initiative to make its services available to people who might be able to benefit from them.

Assessment and diagnosis

A client who is accepted by the agency to which he or she has applied—or to which he or she has been referred—is assigned to a social worker. The social worker has the task of determining in greater detail and in greater depth what the client's problem is or, more often, what the problems are. The social worker also has the task of ascertaining what current resources the client has for dealing with the problems and what other resources might be developed.

Resources fall into three general categories (as discussed in Chapter 2)—wealth, organization, and ideas. The client's income will usually need to be evaluated for its sufficiency or insufficiency. Further, the client's potential access to additional sources of income may often be a significant element in working out solutions to the client's problems. Does the client need and is she eligible for unemployment insurance, public assistance, social security benefits, food stamps, workmen's compensation? Would this client be eligible for job training that would pay a stipend during training? These and similar questions will often form a part of the social worker's assessment of the client's situation.

Organization is a resource that is relevant to the client's situation from a variety of perspectives. For example, the client's own family has a particular organization that affects the client's problem and, with increasing frequency, is coming to be regarded as the source of many problems.[16] But the client's family may also be a significant source of support. Husbands and wives may quarrel or fight, and parents and children may be severely at odds. Such problems may be in the forefront of attention when clients seek help, while the ways in which the family members do or might help each other may have escaped their notice under the stress of the problems that bring them to the agency. Various kinds of help from relatives may be an important resource.

Other organizations are also significant. The client's membership in various organizations may be important sources of support. A woman who has never worked may gain self-esteem by getting a job and thus becoming a member of a work organization. A person who suffers a loss such as death of a spouse may be greatly helped through the period of bereavement by being part of religious and social organizations. The organizations that a client belongs to may be important either in helping the client to deal with problems or in preventing those problems from becoming worse than they are. The social worker will usually assess these organizational supports in the client's life.

The importance of ideas as a resource has been emphasized throughout this book. What ideas does the client have about how the problems arose? What other ideas about cause or origin does he or she consider? What ideas does he or she have about what might be done? Why those particular ideas? In short, the range of ideas the client brings to the situation affects how the social worker can proceed to help. Ideas that are embedded in deeply held values will not change quickly. Ideas that are based on what the client heard from a friend or on television might change somewhat more easily. A client's ideas based on deeply held values may clash with the social worker's ideas. The social worker may regard the client's ideas as an obstacle to solving the problem, or may recognize the client's ideas as a resource despite their difference from the social worker's viewpoint.[17]

Finally, the worker's assessment of the client's resources includes a category whose importance became clear in Chapter 9. Personality is a resource the social worker assesses carefully, particularly that aspect of personality known as *coping mechanisms*. How does the client deal with his problems?

> . . . the child who typically handles fear of failure in the classroom by throwing his books on the floor, the office worker who deals with job pressures by excessive drinking, and the submissive wife who harbors deep resentment toward her husband and who handles it by becoming even more docile and outwardly sweet— all provide useful information to the worker for the later task of planning with the client for alternative ways of dealing with problem situations.[18]

The examples in the quotation are instances of inadequate coping skills, but the social worker does not look merely for inadequacies. It is equally important to gain a clear picture of the ways in which the client copes successfully. A good sense of humor, the ability to say no to unwelcome pressure, the ability to work with others, the ability to take certain kinds of initiative, a willingness to think about one's own actions and their consequences—these are but a few of the coping mechanisms that clients might have available in dealing with their problems and that might, with appropriate guidance, serve them in their current difficulty. The social worker can discern the presence of at least some of these resources from the client's accounts of various aspects of his situation. Other coping skills may not become apparent until some time has gone by and the worker gets to know the client better.

After assessing the client's current situation, including problems stated by the client, problems the worker may have noted that the client did not directly report, and various resources for dealing with the situation, the worker makes a diagnosis—essentially a formulation of the basic problems that the client is facing. The purpose of the diagnosis is for the worker to better understand the client's situation and problems and to proceed from this understanding toward a plan of action for giving help. The diagnosis is not a label but a summary of the client's social and personal situation, including his or her wishes concerning desired directions for change. Thus, for example, a husband who has been deserted by his wife and left with young children may wish for a reconciliation and for return to the marriage. The assessment and diagnosis may lead worker and client to some tentative conclusion concerning how likely this outcome is and what steps might be taken to accomplish it. On the other hand, the man may not wish a reconciliation. The diagnosis then would involve the problems he faces in proceeding with his new life situation—whether or not he works and his job situation is stable, what other sources of income might be necessary, what kinds of assistance he might need in dealing with and caring for his children, and so on.

Unlike medicine or psychiatry, social work does not have a manual of standard diagnoses. A diagnosis in social work is a reasoned summary of the client's situation. One theorist states that

> assessment and social diagnosis may be described as a joint process through which worker and client explore and assess the physical, psychological, and social conditions as they impinge upon the client and then attempt to relate their findings to the range of social problems experienced by the client in a manner that yields objectives for change as well as a plan of action.[19]

Establishing a contract

The notion of a contract has entered social work in recent years. The term emphasizes that what will be done in a worker-client relationship is being determined not by the worker alone but by the worker and the client arriving at an agreement of what they will try to accomplish together. Unlike legal contracts, the contract arrived at between social worker and client is not enforceable in a court; neither party can have a legal penalty imposed if the other fails to live up to the agreement. But the social work contract focuses the goals of the relationship, directs effort toward what will be done, and makes clear what kinds of things lie outside this particular helping relationship.

Contracts may involve both negotiable and nonnegotiable items. For example:

> A non-negotiable condition of a contract with a young boy may be that he cannot hit the social worker under any conditions; he may yell and scream, for example, but he cannot touch. Whether the social worker meets with the boy for fifteen minutes a day or an hour, however, may be mutually discussed and agreed to.[20]

Contracts may be important also as a way of letting the client know that the client is expected to work in this relationship. A fairly common misconception among beginning clients is that they bring their problem to a social worker and the social worker hands them a solution. The social worker may begin to dispel this illusion by proposing the contract. Thus:

> The art of contracting is usually as informal as, "Look, suppose we get together again next week at this time. I'll check out what you have to do to get unemployment insurance and you can check out the hotels to decide where you want to live, OK?" Contracts with sophisticated adults appear more formal; those with children appropriately on their level.[21]

The term *contract* is not yet in universal use in social work. In many quarters, workers continue to refer to a "working agreement about goals" or some similar phrase, preferring the less businesslike sound of the phrase, while those who like the term contract prefer its presumptively more precise connotation, with its suggestion of a more hard-nosed attention to reality. Regardless of the term used, the task of the worker-client activity sequence, after intake and assessment and diagnosis, is to establish what is to be attempted in the helping relationship.

Establishing and maintaining a treatment relationship

While satisfactory help may, under certain circumstances, be obtained in a single encounter between worker and client, more commonly several or many meetings are useful or necessary. Establishing and maintaining a relationship is not something that begins after a contract is negotiated, even though it is presented at this point. A relationship begins when a client comes to the agency. If the client is accepted by the agency for service, the relationship is strengthened a bit. If the social worker who will deal with the client is different from the intake worker, the relationship undergoes some uncertainty while the client deals with a new person and perhaps finds it necessary to say all over again some of the things that were told to the intake worker. Exploring the contract introduces additional uncertainties.

A relationship in which a client seeks help is fraught with contradictions. A person who seeks help is also very often reluctant to be in that position, even when the problem is burdensome. In American society, with the strong value it places on "standing on one's own feet," admitting to oneself and others the need for help is often difficult, perhaps felt as a sign of personal failure. Accepting help means becoming partially dependent in an unaccustomed way. The helping process imposes obligations of time and effort.[22] So the client is often ambivalent about seeking help and entering into a helping relationship. The client wants to be there and also does not want to be there. Ambivalence shows up in many ways. A client may be late for an appointment. A client may not talk about matters that he or she considers too shameful or discrediting. Appointments may be canceled by the client at the last minute. In short, the client may resist the process of being helped while at the same time seeking it. The helping situation is one in which the client's social honor and moral reputation are exposed to examination. Painful judgments and self-judgments may be made. The parent who abuses a child, the alcoholic, the elderly person who can no longer function as a self-sufficient person, the truant child—these are but a small sampling of people in problem situations that render them vulnerable to loss of honor in their own eyes and in the eyes of others as they come to face unpleasant facts about themselves or their circumstances in the company of a social worker whose attention is explicitly focused on them.

When things go well, the client gains trust in the worker and in the situation of being helped. With additional meetings, the client comes to feel that the situation is beginning to be helpful. As in the case of Miss Brown, which was presented in the Prologue to this book, the client may come to feel that "I ain't so bad" and that the problems are not insurmountable. The social worker, guided by the value of respecting the client, remains nonjudgmental, and the client becomes better able to explore aspects of the problem that had remained covered. The successful social work situation is one in which the worker has been able to create and sustain an atmosphere conducive to the client's delving into his or her problems despite the misgivings that initially were deterrents in exploring them.

Evaluation

When a relationship between a worker and a client has proceeded for a time, a change in the client's situation usually occurs. At some point, the client or the worker may want to assess what has been happening and how satisfactory the change is. One or the other may raise the issue, and together they evaluate how well the contract is being fulfilled. As our example of Miss Brown and her worker made clear, client and worker do not necessarily agree on their evaluation. Miss Brown was satisfied that she had dealt with her problem. Her social worker agreed that she had been helped over her immediate crisis but believed that Miss Brown had only scratched the surface of her problems.

Termination

There comes a time when the relationship between client and worker ends. Termination of this relationship can come about in different ways. It may have been agreed early on that the relationship would terminate when a certain goal or goals had been achieved. The evaluation phase may result in agreement that the client's goals have been reached. On the other hand, as the case of Miss Brown again indicates, termination may come when the client feels that she has gained what she wanted, even though the social worker believes the client should not terminate the relationship. Termination can occur when a social worker leaves to take a job in another agency; the client must then decide whether to continue with another worker in the agency or to terminate the relationship not only with the departing worker but with the agency as well.

For purposes of analyzing what goes on in a worker-client relationship the phases of the activity sequence have been presented as distinct, but human interactions do not unfold in neat sequences. Phases overlap. The activities of various phases occur in mixed order. Evaluation, for example, is not necessarily a one-time event, occurring only toward the end of a relationship. It may take place on more than one occasion as either client or worker raises a question as to whether "we are getting anywhere." A conceptual scheme for analyzing human events is a useful tool for understanding them but it is not a rigid blueprint to which all actions conform.

It will be useful to illustrate the activity sequence just presented with two case examples drawn from published case material. However, since studies are often published for purposes that do not require full reporting on every phase, information on all phases of the sequence is not always available. Although there will be some gaps in the material, the following two studies should help to amplify understanding of the various phases.

Activity Sequence in a Public Welfare Department Protective Services Unit

The first example is taken from a report from the Milwaukee County Department of Public Welfare in Wisconsin.[23] The Protective Services Unit of this department deals with complaints of child abuse and neglect.

Intake

The intake procedure in this agency usually begins with a referral by the court or by the police. When either of these referring agencies believes that a child should be removed from its home immediately because of danger to the child's physical, emotional, or social development, the supervisor of the Protective Services Unit ascertains whether the family is currently receiving services from a branch of the welfare department and, if so, whether the social worker already working with the family is able to act immediately. If not, the Protective Services Unit assigns its own worker, who visits the family's home. The first visit may be preceded by a letter. If not, the worker explains on his first visit who he is, why he is visiting the family, and the agency he represents. He explains that he wants to help the family, not make trouble for it.

Assessment of needs and diagnosis

The assessment of needs usually takes place in the client's home, not in the agency office. For example, a worker found Mr. E at home with six small, frightened children. Mrs. E had left after Mr. E returned home from the House of Correction, after a term for drunken and disorderly conduct. Mrs. E was found wandering the streets, and reported having been beaten by her husband when he first came home. The assessment and diagnosis process revealed the following needs:

(1) Emergency shelter for the mother and six children.
(2) Escorting of Mrs. E to the District Attorney's office to file an assault and battery complaint against her husband.
(3) Help for Mr. E with his personality problems.
(4) Need to counsel and support Mrs. E.
(5) Need for assistance to Mrs. E by a skilled homemaker to help her improve her housekeeping skills, especially in preparing meals and handling money.

In sum, Mr. E was diagnosed as an immature personality who had never supported his family adequately, drank excessively, and blamed others for his failings. Mrs. E was diagnosed as an inadequate homemaker who needed help to get a better hold on her household functioning.

The "contract"

The contract in neglect and abuse cases is not negotiated so much as imposed, at least in the beginning. Thus:

In the Protective Services Unit, the social worker conducts most of the casework sessions in the client's home, using the techniques of aggressive, reaching-out casework. He does not wait for the client to ask for help with the problems that are overwhelming him, and often causing him to neglect or abuse his children, but actively seeks to stabilize the family's physical and social environment as quickly as possible. Having once stabilized the environmental situation, he involves family members in individual or group casework sessions according to the needs of the case and the family members' ability to participate in treatment. He withdraws from the situation only after the family members have gained a measure of self-sufficiency and the family's balance has been restored.[24]

This is, of course, a summary of the general procedure. The initial contract is imposed by the worker. After the situation has been stabilized, the worker assesses the family's readiness to proceed further. There is an implication of worker-client negotiation in this second phase.

Development of a treatment relationship

The worker's account of how relationships are developed with clients is contained in the statement that the worker "involves family members in individual or group casework sessions according to the needs of each case and the family members' ability to participate in treatment." There is one further point in the report bearing specifically on the development of relationships with clients: The social worker in these situations has the authority of the court behind him, but calls upon that authority sparingly. The worker endeavors to shift from the initial imposed relationship to an unforced relationship.

Evaluation of progress

The report evaluates the progress in the E family case by noting the following developments:

(1) Mrs. E has applied for a legal separation from her husband.
(2) After release from another term in the House of Correction, Mr. E's visits to his children were regulated and supervised by the social worker.
(3) Mr. E was helped in finding a job after his release, and he contributes support payments to the children and has begun "to demonstrate a capacity for responsible parenthood."
(4) Mrs. E's stuttering has almost disappeared after casework counseling.
(5) Mrs. E has improved as a homemaker; the physical and emotional climate in the home is more stable and secure.

Termination

Termination is not reported specifically for the E case. However, as noted above, termination generally occurs when a family has gained some self-sufficiency and internal balance, so that the abuse or neglect of the children is no longer occurring.

Activity Sequence in a Family Welfare Agency

The second example is based on a report from a voluntary agency, the Family and Children's Service in Pittsburgh.[25] This agency decided to try outreach to poor families that were not making use of the agency's services. They wanted to serve clients "who had never found a social agency that had any value or could be trusted" and who "were very disorganized or too discouraged to be able to make use of community resources."

Intake

The agency selected a slum area known as the Hill, with a large proportion of black single-parent families. Clients were obtained by social workers' going door-to-door on each street in the area. Eventually each social worker had a full caseload, and door-to-door canvassing was stopped. New cases came by referral from persons in the initial caseload and by referral from schools and hospitals in the area.

Assessment and diagnosis

In this program, assessment and diagnosis could not be treated as a single phase. Rather, it took place at different points in the relationship. Thus there was a "critical effort at first contact . . . to determine something the potential client wants." The cumulative life experience of these potential clients had been "poverty, desertion by important people in their lives, discrimination, and pushing around." It was necessary for the social workers to demonstrate that they could be helpful—by identifying some tangible need of the client on the first contact and meeting it. Clients wanted such help as a better place to live, furniture, clothing; help in dealing with a child's school problem; help with a problem related to public housing, public assistance, or the court.

After this initial assessment and diagnosis, and after the social workers gave help with the clients' stated needs, relationships between clients and workers could develop. Some of these lasted as long as four years. During these extended periods of client contact, fuller, more detailed assessments and diagnoses could be made.

Establishing a contract

Again, establishing contracts with the clients in this program was not a one-time event that took place at the beginning of the contacts and then held for the duration. Instead, the contracts were open-ended, developing as the workers became more knowledgeable in offering help and the clients became more aware of the potential for change in themselves and in their circumstances. The report provides an interesting glimpse of one aspect of negotiating contracts between these workers and clients:

> Often we are shocked by a sudden realization that we and a client are not understanding each other and communicating. The client's perception of us may be quite different from the way we think he sees us. We may pride ourselves on being nonjudgmental, but the client expects us to judge him. Of course, we are judging in some respects, and we ought to let him know how we really feel. Or we may think we are accepting the client and his behavior, but since he does not expect us to do this, we have to show our acceptance. . . . we expected them to want to be accepted "as is . . .". But this is not what we hear. They seem to find real value in the caseworker—now proven to be a real help agent—who has expectations of them *and* confidence that they can make it. The expectations must be centered about something that can be realistically achieved.[26]

What this report reveals about the later phases of negotiating a contract is that the clients wanted the social workers to present some expectations for change and some confidence that they could change; they did not want mere acceptance of them as they were. After this type of contract was negotiated, clients were able to change in ways that both they and the worker wanted.

> Some say positively and proudly, "Look, see how well I can meet your expectation!" Some convert this feeling to a guilt force: "I can't let you down." But all seem to feel the greater expectation of the worker as evidence of faith in the client.[27]

Development of a relationship

It is evident that the development of a worker-client relationship began with the initial contact, when the worker discovered a pressing, tangible need that could be quickly met and then met it. The relationships were further solidified by the offering of further tangible assistance:

Workers may at times help clean house, set hair, repair or make clothing. Teaching is less involved in these activities than being in the situation with the client and working along with him. To be involved to this extent with any client also requires close involvement with all members of the client family—boy friends, meaningful neighbors (pseudo-greater family) and relatives. If the worker can understand what the client sees as life, can see meaningfully through the client's perspective, then the client and his family trust the worker as a person who has more answers than they have—that is, as a resource for options. They confide in him, imitate him, and begin to incorporate him as a model.[28]

Once the relationships with clients had developed, assessment of additional needs took place and additional services were offered. Thus homemaker services were provided to aging and handicapped people as well as to younger women who needed to learn more about housekeeping and child care. Therapy groups were formed and many of the women developed new areas of competence through the group activities.

Evaluation

The authors of the report judged that most of the activities had been successful. Over a four-year period, more than nineteen hundred families were served by the project, about 25 percent of the Hill community. Success was judged not only on the basis of numbers served but also on the basis of three general goals set at the beginning of the program: (1) to relieve overwhelming environmental stresses, (2) to modify behavior patterns, and (3) to change attitudes. The evaluation of the program is summarized as follows:

> Most of the families are still with us and still need our help, but they have made some distinct gains. They have a somewhat more optimistic outlook on life. They can and do assume more initiative in helping themselves. The self-help is uneven, depending more on their mood and circumstances than on the nature of the task. We have moments when we are proud of almost all of them, and some consistently demonstrate behavior directed toward expanding goals for themselves. With some clients, agreement on focus and goals is easy. With others it is difficult to discover where we and the client can meet in a working relationship. Is it in creating something new, such as a dress or something to eat? Is it in moving toward employment? Is it in fixing up the client's house? Or is it in controlling his behavior in order to keep him out of trouble? It has required infinite patience and imagination to start over again and try a different approach when previous efforts have not worked.[29]

These two actual case studies were chosen because they offer reasonably full illustrations of the activity sequence in social work. The next section deals with the various roles of the social worker.

Social Worker Roles

As the case studies made clear, the contemporary social worker is required to shift from one activity to another as the developing situation and the developing relationship with the client make necessary. To help a particular client, the social worker may work with an individual, organize a group, or speak on behalf of a client to a court, to a landlord, to a government agency. This diversity of activities conveys perhaps the essential meaning of *generic* social work. Instead of defining their functions and roles as either casework or group work or community organization, social workers do whatever needs to be done with whatever combination of methods the particular case requires. Social workers are generalists. As social workers shift activity, they also shift role. The multiple roles of the contemporary social worker have been itemized by one student of the field as follows:

. . . a *counselor,* who advises, listens, provides resources.

. . . an *administrator,* who oversees agency functions, sets policy, allocates resources, develops programs.

. . . a *consultant,* who provides outside expertise, assesses programs, acts as staff teacher and administrative guide.

. . . a *referral agent,* who suggests other services and alternate sources of help to consumers [clients].

. . . a *broker,* who intervenes between agency and consumer.

. . . a *therapist,* who provides psychotherapeutic services for individuals, families, and groups.

. . . an *advocate,* who represents consumers [clients].

. . . an *outreach worker,* who looks for, and offers services to, people who are unaware of existing resources.

. . . a *social planner,* who determines and plans for the services needed by a community.

. . . a *social activist,* who promotes and politics for social change.[30]

FIELDS OF PRACTICE

This section provides an introduction to the work of social workers from the vantage point of the different fields of practice. Social workers work in (1) fields in which the work is controlled by social workers, (2) fields in which social work is an adjunct service to the major purpose of the program, and (3) fields in which the role of social work is unsettled, shifting from time to time in response to changes in ideas about social work's role. The first type of situation includes family service and child-serving agencies, work with the elderly, certain kinds of recreational programs, adoption, and foster care. In these fields, social workers are substantially in charge of the program.

The second type of situation consists of fields in which social workers work in a host agency, that is, an agency devoted to a primary purpose other than social work but in which social work plays a significant role. Medical and school social work are good examples of these fields. The social work function in these agencies is to help the agency achieve its major purpose, recovery from illness and quality education, respectively.

The best example of the third kind of situation is public assistance. The social worker's role in the public assistance system probably changes more frequently and more drastically than the social worker's role in most other fields of social work.[31]

Family and Child Welfare

The family service field is perhaps the oldest of the fields of practice, since its origins go back to the Charity Organization movement. Strengthening and supporting family life and protecting children from damage to their health, social functioning, and personalities are long-established goals of professional social work and its preprofessional predecessors.

In earlier times, strengthening the family would have meant a fairly definite effort toward keeping the family intact and encouraging everybody to lead a conventional family life. In recent times, with the diversification of life styles and family forms, social work is no longer directed to sustaining a single type of family. Problems are taken as they come, and clients' own preferences (or the realities of their situation) more often provide the framework within which help is offered. The reality is that there are many single-parent families, and the problems of those families must often be dealt with without any expectation that the parent will marry or remarry. If a single-parent family is having a problem functioning, the social worker tries to help it become a better-functioning single-parent family with fewer problems.

Helping families to function better is a goal in various fields of social work practice. Medical social work, for example, which is practiced in hospitals, nursing homes, and other medical settings, involves helping families function under the stress of the illness of a family member. This section on family and child welfare as a practice field focuses on agencies that deal with a broad spectrum of family problems and that do not require a particular problem—such as illness—as a qualification for being served.

What then are the types of family and children's problems dealt with in this field of practice and what means are used?[32]

Family poverty

Family casework had its origins in the COS movement, with pauperism as the initial problem (see Chapter 9). After the federal government took over relief functions in the Great Depression, family service agencies no longer handed out money to clients. In modern times, family social work retains several functions with regard to family poverty. First, the family service agency worker knows about the different kinds of income maintenance programs that exist and helps clients apply for types of income maintenance for which they are eligible. A second function is to assist clients to become more knowledgeable about and skilled in managing their economic resources. This can take many forms; for example, helping poor people avoid making purchases that are exorbitant in price and in installment interest payments. Third, the social worker helps clients deal with attitudes of defeatism, powerlessness, and impaired self-esteem, which usually accompany poverty. These same attitudes also afflict persons who have had a moderate or comfortable standard of living but suffer a decline in standard of living as a result of prolonged unemployment; in today's world, they often join the poor as social work clients.

Continuing poverty, and a sudden decline from an adequate standard of living, are both stressful events that have an impact on the social psychology of the family. What people expect of one another is partly shaped by their financial circumstances. Economic deprivation, whether customary or sudden, often leads to anger, blame, and interpersonal strife. Justifiably or not, family members find fault with those nearest at hand, since they do not have access to those who make economic decisions. Consequently social workers who assist families with economic problems often, though not invariably, find that they must also deal with emotional problems that are related to the financial ones.

Much of family social work is related to some phase of the family life cycle. While this is not the only perspective, it is a particularly useful one for introductory purposes.

Family formation

Family formation occurs through two steps: (1) initiating some kind of interpersonal relationship, usually with a sexual relationship as a component, and (2) having a baby. The preferred sequence in this society is that two adults, of at least minimally approved legal age, first marry and then have a child. Many persons follow this pattern; however, there are many variations from this sequence. Some marry and choose not to have children. Some marry but are unable to have children and so look to adopt a child. Some have a baby without marrying, and many of these are below the approved minimal age for marriage.

Family formation results in numerous changes, some of which cause problems, and for which social workers are called upon to give services. Young unmarried mothers perhaps constitute the most conspicuous category of problem, since they arouse public concern on several counts. There is the longstanding concern about the cost of the mother and child to the taxpayer, a concern that goes back to Elizabethan times. However, there are in addition new kinds of concerns that were not present in Elizabethan society. One is the concern with helping the young mother (often a teenager) cope with the responsibility of a baby before she has reached full adulthood according to modern standards of what constitutes adulthood. The young mother's own personal development is a focus of contemporary social work. A second is concern that the baby grow up to be healthy in all respects. These two concerns together raise questions about whether the mother will keep the baby or give it up for adoption; whether or not she will marry the father; where she will live and with whom; what kinds of practical and emotional support are available or will be needed so that she can function adequately in her new situation. Helping young mothers work out these and related problems is part of the work of family social work.

Social workers also work in the family planning field, which involves sexual counseling, counseling about contraception and abortion, and counseling about the relationship of these aspects of family planning to the values and goals of each partner in the marriage.

Parent-child relations

Difficulties between parents and children have always existed, but whereas in the past parents and children were expected to work out these problems in their own way (usually the parents' way), in the contemporary world it has become increasingly common to call upon expert advice. Psychiatrists and psychologists as well as social workers help with parent-child problems. All attempt to carry out some form of treatment that will improve the parent-child relationship from the perspectives of both parent and child (and sometimes to satisfy an outside authority such as the school or the court, as well).[33]

Often parent-child treatment is initiated in response to a parental complaint about some unacceptable behavior of the child. A fairly common feature of the treatment process consists of helping the parent or parents to understand how they are contributing to the production of the behavior they disapprove of.[34] Social workers may conduct treatment with the child, with or without one or both parents, may conduct family therapy with the family as a group, or may use other treatment procedures appropriate to the particular situation. Often a psychiatrist serves as a consultant to the agency and may be called upon to offer advice concerning the best way to proceed. A staff psychologist may also conduct an independent evaluation of the child and family. Psychiatrist, psychologist, and social workers then hold a conference to discuss the case, each contributing data and interpretations from the vantage points of their particular disciplines to arrive at a plan of action.

Between the end of World War I and the beginning of the War on Poverty, when social work was heavily dominated by psychoanalytic ideas, problems of parent-child relations tended to be regarded as largely self-contained, that is, as problems of parental personality difficulty giving rise to personality and behavior difficulty in the child. The War on Poverty, together with the various social movements of the 1960s, generated a new awareness that family relationships and interpersonal relationships in general are embedded in and affected by the prevailing economic and social conditions in the society. For example, if parents are thwarted in their expectations for decent housing or are unemployed, traditional casework services that focus only on the family's emotional situation is likely to prove insufficient or ineffective. One social work researcher has concluded that "casework is no substitute for adequate material resources, that baccalaureate-level social workers can handle the service delivery if supervised properly, and that multiservice projects, including help with such specific areas as child rearing, health care, and homemaking, are more effective than interpersonal counseling."[35]

Decisions as to which services are most suitable in a particular case are, of course, part of the process of assessment and diagnosis. The important point is that assessment and diagnosis of parent-child relations are now understood to require not only psychological understanding of the relations but economic and social understanding as well.

The empty nest

The empty nest refers to the stage of family life in which all the children have grown up and moved out of their parents' home. This situation, like all life transitions, is often stressful to the parents. (The "empty nest" refers to their home. Of course, departure usually involves stress for the offspring as well, as they endeavor to establish themselves independently in the adult world.) Parents who have focused great energy and attention on child rearing are deprived of this focus when the last child leaves home. Reorganization of their attention and activities is necessitated. Problems between the spouses that may have been disregarded over the years may come to the fore when the children are no longer at home to occupy their efforts. Parents and children may also need to work out new patterns of relationship with each other.

Marriage dissolution

Marriages dissolve as a consequence of divorce, desertion, or the death of a spouse. Both partners or the remaining partner generally experiences considerable distress that may take an extended period of time to recover from, and social workers are often called upon to help in these painful life transitions. Since the early 1970s, there has been an increase in the formation of "self-help" groups. People experiencing a similar type of problem join together to help each other, and themselves, by discussing their shared plight and exploring ways of overcoming it. Social workers often assist in the formation of such groups among, say, widows or divorced mothers of young children, and help to guide the group. (Self-help groups are discussed more fully in Chapter 11.)

Family life education

Family service agencies attempt to increase knowledge about family relationships as a strategy for preventing family problems. Social workers serve as consultants to educational programs, and they may engage in public speaking and writing in order to increase public understanding of some common problems in family life.

In small communities, the family service agency may be an all-purpose agency. Its social workers may offer services in outposts such as an industrial plant or a housing project. The concept of family social service has spread sufficiently so that some corporations and labor unions hire social workers. In this type of situation, sometimes called industrial social work, the focus is on helping workers to function more effectively in the workplace, and to deal with family problems that might be interfering with effective work performance.

Child neglect and abuse

In American society (as well as in most industrial societies), the care of children is entrusted to their parents (or other adults, if parents are not available). Parents have considerable leeway in how they exercise this care. Families are not closely supervised organizations. Family privacy is a strong value. Further, autonomy of adults in conducting their family life is also a basic expectation. But parents do not have absolute leeway, and American society has developed procedures for intervention by the state if the parents engage in acts that are defined by the legal system as child neglect or child abuse. Child abuse takes two principal forms: (1) physical punishment leading to injury, (2) adult sexual activity with a child.

The concept of neglect is somewhat more ambiguous; it clearly covers the failure of the adults to provide such necessities as adequate food, shelter, clothing, and medical attention. It also includes leaving a very young child unattended. Some child welfare specialists would include such other situations as the child not having an adequate place to sleep, and the child's experiencing of "unwholesome or demoralizing circumstances in his home—violence, excessive quarreling, parental dishonesty, defiance of proper authority in society, or lack of love or concern for each other's welfare among family members."[36]

The case study presented earlier of a Protective Services Unit in a county department of public welfare is typical of the social work role in child abuse and neglect cases, at least in one respect, namely, that the clients are involuntary. They become clients as a result of someone's complaint to a court or the police or some other agency. Typically the social worker works with the mother of the abused or neglected child. In this type of case, the social worker is often sorely tested by the mother's resistance to cooperating. Thus social workers report interviews in which the client keeps the television set blaring, or leaves the room, or allows the child to be aggressive toward the worker. The social worker who hopes to have an impact has to be able to withstand and wait out such resistance, while also attempting to establish ways of being helpful. The behavior of the mother reflects the fact that often she herself is a deprived person who needs help.[37]

The social worker may offer direct services to the child. Some agencies offer summer day camps, tutoring programs, and other services for children. A fundamental decision that must be made in each case of child abuse or neglect (often the two occur together) is whether the families can safely care for the child or whether the child must be removed from the home for its own protection.

Foster care

Foster care is full-time care of a child outside the child's own home. The child may be cared for in a foster family home, a group home run by an agency, or in an institution. Foster care is intended to be temporary—until the child's own family can resume care or until the child reaches the age of legal maturity. Situations that call for foster care include: child abuse and neglect, out-of-wedlock birth, separation or divorce of parents, parental incapacity due to illness, and mental illness.[38] The social worker must decide whether foster care is necessary and, if so, what kind would be best for the child. In addition to these two tasks, the social worker must (1) help the child separate from the parents and move into the new situation, (2) monitor the placement to see that appropriate care is being provided, (3) help the foster parents or child-care staff to carry out their responsibilities, and (4) plan for the termination of the care at the appropriate time.[39]

Adoption

Adoption has been defined as

> a social and legal process whereby the parent-child relationship is established
> between persons not so related by birth. By this means a child born to one set
> of parents becomes, legally and socially, the child of other parents, a member of
> another family, and assumes the same rights and duties as those that obtain be-
> tween children and their biological parents.[40]

A substantial proportion of children placed for adoption were born to unmarried
parents; others are children of parents who have been judged abusive or neglect-
ful, or who are too ill to care for them, or who have died. The number of babies
available for adoption in American society has decreased somewhat in recent
years, with increased use of contraception and abortion. There has also been a
decrease in stigma attached to illegitimacy, so that some mothers who previously
would have given their babies up for adoption now keep them.

Social workers' tasks in the adoption process fall into three major categories:
(1) service to natural parents, (2) placement, and (3) postplacement supervision.
In the first category, the social worker explores the circumstances of the natural
parents, including alternatives to surrendering the baby for adoption. Do the
unmarried parents want to keep their baby? Do the biological mother and father
intend to marry? Does the biological mother want to keep her baby? What kinds
of assistance do the parents (or the single parent) need to deal with the experience
of having a baby? Is the mother and/or the father a relatively isolated person or
part of a kin group whose members can provide considerable material and
emotional assistance?

Placement involves evaluating applications from people who want to adopt
a child in order to find suitable adoptive homes. A couple that has been evaluated
as suitable, and the child to be adopted, must then be matched according to some
criteria. These can be highly individual. At one time, the matching process was
confined within narrow limits; social agencies tried to match adoptive parents
and child on such dimensions as ethnic background, religion, and even on such
dimensions as intellectual potential of the child, body build, and complexion.
This has changed today, and adoptive parents are reminded that even in natural
families, close matching of physical, intellectual, and emotional characteristics of
parents and children are not routine occurrences.

The adoptive child who is beyond infancy is given help in preparing to live
with and become part of a new family. The adoptive parents are also given help
in preparing for their new roles. Information is given, questions are answered.
One or more meetings are then arranged between adoptive parents and child.

Adoption is a legal process that goes through various steps until a court issues
a final adoption decree. Until the decree is issued, the social worker may continue
to work with the adoptive parents and child and offer whatever kinds of help
are felt to be needed.[41]

Medical Social Work

Medical social work focuses on the problems of patients and their families. Medical social workers are employed primarily in hospitals but increasingly in such other kinds of medical service organizations as public health agencies, nursing homes, and rehabilitation programs. It is estimated that about forty thousand social workers work in the health field. About half the seventy-two hundred hospitals in the United States have social services departments or provide social services.[42]

Social work in the health care field is based on certain premises concerning the relationship of medical problems to social and psychological factors. These premises are:

(1) Maintenance of good health and recovery from illness are affected by social, cultural, and economic conditions.

(2) Illness of a family member often disrupts the equilibrium of the family and affects the coping abilities of both the patient and the other family members.

(3) Medical treatment may sometimes be incomplete, or even impossible, if the patient and the family do not receive social support and counseling.

(4) Community action is necessary to assist many people to make use of medical services.

(5) Collaboration between medical personnel and personnel from other disciplines is often effective in solving sociomedical problems.[43]

The social worker's work in patient care can be thought of in terms of three phases: (1) preadmission, (2) inpatient, and (3) discharge planning and aftercare. The preadmission phase includes such work as planning for the care of children during the time that a parent must be hospitalized. The discharge and aftercare phase includes such work as arranging for services needed after discharge from the hospital, such as home health care and homemaker help. The bulk of the work, however, usually takes place during the inpatient phase.[44]

Patients may be referred to the social worker by the medical and nursing staff or may directly request to see a social worker. The patient's family may seek the social worker's help. The worker plays a supportive role—helping to alleviate anxieties about the illness, helping patient and family understand the consequences of a particular ailment, helping to take care of matters that the patient worries about. Social workers are also called upon to work with dying patients and their families.[45]

In addition to working directly with patients and their families, hospital social workers have been moving toward the advocate role. Specifically, they work to change the hospital organization in order to bring about an improved level of patient care. For example, a social worker pressed the medical staff of a hospital to offer improved emergency services to rape victims.[46] Hospitals, like most organizations, are organized for the convenience of their staff members. Social workers sometimes play a specific role in working for improved patient care and comfort.

Mental Health

The field of mental health and mental illness has become increasingly complex because there is great disagreement over how to understand these phenomena. There is constant controversy and shifting of ideas about how to diagnose and treat conditions of mental disturbance. The mental hospitals or "insane asylums" that were built in the nineteenth century as part of the general trend toward indoor relief were, by the mid-twentieth century, often regarded as useless and even damaging to those they were supposed to help. "Deinstitutionalization"—discharging mental patients from hospitals and returning them to the community—accelerated in the 1960s. To replace the hospitals, a new type of institution came into existence—the community mental health center. The Community Mental Health Centers Act of 1963 provided federal funds for centers built so they are accessible to the population they are meant to serve. (The area in which the population to be served by a particular agency lives is known as the agency's "catchment area.") As of 1975, some six hundred centers had been built throughout the United States.[47] However, mental hospitals have not totally disappeared; they continue with reduced numbers of patients.

Social workers began working in mental hospitals early in the century, and they became very active in the child guidance clinics. (See discussion of child guidance clinics in Chapter 9.) Today, it is estimated that 42 percent of the staff of all mental health facilities are social workers, 31 percent psychiatrists, 22 percent psychologists, and 5% psychiatric nurses.[48]

The social worker collaborates with the psychiatrist and the psychologist in assessing the disturbance in the patient and in the patient's family. The social worker is sometimes considered the most expert of the three in analyzing family relationships and may have a major role in this aspect of the assessment. Experienced social workers often gain the credibility and authority to function autonomously, both in assessment and in treatment. Fullest autonomy is attained by social workers in private practice, estimated to number about twelve thousand.[49] Most of those in private practice offer counseling or treatment of emotional problems or mental illness.

Social work in the mental health field—usually known as psychiatric social work or, more recently, as clinical social work—involves various types of treatment or therapy. One significant activity is known as *crisis intervention*—helping someone get over an acute experience of heightened anxiety or extreme depression. Marital counseling and treatment of the entire family also are widely used procedures; such counseling and treatment may be short-term or long-term, depending on the particular case, the particular worker, and the particular agency. It is evident from this brief description of social work in the mental health field that this field overlaps considerably with the field known as family and child welfare. This overlap provides part of the rationale for social work's movement toward "generic" practice, as separate fields of practice are not as sharply defined as they once were.

As noted earlier in this chapter, the distinction between undergraduate- and graduate-level preparation in social work does not provide consistently maintained criteria throughout the country for job qualifications; in some places a B.S.W. might do work that only an M.S.W. would be allowed to do in other places. The National Association of Social Workers endeavors, however, to establish graduate-level training as a firm criterion for doing clinical social work. It endeavors to persuade the state governments to license clinical social workers and to require that they not only have a master's or doctor's degree in social work but also several years of supervised experience after the master's degree before qualifying for a license.[50] The goal of establishing these criteria reflects the view that emotional problems and mental illness are the most highly specialized and intellectually demanding areas that social workers deal with and that qualifications for work in this field must therefore be set at a higher level than those for other fields of social work. From a sociological point of view, this goal can be understood as reflecting the fact that clinical social workers both work and compete with psychiatrists and clinical psychologists, who have received M.D. and Ph.D. degrees, respectively, and have received extensive supervision. To work and compete as equals requires approximate equivalence in training and credentials. There are, however, some tasks in mental health agencies that are performed by B.S.W.-level staff, and these opportunities may increase.[51]

School Social Work

School social work was established early in the century and has gone through several phases. At the beginning, the focus was on school-community relations. School procedures were explained to immigrant parents; their children were assisted through providing them with adequate food and clothing.[52] Efforts were made to reduce truancy and juvenile delinquency. From the 1930s to the 1960s, the focus shifted from home and community to the individual child's emotional adjustment; the social worker did casework with the child.

> The problems of children in school were viewed as arising mostly from personal characteristics or those of parents. The impact that school policies and community conditions had on pupils was almost unrecognized. School social workers mini-

mized the importance of their responsibilities for leadership in modifying school and community conditions.[53]

Individual service to children remains the main activity in school social work, but some changes are occurring. Social workers are shifting from an emphasis on mental health to an emphasis on helping pupils achieve educational goals. There is also some shift from individual casework to working with the school as an organization. This involves such activities as (1) working with school administrators in developing school policies that advance the overall welfare of the children, (2) developing services for specific categories of problems that occur with some frequency, and (3) developing and maintaining liaison with other agencies such as corrections, mental health, legal services for children, and family and child welfare. Financial pressures on school systems are slowing down this shift, but the idea has developed that school social work should work with community resources in an updated way.[54]

Social Work with the Aging

Social work with the elderly—or the aging, as the field is more commonly termed—is a growing area because the number of elderly people is increasing and because traditional concepts of family responsibility have altered. The elderly population in the United States, defined as people over age sixty-five, increased from 3 million in the early 1900s to 20 million in 1970; it is expected to be more than 28 million in the year 2000.[55] In those earlier years, it was customary for elderly people to live with grown children or with other relatives. When that was not possible, they lived in the county almshouse or poorhouse. Since World War II, it has become less customary for elderly parents to live with grown children. Although some live in special residential communities for the elderly, many live in traditional housing, interspersed in the general population.

Decreased income, physical mobility, and social ties are fairly common problems of the elderly. These and related problems set the agenda for social work with the elderly. This is a relatively new field:

> Until recently, few social workers saw services to elderly clients as the chief aim of their work. Elderly clients were supposed to adapt themselves to the existing service delivery systems instead of receiving services delivered to their specific requirements in mind. Long waiting lines, scattered offices, inconvenient locations of facilities, steep stairs, and insistence on office visits pose special hardships for the elderly.[56]

Social service agencies devoted specifically to the elderly are still not very widespread, although "senior citizens centers" have begun to develop. These provide meals and recreation for elderly people, working toward the double goal of helping them to maintain adequate nutrition and interpersonal ties. Transportation to the center may be provided. Elderly persons who cannot easily leave their residence may have hot meals delivered under a program commonly called "meals on wheels."

Title XX of the Social Security Act (see Chapter 9) may help to increase the services available to the aging. For example, New York State's plan for use of its federal funds includes the following services for the aging:

Social Group Services for Senior Citizens
DEFINITION: Those services provided to older adults, through specialized community facilities which serve as focal points for their concerns, needs, and interests for such multiple purposes as combating isolation, preventing or delaying physical and mental deterioration, diminishing the effects of loss of role and status, providing centralized accessibility to services and enabling the aged to remain in their homes or community for as long as possible. Services available in these centers may include any or all of the following:
   (a) Information and Referral
   (b) Nutrition (congregate meals)
   (c) Counseling
   (d) Employment Counseling
   (e) Recreation and Education Programs
   (f) Transportation to and from User's Home and Facilities
   (g) Health Maintenance Services
   (h) Community Service Volunteer Opportunities
   (i) Leadership Development
   (j) Facilitation of Other Agencies' Services
   (k) Advocacy
   (l) Outreach[57]

There is great emphasis on helping elderly people to maintain a normal social life, including providing opportunities for them to be employed, to serve as volunteers in community service, to develop leadership qualities, and in general to help them to compensate for the effects of the loss of role and status that occurs when the family home becomes an empty nest and the productive worker is obliged to retire. The challenge to the social worker is to see the elderly person as an individual and not to succumb to stereotyped ideas of elderly people as uniformly incapable of functioning independently in society.

Fulfillment of the need for individualization in a society which stereotypes the aged and relegates them to a lower status is perhaps the primary service a social worker can render in any agency with elderly clients. This is particularly true concerning the institutionalized aged, whose helplessness renders them vulnerable to mass treatment and denial of their individuality.[58]

As the number of elderly people increases, there will be increased need for agencies for those who do not have to be hospitalized but who do require a protected environment that provides some medical care. The nursing home is the major type of agency that has developed for this purpose. Nursing homes have seldom had social workers on their staffs but this is changing since social workers are seen as being able to offer:

(1) Services to the resident, including casework, group work, discharge planning, and advocacy;
(2) Services to the families of residents, including helping them express their feelings about the relative's disability and increasing their capacity to work with the staff in meeting the resident's needs;
(3) Training to the nursing home staff to understand the needs of elderly people; and
(4) Outreach activities in the community to increase public awareness of the needs of the elderly.[59]

The social worker can help staff and family members develop attitudes that foster a more active, less fearful style of life for the elderly client.[60]

Social Work in Corrections

Corrections is the term widely used to refer to efforts to change people convicted of breaking the law so that they will not break the law in the future. The term includes a complex mixture of punishment and help. Thus sending people to prison for crimes is intended to deter them from committing future crimes. However, various efforts may be made to help them at the same time that they are being punished with a prison term. Some prisons offer training for work, and some offer various kinds of counseling or therapy.

Social work has played a role in the prison system, but not a large one. For one reason, "Attempting to change criminals into noncriminals in an environment generally alien to middle-class life-styles demands techniques that most social workers are ill-equipped to deliver."[61] A second reason relates to the very nature of the situation. Prison administrators sometimes require that prisoners become involved in treatment programs. Coercing treatment violates the basic ethical principle of social work that emphasizes the client's right to choose. Social workers are caught in a conflict between the principles on which their occupation is based and the demands of the organization for which they work, when that organization is a prison.[62] Nevertheless, they can be helpful in working with the families of prisoners, in serving as advocates for prisoners, and sometimes in direct work with prisoners themselves.

Not everyone convicted of a crime is sent to prison. Some may be put on probation, that is, be placed in a status where they must report periodically to a probation officer who seeks to assure that the person is "keeping out of trouble." The decision to place individuals on probation instead of sending them to prison is made by a judge, who relies heavily on pre-sentence reports. These are often the work of a social worker employed by the court who investigates convicted individuals' backgrounds and the circumstances of the crimes and then makes a recommendation to the court. A similar process occurs in juvenile courts, which deal with "juvenile delinquency" rather than crimes. A juvenile (a minor) who is placed on probation will often be required to enter a treatment relationship with a probation officer; the relationship is necessarily difficult because the probation officer is both a social worker and an officer of the court; the two roles do not mesh smoothly.[63]

Community Organizing

In the preceding chapter, community organizing was identified as one of the basic methods of social work. Community organization is a distinctive field of practice as well as a method used by all social workers. Some social workers specialize in community organizing, just as others specialize in medical social work or work with children. Not as many social workers enter the field of community organization as did in the activist 1960s when the civil rights movement and the War on Poverty made it especially popular. The field continues to exist, however, and there is always some possibility that a change in circumstances may once again bring it to prominence.

Community organizers seek to bring about social change.[64] They help people in a particular locality become more effective in attaining desired goals. A frequent goal is getting a service-providing organization (for example, a branch of government or a social agency) to give better service. The organization will not improve its service unless those who feel it to be inadequate can themselves become capable of organized effort and generate effective pressure.

Those who are to be organized are known as the social worker's *constituency*. A worker begins to work with a constituency at the invitation of a sponsor. The sponsor might be a small community group who may eventually become part of the larger constituency, or the sponsor might be a foundation that wishes to encourage a certain kind of community activity. The organizer's work can be analyzed into a number of steps.

First, the organizer must *study the community* in order to understand the various groupings, issues, and points of view within it. Then, the organizer begins to *develop a constituency* by explaining his purpose through public meetings and private discussions. The private discussions are held with "the victims of social problems, apparent community leaders, relevant agency officials and/or groups with an interest in the problem."

In time, the worker may *work with some existing groups* in the community or may *help new groups to get started.* He helps the groups to function as groups and to discuss the issues that are important in the community, helping the groups to clarify the problems and issues. This activity is known as *problem analysis* and consists of helping the groups develop answers to four main questions: "Who is it that is suffering? What are the characteristics of the victims? What is it that they suffer from? And what other work has been done on the problem?"[65] During problem analysis, the community organizer also helps the participants develop an identification with their emerging groups and a commitment to their purposes.

Once a stable group or groups have been formed and are committed to working toward a goal, the worker tries to *broaden support by building a coalition,* that is, getting other groups to work together with the one(s) he has been working with so that more people will be working for the goal.

Once a coalition pressing for change has been assembled, attention is directed toward the "target" of change, the organization whose ways the constituency wants changed. The worker and the coalition have several ways of *acting toward the target agency.* The way that is selected depends upon many factors. When prospects for change seem favorable, the worker and his coalition may engage in persuasion. When bringing about change seems more difficult, they engage in "campaign tactics," such as political maneuvering, getting third parties to put pressure on the target, and negotiating with the target agency. An example of campaign tactics is the following:

> A group of slum tenants who wished to force their landlord to make repairs scheduled a picket line demonstration at his suburban home. Wiser persons advised the group to postpone the demonstration, so that news of its imminence might be "leaked" to the landlord. The threat brought the landlord to the bargaining table and, ultimately, he was persuaded to make the repairs.[66]

Finally, if resistance to change seems very strong, the community organizer and his constituency may engage in direct actions such as public protests and demonstrations, noncooperation tactics such as boycotts, and physical obstruction such as a sit-in in an agency to prevent it from conducting its normal business. Direct interventions can be dangerous to the participants and often are violations of law.

SUMMARY

The purpose of this chapter has been to provide an introductory description of the work that contemporary social workers do. The work has been described

The first vantage point is that of method, the basic ways of working. The three traditional methods of social work have been casework, group work, and community organization. Social workers have usually become specialists in one of these methods. Since the 1960s and 1970s, efforts have been made to replace these methods with a "generic" method that emphasizes the interdependence of individuals, groups, and communities. The social worker is thus expected to be able to function more flexibly than in the past, turning attention as needed from individual to group to community in any sequence that the particular problem requires. Several new terms have been proposed to replace the terms for the traditional three methods, but none of the new terminology has yet gained the wide degree of acceptance enjoyed by the older terms.

The second vantage point in describing the work of social work is that of activity sequence. Work on a problem can be analyzed into a set of activities that occur in rough sequence beginning with intake—acceptance of the problem by agency and worker—and proceeding through assessment and diagnosis, establishing a contract, establishing and maintaining a treatment relationship, evaluation of the work, and termination of the relationship. Two illustrations of the activity sequence were presented.

The third vantage point is that of fields of practice. Social work is organized around certain clusters of problems, population groupings, and social institutions. A particular cluster of problems, population group, or social institution may be the basis of a field of practice. The work that social workers do in the major fields of practice was briefly described.

Notes

[1] Beulah Roberts Compton, *Introduction to Social Welfare and Social Work* (Homewood, Ill.: Dorsey Press, 1980), p. 567.

[2] This point is made both by Compton, *Introduction to Social Welfare;* and by Ralph Dolgoff and Donald Feldstein, *Understanding Social Welfare* (New York: Harper & Row, 1980), pp. 273–275.

[3] Helen Harris Perlman, *Perspectives on Social Casework* (Philadelphia: Temple University Press, 1971), p. 35.

[4] Howard Goldstein, *Social Work Practice: A Unitary Approach* (Columbia, S.C.: University of South Carolina Press, 1973), p. 47.

[5] Sar A. Levitan, *The Great Society's Poor Law* (Baltimore: Johns Hopkins Press), pp. 133ff.

[6] Goldstein, *Social Work Practice*, p. 47; Allen Pincus and Anne Minahan, *Social Work Practice: Model and Method* (Itasca, Ill.: F. E. Peacock, 1973).

[7] This is a highly condensed summary of Francis P. Purcell and Harry Specht, "The House on Sixth Street," in Pincus and Minahan, *Model and Method*, pp. 289–299.

[8] Irving A. Spergel, "Social Development and Social Work," in Simon Slavin, ed., *Social*

Administration (New York: Haworth Press and Council on Social Work Education, 1978), p. 24.

[9]*Ibid.*

[10]*Ibid.*, p. 26.

[11]Sheila B. Kamerman et al., "Knowledge for Practice: Social Science in Social Work," in Alfred J. Kahn, ed., *Shaping the New Social Work* (New York: Columbia University Press, 1973), p. 102.

[12]*Ibid.*, pp. 111–112.

[13]F. M. Loewenberg, *Fundamentals of Social Intervention* (New York: Columbia University Press, 1977), p. vii.

[14]This presentation of activity sequence draws upon Allan R. Mendelsohn, *The Work of Social Work* (New York: New Viewpoints, 1980), Chapter 6; Toni Tripodi et al., *Social Workers at Work* (Itasca, Ill.: F. E. Peacock, 1972), pp. 4ff; and James K. Whittaker, *Social Treatment* (Chicago: Aldine, 1974), Chapter 5.

[15]Mendelsohn, *Work of Social Work*, p. 135.

[16]The study of families as organizations remains an underdeveloped area in the social sciences and in psychology, although family therapy has mushroomed as an applied field. Some studies have been done. Differences in family organization within one spectrum of American families ranging from upper middle class to working class are portrayed in Robert D. Hess and Gerald Handel, *Family Worlds* (Chicago: University of Chicago Press, 1959; Phoenix edition, 1974). Contrast between relatively well organized working-class and relatively disorganized lower-class American families is presented in Joseph T. Howell, *Hard Living on Clay Street* (Garden City, N.Y.: Anchor Books, 1973). Different family organizations that have produced severe emotional disturbance in children are explored in Jules Henry, *Pathways to Madness* (New York: Vintage Books, 1973). The impact of work on family organization is explored by Chaya Piotrkowski, *Work and the Family System* (New York: Free Press, 1979). Volumes that attempt to present general frameworks for studying families as organizations include Gerald Handel, ed., *The Psychosocial Interior of the Family*, 2nd ed. (Chicago: Aldine, 1972); and David Kantor and William Lehr, *Inside the Family* (San Francisco: Jossey-Bass, 1975).

[17]Social workers and clients often have very different ideas about how adults should relate to their families; see Hope J. Leichter and William E. Mitchell, *Kinship and Casework* (New York: Russell Sage Foundation, 1967).

[18]Whittaker, *Social Treatment*, p. 123.

[19]*Ibid.*, p. 120.

[20]Mendelsohn, *Work of Social Work*, p. 149.

[21]*Ibid.*

[22]This formulation draws upon the excellent paper by David Landy, "Problems of the Person Seeking Help in Our Culture," in *Social Welfare Forum 1960*, National Conference on Social Welfare (New York: Columbia University Press, 1960).

[23]Ernest A. Herre, "Aggressive Casework in a Protective Services Unit," in Tripodi et al., *Social Workers at Work*, pp. 12–18.

[24]*Ibid.*, p. 15.

[25]Henry Freeman et al., "Can a Family Agency Be Relevant to the Inner Urban Scene?" in Tripodi et al., *Social Workers at Work*, pp. 44–56.

[26]*Ibid.*, p. 51.

[27]*Ibid.*

[28]*Ibid.*, p. 49.

[29]*Ibid.*, p. 53.

[30]Mendelsohn, *Work of Social Work*, pp. 14–15.

[31]This analysis is drawn from Robert Morris and Delwin Anderson, "Personal Care Services: An Identity for Social Work," *Social Service Review*, Vol. 49, No. 2 (June 1975), pp. 157–174.

[32]Here I draw on the useful classification of family and children's problems presented by Elizabeth A. Ferguson, *Social Work—An Introduction*, 3rd ed. (Philadelphia: Lippincott, 1975), Chapters 3 and 4.

[33]Whittaker, *Social Treatment*, lists twenty-one different forms of treatment used in social work, most of them applicable to parent-child problems; see Appendix, pp. 200–247.

[34]A classic study of such processes is Ezra F. Vogel and Norman W. Bell, "The Emotionally Disturbed Child as the Family Scapegoat," in Norman W. Bell and Ezra F. Vogel, eds., *A Modern Introduction to the Family* (New York: Free Press, 1960). Reprinted in Handel, ed.; *Psychosocial Interior*.

[35]Ferguson, *Social Work*, p. 136. For a thorough study of the impact of poverty and discrimination on parent-child relations in black families, see Lee Rainwater, *Behind the Ghetto Walls* (Chicago: Aldine, 1970).

[36]Lela B. Costin, *Child Welfare: Policies and Practice* (New York: McGraw-Hill, 1972), p. 260.

[37]*Ibid.*, p. 281.

[38]*Ibid.*, p. 321.

[39]*Ibid.*, p. 331.

[40]*Ibid.*, p. 359.

[41]This account of social work in adoption draws primarily on Costin, *Child Welfare*, Chapter 12.

[42]Neil F. Bracht, *Social Work in Health Care* (New York: Haworth Press, 1978), p. 4.

[43]*Ibid.*, pp. 23–24.

[44]*Ibid.*, pp. 170–180.

[45]Shirley H. Wattenberg, "Health," in Donald Brieland et al., *Contemporary Social Work*, 2nd ed. (New York: McGraw-Hill, 1980), pp. 268–270; Ferguson, *Social Work*, pp. 286ff.

[46]*Ibid.*

[47]Anthony J. Vattano, "Mental Health," in Brieland et al., *Contemporary Social Work*, p. 282.

[48]Bracht, *Social Work in Health*, p. 4.

[49]Betty L. Baer and Ronald Federico, *Educating the Baccalaureate Social Worker* (Cambridge, Mass.: Ballinger, 1978), p. 9.

[50]Vattano, "Mental Health," p. 295.

[51]Ferguson, *Social Work*, pp. 325, 351.

[52]*Ibid.*, p. 179.

[53]Lela B. Costin, "Social Work in the Schools," in Brieland et al., *Contemporary Social Work*, p. 246.

[54]*Ibid.* See also Arthur P. Michals, Daniel E. Cournoyer, and Elizabeth L. Pinner, "School Social Work and Educational Goals," *Social Work*, Vol. 24, No. 2 (March 1979), pp. 138–141.

[55]Lu Pearman and Jean Searles, "Unmet Social Service Needs in Skilled Nursing Facilities," in Bracht, *Social Work in Health*, p. 184.

[56]Ferguson, *Social Work*, p. 268.

[57]*Comprehensive Annual Social Services Program Plan for New York State, October 1, 1979 to September 30, 1980* (Albany, N.Y.: Department of Social Services, September 1979), p. 77.

[58]Ferguson, *Social Work*, p. 271.

[59]Pearman and Searles, "Unmet Social Service Needs," p. 185.

[60]Ferguson, *Social Work*, p. 274.

[61] John C. Watkins, Jr., "Juvenile and Criminal Justice," in Brieland et al., *Contemporary Social Work*, p. 331.

[62] *Ibid.*, p. 330.

[63] David H. Robertson, "The Juvenile Court—and Bill—and Authority," in Arthur E. Fink et al., *The Field of Social Work*, 6th ed. (New York: Holt, Rinehart and Winston, 1974), pp. 214ff.

[64] The following highly condensed account of community organization draws primarily on George Brager and Harry Specht, *Community Organizing* (New York: Columbia University Press, 1973).

[65] *Ibid.*, p. 109.

[66] *Ibid.*, p. 330.

VARIETIES OF SOCIAL WELFARE INSTITUTIONS

Social Service

Charity Organization Society
Child guidance clinic
Community chest
Council of Social Agencies
Family service agency
Federation of social agencies (also called associated charities)
Group work agency
Hospital social service department
Hot line
Neighborhood information center
Neighborhood legal services center
Private practice
Public social agency
Psychiatric clinic
Social reform movement
Social service exchange
Social settlement (or settlement house)
United Way
Voluntary social agency
Visiting teacher (school social work)

Significant Figures in Social Service

Jane Addams—Co-founder and longtime director of Hull House in Chicago, most famous American settlement house; vigorous leader of social reform movements; helped define social work as a social reform occupation

Samuel Barnett—Anglican clergyman who conceived the concept of the settlement house and established the first one, in London

Grace Coyle—Developed the first conceptualization of group work as a social work method

Sigmund Freud—Viennese psychiatrist who conceived and developed psychoanalysis as a theory of personality development and functioning and as a theory of treatment of mental illness; psychoanalysis, as developed by Freud and his followers, became the most influential idea system in social work, especially in casework

Mary Richmond—Developed the first conceptualization of casework as a social work method, prior to Freud's influence on the field

Significant Dates in Social Service

1869—First Charity Organization Society founded in London

1877—First Charity Organization Society founded in the United States, in Buffalo

1884—First settlement house established, Toynbee Hall in London

1886—First settlement house in United States, Neighborhood Guild in New York

1889—Hull House, most famous settlement house, established in Chicago

1898—New York Charity Organization Society establishes a Summer School of Philanthropy, first formal institution for training social workers

1917—Mary Richmond's *Social Diagnosis* published

1930—Grace Coyle's *Social Process in Organized Groups* published

1962—Community organization practice recognized as a social work method by Council on Social Work Education

1962—Public Welfare Amendments of 1962, providing federal reimbursement to states for social casework services as major strategy to remove people from AFDC rolls

1967—Casework services as strategy to remove recipients from AFDC rolls judged unsuccessful; replaced by new strategy of work incentives (WIN) to reduce welfare rolls

1974–1975—Title XX adopted and put into effect; provides federal reimbursement to states for wider array of social service costs than did 1962 amendments

1970s to present—Social work moving away from its traditional conceptualization of three distinct methods toward a conceptualization that emphasizes the interrelationship of individuals, groups, communities, organizations, and social segments, and applies generic methods to these interrelationships

Mutual
Aid

VI

Three Concepts
of Mutual Aid

11

Charity, public welfare, and social service—all involve relationships of inequality. People who have more of something give some of it to those who have less of that thing. The wealthy and well-off give charity to the poor. In public welfare, taxes are collected from those who can afford to pay them, and some of this money is distributed or transferred in the form of public assistance to those who do not have enough, or to social welfare service institutions (for example, for child care or elderly care) that serve those whose resources are insufficient for them to manage without public welfare help. Social service, too, is based on a relationship of inequality: a person with particular skills and knowledge works with a person or group with fewer of these skills and knowledge. There is a flow of help from helper to helped. And the distinction between helper and helped is clear.

Although there were times when the wealthy believed that the poor helped the rich by giving the rich the opportunity to be helpful, this notion never succeeded in transforming charity into a relationship of equality. There was seldom much doubt that the rich could give more than the poor could give in return. The poor could give honor, as in ancient Greece, or they could give gratefulness as the COS expected, but neither was truly seen as equal to the donations they had received.

In contrast to these forms of social welfare, the concept of mutual aid is based on a relationship of equality. There is no clear distinction between helpers and helped; helpers and helped are or can be the same individuals.

People who give each other mutual aid have a shared identity. They form a group on the basis of what they have in common, such as the same occupation, the same ethnic group, residence in the same neighborhood, or the same problem. These and other similarities have led people to develop what Franklin Giddings, an early sociologist, called a "consciousness of kind."

There have been three major versions of the concept of mutual aid. The concept of *mutual insurance* dates back at least to ancient Roman times and is still operative today. People in the same occupation banded together and contributed to a common fund; a member who became ill received payments from the fund. The members thus insured each other.

During the War on Poverty in the 1960s, the concept of mutual aid known as *community action* became prominent. The basis of association was shared neighborhood, and its goal was to gain political power in order to influence the decisions affecting the neighborhood.

The third version of mutual aid, *self-help groups,* came to prominence in the 1970s. The basis of association was a problem all group members had that led them to join together for the purpose of mutual aid. For this reason, the term *mutual help groups* might be a more accurate designation. The earliest known of the self-help groups was Alcoholics Anonymous, created in the 1930s by people who had a drinking problem who met together to help each other through confession of their problem and discussion. Subsequently, the self-help group concept has been adopted by persons with many other kinds of problems.

The members of a self-help group conceive of themselves as being "in the same boat." In contrast to charity's distinction between rich and poor, and social services' distinction between the expert helper and the client in need of help, there is no distinction between helper and helped in mutual aid. In the actual functioning of community action groups and self-help groups, expert advisors may be called in to assist, but they function as auxiliaries; they are *facilitators,* not leaders dominating the groups. Community action and self-help groups both emerged from dissatisfaction with traditional forms of aid, both public and private (for example, welfare, traditional social worker–client relationships, psychoanalysis), though certain kinds of social work assistance are often accepted in community action and in self-help groups.

Despite their differences, the three main categories of mutual aid exemplify a common principle and a powerful impulse in human society: the principle of voluntary action, of people joining together in associations of their own devising and under their own direction; and the impulse to be in charge of one's own life, to be autonomous.

To be sure, pure autonomy and pure voluntarism are accepted as realistic only in the doctrine of anarchism, which conceives of society as existing entirely through voluntary cooperation.[1] Such thorough escape from outside constraint is not found in any of the versions of mutual aid, nor in the persons who join in these endeavors. They have still been members of societies characterized by uneven distribution of power, and have therefore been at least somewhat constrained by groups and organizations and governments not entirely of their choosing. Mutual aid nonetheless has been a principle that, put into action, has enabled people to feel that they have gained some control over their lives and the ability to solve at least some of their problems.

MUTUAL INSURANCE

Mutual insurance is probably the oldest form of mutual aid. Occupational groupings in the Roman Empire—known as *collegia*—were mutual insurance groups. The members of each association made monthly contributions into a common fund. Mutual insurance has continued into the present; the associations whose members insure each other are sometimes based upon occupation, sometimes upon neighborhood, sometimes upon ethnic group membership, or upon other memberships that lead people to develop a consciousness of kind.

Medieval Fraternities and Guilds

During the Middle Ages, many local voluntary associations called fraternities or guilds were organized. Some of these appear to have originated (at least those in England) as groups associated with a parish church, while others developed as associations of workers in a particular craft. The organization of the craft guilds developed out of efforts to gain the right to establish voluntary associations, an effort that was directed at the established authority of feudal lords. Both the craft guilds and the parish fraternities included among their goals the mutual aid of members who became ill or experienced a misfortune that led to loss of income. Thus one parish fraternity provided that "if any brother or sister fall into poverty by way of robbery or accident of fire or by any other misfortune, not through his own fault, and he have not wherewith to live or help himself he shall every week have fourteen pence."[2] Most of the fraternities required that the member pay dues for seven years before being eligible for relief.

Friendly Societies

Independently of the guilds and parish fraternities, poor people in England in the eighteenth century formed mutual aid societies known as friendly societies. These seem to have arisen at first on the initiative of poor people themselves, although they later caught the attention of more powerful people who encouraged their formation and growth.[3] There were many varieties of friendly societies: for example, workers in a particular trade, residents of a particular locality, or even the clientele of a particular alehouse. Most were local clubs that combined sociability with mutual insurance.[4] They collected subscriptions from members, and the money was set aside for giving assistance to the members in a great variety of misfortunes: income maintenance of members or their dependents in sickness, old age, widowhood, orphanhood, death, shipwreck, when traveling in search of employment, loss by fire of the tools of the member's trade.[5]

Toward the end of the eighteenth century, when the costs of the Poor Law were being experienced as very burdensome, the friendly societies caught the attention of powerful people in England. Self-help was part of the spirit of the age, and one of the proposals for abolishing the Poor Law altogether called for a national organization of friendly societies. All classes of people would be compelled to contribute; those who failed to do so would have to wear a badge that said "DRONE in large letters of red cloth—unless, of course, they were members of the upper classes." Benefits would be paid to those in need, except to the drones, who would have to undergo a workhouse test.[6] This scheme, developed by a minister, was not adopted. It is of interest as an indication of the idea of the time that poverty was caused by workers' lack of foresight, their failure to plan for the future by saving and insuring against future loss of income. The belief seemed to be that if everyone contributed to a friendly society, no one would ever have to be supported from the poor rate.

Instead of compelling membership in friendly societies, a law was passed in 1793 that *encouraged* their growth by giving members a privilege: members would be exempt from removal from a parish under the Law of Settlement and Removal (see Chapter 5) until they were actually chargeable with dependency, rather than merely on suspicion that they might become chargeable. It took two more years for this privilege to be extended to single women who were pregnant.[7] Friendly societies did flourish in the United Kingdom (England, Wales, Scotland, Ireland), and about a hundred years later there were almost twenty-five thousand friendly societies, with more than 4 million members.[8]

It is noteworthy that it was in the intense climate of anti–Poor Law sentiment and the search for self-help schemes that the idea of the *savings bank* was first conceived. In 1795, an Anglican clergyman proposed a plan for a "Provident Parochial Bank, expressing a hope that a reasonable rate of interest might lead the poor to shun poor relief, and perhaps even the ale-house."[9] The first savings banks were those established in Scotland a few years later. For a time, there was a debate in Great Britain over the relative merits of the savings bank and the friendly society as avenues of self-help. Although there is evidence that domestic servants and artisans had money to deposit in the new savings banks that sprung up, laborers did not; they "remained true to their clubs, and it is club membership, and not savings bank deposits, which provide most evidence of the activities of the poor to help themselves."[10]

Fraternal insurance

Friendly societies were local clubs, organized by people who knew or could know each other personally. The early nineteenth century saw the extension, and to some extent the transformation, of the local friendly society to a national scale. According to one account, a stonemason was dissatisfied with the emphasis on feasting and drinking that had developed in many of the societies, and he determined to reform them. He organized a group called the Order of Odd Fellows in Manchester in 1912 as a first step in creating a national organization of independent local lodges affiliated with a national office that would supervise the mutual insurance activities of the organization. This organization, the Manchester Unity —of the Independent Order of Odd Fellows—was the first of many national fraternal organizations that provided mutual insurance benefits to their members.[11] The concept also developed in the United States; according to one disputed account, the first American fraternal benefit association was the Ancient Order of United Workmen, established in 1868.[12] However, this claim does not take account of mutual insurance societies founded much earlier by immigrants.

Immigrant Societies

There is some evidence that the friendly societies in England originated not among the English but among immigrants to England, French Huguenots (Calvinist Protestants) who fled Roman Catholic domination in France. The first such society dates from 1687.[13] In an unfamiliar country, the shared origin and distinctive identity of groups of immigrants led them to turn to each other for mutual support. Immigrants to the American colonies banded together in this way, on the basis of nationality, or religion, or both. The first such society in the American colonies was the Scots Charitable Society, organized in Boston in 1657. In its charter, the group stated that it was organized "for the relief of ourselves and any other for which . . . we may see cause."[14] Other societies were established in the eighteenth century, and still others in the nineteenth century, after the colonies became a nation and immigration increased. English, Welsh, Irish, Scotch, German, French, Swiss, Jews, Belgians, Italians, Dutch, Scan-

dinavians, Cubans, and Puerto Ricans—all established benevolent societies in
New York City during the first half of the nineteenth century. The mutual aid
societies provided income benefits during periods of illness of members and, in
the event of the death of a member, paid funeral expenses. Some mutual aid
societies were organized on the basis of occupation rather than national origin
or religion, and some immigrants joined existing fraternal orders such as the Odd
Fellows. By the end of the Civil War in 1865, almost every nationality group
in New York had at least one benevolent society.[15]

Mutual Insurance and Social Insurance

The concept of mutual insurance and the concept of social insurance (see Chapter 7) have a certain similarity, although there are also significant differences
between them. Mutual insurance originates in face-to-face groups or other small-
scale groups whose members have a distinctive identity—based on locality,
occupation, ethnic group, religion, or membership in the club—that sets them
apart from others in the society. Social insurance is insurance for the entire
population of a nation, or for everybody in the nation who has a particular
experience such as unemployment or old age that interrupts income. Social
insurance is thus widely inclusive rather than exclusive to those who share a
distinctive loyalty.

Despite the obvious differences, there are nonetheless some similarities. In
England, social insurance was based on citizenship. Social insurance took on the
aspect of citizens insuring each other for at least a national minimum standard
of living. This principle was quite different from the Poor Law principle that
singled out a category of paupers. After World War II, "It became acknowledged on virtually all sides that one of the perquisites of British citizenship was
the right to the minimum standard of existence."[16]

The designers of the American social security program made use of the
concept of self-help by requiring contributions from earnings in order to qualify
for old-age and related benefits.

> It was precisely this old and venerable legacy of self-help that furnished the
> new theme needed to justify the unavoidable program of old-age protection. In
> this respect America deviated markedly from European precedents. As J. Douglas
> Brown has explained: "We wanted our government to provide a mechanism
> whereby the individual could prevent dependency through his own effort." There
> was something ironic in this emphasis on self-help, since American workers had
> been much less inclined than Europeans to help themselves through friendly
> societies. Nevertheless, it was a shrewd formula, for it put a veneer of individual-
> ism over the inevitable element of compulsion.[17]

The major similarity between mutual insurance and social insurance is that both are programs for people who are joined together on the basis of some similarity to provide income for the members of the group who experience a need for it. The major difference is that mutual insurance is voluntary, whereas social insurance is compulsory. The idea that the national state should compel its citizens to pay taxes to assure each other of a minimum income after retirement in old age (and disability and survivor benefits) is widely accepted today. But it is not universally accepted. Nobel prize-winner economist Milton Friedman, one of the staunchest modern-day defenders of traditional laissez-faire ideas, believes that the concept of compulsory insurance is a dangerous and unwarranted infringement of personal liberty. He would like to see a return to voluntary self-help.

COMMUNITY ACTION

Community action acquired the connotation of mutual aid after a time, but it did not have it when the concept was first introduced. Disagreement over the meaning of the term became a source of fierce political conflict during the 1960s.

The Introduction of Community Action

Community action was an aspect of the Economic Opportunity Act of 1964, which authorized the War on Poverty that was to lead to the Great Society. (See Chapter 6.) The act had seven titles (sections), each giving the legal basis for a particular program in the overall "war." There were titles dealing with work training for youth and relief recipients, with loans for marginal farmers; and with other programs.[18] The section of law defining what a community action program is stated:

> The term "community action program" means a program
> (1) which mobilizes and utilizes resources, public or private, or any . . . geographic area . . . in an attack on poverty;
> (2) which provides services, assistance, and other activities . . . to give promise of progress toward elimination of poverty or a cause or causes of poverty . . . ;

(3) which is developed, conducted, and administered with the maximum feasible
     participation of residents of the areas and members of the groups served; and
(4) which is conducted, administered, or coordinated by a public or private
     nonprofit agency (other than a political party), or a combination thereof.[19]

Congress did not explain what it intended by the phrase "maximum feasible
participation of residents of the areas and members of the groups served," and
the expression became a battleground on which a war within the War on Poverty
was fought; this was a war for control of the programs to fight poverty and for
jobs within the programs.

The act established a new federal agency, the Office of Economic Opportunity (OEO), to supervise the new programs. Each participating community was
to establish a Community Action Program (CAP)—also known as a Community
Action Agency (CAA)—that would receive money from OEO and make decisions on how to spend the money. The CAP would also coordinate antipoverty
efforts under the jurisdiction of established government departments; there were
some four hundred different programs that then granted money to local communities for one or another social welfare purpose.[20]

The people running each CAP were supposed to come from three groupings:
(1) representatives of established social welfare agencies, (2) representatives of
"leadership groups" such as labor, business, religion, and minority groups, and
(3) representatives of the local poor.[21] There were disputes in many communities
over such questions as: What proportion of the policy-making bodies of the
CAPs should be representatives of the poor? How should they be chosen? Early
in 1965, OEO "suggested unofficially that policymaking bodies for CAPs include approximately one-third representation of low-income groups, chosen
wherever feasible in accordance with 'democratic techniques.' "[22] The poor were
thus to be brought into a coalition with established leaders and professionals. But
in many target areas—the areas in which the CAPs were to concentrate their
activities—minority group leaders argued that people from the target area should
be a majority of the board members and should control the program.[23] How
could such a claim be justified? The answer lies in a new theory of dependency
and poverty that began to emerge at that time.

Poverty as Lack of Power

Poverty was first seen simply as a condition in which a person lacked the material
necessities of life. This is the view of poverty that has come down to us over the
longest stretch of history, and it is by no means obsolete today. A second view
appeared perhaps as early as the fifth century A.D., when Augustine introduced
the idea that some poor were undeserving of charity. His view implied that some

deficiency of character was the cause of poverty. Nineteenth-century Victorians were not concerned about poverty so much as about pauperism, the condition not only of being poor but of being absolutely dependent upon outside assistance. They saw pauperism as due to a deficiency of character and sought to correct the deficiency first by threatening to put people into workhouses and later by friendly visiting. The rise of psychoanalysis led to subtler understandings of character and motivation than had been available before; one result was that social work was tempted to overlook the reality of the lack of material resources in poverty and to overemphasize psychological interpretations and treatment.

In the 1960s, the lack of a significant role in collective decision making was seen as a fundamental cause of poverty. Powerlessness was a new concept to explain poverty. Unquestionably, the civil rights movement contributed significantly to the development of this view. From the day in 1955 when Rosa Parks, a black woman in Montgomery, Alabama, refused to sit in the back of the bus as had been required of blacks by whites, the power to make decisions began to be seen as a significant means of change for people who were excluded from the routine benefits of American society. As the civil rights movement gathered strength over the next several years, participation in decision making became an increasingly important goal; by 1966, this goal had resulted in the transformation of the civil rights movement into the black power movement.[24] The elimination of political dependency was a principal aim among blacks.

The notion of the lack of political power as the cause of poverty was one of two main concepts of community action in the views of those who formulated the Economic Opportunity Act. The other was the more traditional notion of individual change. The two views have been contrasted as follows:

> Those who interpreted the idea of community action in terms of the expansion and more efficient allocation of services implicitly supported a category of objectives that center upon the principle of *individual change.* The notion here is that the poor lack certain characteristics requisite to achieving success in the competitive arena of middle-class America. The main objective is to rectify these deficiencies through the provision of health, legal, occupational, educational, and social services. Other objectives implicit in this category involve the promotion of social control and uniform standards of behavior.
>
> The second category of objectives is suggested by those who interpreted community action as signifying an attempt to increase the political power of the poor. In this category, the central principle is the *democratization of social welfare.* Poverty is understood not just as a lack of material goods, but also as a sense of impotency and a lack of dignity and self-respect. This principle includes the assurance of civic as well as economic self-sufficiency. Here the main objective is to involve the poor not only as clients of welfare services, but as participants in the planning and implementation of these services. This involvement implies a change in the decision-making structure of the institutions that serve the poor, one that would allow them access to this structure and permit influence upon the

decisions made therein, thus providing leverage to obtain a more equitable distribution of goods and services.[25]

With the theory of powerlessness as an explanation of poverty, the goal of gaining majority control of CAPs was quite logical. The *Community Action Program Guide* issued by the OEO seemed to support this idea:

> The long range objective of every community action program is to effect a permanent increase in the capacity of individuals, groups, and communities afflicted by poverty to deal effectively with their own problems so that they need no further assistance.[26]

Power Struggles

Traditionally, in the United States, when the federal government gives money to local governments to carry out a national purpose, the money goes to state and local government departments that are under the influence, if not the control, of the governor, mayor, or county board of supervisors. The CAPs represented a significant departure from this system. Money was being channeled from the federal treasury directly to local CAPs, with the mayors having no control except what they could gain through political struggles. Elected officials help to assure their reelection through political appointments and through providing their constituents with desired services. The mayors therefore did not like seeing these activities pass into hands beyond their control. And they did not sit still and let the CAPs go their own way. They fought for control, and after three years, they succeeded in getting Congress to change the Economic Opportunity Act in 1967 so that the CAPs came under control of the city governments.[27]

Evaluation of Community Action

Community action was a decided innovation in the development of social welfare. As the concept of local community control gained momentum, fierce conflicts erupted in one city after another. Most local political leaders and professional social workers remained adamantly opposed to giving decision-making authority to people who generally had little education and little experience in making organizational decisions, and many of whom had been (or still were) recipients of public assistance and clients of diverse social welfare agencies. The OEO, directed by Sargent Shriver, brother-in-law of the late President

Kennedy, supported the concept of community control, as did some professors of social work and some practicing social workers.

There were over a thousand community action agencies by the time Congress trimmed their authority. Did they contribute anything to social welfare except conflict? Answers to this question are bound to vary. Daniel Patrick Moynihan, who was Assistant Secretary of Labor in the Kennedy administration and a member of the committee that planned the Economic Opportunity Act of 1964, said that "maximum feasible participation" of the residents was, in his view, "maximum feasible misunderstanding."[28] Moynihan believed that as the concept of participation was put into practice, it could not work because it failed to take account of existing social relationships. The people who seized upon the idea of "maximum feasible participation" and turned it into the notion of community control were completely unrealistic in their expectations. The result, he later wrote, was that "the social history of the 1960's is . . . littered with the wreckage of crash programs that were going to change everything and in fact changed nothing."[29] In response to this, others have said: "Even wrecks alter the landscape, marking a path of leadership that perhaps had to be explored."[30] Despite the ultimate failure of the CAP, it was successful in that it gave rise to

a movement to protect the right of the poor, and all politically disadvantaged minorities to be heard, which over the decade has profoundly influenced our conceptions of democracy. If these rights can be secured and applied, at every level of government, to a more open process of arbitrating the allocation of resources, then the experiment of community action may be vindicated after all.[31]

SELF-HELP GROUPS

Self-help groups are:

voluntary, small group structures for mutual aid and the accomplishment of a special purpose. They are usually formed by peers who have come together for mutual assistance in satisfying a common need, overcoming a common handicap or life-disrupting problem, and bringing about desired social and/or personal change.[32]

Such groups are small enough that they can have face-to-face meetings; groups organized to deal with the same kind of problem in different localities may be linked as branches or chapters of a national organization.

The number of such groups has proliferated considerably in the 1960s and

1970s. Americans have been noted as being willing to organize groups and associations for almost any purpose. As early as 1835, in one of the most celebrated books ever written about the United States, Alexis de Tocqueville, a French aristocrat who had visited the country a few years before, wrote:

> In no country in the world has the principle of association been more successfully used or applied to a greater multitude of objects than in America. . . . In the United States associations are established to promote the public safety, commerce, industry, morality, and religion. There is no end which the human will despairs of attaining through the combined power of individuals united into a society. . . . If it is proposed to inculcate some truth or to foster some feeling by the encouragement of a great example, they form a society. . . . As soon as several of the inhabitants of the United States have taken up an opinion or a feeling which they wish to promote in the world, they look out for mutual assistance; and as soon as they have found one another, they combine.[33]

The longstanding penchant of Americans for forming groups and associations waxes and wanes, and it takes different forms at different times. In the 1930s, there were intense efforts to organize labor unions, and the Townsend movement was a significant nonlabor organization that flourished at that time (see Chapter 8). The 1940s and 1950s were fairly quiescent, first because the country was engaged in World War II, and then because after men returned home from the armed forces, people sought satisfaction in private life. A new era of forming associations for public purposes was initiated by the civil rights movement, as blacks realized that they were still left out of the economically flourishing and socially comfortable postwar society that seemed to be developing for most people. Not long after blacks began organizing for their civil rights, some women launched a movement to alter their position in American society. An important early activity in this movement was "consciousness-raising," an activity in which small groups of women met and, through discussion, became aware of feelings about being women, about their relation to men, and about the predominant power of men in society. (Most of the activity in the women's movement came after the anti-war movement.)

The concept of consciousness-raising appears to have been borrowed from psychoanalysis. Psychoanalysis, as noted in Chapter 9, emphasized the importance of unacceptable feelings and impulses that have become unconscious; the purpose of psychoanalytic treatment was to help the patient solve conflicts and cope with anxiety by becoming conscious of these feelings. Although psychoanalysis was originally an individual treatment procedure, Freud's ideas had been extended by workers who developed ideas and procedures of psychoanalytic group therapy. Consciousness-raising thus was an adaptation of a professional concept to the purposes of the self-help groups that made up the women's movement.

Another dimension of self-help was added in the late 1960s. As we sank into an undeclared war in Vietnam during the Johnson administration, a small protest against the war grew to major proportions, eventually succeeding in forcing the American government to terminate the war. The anti–Vietnam War movement was a massive repudiation of official authority. The planning for the war had been carried out by many people who had been regarded as among "the best and the brightest," as one journalist termed them. Here was expert authority gone wrong. "The best and the brightest" kept saying that the war was important for the country's security and that it would be won in a short time. Instead, the war dragged on, and the reasons for U.S. involvement in it seemed ever more dubious to more and more people. Professional experts in military affairs and in international relations were seen as fallible, and official authority similarly was seen as fallible and undependable. Officials and experts alike were condemned for waging an immoral war. The public disenchantment with government that began in the Johnson administration was further intensified by the criminal offenses of the Nixon administration; the attorney general of the United States in that administration, the highest law enforcement officer in the country, went to prison for obstructing justice, and the president, threatened with removal from office for the same offense, resigned.

This dissatisfaction with professionals who claim to know better than average people what should be done, and with official authorities who are perceived as more undependable than ever, gave new impetus to the tradition of Americans organizing for their own purposes. There were also specific models to follow or adapt.

The pioneer organization of modern self-help groups was Alcoholics Anonymous (AA), founded in the early 1930s, although a somewhat similar group existed for a short time a century earlier.[34] AA began as a small group in Akron, Ohio; by 1975, it had become an association of about twenty-seven thousand affiliated groups, with more than half a million members.[35] It became the exemplar for later groups composed of members who faced a problem that they felt set them apart from the larger society. Thus the 1950s saw the founding of such groups as Narcotics Anonymous and Gamblers Anonymous; and the 1960s, Overeaters Anonymous, Neurotics Anonymous, and Parents Anonymous (for parents who abuse children).

In addition to groups formed among people who engage in behavior that they believe is undesirable and should be changed, there are also self-help groups among people who suffer from a particular medical problem: Make Today Count, for people who have cancer; Mended Hearts, for people who have had heart attacks; Emphysema Anonymous, for persons who suffer from that lung disease. There are also self-help groups for families of people who are suffering from a particular condition, such as groups for parents of children who have cancer and groups for parents of retarded children.[36] It is estimated that there are over a half million different self-help groups, presumably mostly in the United States, but also including foreign branches of AA, which is now an international organization.[37]

The many self-help groups differ in their internal organization. Some like AA are said to be quite authoritarian; members who backslide into drinking are publicly condemned and shamed.[38] The great number and variety of self-help groups that have been formed suggest that self-help may be regarded as a social movement—a collective enterprise that seeks to establish a new order of life— but it differs somewhat from most social movements. People usually join a self-help group to bring about some change in themselves; most social movements are focused on bringing about change in the larger society, and members expect to defer their personal gratifications until the desired change in society has been accomplished.[39]

Self-help groups are, for the most part, made up of people who have a problem that causes them anxiety and/or to feel stigmatized. Persons who are stigmatized face the problem of being accepted by others.[40] In joining a self-help group, they seek either to conform to the norms of society, or to change those norms to include acceptance of their behavior or condition.[41] Thus the person who joins AA or Gamblers Anonymous is trying to change his own behavior and to conform to the norms of society. Most self-help groups probably are at least partially focused on self-change. Self-help groups in the women's movement, however, focus not only on changing the members themselves but also on changing the norms of society.[42]

How Self-Help Groups Work

The effectiveness of self-help groups has not been widely studied. Perhaps the most one can say is that members very often feel they benefit from belonging, and that is not an inconsequential benefit. There are some quantitative studies of effect: AA reports that 60 percent of its members stay sober for a year, and 40 percent for two years or longer.

Several explanations have been offered for how and why self-help groups work. One is that speaking in a group helps not only the others but the speaker as well. That person feels effective, competent, and knowledgeable, and is taking the normative stand that the group is working toward. The speaker may also be persuading himself or herself to follow the norm while working at persuading the others. Since this helper role is usually played by every member of the group at one point or another, all benefit personally while helping others.

A second explanation is the effect of group support. The members recognize that they are all in the same boat. Each one wants to be accepted by the others as someone with a problem, instead of being condemned for having the problem. Mutual acceptance helps create conditions in which problem solving can go forward.

Third, each group has an ideology, a set of ideas about how that type of problem develops and what must be done about it. Some groups have very specific teachings that members learn and recite at the start of each meeting. These groups provide their members with a set of shared beliefs that strengthens the importance of the organization and its goals. The ideology often involves criticism of social welfare professionals, social agencies, and the larger society that imposes stigma.[43]

Self-Help and Professional Help

It has been observed that the rise of self-help groups

> is a profound critique of professionalism. . . . Self-help mutual aid groups have developed, in large measure, because of the unwillingness and inability of professional organizations to deal with . . . problems, and because of such organizations' overly intellectualized orientation, excessive credentialism, and limited reach in regard to various populations.[44]

These alleged shortcomings of professional practice and established agency service notwithstanding, the actual relationship between professional help and self-help is often a complementary one.

Professionals often help to organize self-help groups and to facilitate their functioning. Professionals may teach their skills to the group in order to enhance its effectiveness. Although some professionals are tempted to dominate self-help groups and others find them unacceptably amateurish, collaboration between social workers and self-help groups is, nevertheless, not uncommon.

The distinction between self-help groups and professional social work relationships has been clearly delineated by Alfred Katz:

> . . . self-help groups . . . can provide for many people . . . a resource for life support and sometimes life change that has qualities different in kind from and in some ways transcending those available from professional sources. Among these are . . . opportunities for peer support, for identity establishment, for personal change and self-validation, as well as for simple socialization and an array of concrete benefits. They achieve these through group contacts and group life . . . in ways that professional relationships and contact can never duplicate. Above all they offer the status of reciprocal equality in social relationships. Whatever else we may think about professionalism, it can never really supply a climate or status of egalitarianism. Professional relationships always carry the burden of super- and subordination, of "authority," while in the self-help group the relationship is a horizontal one between equals and peers—peers in the possession of a common problem but also peers in the possession of a common social status.[45]

Katz concludes that in order for self-help groups to have any effect on the larger social environment, they require allies, who should be "the most concerned and flexible, the least bureaucratically minded, among professionals—those whose greatest commitments are not to professional or personal status and to system maintenance but to human welfare and the full flowering of human potential."[46] He thus calls for concerned social workers to support self-help groups. He regards the ideas of professional social service and self-help as compatible when combined appropriately.

SUMMARY

Mutual aid is a concept of social welfare that is based upon a relationship of equality among the participants. Helpers and helped are the same individuals, persons who have banded together on the basis of something they all have in common—occupation, community, ethnic group, religion, and similarity of problem or affliction have served as bases on which people have formed mutual aid groups.

Mutual aid is an effort people make to help themselves and each other as equals, minimizing the role of authority, whether this be government authority based on power or authority of the expert, based on knowledge, skill, and professional status. Nonetheless, as with all forms of social welfare, pure examples of the concept do not occur in reality, only approximations to them. Mutual aid groups often receive help from professionals, from organizations, and from government. Self-help groups may themselves become part of organizations that necessarily have some bureaucratic aspects to them.

Three main types of mutual aid groups have been distinguished on the basis of the type of help given. The oldest type of help is the mutual insurance group, exemplified in the ancient Roman *collegia,* the medieval guilds, the eighteenth-century friendly societies, and the immigrant societies that developed in the American colonies and nation. All of these types of groups provided their members mutual insurance; the group shared the risk of loss of income, and provided income maintenance and burial expenses.

Community action groups developed on a neighborhood basis during the War on Poverty in the 1960s. Neighborhood groups banded together to gain and share power, which they sought to take away from established political and social welfare organizations. They sought to share power among themselves, in the belief that neighborhood-based decision making would result in greater benefits to the residents. Decision-making power was regarded as a benefit in its own right because it gave people more control over their lives. It was seen also as increasing self-confidence, thereby enabling the residents to be able to compete more effectively in the wider society, both economically and politically. The local authority was seen also as yielding economic benefits in the short run by employing many residents, particularly in black and Hispanic neighborhoods, who had difficulty finding employment in the private sector.

Mutual aid groups based on shared problems first became a significant part of the social welfare world with the rapid success of Alcoholics Anonymous in the 1930s. The basic concept, transferred to other problems, gained rapid momentum only in the 1960s and 1970s. The various self-help groups differ in structure, but the central thrust is members' helping each other to recognize what kind of a problem they have and how they can solve it. Virtually all groups try to help the members change themselves in some way, but some also seek to change society's norms concerning their particular problem or status. Self-help groups share neither financial risk nor political power but feelings, insights, encouragement, and emotional support.

VARIETIES OF SOCIAL WELFARE INSTITUTIONS
Mutual Aid

Collegia	
Community Action Agencies	Guilds
Fraternal insurance	Immigrant societies
Friendly societies	Self-help groups

Notes

[1]George Woodcock, ed., *The Anarchist Reader* (Glasgow, Scotland: Fontana/Collins, 1977), "Anarchism: A Historical Introduction."

[2]In George Unwin, *The Guilds and Companies of London,* 4th ed. (London: Frank Cass, 1963), p. 119.

[3]J. E. Poynter, *Society and Pauperism* (London: Routledge & Kegan Paul, 1969), pp. xix, 35–39.

[4]*Ibid.,* p. 36.

[5]E. W. Brabrook, *Provident Societies and Industrial Welfare* (London: Blackie & Son, 1898), pp. 41–42.

[6]Poynter, *Society and Pauperism,* pp. 37–38.

[7] *Ibid.*, pp. 7, 38.

[8] Brabrook, *Provident Societies,* p. 55.

[9] Poynter, *Society and Pauperism,* p. 39.

[10] *Ibid.*, p. 294.

[11] Walter Basye, *History and Operation of Fraternal Insurance* (Rochester, N.Y.: Fraternal Monitor, 1919), p. 28.

[12] *Ibid.*, pp. 9, 13–14.

[13] Brabrook, *Provident Societies,* p. 45.

[14] From the Charter of the Scots Charitable Society, in Walter I. Trattner, *From Poor Law to Welfare State* (New York: Free Press, 1974), p. 32.

[15] Robert Ernst, *Immigrant Life in New York City, 1825–1863* (New York: King's Crown Press of Columbia University, 1949), pp. 32–33, 125–127.

[16] Gaston V. Rimlinger, "American Social Security in a European Perspective," in William G. Bowen et al., eds., *The Princeton Symposium on the American System of Social Insurance* (New York: McGraw-Hill, 1968), p. 215.

[17] *Ibid.*, pp. 220–221.

[18] Ralph M. Kramer, *Participation of the Poor* (Englewood Cliffs, N.J.: Prentice-Hall, 1969), p. 1.

[19] Economic Opportunity Act of 1964, in Levitan, *Great Society's Poor Law,* p. 110.

[20] Kramer, *Participation,* p. 1

[21] Daniel Patrick Moynihan, *Maximum Feasible Misunderstanding* (New York: Free Press, 1969), p. 97.

[22] Paul E. Peterson and J. David Greenstone, "Racial Change and Citizen Participation: The Mobilization of Low-Income Communities through Community Action," in Robert H. Haveman, ed., *A Decade of Federal Antipoverty Programs* (New York: Academic Press, 1977), p. 257.

[23] Kramer, *Participation,* p. 10.

[24] Lewis M. Killian, *The Impossible Revolution?* (New York: Random House, 1968), pp. 112ff.

[25] Neil Gilbert, *Clients or Constituents* (San Francisco: Jossey-Bass, 1970), p. 29.

[26] From the *Community Action Program Guide,* in Kramer, *Participation,* p. 10.

[27] Kramer, *Participation,* p. 262.

[28] Moynihan, *Maximum Feasible Misunderstanding.*

[29] Daniel P. Moynihan, in Peter Marris and Martin Rein, *Dilemmas of Social Reform,* 2nd ed. (Chicago: Aldine, 1973), p. 241.

[30] Marris and Rein, *Dilemmas,* p. 241,

[31] *Ibid;* p. 296.

[32] Alfred H. Katz and Eugene I. Bender, *The Strength in Us—Self-Help Groups in the Modern World* (New York: New Viewpoints, 1976), p. 9.

[33] Alexis de Tocqueville, *Democracy in America* (New York: Alfred A. Knopf, 1945), Volume I, pp. 191–192; Volume II, pp. 106, 109. Volume I was first published 1835; Volume II was first published in 1840.

[34] Edward Sagarin, *Odd Man In—Societies of Deviants in America* (Chicago: Quadrangle, 1969), p. 34; Alan Gartner and Frank Riessman, *Self-Help in the Human Services* (San Francisco: Jossey Bass, 1977), p. 5.

[35] Gartner and Riessman, *Self-Help,* p. 25.

[36] *Ibid.*, Table 1, p. 24, and Appendix A, pp. 159–176.

[37] *Ibid.*, p. 6.

[38] *Ibid.*, p. 26

[39] Katz and Bender, *Strength in Us,* pp. 26–30.

[40]Erving Goffman, *Stigma* (Englewood Cliffs, N.J.: Prentice-Hall, 1963), pp. 1–19.

[41]Sagarin, *Odd Man In*, p. 21.

[42]See, for example, Janet Norman, "Consciousness-Raising: Self-Help in the Women's Movement" in Katz and Bender, *Strength in Us*.

[43]The preceding four paragraphs draw on Gartner and Riessman, *Self-Help*, Chapter 4.

[44]*Ibid.*, p. 12.

[45]Alfred H. Katz, "Self Help Groups and the Professional Community," in *The Social Welfare Forum, 1975* (New York: Columbia University Press/National Conference on Social Welfare, 1976), p. 151.

[46]*Ibid.*, p. 153.

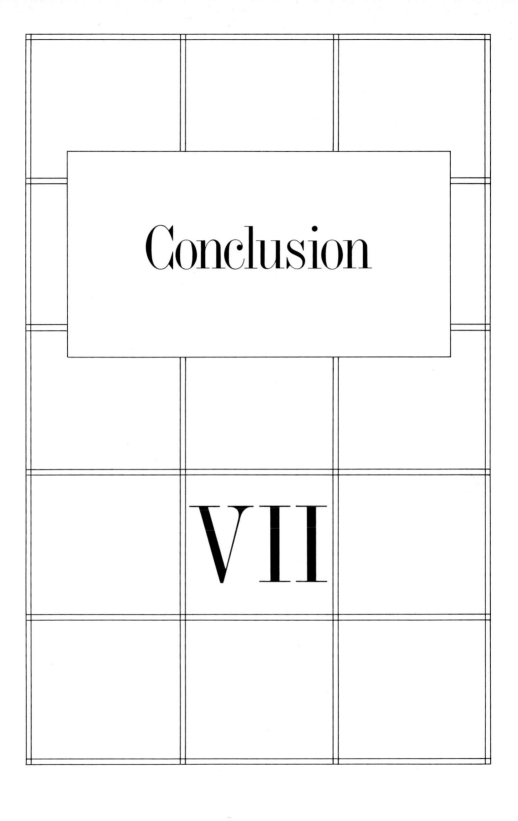

Conclusion

VII

Enduring Issues in Social Welfare

12

The origins of contemporary social welfare institutions are traceable to concepts of religious morality that developed in Judaism and Christianity and to concepts of civic responsibility that developed in the Greek city-states, the Roman Republic, and the Roman Empire. The concepts of morality and civic responsibility became intertwined as Christianity arose and developed in the Roman Empire.

However, social welfare is not understandable simply in terms of morality and responsibility. Roman emperors distributed enormous amounts of free food to crowds as a way of maintaining control over the populace. This logic, updated to fit modern conditions, was adopted by Bismarck eighteen centuries later when he introduced social insurance into Germany. Considerations of controlling a potentially rebellious population played some part in the introduction of social insurance into Great Britain and the United States as well. Social welfare has been marked by considerations of social control throughout its history. It has, in fact, been argued that *public* welfare, at least, has nothing to do with morality or responsibility and is understandable only as social control.[1]

But if social control, or the wish of the well-off to keep what they have, were the only issue in social welfare, it would be hard to see why the old, the disabled, the vagrant, the poor have not simply been routinely killed off—unless some concepts of morality and responsibility, as well as self-interest, have had a restraining effect.

To be sure, contributions have not always been given just for the benefit of the unfortunate. The Greek philanthropists wanted honor in exchange for their civic-minded donations, and the medieval merchants wanted assurance of eternal salvation in exchange for theirs.

Self-interest is seldom far from social welfare, but social welfare is not reducible to self-interest in disguise. There is too much evidence that people have been genuinely concerned about poverty and baffled about what to do about it. Inequality of condition has not been taken for granted in Western society. Much effort has gone into trying to understand it, and trying to justify it as well as do something about it. The activities that go into social welfare are complex in intention and motivation. People want to "do good," but they do not want it to cost them too much. Sometimes the costs and frustrations of dealing with social dependency engender great animosity in those who are not as dependent. They do not want to pay the price and they do not want the responsibility; they look for reasons to turn away, to not pay the cost of social welfare.

However, instead of seeing social welfare purely as an expression of morality and civic responsibility or purely as attempts by the well-to-do and powerful to give up as little as possible in order to keep what they have, social welfare is more accurately regarded as an expression of conflicting values, attitudes, and motivations.

Throughout the many forms that social welfare concepts and institutions have taken, there are some social welfare issues that have endured to this day—issues on which there is no general agreement, and that are considered and reconsidered in discussions of "social policy." Social policies guide decision making with regard to social welfare and social service programs.[2] In earlier periods, when societies were simpler, few questions had to be considered at one time in making social policy. In modern times, as societies have grown more and more complex, policy making has come to require consideration of many questions simultaneously. Each of the sections in this chapter deals with one of the questions that need to be considered in modern social policy making.

SHOULD THE POOR BE HELPED OR PUNISHED?

The oldest ideas in Western thought concerning how the poor should be treated are the Judaic, which prescribe kindness, consideration, and material help. These ideas were adopted virtually unaltered by Christianity which later added ideas of its own. Judeo-Christian thought retains influence to this day, after some three thousand years, not only in Western society but outside of it. For example, in 1979, a Roman Catholic nun, Sister Teresa, was awarded the Nobel Peace Prize for her work in feeding, sheltering, and obtaining medical care for the destitute in Calcutta, India. Her activities are guided by ideas of ancient origin, and many other people, less celebrated, are similarly guided.

But the Christian obligation to be charitable has not always been fulfilled in Christian countries. At times, the obligation has been considered unbearably burdensome. Between the fourteenth and sixteenth centuries in England, poor people who wandered out of their own districts could be subjected to brutal punishments, such as whipping, or branding with a hot iron, or even death. Persons dependent on public relief have at times, been publicly shamed by being forced to wear distinguishing badges, such as "P" for pauper.

In the eighteenth century, the concept of deterring the poor from seeking help gained favor. The workhouse, originally intended to be helpful to the poor by giving them work, was instead used as a punishment for destitution and a deterrent to obtaining aid. Parishes had the right to refuse aid to those requesting it unless they and their families entered the workhouse. This deterrent policy became national law in Great Britain with the adoption of the New Poor Law in 1834. The poor were punished by being deprived of the liberties enjoyed by other citizens. Even after this "workhouse test" was abolished, persons receiving public funds were deprived of the right to vote.

The punishments just described were prescribed by law. Even when the laws themselves do not call for punishments, they may be inflicted in the way the laws are carried out. The punishments referred to here are coercion, intimidation, and denial of benefits to which a person might be entitled by law. Public welfare departments, in particular, have often subjected clients to coercion and intimidation.

> The recipients of social services are . . . subject to a variety of behavioral rules reflecting the agency's notions as to what is good for the recipient; the rules are administered in a seemingly informal manner highly individualistic to the particular worker that the client is dealing with; and, as a practical matter, the client has no real alternative but to submit.[3]

It is impossible to do away with all administrative discretionary power. But it is possible to reduce the capriciousness with which agencies treat clients. First, however, those who make policy must decide that it is important to administer social welfare organizations in ways that minimize punishment of the clients; then they must invest the time, ideas, money, and staff to accomplish the goal.

WHO IS TO BLAME?

Poverty in Western society seems always to have called for an explanation. Since ancient times, people in Western communities have been able to produce surpluses of wealth and thereby rise above a subsistence standard of living. In communities where many had at least a subsistence standard and some had a better standard, the condition of people with less than subsistence had to be explained. For a considerable time, this condition was explained as being due to God's will. For unknown reasons, the all-powerful Ruler of the Universe chose to bring misfortune to some.

With the quickening pace of economic activity in the Middle Ages, new ideas began to develop. Poverty began to be regarded, particularly in the case of able-bodied men who did not work, as willful, a deliberate, obstinate choice. In contrast, the Elizabethan Poor Law of 1576 recognized for the first time that some able-bodied men were unemployed because they could not find work. Since that time, these two views of poverty have competed.

There are two broad explanations of poverty. One is an explanation in terms of individual character. The other is an explanation in terms of the way society is organized. The first has come to be called "blaming the victim," since it implies that poor people are responsible for their own condition.[4] The second might be called "blaming society." These opposite viewpoints can also be referred to as the "pathology theory" and the "structural theory." The pathology theory attributes poverty to deficiencies in the character of the poor: laziness, self-indulgence, lack of ambition. This theory has a number of variations. Perhaps the most important is the one that attributes the personality deficiencies of the poor to the culture in which they have been socialized—"the culture of poverty"—and in which they continue to live. The structural theory

> explains poverty in terms of the conditions under which the poor live: poor housing and education, lack of income, lack of adequate jobs, inadequate health care. The structuralists argue that the deviant behavior characteristics pathology theorists ascribe to the poor are merely adaptations to a hostile environment. Both theories may agree on the behavioral characteristics of the poor—crime, ill-health, inability to obtain adequate work, defiance, and so on—but differ about what to do about them. The pathology theorists or culturalists seek reformation of the poor; the structuralists would change the environment in which the poor live.[5]

These two explanations of poverty lead in different directions concerning what steps should be taken to both raise the standard of living of poor people and reduce their so-called deviant behavior. The structuralist explanation places the burden of action on society, for example, in the form of creating jobs, recruiting and training people for jobs, and providing income to the poor to enable them to participate as full members of society. The pathology theory places the responsibility on the poor person to change; this approach emphasizes the importance of psychologically oriented social work counseling services. This approach was incorporated into the 1962 amendments to the Social Security Act.[6]

While there is a clear distinction as to what types of measures are likely to be most effective, and also a clear distinction in moral tone, between the pathology theorists and the structural theorists, they may not be as far apart in their views as proponents of each theory believe. As often occurs, the correct explanation may be somewhere in the middle. A leading critic of the concept of the "culture of poverty" as an explanation of why poor people remain poor, has, nevertheless, observed that

> there is certainly empirical evidence of pathology, incompetence, and other kinds of inadequacy among the people of the ghettoes and slums, as there is in the rest of society. There can be no doubt that living in poverty has its own destructive effect on human capacities and that these impairments become part of the whole process perpetuating deprivation. The vital questions are, how important are the internal disabilities of the lower class, and how are they related to significant external factors? An incomplete but important answer seems plain already: subcultural disabilities are definitely not the whole problem and almost certainly not the principal problem.[7]

As noted earlier, the discovery that the Elizabethans made that some people who want work cannot find it is a discovery that tends to be forgotten from time to time. Western thought has been dominated by individualist ideas for four hundred fifty years, with the result that many believe that anyone who wants a job can find one. Yet for now and for the foreseeable future, economists believe that an unemployment rate in the United States of 5 percent or even higher must be considered "normal." That is, modern American society cannot and will not be able to provide employment to all those who want to work. With such a structural condition, the pathology theory does not seem very appropriate.

One version of the pathology theory emphasizes the importance of family relationships. The disturbed behavior of an individual is traced to problems in family relationships. There are no doubt many causes of family pathology. One of them is unemployment. It has been known for at least forty years, since research was done on the effects of unemployment during the Great Depression, that unemployment of the breadwinner introduces profound psychological disturbances into the family.[8] Thus an economic policy that does not lead to full employment can be blamed for contributing to family and individual pathology. Some economic planners may have good reasons for avoiding full employment because it contributes to inflation, but the consequences of making this choice should be understood.

There was a time when most kinds of social pathology were explained by "broken homes." It has long been understood that this explanation is too simple; alcoholism, delinquent behavior, criminal behavior, mental illness, narcotics abuse, and other forms of social and psychological pathology cannot all be attributed to a family background in which there has been a divorce or the desertion of one parent. At the same time, there is no clear interest served by encouraging desertion. Since 1961, the law governing AFDC has allowed states to provide aid to families with an unemployed father in the home. Yet only about half the states have instituted such programs. The other states provide aid only to families in which there is no father in the home, thereby encouraging unemployed fathers to desert their families so the families can become eligible for aid. Although according to the prevailing values of American society, desertion would be a form of irresponsibility, when a father who cannot get a job deserts his family in order for the family to qualify for subsistence, he may be demonstrating responsibility rather than its opposite.[9]

DO THE POOR
HAVE THE SAME RIGHTS
AS OTHER PEOPLE?

Ever since the deterrent theory of poor relief was introduced in the eighteenth century, efforts have been made to limit the rights of poor people who received benefits to which they were legally entitled. The workhouse test deprived them of the right to move around as freely as others; they were subjected to the control and discipline of workhouse administrators. Later, after the workhouse test was abandoned and outdoor relief had been restored, people receiving relief in Great Britain were deprived of political rights, particularly the right to vote.

AFDC recipients in the United States have been subjected to invasions of privacy that were later ruled illegal. Prior to the enactment of AFDC-UP in 1961, all AFDC recipients had to be families without a male in the home in order to qualify for assistance. Since many women on AFDC continued to have children, they were presumed to have an ongoing relationship with a man who might be considered a "substitute father" and therefore legally responsible for financial support of the woman and her children, whether married to her or not. It was assumed that women would deny such relationships. Consequently welfare workers resorted to surprise nighttime visits to the homes of AFDC recipients to try to find "a man in the house." These "midnight raids" were often made without a search warrant. The public welfare caseworkers who made the visits would gain entrance to the homes by threatening clients with cutoff of benefits unless they were allowed entry to make an inspection.[10] In 1968, the U.S. Supreme Court ruled that "destitute children who are legally fatherless cannot be flatly denied federally funded assistance on the transparent fiction that they have a substitute father."[11] Some months prior, the federal government had issued new standards to the state governments calling upon them to avoid practices that violated the constitutional rights of client-recipients.[12] With the Court decision, unannounced visits were rendered illegal.

Another type of deprivation of rights, or at least unequal protection of rights, has been the failure of state governments to seek out persons who might be entitled to public assistance but who have not themselves applied for it.

> The Social Security Administration . . . works vigorously to inform a broad public of entitlements to old-age payments, advertising on radio and in newspapers, and deploring the fact that some benefits go unclaimed. Similarly, a massive publicity campaign . . . was conducted several years ago to inform the aged of their rights under Medicare. By contrast, potential welfare recipients are never sought out; rather, they are fended off. Welfare statutes, for example, are elaborated into voluminous procedural manuals, often so complicated that they are not quite comprehensible even to those who administer them. . . . the poor do not know the regulations, and welfare officials are not disposed to do much instructing.[13]

WHO SHOULD PAY?

The history of social welfare can be looked at in terms of the changes that have occurred in who pays the cost of the benefits that society distributes—especially the cost of subsistence for the poor, and since industrialization, the cost of subsistence for the working poor during illness and when they reach old age and can no longer work. With the currency of the concept of the welfare state, there is a further issue of who should pay for the wide variety of benefits that all citizens might want.

In ancient times, when the question concerned only those without means of livelihood, there appears to have been but a single answer: Individuals with means should pay for those without them—voluntarily or, if necessary, under pressure to "volunteer" donations. This answer persisted into the Middle Ages, as St. Thomas Aquinas struggled to arrive at a definition of "surplus," from which wealthy individuals were to make their charitable contributions. Perhaps the last serious advocate of voluntary support of the poor was President Herbert Hoover, who expected private charity to bear the brunt of the cost of relieving hardship as the Great Depression spread.

The Elizabethan Poor Law of 1572 introduced the poor rate, a local tax that each parish was to collect to support its own poor. This led the parishes to adopt regulations to keep strangers out, lest parishioners' taxes rise to pay the cost of somebody else's poor. Their efforts were facilitated by the enactment of the Law of Settlement and Removal in 1662. The localism of the English parish was carried to the American colonies. When the colonies became states in the new nation, each state became responsible for its own poor. Anyone coming into one state from another had to meet a lengthy residence requirement before becoming eligible for public assistance in the new state. Residence laws of this kind were declared unconstitutional in 1968.

With the development of an industrial economy guided by the values of individualism and laissez-faire, the expectation was that people would pay their own way. Individuals were expected to anticipate contingencies that might deprive them of income. Savings banks for individual savings and friendly societies for mutual insurance appeared in the eighteenth and nineteenth centuries. Savings banks were also established in the United States, though friendly societies did not flourish in the United States as they did in England.

Interest in maintaining the stability of nation-states led to the adoption of social insurance in which all citizens paid, through taxes, for certain benefits of income and health care costs. Even with nationwide social insurance programs paid for out of citizens' taxes, there remain questions of who should pay.

For example, in the United States, the Social Security Act provided that the social security tax would be a certain percentage of a portion of a person's earnings. In 1981, the tax was 6.65 percent of the *first* $29,700 of a person's annual earnings. Thus a person earning $29,700 a year would pay $1,975 in social security tax. A person earning $59,400 would also pay $1,975 in social security tax. That would be 6.65 percent of the first $29,700 of earnings—but only 3 percent of actual earnings. A person earning $5,000 would pay $332.50 in social security tax, 6.65 percent of total earnings. Every earner pays the same percentage of income as tax up to the first $29,700 of income. But as the example indicates, those earning more than the $29,700 earnings base pay a smaller percentage of their overall income. Low-income earners will receive lower retirement benefits than medium- and high-income earners because benefits are partly related to income. Questions have been raised as to the fairest way of taxing people to pay for social security. The social security tax is a *flat-rate tax;* that is, everyone pays the same rate of tax—on the first $29,700 of earnings. The federal income tax, is, by contrast, a *progressive tax.* In general (disregarding "loopholes" for the sake of the discussion), the higher the income, the higher the tax. Some observers believe that the social security program should be financed not by the special, flat-rate tax but out of general tax revenues, of which the tax on income is a large part. Social security contributions would thus be more proportionate to earned income. The technicalities of the arguments on this issue are beyond the scope of this book. The purpose here is not to argue for or against any particular method of payment but simply to indicate that the existing system of payment is only one answer to the question of who should pay for social security. Other answers are possible.

Social security is compulsory. Everybody in covered employment must pay the social security tax. However, economist Milton Friedman argues that in a free society no one should be compelled to buy annuities to provide for old age: "If a man knowingly prefers to live for today, to use his resources for current enjoyment, deliberately choosing a penurious old age, by what right do we prevent him from doing so?"[14] This particular argument overlooks one aspect of the social security system: The tax that employees pay out of their wages or salaries is matched by payments made by their employers. So it is not merely workers who are compelled to save for old age, but also their employers who are compelled to contribute to the retirement income of those from whose work they have profited. Friedman's argument does not deal with the concept of employer responsibility for employee retirement income.

The question of who should pay for whom is an ongoing one in social welfare. Answers depend partly on values—what kind of income inequalities are considered desirable or undesirable—and partly on technical considerations—what the actual effects are of any particular system of payments. In the immediate future in the United States, the question is likely to be debated most intensely with regard to medical care. Except for those eligible for Medicare and Medicaid and for those whose medical costs are partly or mostly paid through employer-paid health plans, most Americans pay for their own health costs. Sharing the costs through national health insurance will be one of the major policy questions before the country for the next several years.

WHO SHOULD DECIDE?

There are numerous decisions to be made in the field of social welfare. A major trend over the past several hundred years is that governments have been making more and more of the decisions. As just noted, Milton Friedman—and others (including, since 1981, the Reagan administration), believe that modern governments make too many decisions that should be left to individuals. Friedman favors voluntary charity taking over in situations in which individuals have failed to provide for themselves. He appears to believe that the Great Depression was a unique occurrence that cannot happen again and that therefore we need not fear that private charity would be swamped again, as it was then, provided we create conditions that would once again encourage large-scale charity.[15]

So one question here is, Which decisions should be left to the single individual or household decision-making unit and which should be made by government? Another is, Which level of government should make decisions? The community action program represented an effort to have certain kinds of decisions made at a neighborhood level, instead of at the city, state, or national level. The political conflict that followed from that effort was disruptive to society. The participation concept tended to pit black and Chicano neighborhoods against white politicians.[16] But in the view of some students of the community action movement:

> . . . black leaders and citizens responded so vigorously to the call for maximum feasible participation largely because they felt excluded from the political process. In effect, a concern with this political exclusion assumed a higher priority than any attack on economic deprivation. Using poverty as a term to justify efforts to increase black political participation consequently took priority over using it as a guide to attacking economic deprivation.[17]

While this effort at community action eventually failed, it did bring new black middle-class leaders into government. As another scholar notes, "If we look at the spread of the neighborhood government movement in our cities today and the emergence of subcity units of government, we must trace this back to the community action program."[18]

How much and what kinds of decision making can be accomplished at a neighborhood level are not easy questions to answer on the basis of current experience, but it seems likely that efforts to keep this idea alive will continue. The events of the 1960s left a legacy of sentiment that the increasing power of large-scale bureaucracy should not be allowed to go unchecked, that there should be "grassroots" participation in decision making. Further impetus in this direction was provided in the 1970s by the political theme introduced by the Nixon administration and continued in both the Ford and Carter administrations: "Don't look to government to solve all your problems." With this as a backdrop, local-level decision making will continue to be examined and tried as an alternative to decision making at higher levels of government.[19]

The issue of decision making exists also between professionals and lay people. The self-help group, perhaps a bland successor to the community action movement, is another effort of people to assume a larger measure of control over their lives. Self-help groups are not necessarily antagonistic to professional social work, but there is considerable potential for conflict, as social work professor Carol H. Meyer has observed:

> [There] is the question of the relationship of social work practice to indigenous self-help groups. It may prove to be a test of the humanistic (as opposed to the

professional) commitment of social workers as to whether or not there will be a working relationship between these helping efforts.[20]

And Meyer has noted another arena of conflict over decision making:

> Consumerism is everywhere, and social workers, to the extent that they are exposed to the public view, will not be the last to hear demands upon their skills and knowledge. Consumerism will test our mettle; the people we serve will let us know whether or not they are being served as they really want.[21]

Meyer's expectation thus is that clients will play a greater part in deciding how the social worker should function in the professional-client relationship; this represents a shift from the traditional balance of influence in that relationship. One of the hallmarks of a profession has been that the professional has decided what was best for the person being served, although social work, more than most professions, has emphasized respect for the client's values and goals.

The search for an acceptable balance between decisions made by individuals or small groups and decisions made by people holding formal authority (government or professional) is likely to continue. Both government and professional authority have expanded in the nearly half century since the New Deal; the community action movement and the self-help movement represent efforts to recover some of the decision-making power that ordinary citizens feel they have lost.

WHAT IS THE EFFECT OF RECEIVING WELFARE ON INCENTIVE TO WORK?

The allowance system of the late eighteenth century, generally known as the Speenhamland system, led eventually to a "welfare backlash" (the modern term), a rise of resentment by taxpayers. The backlash response to the Speenhamland system was the New Poor Law of 1834; outdoor relief was to be terminated, and the poor who claimed relief were made to enter the workhouse. The workhouse test would deter anyone hoping to obtain relief without working. This is the immediate heritage of concern about the effects of help on willingness to work, although the origins of such concern go back at least as far as the Statute of Laborers of 1349, following the Black Plague.

The rapid expansion of the public assistance rolls ("welfare rolls") in the

1960s again stimulated widespread belief that the United States was supporting a growing number of people who were losing all incentive to work and were becoming members of a permanent welfare class. In 1967, Congress took steps to counter this seeming trend by adopting the Work Incentive Plan (WIN). In 1970, President Nixon attempted, unsuccessfully, to have Congress pass a new welfare program, referred to as "Workfare," that would have increased incentive to work.

In all of these efforts, however, there was a lack of solid information about the relation between receiving public assistance and the willingness or incentive to work. Only gradually have research efforts been undertaken to obtain more precise information instead of relying on beliefs and prejudices. One study showed that common beliefs about welfare recipients are erroneous. Welfare recipients were shown to have the same kinds of life aspirations and work ethic as middle-class employed people. A fundamental difference, however, was that many of the women on welfare had failed at work and lacked confidence in their ability to get and keep a job. Thus what they require is not an incentive to work but a chance to experience success in a job that pays enough to support them.[22]

A more recent study called into question the existence of a large, permanent welfare class.[23] The research investigators defined a welfare class as consisting of people who meet all three of these conditions: (1) going on welfare at all, (2) staying on welfare for a period of years, and (3) being heavily dependent on welfare during those years. The duration characteristic would be met by individuals who had been on welfare for at least six or seven years; the dependence characteristic would be met by individuals dependent on welfare for more than 50 percent of their income during those years. They studied a group of women who were between the ages of 18 and 54, in 1968, and they followed their sources of income for a seven-year period. They concluded that of the 2.7 million women likely to be on welfare in any given year, only a little more than 20 percent could be considered members of the welfare class, as they defined it. The others had either short- or medium-term stays on welfare.

The study of sources of income revealed that apart from the welfare class, women on welfare received income from diverse sources: earnings of the male head of family and from the woman herself and children's earnings. Some income was obtained from alimony and child support payments, from food stamps, and from public and private transfer payments. (*Transfer payments* are payments made outside a market situation. Public transfers include payments from workmen's compensation, unemployment insurance, and social security. Private transfer payments include money given by relatives, as well as alimony and child support payments.)

The investigators examined the life situation of a subsample of women who received welfare. They discovered three patterns of welfare use: (1) Some women used welfare as an aid in the transition from one life situation to another. They were "digging out" from a difficulty caused by divorce, widowhood, illness, or some other sharp change in family circumstance. (2) A second group seemed "locked in" to welfare use because they "lack a social support system to aid them in altering their situation; the family's potential to create a change in its circumstances appears limited."[24] (3) A third group consisted of women who could obtain income in other ways

> but who opt to rely upon welfare as the stable foundation for their income package. ... Basically, women who follow this pattern acquire income from a wide variety of sources in addition to their AFDC grant. These include: help (reported and unreported) from boyfriends and from relatives, free lunches and child care, small social services payments, and income from earning on an *ad hoc* or as-needed basis, although by and large these women seek income sources other than their own wages.[25]

About half of those in the welfare class were estimated to be in the "digging out" pattern, and a quarter each in the other two patterns.

While evidence on the overall question is still only sketchy, it appears that negative public beliefs about the receipt of welfare are greatly exaggerated. There do indeed seem to be people who live off public assistance as an alternative to working, but they appear to be only a small fraction of those who receive public assistance. The public mistakes them for the major fraction.

WHO SHOULD BE HELPED?

It is widely believed in the United States that most people are self-supporting and independent, while a noticeable but too large minority are dependent. However, the notion that society can simply be divided into two broad classes of people, taxpayers and "tax-eaters," is a gross oversimplification.[26]

Social welfare theorist Martin Rein has observed:

> All of us are dependent during major and important periods of our lives. No one finds this strange or reprehensible. What does cause great, and rising, concern is *public* dependency.[27]

But, in fact, not all public dependency causes concern. There are forms of dependency that have come to be fully accepted as part of the American way of life. And some are acceptable because they go by names other than dependency or welfare, and because those who benefit from these (welfare) payments that are not usually called welfare payments have additional sources of income.

The U.S. government donates money through subsidies to various businesses. A subsidy is "a direct pecuniary aid furnished by a government to a private commercial enterprise, . . . a grant or contribution of money."[28] The government has been giving subsidies for a long time. In the nineteenth century, the newly developing railroads were given grants of government-owned land valued at more than $400 million.[29] In the 1930s, when farmers' income fell drastically, the government began providing money to farmers called "price supports." The money was not given directly as a gift, however. The government would set a price for each crop, and the farmers would sell as much of their crop at that price as they could. The surplus—what could not be sold in the market at that price—was bought by the government and stored in warehouses. In 1973, when instead of crop surpluses there were crop shortages, the government adopted a new plan by which it simply sent checks to farmers.[30] Farm subsidies are not called welfare, but Milton Friedman, and some other economists, consider them to be a form of welfare.[31]

The government makes other kinds of gifts. It often advances money to corporations to develop a new product. New products that are developed with these public funds are often given to the company, without the government sharing in the proceeds of the product sales.

The government often justifies the giving of subsidies and property grants by relating the practice to some public policy. Analysis of the validity of each justification cannot be attempted here. The important point is that large and prosperous corporations receive benefits and undertake projects free of financial risk to themselves, out of *public funds.* The increase in the number of such cases has led Leonard Baker to argue that we are moving toward "the guaranteed society," a society in which, in effect, everybody is guaranteed a subsidy.[32] Baker is in favor of help that assures opportunity to a business, but not in favor of help that guarantees its success.

Virtually all segments of society receive some kind of help from public sources and in that sense are dependent upon public funds. The dependency is highly visible in some cases and hidden in others because of the way the funding is arranged. The question to be answered, then, is not, Who should be helped? but, *What kinds of help are appropriate for each situation?*

Notes

[1]Frances Fox Piven and Richard A. Cloward, *Regulating the Poor: The Functions of Public Welfare* (New York: Vintage, 1971).

[2]Alfred Kahn, *Social Policy and Social Services,* 2nd ed. (New York: Random House, 1979), p. 67.

[3]Joel F. Handler, *The Coercive Social Worker* (Chicago: Rand McNally, 1973), p. 143.

[4]See William Ryan, *Blaming the Victim* (New York: Pantheon Books, 1971).

[5]Handler, *Coercive Social Worker*, p. 5.

[6]*Ibid.*, pp. 120–123. See also Gilbert Y. Steiner, *The State of Welfare* (Washington, D.C.: Brookings Institution, 1971), pp. 35–40.

[7]Charles A. Valentine, *Culture and Poverty* (Chicago: University of Chicago Press, 1968), p. 145.

[8]For a brief summary and selected references on this point, see Gerald Handel, "Sociological Aspects of Parenthood," in Debra P. Hymovich and Martha Underwood Barnard, eds., *Family Health Care*, Vol. I, 2nd ed. (New York: McGraw-Hill, 1979), pp. 44–46.

[9]Elliott Liebow's study of a group of black "streetcorner men" is illuminating on this point. See Elliot Liebow, *Tally's Corner* (Boston: Little, Brown, 1967), Chapter 3.

[10]Robert M. O'Neil, *The Price of Dependency* (New York: Dutton, 1970), pp. 273–276.

[11]In Frances Fox Piven and Richard A. Cloward, *Regulating the Poor: The Functions of Public Welfare* (New York: Vintage Books, 1971), pp. 308–309.

[12]O'Neil, *Price of Dependency* p. 274.

[13]Piven and Cloward, *Regulating the Poor*, pp. 151–152.

[14]Milton Friedman, with the assistance of Rose D. Friedman, *Capitalism and Freedom* (Chicago: University of Chicago Press, 1962), p. 188. Friedman later advocated a negative income tax.

[15]*Ibid.*, pp. 188, 190–191.

[16]Daniel P. Moynihan, *Maximum Feasible Misunderstanding* (New York: Free Press, 1969), pp. 132–136.

[17]Paul E. Peterson and J. David Greenstone, "Racial Change and Citizen Participation: The Mobilization of Low-Income Communities Through Community Action," in Robert H. Haveman, ed., *A Decade of Federal Antipoverty Programs* (New York: Academic Press, 1977), p. 277.

[18]Milton Kotler, "Discussion", in Haveman, *Decade*, p. 282.

[19]For a detailed exploration of this issue, see Charles F. Grosser, *New Directions in Community Organization* (New York: Praeger, 1973).

[20]Carol H. Meyer, "Direct Services in New and Old Contexts," in Alfred J. Kahn, ed., *Shaping the New Social Work* (New York: Columbia University Press, 1973), p. 45.

[21]*Ibid.*, p. 35.

[22]"Do the Poor Want to Work?" *The Brookings Bulletin*, Vol. 9, No. 3 (Summer 1972), pp. 1–3. This is a summary of Leonard Goodwin, *Do the Poor Want to Work?* (Washington, D.C.: Brookings Institution, 1972).

[23]Martin Rein and Lee Rainwater, "Patterns of Welfare Use," *Social Service Review* (December 1978), pp. 511–534.

[24]*Ibid.*, p. 530.

[25]*Ibid.*, p. 531.

[26]For an empirical study indicating that a similar distinction is used by ordinary citizens in one California city, see John U. Ogbu, *The Next Generation: An Ethnography of Education in an Urban Neighborhood* (New York: Academic Press, 1974).

[27]Martin Rein, *Social Policy* (New York: Random House, 1970), p. 85.

[28]*The Random House Dictionary*, college ed. (New York: Random House, 1969), p. 1310.

[29]Leonard Baker, *The Guaranteed Society* (New York: Macmillan, 1968), p. 6.

[30]A. Dale Tussing, *Poverty in a Dual Economy* (New York: St. Martin's Press, 1975), pp. 64, 121.

[31]Friedman, *Capitalism and Freedom*, p. 181; Tussing, *Poverty in a Dual Economy*.

[32]Baker, *Guaranteed Society*.

References

ANDERSON, MARTIN. *Welfare* (Stanford, Calif.: Hoover Institution Press of Stanford University, 1978).

ANDREWS, F. EMERSON. *Corporation Giving* (New York: Russell Sage Foundation, 1952).

ANDREWS, F. EMERSON. *Philanthropic Giving* (New York: Russell Sage Foundation, 1950).

AXINN, JUNE, AND LEVIN, HERMAN. *Social Welfare* (New York: Dodd, Mead, 1975).

AYDELOTTE, FRANK. *Elizabethan Rogues and Vagabonds*, Oxford Historical and Literary Studies, Vol. I (Oxford, England: Clarendon Press, 1913).

BAER, BETTY L., AND FEDERICO, RONALD. *Educating the Baccalaureate Social Worker* (Cambridge, Mass.: Ballinger, 1978).

BARNES, HARRY ELMER. *An Economic History of the Western World* (New York: Harcourt, Brace, 1937).

BASKERVILLE, GEOFFREY. *English Monks and the Suppression of the Monasteries* (London: Jonathan Cape, 1937).

BASYE, WALTER. *History and Operation of Fraternal Insurance* (Rochester, N.Y.: Fraternal Monitor, 1919).

BECK, BERNARD. "The Military as a Welfare Institution," in Charles C. Moskos, Jr., ed., *Public Opinion and the Military Establishment* (Beverly Hills, Ca.: Sage Publications, 1971).

BECK, BERNARD. "Welfare as a Moral Category," *Social Problems*, 14:258–277 (Winter, 1967).

BEN-SASSON, H. H., ed.. *A History of the Jewish People* (Cambridge, Mass.: Harvard University Press, 1976).

BERNARD, L. DIANE. "Education for Social Work," *Encyclopedia of Social Work*, Vol. 1, 17th ed. (Washington, D.C.: National Association of Social Workers, 1977).

BISNO, HERBERT. "How Social Will Social Work Be?" *Social Work*, Vol. 1 (April 1956).

BLOCH, MARC. *Feudal Society.* Vol. I, *The Growth of Ties of Dependence.* Translated by L. A. Manyon. (Chicago: University of Chicago Press, Phoenix Edition, 1964).

Booth, Philip. *Social Security in America* (Ann Arbor, Mich.: University of Michigan/Wayne State University Institute of Labor and Industrial Relations, 1973).

Brabrook, E. W. *Provident Societies and Industrial Welfare* (London: Blackie & Son, 1898).

Bracht, Neil F. *Social Work in Health Care* (New York: Haworth Press, 1978).

Brager, George, and Specht, Harry. *Community Organizing* (New York: Columbia University Press, 1973).

Bremner, Robert H. *American Philanthropy* (Chicago: University of Chicago Press, 1960).

Bremner, Robert H. *From the Depths: The Discovery of Poverty in the United States* (New York: New York University Press, 1956).

Brilliant, Eleanor L. "Private or Public: A Model of Ambiguities," *Social Service Review*, Vol. 47, No. 3 (September 1973).

Brinton, Crane, *Ideas and Men.* (New York: Prentice-Hall, 1950).

Brown, Josephine Chapin. *Public Relief, 1929–1939* (New York: Henry Holt, 1940).

Brown, J. Douglas. *An American Philosophy of Social Security* (Princeton, N.J.: Princeton University Press, 1972).

Bruce, Maurice. *The Coming of the Welfare State* (London: B. T. Batsford, 1961).

Burke, Vincent J., and Burke, Vee. *Nixon's Good Deed* (New York: Columbia University Press, 1974).

Bruno, Frank J., with chapters by Louis Towley. *Trends in Social Work, 1874–1956*, 2nd ed. (New York: Columbia University Press, 1957).

Cantor, Norman. *Medieval History,* 2nd ed. (New York: Macmillan, 1969).

Carson, Deane. "Companies as Heroes? Bah! Humbug!!" *New York Times,* December 25, 1977.

Caudill, Harry M. *Night Comes to the Cumberlands* (Boston: Little, Brown, 1963).

Chambers, Clarke A. *Seedtime of Reform—American Social Service and Social Action, 1918–1933* (Minneapolis, Minn.: University of Minnesota Press, 1963).

Checkland, S. G., and Checkland, E. O. A., eds., *The Poor Law Report of 1834* (Harmondsworth, England: Penguin Books, 1974).

Clough, Shepard Bancroft, and Cole, Charles Woolsey. *Economic History of Europe* (Boston: D. C. Heath, 1941).

Cloward, Richard A., and Epstein, Irwin. "Private Social Welfare's Disengagement from the Poor: The Case of Family Adjustment Agencies," in George A. Brager and Francis P. Purcell, *Community Action Against Poverty* (New Haven, Conn.: College and University Press, 1967) and in Mayer Zald, ed., *Social Welfare Institutions* (New York: Wiley, 1965).

Coleman, Richard P., and Rainwater, Lee. with Kent A. McClelland. *Social Standing in America* (New York: Basic Books, 1978).

Comprehensive Annual Social Services Program Plan for New York State, October 1, 1979 to September 30, 1980 (Albany, N.Y.: Department of Social Services, September 1979).

Compton, Beulah Roberts. *Introduction to Social Welfare and Social Work* (Homewood, Ill.: Dorsey Press, 1980).

Con Edison, *Customer News,* January, 1975.

Costin, Lela B. *Child Welfare: Policies and Practice* (New York: McGraw-Hill, 1972).

Costin, Lela B. "Social Work in the Schools," in Donald Brieland, Lela B. Costin, Charles R. Atherton and others, *Contemporary Social Work,* 2nd ed. (New York: McGraw-Hill, 1980).

Coulton, G. G., *The Medieval Scene* (Cambridge: Cambridge University Press, 1930).

Cowan, Edward. "Califano Says Shift on Social Security Could Be Permanent," *New York Times,* May 11, 1977.

Cowan, Edward. "Congress Told Social Security Fund Needs New Money," *New York Times,* August 6, 1979.

COWING, CEDRIC B. *The Great Awakening and the American Revolution: Colonial Thought in the 18th Century* (Chicago: Rand McNally, 1971).

COX, FRED M., ERLICH, JOHN L., ROTHMAN, JACK, AND TROPMAN, JOHN E., eds.. *Strategies of Community Organization* (Itasca, Ill.: F. E. Peacock, 1974).

CREECH, MARGARET. *Three Centuries of Poor Law Administration* (Chicago: University of Chicago Press, 1936).

CRONER, HELGE B., comp. *National Directory of Private Social Agencies* (Queens Village, N.Y.: Social Service Publications, 1977–1978).

DAVIS, ALLEN F. *Spearheads for Reform: The Social Settlements and the Progressive Movement, 1890–1914* (New York: Oxford University Press, 1967).

DE SCHWEINITZ, KARL. *England's Road to Social Security* (New York: A. S. Barnes, 1972). First published in 1943.

DE TOCQUEVILLE, ALEXIS. *Democracy in America* (New York: Knopf, 1945).

DOLGOFF, RALPH, AND FELDSTEIN, DONALD. *Understanding Social Welfare* (New York: Harper & Row, 1980).

EISENSTADT, S. N., ed. *The Protestant Ethic and Modernization—A Comparative View* (New York: Basic Books, 1968).

ELMAN, RICHARD M. *The Poorhouse State—The American Way of Life on Public Assistance* (New York: Pantheon, 1966).

Encyclopedia of Religion and Ethics, Vol. 3 (New York: Charles Scribner, 1922).

Encyclopedia of the Social Sciences (New York: Macmillan, 1931).

EPSTEIN, ISADORE. *Judaism—A Historical Presentation* (Baltimore: Penguin Books, 1959).

ERIKSON, KAI T. *Everything in its Path.* (New York: Simon and Schuster, 1976).

ERNST, ROBERT. *Immigrant Life in New York City, 1825–1863* (New York: King's Crown Press of Columbia University, 1949).

FERGUSON, ELIZABETH A. *Social Work, An Introduction,* 3rd ed. (Philadelphia: Lippincott, 1975).

FINE, SIDNEY. *Laissez Faire and the General-Welfare State* (Ann Arbor, Mich.: University of Michigan Press, 1964).

FRASER, DEREK. *The Evolution of the British Welfare State* (New York: Barnes & Noble, 1973).

FREEMAN, HENRY, HOFFMAN, MARY ELLEN, SMITH, WINIFRED, AND PRUNTY, HOWARD. "Can a Family Agency be Relevant to the Inner Urban Scene?" *Social Casework,* Vol. 51, No. 1 (1970).

FREIDEL, FRANK. *America in the Twentieth Century,* 3rd ed. (New York: Knopf, 1970).

FREMONT-SMITH, MARION R. *Philanthropy and the Business Corporation* (New York: Russell Sage Foundation, 1972).

FRIEDLANDER, WALTER A., AND APTE, ROBERT Z. *Introduction to Social Welfare,* 4th ed. (Englewood Cliffs, N.J.: Prentice-Hall, 1974).

GAGLIARDO, DOMENICO. *American Social Insurance,* rev. ed. (New York: Harper & Brothers, 1955).

GARRATY, JOHN A. *Unemployment in History—Economic Thought and Public Policy* (New York: Harper & Row, 1978).

GARTNER, ALAN, AND RIESSMAN, FRANK. *Self-Help in the Human Services* (San Francisco: Jossey-Bass, 1977).

GERMAIN, CAREL. "Casework and Science: A Historical Encounter," in Robert W. Roberts and Robert H. Nee, eds., *Theories of Social Casework* (Chicago: University of Chicago Press, 1970).

GILBERT, NEIL. *Clients or Constituents* (San Francisco: Jossey-Bass, 1970).

GILBERT, NEIL. "The Transformation of the Social Services," *Social Service Review* (December 1977).

GODFREY, WALTER H. *The English Almshouse—With Some Account of Its Predecessor, the Medieval Hospital* (London: Faber and Faber, 1955).

GOFFMAN, ERVING. *Stigma* (Englewood Cliffs, N.J.: Prentice-Hall, 1963).

GOGUEL, MAURICE. *The Primitive Church,* trans. H. C. Snape (New York: Macmillan, 1964).

GOLDSTEIN, HOWARD. *Social Work Practice: A Unitary Approach* (Columbia, S.C.: University of South Carolina Press, 1973).

GOODE, WILLIAM J. "The Theoretical Limits of Professionalization," in Amitai Etzioni, ed., *The Semi-Professions and Their Organization* (New York: Free Press, 1969).

GRANT, ROBERT M. *Augustus to Constantine—The Thrust of the Christian Movement into the Roman World* (New York: Harper & Row, 1970).

GRANT, ROBERT M. *Early Christianity and Society* (New York: Harper & Row, 1977).

GRAY, B. KIRKMAN. *A History of English Philanthropy—From the Dissolution of the Monasteries to the Taking of the First Census* (New York: Augustus M. Kelley, 1967). First published in 1905.

GREEN, R. W., ed. *Protestantism and Capitalism—The Weber Thesis and Its Critics* (Boston: D. C. Heath, 1959).

GREENWOOD, ERNEST. "The Attributes of a Profession," in Paul E. Weinberger, ed., *Perspectives on Social Welfare,* 2nd ed. (New York: Macmillan, 1974) and in Mayer Zald, ed. *Social Welfare Institutions* (New York: Wiley, 1965).

GUMMER, BURTON. "Is the Social Worker in Public Welfare an Endangered Species?" *Public Welfare,* Vol. 37, No. 4 (Fall 1979).

HALMOS, PAUL. *The Personal Service Society* (New York: Schocken Books, 1970).

HANDEL, GERALD, ed. *The Psychosocial Interior of the Family,* 2nd ed. (Chicago: Aldine, 1972).

HANDEL, GERALD, review of Paul Halmos. "The Personal Service Society," *American Sociological Review,* Vol. 36, No. 5 (October 1971).

HANDEL, GERALD, review of Nicholas N. Kittrie. "The Right to Be Different," *Social Casework,* Vol. 54, No. 7 (July 1973).

HANDLER, JOEL F. *The Coercive Social Worker* (Chicago: Rand McNally/Markham, 1973).

HANDLER, JOEL F. *Reforming the Poor* (New York: Basic Books, 1972).

HANDS, A. R. *Charities and Social Aid in Greece and Rome* (Ithaca, N.Y.: Cornell University Press, 1968).

HAY, DENYS. *The Medieval Centuries* (London: Methuen, 1964).

HAVEMAN, ROBERT H., ed. *A Decade of Federal Antipoverty Programs* (New York: Academic Press, 1977).

HAY, J. R. *The Origin of the Liberal Welfare Reforms, 1906–1914* (London: Macmillan, 1975).

HENRY, JULES. *Pathways to Madness* (New York: Vintage, 1973).

HERRE, ERNEST A. "Aggressive Casework in a Protective Services Unit," *Social Casework,* Vol. 46, No. 6 (1965) and in Tripodi et al., *Social Workers at Work.*

HESS, ROBERT D., AND HANDEL, GERALD. *Family Worlds* (Chicago: University of Chicago Press, 1959; Phoenix edition, with new preface, 1974).

HILL, CHRISTOPHER. *Reformation to Industrial Revolution—The Making of Modern English Society,* Vol. I, 1530–1780 (New York: Pantheon, 1967).

HILL, CHRISTOPHER. *Society and Puritanism in Pre-Revolutionary England* (New York: Schocken, 1964).

HILLERBRAND, HANS J. *The World of the Reformation* (New York: Scribner's, 1973).

HOBSBAWM, E. J. *Industry and Empire—The Pelican Economic History of Britain, Volume 3, From 1750 to the Present Day* (Harmondsworth, England: Penguin Books, 1969).

The Holy Scriptures—According to the Masoretic Text—A New Translation (Philadelphia: Jewish Publication Society of America, 1937).

HOWELL, JOSEPH T. *Hard Living on Clay Street* (Garden City, N.Y.: Anchor Books, 1973).

HUNTER-GAULT, CHARLAYNE. "Tri-State United Way Is Accused of Shortchanging Black Groups," *New York Times*, October 12, 1977.

International Encyclopedia of the Social Sciences (New York: Macmillan, 1968).

JAMES, MARGARET. *Social Problems and Policy During the Puritan Revolution, 1640–1660* (London: Routledge, 1930).

JERNEGAN, MARCUS WILSON. *Laboring and Dependent Classes in Colonial America, 1607–1783* (Chicago: University of Chicago Press, 1931).

JOHNSON, ALEXANDER. *The Almshouse* (New York: Russell Sage Foundation, 1911).

JOHNSON, EARL, JR., in Robert H. Haveman, ed., *A Decade of Federal Antipoverty Programs* (New York: Academic Press, 1977).

JONES, GARETH. *History of the Law of Charity, 1532–1827* (Cambridge: Cambridge University Press, 1969).

JORDAN, WILBUR K. *Philanthropy in England, 1480–1660* (New York: Russell Sage Foundation, 1959).

JUSSERAND, J. J. *English Wayfaring Life in the Middle Ages (XIVth Century)*, 3rd ed. trans. Lucy Toulmin Smith (London: T. Fisher Unwin, 1925).

KADUSHIN, ALFRED. "The Knowledge Base of Social Work," in Alfred J. Kahn, ed., *Issues in American Social Work* (New York: Columbia University Press, 1959).

KAHN, ALFRED J., ed. *Shaping the New Social Work* (New York: Columbia University Press, 1973).

KAHN, ALFRED. *Social Policy and Social Services*, 2nd ed. (New York: Random House, 1979).

KAHN, ALFRED J., AND KAMERMAN, SHEILA B. *Not for the Poor Alone* (Philadelphia: Temple University Press, 1975).

KAIM-CAUDLE, P. R. *Comparative Social Policy and Social Security* (New York: Dunellen, 1973).

KAMERMAN, SHEILA B., DOLGOFF, RALPH, GETZEL, GEORGE, AND NELSEN, JUDITH. "Knowledge for Practice: Social Science in Social Work," in Alfred J. Kahn, ed., *Shaping the New Social Work* (New York: Columbia University Press, 1973).

KANTOR, DAVID, AND LEHR, WILLIAM. *Inside the Family* (San Francisco: Jossey-Bass, 1975).

KATZ, ALFRED H. "Self Help Groups and the Professional Community," in *The Social Welfare Forum, 1975* (New York: Columbia University Press/National Conference on Social Welfare, 1976).

KATZ, ALFRED H., AND BENDER, EUGENE I. *The Strength in Us* (New York: New Viewpoints, 1976).

KAUFMANN, YEHEZKEL. *The Religion of Israel—From Its Beginnings to the Babylonian Exile*, trans. and abr. Moshe Greenberg (Chicago: University of Chicago Press, 1960).

KILLIAN, LEWIS M. *The Impossible Revolution?* (New York: Random House, 1968).

KIRKLAND, EDWARD CHASE. *Dream and Thought in the Business Community, 1860–1900* (Ithaca, N.Y.: Cornell University Press, 1956).

KIRSTEIN, GEORGE G. *Better Giving* (Boston: Houghton Mifflin, 1975).

KITTRIE, NICHOLAS N. *The Right to Be Different* (Baltimore: Johns Hopkins University Press, 1971).

KLEBANER, BENJAMIN J. "Pauper Auctions: The 'New England Method' of Public Poor Relief," *Historical Collections of the Essex Institute*, Vol. 91, No. 3 (July 1955).

KLEBANER, BENJAMIN J. "Poverty and Its Relief in American Thought, 1815–1861," *Social Service Review*, Vol. 38, No. 4 (December 1964).

KLEBANER, BENJAMIN J. "Some Aspects of North Carolina Public Poor Relief, 1700–1860," *North Carolina Historical Review*, Vol. 31, No. 4 (October 1954).

KRAMER, RALPH M. *Participation of the Poor* (Englewood Cliffs, N.J.: Prentice-Hall, 1969).

LANDY, DAVID. "Problems of the Person Seeking Help in Our Culture," *Social Welfare Forum, 1960,* National Conference on Social Welfare (New York: Columbia University Press, 1960). Reprinted in Mayer N. Zald, ed. *Social Welfare Institutions* (New York: Wiley, 1965).

LASKI, HAROLD J. *The Rise of Liberalism* (New York: Harper & Brothers, 1936).

LEIBY, JAMES. *A History of Social Welfare and Social Work in the United States* (New York: Columbia University Press, 1978).

LEICHTER, HOPE J., AND MITCHELL, WILLIAM E. *Kinship and Casework* (New York: Russell Sage Foundation, 1967).

LEKACHMAN, ROBERT. *A History of Economic Ideas* (New York: Harper & Row, 1959).

LEONARD, E. M. *The Early History of English Poor Relief* (Cambridge: Cambridge University Press, 1900).

LEVINE, MURRAY A., AND LEVINE, ADELINE. *A Social History of Helping Services* (New York: Appleton-Century-Crofts, 1970).

LEVITAN, SAR A. *The Great Society's Poor Law* (Baltimore: Johns Hopkins University Press, 1969).

LINDSEY, ROBERT. "United Way Accused of Monopoly in Fight over Charitable Funds," *New York Times,* April 3, 1978.

LINK, ARTHUR S. *American Epoch—A History of the United States Since the 1890s,* Vol. II, 3rd ed. (New York: Knopf, 1967).

LOEWENBERG, F. M. *Fundamentals of Social Intervention* (New York: Columbia University Press, 1977).

LONGMATE, NORMAN. *The Workhouse* (New York: St. Martin's Press, 1974).

LOPEZ, ROBERT S. *The Commercial Revolution of the Middle Ages, 950–1350.* (Englewood Cliffs, N.J.: Prentice-Hall, 1971)

LUBOVE, ROY. *The Professional Altruist—The Emergence of Social Work as a Career, 1880–1930* (Cambridge: Harvard University Press, 1965).

LUBOVE, ROY. *The Struggle for Social Security, 1900–1935* (Cambridge: Harvard University Press, 1968).

LUKES, STEVEN. "Types of Individualism," in Philip P. Wiener, ed. *Dictionary of the History of Ideas* (New York: Scribner, 1973).

McCOWN, CHESTER C. *Man, Morals, and History—Today's Legacy from Ancient Times and Biblical Peoples* (New York: Harper & Brothers, 1958).

McNEILL, WILLIAM H. *The Rise of the West* (New York: Mentor Books, 1963).

MANGUM, GARTH L., AND SENINGER, STEPHEN F. *Coming of Age in the Ghetto—A Dilemma of Youth Unemployment* (Baltimore: Johns Hopkins University Press, 1978).

MANNHEIM, KARL. *Man and Society in an Age of Reconstruction,* trans. by Edward Shils (London: Kegan Paul, Trench, Trubner, 1940).

MARMOR, THEODORE R., ed. *Poverty Policy* (Chicago: Aldine-Atherton, 1971).

MARMOR, THEODORE R., with the assistance of Jan S. Marmor. *The Politics of Medicare* (Chicago: Aldine, 1973).

MARRIS, PETER, AND REIN, MARTIN. *Dilemmas of Social Reform,* 2nd ed. (Chicago: Aldine, 1973).

MARSHALL, J. D. *The Old Poor Law, 1795–1834* (London: Macmillan, 1969).

MARSHALL, T. H. *Class, Citizenship and Social Development* (Garden City, N.Y.: Doubleday Anchor Books, 1965).

MATZA, DAVID. "Poverty and Disrepute," in Robert K. Merton and Robert Nisbet, eds., *Contemporary Social Problems,* 3rd ed. (New York: Harcourt, Brace, Jovanovich, 1971).

MENCHER, SAMUEL. *Poor Law to Poverty Program—Economic Security Policy in Britain and the United States* (Pittsburgh: University of Pittsburgh Press, 1967).

MENDELSOHN, ALLAN R. *The Work of Social Work* (New York: New Viewpoints, 1980).

MEYER, CAROL H. *Social Work Practice: A Response to the Urban Crisis* (New York: Free Press, 1970).

MICHALS, ARTHUR P., COURNOYER, DANIEL E., AND PINNER, ELIZABETH L. "School Social Work and Educational Goals," *Social Work*, Vol. 24, No. 2 (March 1979).

MILES, ARTHUR P. *An Introduction to Public Welfare* (Boston: D. C. Heath, 1949).

MILLER, PERRY. *The New England Mind: From Colony to Province* (Cambridge, Mass.: Harvard University Press, 1953).

MORRIS, RICHARD B. *Government and Labor in Early America* (New York: Harper Torchbooks, 1965).

MORRIS, ROBERT, AND ANDERSON, DELWIN. "Personal Care Services: An Identity for Social Work," *Social Service Review*, Vol. 49, No. 2 (June 1975).

MOWAT, CHARLES LOCH. *The Charity Organization Society, 1869–1913—Its Ideas and Work* (London: Methuen, 1961).

MOWBRAY, ALBERT H., BLANCHARD, RALPH H., WILLIAMS, C. ARTHUR, JR. *Insurance: Its Theory and Practice in the United States*, 6th ed. (New York: McGraw-Hill, 1969).

MOYNIHAN, DANIEL P. "The Crisis in Welfare," *The Public Interest*, No. 10 (Winter 1968).

MOYNIHAN, DANIEL P. *Maximum Feasible Misunderstanding* (New York: Free Press, 1969).

MOYNIHAN, DANIEL P. "The Professionalization of Reform," *The Public Interest*, No. 1 (Fall 1965).

MULLER, HERBERT J. *Freedom in the Western World* (New York: Harper & Row, 1963).

MULLER, HERBERT J. *The Uses of the Past* (New York: Oxford University Press, 1952).

MUNNELL, ALICIA H. *The Future of Social Security* (Washington, D.C.: Brookings Institution, 1977).

NELSON, DANIEL. *Unemployment Insurance—The American Experience, 1915–1935* (Madison, Wisc.: University of Wisconsin Press, 1969).

New York Times, January 28, 1975, May 11, 1977, August 6, 1979.

New York Times, March 10, March 11, March 12, 1971.

NEWMAN, DOROTHY K., et al. *Protest, Politics, and Prosperity—Black Americans and White Institutions, 1940–1975* (New York: Pantheon, 1978).

NORMAN, JANET. "Consciousness-Raising: Self-Help in the Women's Movement," in Katz and Bender, *The Strength in Us.*

OWEN, DAVID. *English Philanthropy 1660–1960* (Cambridge: Belknap Press of Harvard University Press, 1964).

Oxford English Dictionary (Oxford: Oxford University Press, 1933).

PATTI, RINO J., AND RESNICK, HERMAN. "Changing the Agency from Within," *Social Work*, Vol. 17, No. 4 (July 1972).

PEARMAN, LU, AND SEARLES, JEAN. "Unmet Social Service Needs in Skilled Nursing Facilities," in Bracht, *Social Work in Health.*

PERLMAN, HELEN HARRIS. *Perspectives in Social Casework* (Philadelphia: Temple University Press, 1971).

PETERSON, PAUL E., AND GREENSTONE, J. DAVID. "Racial Change and Citizen Participation: The Mobilization of Low-Income Communities through Community Action," in Robert H. Haveman, ed., *A Decade of Federal Antipoverty Programs* (New York: Academic Press, 1977).

PHELAN, JAMES, AND POZEN, ROBERT. *The Company State—Ralph Nader's Study Group Report on Dupont in Delaware* (New York: Grossman, 1973). Introduction by Ralph Nader.

PINCUS, ALLEN, AND MINAHAN, ANNE. *Social Work Practice: Model and Method* (Itasca, Ill.: F. E. Peacock, 1973).

PIOTRKOWSKI, CHAYA. *Work and the Family System* (New York: Free Press, 1979).

PIRENNE, HENRI. *Economic and Social History of Medieval Europe,* trans. I. E. Clegg (New York: Harcourt, Brace & World, 1937).

PIVEN, FRANCES FOX, AND CLOWARD, RICHARD A. *Regulating the Poor* (New York: Vintage, 1971).

Pocket Data Book, USA 1976 (Washington, D.C.: U.S. Government Printing Office, 1976).

POLANYI, KARL. *The Great Transformation* (New York: Rinehart, 1944).

POOLE, AUSTIN. *Obligations of Society in the XIIth and XIIIth Centuries* (Oxford: Oxford University Press, 1946).

POUND, JOHN. *Poverty and Vagrancy in Tudor England* (London: Longman, 1971).

POYNTER, J. R. *Society and Pauperism—English Ideas on Poor Relief, 1795–1834* (London: Routledge & Kegan Paul, 1969).

RAINWATER, LEE. *What Money Buys* (New York: Basic Books, 1974).

REIN, MARTIN. *Social Policy* (New York: Random House, 1970)

REIN, MARTIN. AND RAINWATER, LEE. "Patterns of Welfare Use," *Social Service Review* (December 1978).

REINHOLD, ROBERT. "Public Found Against Welfare Idea But in Favor of What Programs Do," *New York Times,* Aug. 3, 1977.

RICHAN, WILLARD C., AND MENDELSOHN, ALLAN R. *Social Work—The Unloved Profession* (New York: New Viewpoints, 1973).

RICHMOND, MARY E. *What Is Social Casework?* (New York: Arno Press and New York Times, 1971). Originally published by the Russell Sage Foundation in 1922.

RIMLINGER, GASTON V. "American Social Security in a European Perspective," in William G. Bowen, Frederick H. Harbison, Richard A. Lester, Herman M. Somers, eds., *The Princeton Symposium on the American System of Social Insurance* (New York: McGraw-Hill, 1968).

RIMLINGER, GASTON V. *Welfare Policy and Industrialization in Europe, America, and Russia* (New York: Wiley, 1971).

ROBERTSON, DAVID H. "The Juvenile Court—and Bill—and Authority," in Arthur E. Fink, *The Field of Social Work,* 6th ed. (New York: Holt, Rinehart and Winston, 1974).

RODGERS, HARRELL R., JR. *Poverty Amid Plenty* (Reading, Mass.: Addison-Wesley, 1979).

ROMASCO, ALBERT U. *The Poverty of Abundance—Hoover, the Nation, the Depression* (New York: Oxford University Press, 1965).

ROSE, MICHAEL E. *The Relief of Poverty, 1834–1914* (London: Macmillan, 1972).

ROSENTHAL, JOEL T. *The Purchase of Paradise* (London: Routledge and Kegan Paul, 1972).

ROSS, AILEEN D. "Philanthropic Activity and the Business Career," *Social Forces,* Vol. 32, No. 3 (1954). Reprinted in Mayer N. Zald ed., *Social Welfare Institutions—A Sociological Reader* (New York: Wiley, 1965).

ROSS, HEATHER L., AND SAWHILL, ISABEL V. *Time of Transition—The Growth of Families Headed by Women* (Washington, D.C.: Urban Institute, 1975).

ROTHMAN, DAVID J. *The Discovery of the Asylum* (Boston: Little, Brown, 1971).

RYAN, WILLIAM. *Blaming the Victim* (New York: Pantheon, 1971).

SABINE, GEORGE H. *A History of Political Theory* (New York: Henry Holt, 1937).

SAGARIN, EDWARD. *Odd Man In* (Chicago: Quadrangle, 1969).

SANDBURG, CARL, *The People, Yes* (New York: Harcourt, Brace, 1936).

SCHNEIDER, DAVID, AND DEUTSCH, ALBERT, *The History of Public Welfare in New York State, 1867–1940* (Chicago: University of Chicago Press, 1941).

SCHOTTLAND, CHARLES I. *The Social Security Program in the United States,* 2nd ed. (New York: Appleton-Century-Crofts, 1970).

SCHOTTLAND, CHARLES I., ed. *The Welfare State* (New York: Harper Torchbooks, 1967).

SMITH, ADAM. *An Inquiry into the Nature and Causes of the Wealth of Nations,* ed. and intro. Edwin Cannan (New York: Modern Library, 1937).

Social Security Handbook, 6th ed. (Washington, D.C.: Government Printing Office, 1978).

SPERGEL, IRVING A. "Social Development and Social Work," in Simon Slavin, ed., *Social Administration* (New York: Haworth Press and Council on Social Work Education, 1978).

SPINDLER, ARTHUR. *Public Welfare* (New York: Human Sciences Press, 1979).

STEINER, GILBERT Y. "Reform Follows Reality: The Growth of Welfare," in Eli Ginzberg and Robert M. Solow, eds., *The Great Society* (New York: Basic Books, 1974).

STEINER, GILBERT Y. *Social Insecurity: The Politics of Welfare* (Chicago: Rand McNally, 1966).

STEINER, GILBERT Y. *The State of Welfare* (Washington, D.C.: Brookings Institution, 1971).

STONE, LAWRENCE. *The Family, Sex and Marriage in England, 1500–1800* (New York: Harper & Row, 1977).

TAWNEY, R. H. *Religion and the Rise of Capitalism* (London: John Murray, 1936).

THOMPSON, JAMES WESTFALL. *Economic and Social History of the Middle Ages (300–1300),* Vol. I (New York: Frederick Ungar, 1959). First published in 1928.

THRUPP, SYLVIA L. *The Merchant Class of Medieval London, 1300–1500* (Chicago: University of Chicago Press, 1948).

TIERNEY, BRIAN. *Medieval Poor Law—A Sketch of Canonical Theory and Its Application in England* (Berkeley and Los Angeles: University of California Press, 1959).

TOREN, NINA. *Social Work: The Case of a Semi-Profession* (Beverly Hills, Calif.: Sage, 1972).

TRATTNER, WALTER I. *From Poor Law to Welfare State—A History of Social Welfare in America* (New York: Free Press, 1974).

TREVELYAN, G. M. *English Social History—A Survey of Six Centuries, Chaucer to Queen Victoria* (Harmondsworth, England: Penguin Books, 1967). First published in 1942.

TRIPODI, TONI, FELLIN, PHILLIP, EPSTEIN, IRWIN, AND LIND, ROBERT, eds.. *Social Workers at Work* (Itasca, Ill.: F. E. Peacock, 1972).

TROLANDER, JUDITH ANN. *Settlement Houses and the Great Depression* (Detroit: Wayne State University Press, 1975).

TURNER, JOHN H., et al., eds. *Encyclopedia of Social Work,* 17th ed. (New York: National Association of Social Workers, 1977).

TUSSING, A. DALE. *Poverty in a Dual Economy* (New York: St. Martin's Press, 1975).

UNWIN, GEORGE. *The Guilds and Companies of London,* 4th ed. (London: Frank Cass, 1963).

VALENTINE, CHARLES A. *Culture and Poverty* (Chicago: University of Chicago Press, 1968).

VAN WERVEKE, H. "The Rise of the Towns," in M. M. Postan, E. E. Rich, and Edward Miller eds., *The Cambridge Economic History of Europe,* Vol. III, *Economic Organization and Policies in the Middle Ages* (Cambridge: Cambridge University Press, 1963).

VATTANO, ANTHONY J. "Mental Health," in Brieland, Costin, Atherton and others, *Contemporary Social Work.*

VOGEL, EZRA F., AND BELL, NORMAN W. "The Emotionally Disturbed Child as the Family Scapegoat," in Norman W. Bell and Ezra F. Vogel, eds., *A Modern Introduction to the Family* (New York: Free Press, 1960).

WALZER, MICHAEL. "Puritanism as a Revolutionary Ideology," in S. N. Eisenstadt, ed., *The Protestant Ethic and Modernization—A Comparative View* (New York: Basic Books, 1968).

WATKINS, JOHN C., JR. "Juvenile and Criminal Justice," in Brieland, Costin, Atherton and others, *Contemporary Social Work.*

WATTENBERG, SHIRLEY H. "Health," in Brieland, Costin, Atherton and others, *Contemporary Social Work.*

WEBB, SIDNEY, AND WEBB, BEATRICE. *English Poor Law History—Part I: The Old Poor Law* (Hamden, Conn.: Archon Books, 1963). First in published 1927.

WEBER, MAX. *The Protestant Ethic and the Spirit of Capitalism,* trans. Talcott Parsons (New York: Scribner's, 1930).

WHITTAKER, JAMES K. *Social Treatment* (Chicago: Aldine, 1974).

WILENSKY, HAROLD, AND LEBEAUX, CHARLES N. *Industrial Society and Social Welfare* (New York: Free Press, 1965).

WILENSKY, HAROLD L. *The Welfare State and Equality* (Berkeley, Calif.: University of California Press, 1975).

WISNER, ELIZABETH. *Social Welfare in the South* (Baton Rouge, La.: Louisiana State University Press, 1970).

WOODCOCK, GEORGE, ed. *The Anarchist Reader* (Glasgow, Scotland: Fontana/Collins, 1977).

WOODROOFE, KATHLEEN. *From Charity to Social Work* (Toronto: University of Toronto Press, 1962).

WYLLIE, IRVIN G. *The Self-Made Man in America—The Myth of Rags to Riches* (New Brunswick, N.J.: Rutgers University Press, 1954).

ZIMBALIST, SIDNEY E. *Historic Themes and Landmarks in Social Welfare Research* (Harper & Row, 1977).

Glossary

Access services Social services which put a client in touch with the particular social agency that can help with the specific type of problem.

Aid to Families with Dependent Children (AFDC) Public assistance program initiated under the Social Security Act of 1935 in which the federal government reimburses the states for a portion of the costs of furnishing subsistence to financially dependent children and their adult caretaker(s).

Allowance system System that developed in late 18th-century England of granting the working poor an allowance in aid of wages to enable their incomes to keep pace with the cost of living as measured by the price of bread ("bread scale"). Also known as the Speenhamland system, named for the town where the most famous allowance system originated.

Almsgiving Donation of money, food, or clothing to those in need.

Almshouse In the Middle Ages a residence for poor people, often built by a wealthy merchant as a philanthropic contribution to his town. In 19th-century and early 20th-century United States, a publicly supported dwelling for the poor; entry into an almshouse was often required as a condition for receiving subsistence aid.

Anxiety Experience of threat to one's wellbeing. Anxiety is differentiated from fear on the basis that the source of a fear is known, while the source of anxiety is usually unknown. Anxiety is perhaps the single most important explanatory concept in psychoanalysis, which attempts to help the patient discover its source and thereby learn to cope with it more effectively.

Associated philanthropy Practice of wealthy businessmen pooling their donations —beginning in 17th century—to support a specific charitable society.

Auction system   System of public assistance that began in New England and spread to other colonies and states. Town officials auctioned poor people who were given for care to the lowest bidder.

Begging   Soliciting alms.

Beneficiary   Role designation for a person who receives income benefits from a social-insurance program. Contrasts with "recipient."

Bequest   Donation of money specified by the donor to be made after his death.

Canon law   Body of law of the Roman Catholic Church. Medieval canon law attempted to formulate a coherent theory of poverty, wealth, and charity.

Capitalism   Economic and political system in which the means of production are privately owned by individuals or companies, and economic activity is regulated by privately negotiated contracts rather than by central-state planning.

Capitalist spirit   Outlook that emphasizes the making of profits and accumulation of wealth as the prime goal of life and that regards money as the major basis for judging the worth of persons as well as of things.

Casework   One of the original basic methods of social work. The social worker provides social services through such activities as counseling, giving information, contacting other agencies to arrange for other services. Casework may be done with individuals, family pairs, or whole families.

Categorical assistance   Public assistance partly paid for by the federal government to persons eligible in one of the four categories established by the Social Security Act of 1935 and later amendments: Aid to Blind, Aid to (Families of) Dependent Children, Aid to Permanently and Totally Disabled; Old-Age Assistance. Before 1935 individual states provided some assistance to people in some categories.

Charitable society   Any of the organizations set up by businessmen in the 17th-to-19th centuries for the purpose of aiding some specific category of socially vulnerable persons—foundlings, destitute boys, unmarried mothers, servant girls, and others.

Charitable trust   Legal arrangement for assuring that money given by a charitable donor is used for the purposes he or she specifies.

Charity   Oldest of the five major ideas of social welfare. A social relationship in which a person with some surplus above subsistence donates money or help in kind to someone with insufficient means of livelihood.

Charity Organization movement   Also known as "scientific charity," this was a late 19th-century social movement aimed at making charity more efficient and reducing pauperism.

Charity schools   Schools established in England during early 18th century by local philanthropists and coordinated by the Society for the Promotion of Christian Knowledge to establish habits of industry and sobriety in poor children in order to prevent them from becoming poor adults who would threaten social stability.

Child guidance clinic   Institution that developed during 1920's for the initial purpose of preventing juvenile delinquency but that evolved into a more general type of agency dealing with emotional problems of children and their families. Almost always run by psychiatrists, the work of the clinics is typically carried out by three-person teams, each consisting of a psychiatrist, a social worker, and a clinical psychologist.

Children's allowances   Family allowances.

Church chest   In early Christian times a chest where donations were put to take care of Christian poor, widows, orphans, prisoners, and captives.

Civil Works Administration (CWA)   New Deal agency to provide employment by building public works.

Civilian Conservation Corps (CCC)   New Deal agency that enrolled young men between ages of 18 and 25 from families on relief and sent them to countryside to work on projects of soil conservation, flood control, reforestation. Part of their monthly pay was sent directly home to their families.

Client   Role designation for a person who receives services from a social-welfare agency or from a professional person who performs the services. Most service professions use the designation "client," the major exceptions being medicine—and, by extension, most non-medical psychotherapy—which uses the designation "patient," and education, which uses the designation "student." Some social workers are beginning to prefer the designation "consumer" as a way of emphasizing the rights of the person who receives the services.

Community action   Type of mutual aid, fostered during the War on Poverty, in which neighborhood-based groups and associations gained or sought to gain decision-making control over social welfare agencies in their neighborhoods. Term is now used more loosely to refer to the neighborhood-based social agencies that were established during the War on Poverty and in which neighborhood residents participate in policy-making but do not control the agency.

Community chest   Single organization, city-wide or county-wide, whose function is to raise funds for all the voluntary agencies affiliated with it in order to minimize competition for funds among agencies and to minimize the number of times citizens are approached for contributions. Community chests, mostly founded after World War I (when community more often referred to a city than to a neighborhood) are now usually known as United Way.

Community organization   Method of social work practice in which the social worker works with the officials of social agencies and with community leaders in planning social services for the community. It may also involve working with citizens' groups and associations.

Contract system   In early New York and elsewhere, system of public assistance which provided that poor people be maintained by payment of public funds to an independent contractor who agreed to be responsible.

Defense mechanism   Concept in psychoanalysis, referring to a person's efforts to avoid experiencing anxiety. Repression is probably the most common defense mechanism.

Deterrence   Effort, especially intensified by the New Poor Law, to discourage poor people from applying for help.

Demogrant   One type of plan for a guaranteed annual income. Each person would receive a standard payment from the government, thus eliminating a means test. Persons with adequate income would, in effect, repay the grant when they pay income taxes. The universality of payment would make it a citizen right and thus presumably remove stigma from the payment.

Dole   Donation of food or money, as was done at monastery gates during the Middle Ages and in relief lines during the Great Depression. Often disparaged as "a handout."

Earnings base   Amount of earned income on which social security taxes are assessed.

Earnings disregard   Amount of earned income that a recipient of public assistance or a beneficiary of social insurance is allowed to earn without having benefits reduced.

Elizabethan Poor Law   Series of laws dealing with support of the poor that were passed during the reign of Queen Elizabeth I in England between 1558 and 1601, when the last comprehensive poor law was passed until the New Poor Law of 1834. The term sometimes includes the laws passed during earlier Tudor reigns, particularly those of Elizabeth's father, Henry VIII, and her brother, Edward VI.

Enclosure movements   Successful, periodic efforts made from Tudor times to the 19th century by large landowners to drive small tenant farmers off the land and enclose the enlarged tracts for profitable sheepraising.

Family allowances   Social-welfare program found in Canada and many European countries, under which the national government provides monthly payments to families with young children. In most countries, it does not involve a means test.

Federal Emergency Relief Administration (FERA)   First New Deal social-welfare agency, whose purpose was to provide funds to localities for direct relief to starving people.

Feudalism   Social and economic system of medieval Europe, organized on basis of lord-vassal-serf relationships in which lower-ranking persons received protection and other benefits in exchange for labor or combat services to higher-ranking persons.

Food stamps   Coupons given without charge to persons below the poverty line; these can be exchanged for food in grocery stores.

Friendly societies   Societies for mutual insurance organized by poor people in England in 18th and 19th centuries. Formation of friendly societies was encouraged by wealthy and powerful people who hoped that this form of mutual aid or self-help would reduce the taxes they had to pay under the Poor Law.

Friendly visiting   Activity of the charity organization volunteer worker who visited poor people in their homes to bring them moral uplift and instruction in order to change their character. Friendly visitors believed that such a change was necessary and sufficient to enable the poor escape from poverty.

Funeral dole   Medieval charitable method of distributing money or food to the poor at a merchant's funeral.

General assistance   Public assistance program administered and funded entirely by states and localities, to give financial aid to persons ineligible for categorical assistance. Also known as Home Relief.

Gleaning of fields   Ancient Israelite charity method of letting poor gather crops left for them after regular harvest.

Gospel of wealth   Term applied mockingly to Andrew Carnegie's idea that millionaires are the people most suited to decide what is best for the community. Carnegie was influenced by Social Darwinism.

Group work   Method of social work practice in which the social worker guides small groups of persons for the purpose of enhancing the members' personality development and social skills or for the purpose of helping members deal with some specific emotional problems. In the latter situation, group work is often called group treatment and is considered a type of psychotherapy.

Guaranteed annual income   Concept of income maintenance that would assure all individuals and families at least a certain minimal annual income. It is usually thought of as replacing public assistance, though some advocates think of it as replacing social insurance also.

Home relief   In early 19th century synonymous with outdoor relief. After 1935, home relief refers to local and state public assistance for persons who do not qualify for categorical assistance. Home relief today is also known as General Assistance.

House of industry   American colonial institution for reducing beggary and pauperism by employing the destitute.

Hospital   In medieval times all-purpose reception center for anyone in need of temporary shelter—sick, homeless, travelers—operated by religious brothers and sisters. In late Middle Ages, most hospitals became almshouses for a group of resident poor, elderly, or disabled people.

Income maintenance   Any social welfare program, whether of a public assistance type or social insurance type, that provides income replacing the loss, or absence, of earned income.

Individualism   Idea that the individual person is the purpose for which society exists. A significant value in western society, underlying the laissez-faire concept that individual pursuit of self-interest is the best principle on which to base economic activity.

Indoor relief   Subsistence given to persons living collectively in a special residential institution, especially a workhouse, although also in other types of asylums.

Institutional concept of social welfare   A concept of social welfare that considers social welfare institutions to be part of the normal array of institutions in modern society, serving all categories of citizens rather than only those with special problems.

Job Corps   Agency of the War on Poverty; it sought to increase employability of youths aged 16 to 21 by teaching them job-related skills while they lived away from home in special residential centers.

Laissez-faire   Name given to the economic beliefs of businessmen, political leaders, and leading thinkers from late 18th century on, emphasizing rights of private property and minimal governmental regulation of the economy.

Less eligibility   Concept introduced in the Poor Law Amendment of 1834 (the New Poor Law) to ensure that anyone receiving public aid for subsistence should receive less than the lowest-paid worker earning his own livelihood, regardless of size of family or any other factor.

Liberalism   Political, economic, and ethical doctrine emphasizing rights of the individual to make free choices, to pursue his or her self-interest, to own property, and to enjoy civil liberties without fear of arbitrary government interference. Liberalism appealed to businessmen, who focused on those aspects of the doctrine emphasizing protection of property because of their tendency to interpret both taxation and government regulation as interference with property.

Macropractice   Generic method of social work, used in work with communities, government welfare departments, social-welfare-coordinating bodies such as United

Way, and other large-scale units. Its purpose is to arrange for the delivery of social services to the ultimate user.

Mandatory law   Law that requires political subdivisions to take the actions specified in the law.

Manor   Medieval village community where unfree peasants (serfs) cultivate the lord's domain in exchange for use of another portion of his estate for their own livelihood; large part of estate remained open to all for grazing, gathering wood, hunting, and trapping.

Maximum feasible participation   Phrase in the Economic Opportunity Act of 1964 establishing the War on Poverty. Intended to encourage participation of poor people in running the new programs, it was widely interpreted by leaders in poor neighborhoods as authorizing local community control of programs. There was no official definition of how much participation of the poor was the maximum that was feasible, until Congress amended the Act in 1966 by setting a limit of one-third of the members of any agency's board of directors as being community residents.

Means test   Financial examination of an applicant for public assistance to discover whether he or she is without adequate means of support.

Medicaid   A federal-state, means-tested program which pays part of the medical expenses of persons receiving public assistance and of persons who are judged "medically needy," that is, needing help to pay medical expenses, though not for subsistence.

Medicare   Federal social insurance program which pays medical expenses of persons over age 65.

Mendicancy   Begging as a way of life. (also mendicity)

Mercantilism   Economic beliefs of 16th to mid-18th century merchants, emphasizing strengthening one's own nation at the expense of others, requiring low wages to workers and high degree of government management of economy.

Micropractice   Generic method of social work, used in work with individuals, families, and small groups for delivering service directly to user. Contrasts with macropractice.

Monastery   Secluded community established by churchmen dissatisfied with church's worldliness and seeking to lead a more holy life. In Middle Ages, monasteries offered a charitable dole of food and drink to any who asked.

Mutual aid   Form of social welfare based on the equality and interchangeability of helpers and helped.

Mutual insurance   One type of mutual aid. A form of insurance in which persons who have a shared social identity insure each other by payments into a common fund. Distinguished from private insurance purchased from a private company and from social insurance organized by the state.

National Youth Administration (NYA)   New Deal agency which provided jobs to high school and college youth so they could remain in school.

Need   Claim to participate in society in accordance with some available or conceivable standard that is considered applicable to oneself.

Negative income tax   One type of plan for a guaranteed annual income. It would use the existing income-tax reporting system. Persons below a certain income level would receive payments from government, the opposite or "negative" of persons above a certain level who pay income tax to the government.

New Deal   Name given to the administration of President Franklin D. Roosevelt, important for its creation of federal role in American social-welfare system.

New Poor Law   In England abolishing the Elizabethan Poor Law and the allowance system and replacing them with nationally supervised compulsory indoor relief. (Also known as Poor Law Reform Act and Poor Law Amendment.)

Old Age Assistance   Public-assistance program initiated under the Social-Security Act of 1935 for providing subsistence to impoverished elderly people. Replaced in 1974 by SSI.

Old Poor Law   Elizabethan Poor Law.

Outdoor relief   Subsistence granted to people while allowing them to continue living in their accustomed dwellings.

Parish   Village or other district that has its own church. In Tudor period, parish became a unit of local government, responsible for care of its own poor.

Pathology theory of poverty   Idea that poor people are to blame for their own poverty because of personal deficiencies.

Pauper   Destitute person who becomes dependent upon continuing charity or public assistance for subsistence. In 19th-century England and America, paupers were considered to be morally and psychologically damaged by their continuing dependency; social welfare thinking and action were more concerned with pauperism than with poverty.

Permissive law   Law that allows a political subdivision to take actions specified in the law but that does not require it to do so.

Philanthropy   Donation by a wealthy person either to a community or to establish a program of continuing help to a specified group. While retaining this meaning in the 20th century, the term is now also used as a more respectable synonym for charity.

poor, The   Category of people whose wellbeing was the original focus of social welfare and has continued as a central focus, although social welfare is now concerned with many other categories as well. In ancient times the poor were those without adequate means of subsistence. In the Middle Ages the term was more general and included the disabled, the aged, the chronically ill, as well as ablebodied people without adequate subsistence. Since the War on Poverty, the poor are officially defined as those whose income falls below the poverty line.

Poorhouse   In Elizabethan times a house which each parish was obliged to maintain widows, aged, sick and infirm people, mothers of illegitimate children, tramps, and paupers awaiting removal to other parishes. In 19th- and 20th-century U.S., a synonym in some states for almshouse.

Poor Law Reform   New Poor Law.

Poverty line   Government-specified amount of income, scaled for size of family and changing from time to time as prices change, which is considered the minimum-adequate income. People with less are said to be "below the poverty line."

Progressive Era   Period in American history, roughly 1890 to 1914, during which there was much reform activity attempting to deal with the social problems caused by industrial capitalism.

Protestant Ethic   A moral doctrine of Calvinist Protestantism which holds that individuals are called to their work by God and that they must therefore be industrious, sober, disinterested in enjoyment (and therefore frugal in spending money) in order to serve God.

Psychoanalysis   A school of psychiatry developed by Sigmund Freud emphasizing the importance of inner conflict and anxiety as causes of mental illnesses.

Public assistance   Income provided by the government out of tax revenues to persons with no other source of income or with inadequate income from other sources. (sometimes called public aid)

Public health   Concept that the health of individuals can be safeguarded or improved by procedures controlling hazards in the environment that potentially affect an entire population.

Public welfare   Form of social welfare in which the public, acting through the state or government, provides public assistance and various social services for dependent members of society.

Quarter of employment   Unit of work for measuring eligibility for social security benefits. Until 1978 a quarter was defined as an actual three-month period in which a person earned at least $50. Since 1978, a quarter is defined by each $250 earned, up to a maximum of $1000, regardless of how the earnings are distributed within the calendar year.

Recipient   Role designation for a person who receives income benefits from a public assistance program. Contrasts with "beneficiary."

Relief   Aid given to alleviate hardship. The term came into widespread use during the Great Depression when many people were "on relief." Today's more or less equivalent term is "on welfare."

Repression   Psychoanalytic concept, one of the defense mechanisms, referring to removal of unacceptable desires and thoughts from conscious awareness.

Residual concept of social welfare   Concept of social welfare that considers the family and the market to be the normal institutions for meeting needs and that therefore regards social-welfare institutions to be the last resort for exceptional cases.

Retirement test   Requirement of the American social-security system that a person be not only of proper age but also be retired from employment in order to receive benefits under the old-age provisions. The retirement test is removed at age 72.

Romanticism   Nineteenth-century movement of thought that expressed dissatisfaction with the intensified interest in money and material goods fostered by industrial capitalism, which it considered dehumanizing. Romanticism sought renewed emphasis on spiritual values; it helped shape both the Charity Organization movement and the settlement house movement.

Self-help group   Group, organized by persons who have a similar personal problem. Its members help each other through the mutual giving and receiving of emotional support, information, advice, criticism, and approval.

Settlement   Right to reside in a particular community. Originated in feudal concept of attachment to land and notion that everyone belongs in a certain place. The English Law of Settlement and Removal of 1662 required people to remain in the parish where they had their settlement unless they could prove they would not become chargeable in another parish. The concept was carried over to the American colonies.

Settlement house Building in a slum neighborhood, occupied as a residence by middle-class people who offer programs of instruction, recreation, and community improvement to the neighborhood.

Social agency Any organization, voluntary or governmental, that delivers social services.

Social Christianity Nineteenth-century movement within Protestantism that emphasized service to humanity as a basic tenet of Christianity.

Social Darwinism Nineteenth-century doctrine which attempted to apply Charles Darwin's biological theory of natural selection and evolution to social phenomena. Social Darwinists believed that the wealthiest people were the most successful, thus demonstrating that they were the "fittest" to make decisions for society.

Social development Essentially equivalent to macropractice.

Social gospel Late 19th-century movement in American Protestantism—a version of Social Christianity—that considered economic and political questions to fall within the scope of Christian ethics and therefore matters of religious concern. Social gospel ministers criticized laissez-faire capitalism.

Social insurance Income payments made when earned income is interrupted by accident, retirement, or unemployment. The payments are based on and related to amounts previously paid into a governmentally-organized fund. Social insurance differs from public assistance by introducing the concept of predictable entitlement to benefits.

Social psychiatry School of psychiatry that developed during the Progressive Era and that emphasized the importance of social influences in causing mental illnesses.

Social security In the United States the term used to refer to the social insurance more formally known as Old Age, Survivors, and Disability Insurance. Established by the Social Security Act. The term was also incorporated into the names of the several government bureaus that, successively, have administered the program.

Social service Provision of help through focused forms of human contact, association, or interaction.

Social treatment Essentially equivalent to micropractice.

Social welfare Twentieth-century term meaning the social organization of concern for persons and groups vulnerable to social disability. Social welfare institutions are types of organizations (voluntary agencies, government departments, workhouses, asylums, monasteries, etc.) that seek to implement current ideas (values, beliefs, knowledge) about the best ways to deal with social disability. The term is applied retrospectively to encompass organizations and ideas current in other times as well as our own. Health and educational institutions are usually included as social welfare institutions in Europe but are considered separate fields in the United States.

Social work Occupation whose practitioners provide certain specialized forms of social service. One of the helping professions that began to develop in the Progressive Era, and the one that traditionally has been most directly concerned with poor people.

Socialism Economic and political system based on state ownership of the means of production and distribution of goods and services. Economic activity is planned by the state to achieve the best outcome for society; the concept is thus the opposite of Adam Smith's that "a hidden hand" brings about society's best interest as a result of individual entrepreneurs striving to gain markets according to their own judgments.

Stewardship of wealth Belief that emerged among medieval merchants and 16th-century English Puritans that the rich do not really own their wealth but have been entrusted with it by God and are therefore obliged to use it in socially constructive ways. Early American colonial leaders adhered to the belief, as did some 19th-century American industrialists who thereby justified extremes of wealth and poverty.

Structural theory of poverty   Idea that poor people are poor because of flaws in the organization or structure of society. By failing to provide adequate education and sufficient jobs for all, the society fails to provide adequate income for all.

Systems approach   A concept of social work method which considers all social work activities to be components of a single, comprehensive or generic method.

Transfer payments   Money shifted from those who first receive it as private income to others who are considered entitled to it. Government transfers are the most significant; they shift money by taxing according to rules concerning who should pay and disburse it according to rules concerning who should receive. Private-transfer payments include categories such as gifts, alimony, and child support payments by a divorced father.

Unemployment compensation   Social insurance to compensate workers for income lost due to involuntary loss of employment.

United Way   Major community organization that raises funds for the voluntary social agencies in a city or region and allocates the funds among the agencies. Successor to the Community Chests.

Voluntarism   Idea that social welfare should rely most heavily on volunteer donations of time and money rather than on government-organized programs.

Voluntary social agency   Agency organized by private initiative and supported by voluntary contributions. In the late 20th century voluntary agencies receive an increasing fraction of support from government funds.

Volunteer   Person who donates time to assist in providing social service.

War on Poverty   Name President Lyndon Johnson gave to his multifaceted program of job-training, skills-upgrading, and community action adopted under the Economic Opportunity Act of 1964.

Welfare   Term that originally meant wellbeing. Around the beginning of the 20th century it began to mean "organized activity to promote wellbeing." It retains both meanings to some extent, but since the middle of the 20th century, the term has most commonly come to mean "public assistance payments to poor people." Many of those receiving payments are widely thought to be either not in need of them or not deserving; welfare is therefore regarded as a less respectable form of income than earned income, inherited income, or income from social insurance.

Welfare state   State which seeks to minimize the economic and social insecurity of its citizens by providing as rights of citizenship income benefits for all hazards that interrupt private income, as well as paying much of the cost of services considered essential to wellbeing, such as medical services, education, daycare services, and a widening range of services that have come to be considered essential.

Work ethic   Protestant Ethic.

Work Incentive Program (WIN)   Adopted in 1967 to increase employment of women receiving assistance under AFDC.

Workhouse   In late 16th century a building where ablebodied unemployed people could be given work. Later, especially in 19th century, a building where poor people were obliged to live if they wished to receive subsistence from public funds.

Working poor   People who have paying jobs but whose earnings are inadequate for support of themselves and their families.

Workman's compensation   Social insurance to compensate workers for income lost and medical expenses incurred from injuries at work. In the United States the federal government does not participate in Workman's Compensation insurance; each state has its own program.

Works Progress Administration (WPA)   Most famous of the New Deal agencies. The successor to the CWA in providing federally-paid jobs.

Index

About the Author

Gerald Handel is Professor of Sociology at The City College and the Graduate Center of the City University of New York. He was born and raised in Cleveland, Ohio, and studied at The University of Chicago where he earned B.A., M.A., and Ph.D. degrees. His previous publications include *The Psychosocial Interior of the Family,* which he edited, and three co-authored books: *The Child and Society* (with Frederick Elkin); *Family Worlds* (with Robert D. Hess); and *Workingman's Wife: Her Personality, World and Life Style* (with Lee Rainwater and Richard P. Coleman).

Historical Periods, Social Developments, Landmark Events	Charity/Philanthropy	Public Welfare
INDUSTRIAL PERIOD 1733, Industrial Revolution		
1776, Adam Smith publishes ideas of laissez-faire capitalism		1795, Speenhamland system begun in England
1830's, Reform period in England		1820's, Indoor relief begins to become the dominant method in U.S.
		1834, New Poor Law in England
1840's, Karl Marx publishes ideas of revolutionary communism		
1865+, Industrialization of U.S. intensifies after Civil War	1869, Charity Organisation Movement, "scientific charity," begun in England; 1877, scientific charity spreads to U.S.	
1890–1960, Development of psychoanalysis		
1890–1914, Progressive Era in U.S.		1900–1929, Individual states in U.S. gradually return to outdoor relief;
WORLD WAR I 1914–1918	Communities organize war chests for relief; evolve into community chests, later United Way	1912, U.S. Children's Bureau organized for child welfare
GREAT DEPRESSION 1929–1939, U.S. economy crippled	President Hoover, 1929–33, emphasizes voluntary charity as remedy	
The New Deal, 1933–39 President Roosevelt		1933, Federal government breaks with tradition, provides emergency relief Work relief programs
		1935, Social Security Act provides income for blind, aged, and dependent children
WORLD WAR II 1939–1945		
Kennedy Administration 1961–63		1961, Food Stamps begun; 1962, Amendments to Social Security Act provide for rehabilitating welfare recipients by casework
The Great Society, 1963–1968, of President Johnson		1964–67, War on Poverty
		1967, Work Incentive Program replaces 1962 casework
Nixon Administration, 1969–74	1970's, dominance of United Way receives some challenges	1969, 1971, Family Assistance Plan proposed as welfare reform
Carter Administration, 1977–1981		1977, Program for Better Jobs and Income proposed as welfare reform